Media Freedom as a Fundamental Right

Domestic constitutions and courts applying international human rights conventions acknowledge the significance of the mass media for a democratic society not only by granting special privileges but also by imposing enhanced duties and responsibilities to journalists and media companies. However, the challenges of media convergence, media ownership concentration and the internet have led to legal uncertainty. Should media privileges be maintained, and, if so, how is 'the media' to be defined? To what extent does media freedom as a legal concept also encompass bloggers who have not undertaken journalistic education? And how can a legal distinction be drawn between investigative journalism on the one hand and reporting on purely private matters on the other? To answer these questions, Jan Oster combines doctrinal and conceptual comparative analysis with descriptive and normative theory, and argues in favour of a media freedom principle based on the significance of the media for public discourse.

JAN OSTER is Assistant Professor for EU Law and Institutions at Leiden University, the Netherlands. He also holds a lectureship for telecommunications law and private international media law at the Mainz Media Institute, Germany.

Cambridge Intellectual Property and Information Law

As its economic potential has rapidly expanded, intellectual property has become a subject of front-rank legal importance. *Cambridge Intellectual Property and Information Law* is a series of monograph studies of major current issues in intellectual property. Each volume contains a mix of international, European, comparative and national law, making this a highly significant series for practitioners, judges and academic researchers in many countries.

A list of books in the series can be found at the end of this volume.

Media Freedom as a Fundamental Right

Jan Oster
Leiden University

CAMBRIDGE
UNIVERSITY PRESS

CAMBRIDGE
UNIVERSITY PRESS

University Printing House, Cambridge CB2 8BS, United Kingdom

Cambridge University Press is part of the University of Cambridge.

It furthers the University's mission by disseminating knowledge in the pursuit of education, learning and research at the highest international levels of excellence.

www.cambridge.org
Information on this title: www.cambridge.org/9781107098954

First published 2015

A catalogue record for this publication is available from the British Library

Library of Congress Cataloguing in Publication data
Oster, Jan, 1978- author.
Media freedom as a fundamental right / Jan Oster.
pages cm. – (Cambridge intellectual property and information law ; 30)
ISBN 978-1-107-09895-4 (Hardback)
1. Freedom of the press. 2. Freedom of information. 3. Freedom of expression. 4. Mass media – Law and legislation. I. Title.
K3255.O88 2015
342.08′53–dc23 2014043420

ISBN 978-1-107-09895-4 Hardback

Contents

Preface and acknowledgements

This book is the result of a long-lasting interest in information and communication law, of various classes on this subject and of several conferences and presentations. Part I of the book builds on and further develops the ideas of an earlier article, 'Theory and Doctrine of "Media Freedom" as a Legal Concept' (2013) 5 *Journal of Media Law* 57. The law is up to date as of early November 2014.

I would like to thank many people who helped me to write this book: Kim Hughes and Richard Woodham at Cambridge University Press for their strong support of this project; the anonymous referees who offered comments on the article in the *Journal of Media Law* and on the manuscript; Claire Schreyer and Katrina Simpson for their invaluable research assistance; Kate Ollerenshaw for her thorough and very supportive copy-editing and proofreading; and my former colleagues at King's College London The Dickson Poon School of Law and my colleagues at Leiden University, Faculty of Humanities, for making my academic life inspiring and rewarding.

Last but not least I wish to thank Eva: this book is as much yours as it is mine.

Table of cases

Human Rights Committee

Committee on the Elimination of Racial Discrimination

International Criminal Tribunal for the former Yugoslavia

Special Court for Sierra Leone

African Commission on Human and Peoples' Rights

African Court on Human and Peoples' Rights

European Court of Human Rights

Österreichischer Rundfunk v. *Austria* [2004] App. no. 57597/00 (admissibility decision) 177
Österreichischer Rundfunk v. *Austria* [2006] App. no. 35841/02 86, 165, 177
Österreichische Vereinigung zur Erhaltung, Stärkung und Schaffung eines wirtschaftlich gesunden land- und forstwirtschaftlichen Grundbesitzes v. *Austria* [2013] App. no. 39534/07 41, 99, 100
Otto-Preminger-Institut v. *Austria* [1994] App. no. 13470/87 116, 122, 243, 244, 245
Özgür Gündem v. *Turkey* [2000] App. no. 23144/93 94, 105, 194, 197, 200, 201
Öztürk v. *Turkey* [1999] App. no. 22479/93 67
P4 Radio Hele Norge ASA v. *Norway* [2003] App. no. 76682/01 222
Pasko v. *Russia* [2009] App. no. 69519/01 206, 211
Pavel Ivanov v. *Russia* [2004] App. no. 35222/04 232
Peck v. *United Kingdom* [2003] App. no. 44647/98 43, 173, 174
Pedersen and Baadsgaard v. *Denmark* [2004] App. no. 49017/99 45, 51, 74, 160, 176, 180, 182, 183, 184
Pentikäinen v. *Finland* [2014] App. no. 11882/10 87
Perinçek v. *Switzerland* [2013] App. no. 27510/08 42, 228, 229, 231, 233, 234
Perna v. *Italy* [2003] App. no. 48898/99 66, 182
Perrin v. *United Kingdom* [2005] App. no. 5446/03 64, 213
PETA Deutschland v. *Germany* [2012] App. no. 43481/09 42, 77
Petrina v. *Romania* [2008] App. no. 78060/01 147, 148, 149
Pfeifer v. *Austria* [2007] App. no. 12556/03 147, 148, 149, 182
Pipi v. *Turkey* [2009] App. no. 4020/03 47, 184
Polanco Torres et Movilla Polanco v. *Spain* [2010] App. no. 34147/06 148
Polat v. *Turkey* [1999] App. no. 23500/94 201
Prager and Oberschlick v. *Austria* [1995] App. no. 15974/90 41, 50, 161, 162, 183
Pretty v. *United Kingdom* [2002] App no. 2346/02 28
Print Zeitungsverlag GmbH v. *Austria* [2013] App. no. 26547/07 74, 163
Radio France and others v. *France* [2004] App. no. 53984/00 31, 42, 50, 67, 74, 77, 78, 86, 138, 147, 148
Radio Twist AS v. *Slovakia* [2006] App. no. 62202/00 206
Raninen v. *Finland* [1997] App. no. 152/1996/771/972 43
Ricci v. *Italy* [2013] App. no. 30210/06 47, 144
Ringier Axel Springer Slovakia, AS v. *Slovakia* [2011] App. no. 41262/05 122, 183
Ristamäki and Korvola v. *Finland* [2013] App. no. 66456/09 185
Roche v. *United Kingdom* [2005] App. no. 32555/96 97

European Commission on Human Rights

European Court of Justice/Court of Justice of the EU

European Commission

Inter-American Court of Human Rights

Inter-American Commission of Human Rights

Australia

Canada

Germany

Federal Constitutional Court (Bundesverfassungsgericht)

United States

Treaties, Conventions, Declarations and Statutes

United Nations and international treaties

Convention against Torture and Other Cruel, Inhuman or Degrading Treatment or Punishment (United Nations Convention against Torture) (1984)
Convention on the Rights of the Child (1989)
[First] Optional Protocol to the International Covenant on Civil and Political Rights (1966)
International Convention on the Elimination of All Forms of Racial Discrimination (ICERD) (1965)
International Convention on the Elimination of Discrimination Against Women (CEDAW) (1979)
International Covenant on Civil and Political Rights (ICCPR) (1966)
International Covenant on Economic, Social and Cultural Rights (ICESCR) (1976)
Universal Declaration of Human Rights (UDHR) (1948)
Vienna Convention on Diplomatic Relations (1961)
Vienna Convention on the Law of Treaties (1969)

African Union

African Charter on Human and Peoples' Rights (AfCHPR) (1981)

Council of Europe

Convention on Access to Official Documents (2008)
Convention for the Protection of Human Rights and Fundamental Freedoms (European Convention on Human Rights – ECHR) (1950)
Convention on the Prevention of Terrorism (2005)
Convention on Transfrontier Television (1989)

European Union

Charter of Fundamental Rights of the European Union (EUChFR) (2007)

Consolidated versions of the Treaty on European Union and the Treaty on the Functioning of the European Union (2012)

Council Framework Decision 2002/475/JHA of 13 June 2002 on combating terrorism, OJ 2002, L 164/3, amended by Council Framework Decision 2008/919/JHA of 28 November 2008 amending Framework Decision 2002/475/JHA on combating terrorism, OJ 2002, L 330/21

Council Framework Decision 2008/913/JHA of 28 November 2008 on combating certain forms and expressions of racism and xenophobia by means of criminal law, OJ 2008, L 328/55

Council Framework Decision 2008/919/JHA of 28 November 2008 amending Framework Decision 2002/475/JHA on combating terrorism, OJ 2008, L 330/21

Decision of the European Central Bank of 4 March 2004 on public access to European Central Bank documents (2004/258/EC), OJ 2004, L 80/42

Directive 95/46/EC of the European Parliament and of the Council of 24 October 1995 on the protection of individuals with regard to the processing of personal data and on the free movement of such data, OJ 1995, L 281/31

Directive 2000/31/EC of 8 June 2000 on certain legal aspects of information society services, in particular electronic commerce, in the Internal Market (Directive on electronic commerce), OJ 2000, L 178/1

Directive 2001/29/EC of the European Parliament and of the Council of 22 May 2001 on the harmonisation of certain aspects of copyright and related rights in the information society, OJ 2001, L 167/10

Directive 2002/19/EC of the European Parliament and of the Council of 7 March 2002 on access to, and interconnection of, electronic communications networks and associated facilities (Access Directive), OJ 2002, L 108/7

Directive 2002/22/EC of the European Parliament and of the Council of 7 March 2002 on universal service and users' rights relating to electronic communications networks and services (Universal Service Directive), OJ 2002, L 108/51

Directive 2002/58/EC of the European Parliament and of the Council of 12 July 2002 concerning the processing of personal data and the protection of privacy in the electronic communications sector (Directive on privacy and electronic communications), OJ 2002, L 201/37

Directive 2003/4/EC of the European Parliament and of the Council of 28 January 2003 on public access to environmental information and repealing Council Directive 90/313/EEC, OJ 2003, L 41/26

Directive 2003/33/EC of the European Parliament and of the Council of 26 May 2003 on the approximation of the laws, regulations and administrative provisions of the Member States relating to the advertising and sponsorship of tobacco products, OJ 2003, L 152/16

Directive 2003/98/EC of the European Parliament and of the Council of 17 November 2003 on the re-use of public sector information, OJ 2003, L 345/90

Directive 2004/18/EC of the European Parliament and of the Council of 31 March 2004 on the coordination of procedures for the award of public works contracts, public supply contracts and public service contracts, OJ 2004, L 134/114

Directive 2006/114/EC of the European Parliament and of the Council of 12 December 2006 concerning misleading and comparative advertising (codified version), OJ 2006, L 376/21

Directive 2010/13/EU of the European Parliament and of the Council of 10 March 2010 on the coordination of certain provisions laid down by law, regulation or administrative action in Member States concerning the provision of audiovisual media services (Audiovisual Media Services Directive), OJ 2010, L 95/1

Directive 2011/92/EU of the European Parliament and of the Council of 13 December 2011 on combating the sexual abuse and sexual exploitation of children and child pornography, and replacing Council Framework Decision 2004/68/JHA, OJ 2011, L 335/1

Regulation (EC) No. 1049/2001 of the European Parliament and of the Council of 30 May 2001 regarding public access to European Parliament, Council and Commission documents, OJ 2001, L 145/43

Regulation (EC) No. 139/2004 of 20 January 2004 on the control of concentrations between undertakings, OJ 2004, L 24/1

Organization of American States

American Convention on Human Rights (ACHR) (1969)

American Declaration of the Rights and Duties of Man (1948)

National Laws (all provisions as amended)

Germany

Basic Law (Grundgesetz) for the Federal Republic of Germany (1949)

Civil Law Code (Bürgerliches Gesetzbuch) (1900)

Civil Procedure Code (Zivilprozessordnung) (1877)

Criminal Law Code (Strafgesetzbuch) (1872)

Criminal Procedure Code (Strafprozessordnung) (1877)

Interstate Treaty on Broadcasting and Telemedia (Rundfunkstaatsvertrag) (1991)
Works Constitution Act (Betriebsverfassungsgesetz) (1952)

United Kingdom

Communications Act (2003)
Contempt of Court Act (1981)
Data Protection Act (1998)
Defamation Act (1996)
Defamation Act (2013)
Royal Charter on self-regulation of the press (2013)

United States

Communications Act (1934)
Communications Decency Act (1996)
Constitution of the United States (1789)
Espionage Act (1917)
Freedom of Information Act (1966)
Securing the Protection of our Enduring and Established Constitutional Heritage (SPEECH) Act (2010)
Sherman Antitrust Act (1890)

Other countries

Austrian Criminal Law Code (Strafgesetzbuch) (1974)
Constitution of Belgium (1831)
Constitution of the Italian Republic (1947)
Constitution of the Netherlands (1815)
Declaration of the Rights of Man and of the Citizen (France) (1789)
Swiss Federal Constitution (1999)

Press self-regulation

Press Complaints Commission (PCC), Editors' Code of Practice (2011)
German Press Council, German Press Code: Guidelines for journalistic work as recommended by the German Press Council (Richtlinien für die publizistische Arbeit nach den Empfehlungen des Deutschen Presserates) (2013)

Reports and other documentary sources

United Nations

Commission on Human Rights

Report of the Special Rapporteur on the Promotion and Protection of the Right to Freedom of Opinion and Expression, Mr Abid Hussain, submitted pursuant to Commission Resolution 1997/27, E/CN.4/1998/40/Add.1

Resolution 2005/38: The Right to Freedom of Opinion and Expression, E/CN.4/RES/2005/38

Resolution 1999/82: Defamation of Religions of 30 April 1999, E/CN.4/1999/167

Commission on Human Rights, Resolution 2000/84: Defamation of Religions of 26 April 2000, E/CN.4/RES/2000/84

Resolution 2001/4: Combating Defamation of Religions as a Means to Promote Human Rights, Social Harmony and Religious and Cultural Diversity of 18 April 2001, E/CN.4/RES/2001/4

Resolution 2002/9: Combating Defamation of Religions of 15 April 2002, E/CN.4/RES/2002/9

Resolution 2003/4: Combating Defamation of Religions of 14 April 2003, E/CN.4/RES/2003/4

Resolution 2004/6: Combating Defamation of Religions of 13 April 2004, E/CN.4/RES/2004/6

Commission on Human Rights, Resolution 2005/3: Combating Defamation of Religions of 12 April 2005, E/CN.4/RES/2005/3

Economic and Social Council

Siracusa Principles on the Limitation and Derogation Provisions in the International Covenant on Civil and Political Rights, UN Doc. E/CN.4/1985/4, Annex (1985)

General Assembly

Document A/5000 of the sixteenth session, 5 December 1961
Resolution 1904 (XVIII): Declaration on the Elimination of All Forms of Racial Discrimination of 20 November 1963, A/RES/1904 (XVIII)
Resolution 53/144: Declaration on the Right and Responsibility of Individuals, Groups and Organs of Society to Promote and Protect Universally Recognized Human Rights and Fundamental Freedoms of 8 March 1999, A/RES/53/144
Resolution 60/150: Combating Defamation of Religions of 16 December 2005, A/RES/60/150
Resolution 61/164: Combating Defamation of Religions of 19 December 2006, A/RES/61/164
General Assembly, Resolution 62/154: Combating Defamation of Religions of 18 December 2007, A/RES/62/154
Resolution 63/171: Combating Defamation of Religions of 18 December 2008, A/RES/63/171
Resolution 64/156: Combating Defamation of Religions of 18 December 2009, A/RES/64/156
Resolution 65/224: Combating Defamation of Religions of 21 December 2010, A/RES/65/224

Human Rights Committee

General Comments

Short name	**Reference**
General Comment no. 11	Article 20 (Nineteenth session, 1983), reprinted in Compilation of General Comments and General Recommendations Adopted by Human Rights Treaty Bodies, UN Doc. HRI/GEN/1/Rev.6 at 133 (2003)
General Comment no. 22	Article 18 (Forty-eighth session, 1993), UN Doc. CCPR/C/21/Rev.1/Add.4 (1993), reprinted in Compilation of General Comments and General Recommendations Adopted by Human Rights Treaty Bodies, UN Doc. HRI/GEN/1/Rev.6 at 155 (2003)
General Comment no. 24	Issues relating to Reservations made upon Ratification or Accession to the Covenant or the Optional Protocols thereto, or in relation to declarations under Article 41 of the Covenant, (Fifty-second session, 1994), UN Doc. CCPR/C/21/Rev.1/Add.6 (1994), reprinted in Compilation of General Comments and General Recommendations Adopted by Human Rights Treaty Bodies, UN Doc. HRI/GEN/1/Rev.6 at 161 (2003)
General Comment no. 25	The right to participate in public affairs, voting rights and the right of equal access to public service (Art. 25), (Fifty-seventh session, 1996), UN Doc. CCPR/C/21/Rev.1/Add.7 (1996), reprinted in Compilation of General Comments and General Recommendations

Short name	Reference
	Adopted by Human Rights Treaty Bodies, UN Doc. HRI/GEN/1/Rev.6 at 168 (2003)
General Comment no. 27	Freedom of movement (Art.12), (Sixty-seventh session, 1999), UN Doc. CCPR/C/21/Rev.1/Add.9 (1999), reprinted in Compilation of General Comments and General Recommendations Adopted by Human Rights Treaty Bodies, UN Doc. HRI/GEN/1/Rev.6 at 174 (2003)
General Comment no. 29	States of Emergency (article 4), UN Doc. CCPR/C/21/Rev.1/Add.11 (2001), reprinted in Compilation of General Comments and General Recommendations Adopted by Human Rights Treaty Bodies, UN Doc. HRI/GEN/1/Rev.6 at 186 (2003)
General Comment no. 31	Nature of the General Legal Obligation on States Parties to the Covenant, UN Doc. CCPR/C/21/Rev.1/Add.13 (2004)
General Comment no. 32	Article 14: Right to equality before courts and tribunals and to a fair trial, UN Doc. CCPR/C/GC/32 (2007)
General Comment no. 34	Article 19, Freedoms of opinion and expression, 12 September 2011, CCPR/C/GC/34

Concluding observations

Short name	Reference
Concluding observations on Algeria (CCPR/C/DZA/CO/3)	Concluding observations on Algeria (CCPR/C/DZA/CO/3) of 12 December 2007
Concluding observations on Costa Rica (CCPR/C/CRI/CO/5)	Concluding observations on Costa Rica (CCPR/C/CRI/CO/5) of 16 November 2007
Concluding observations on Democratic People's Republic of Korea (CCPR/CO/72/PRK)	Concluding observations on Democratic People's Republic of Korea (CCPR/CO/72/PRK) of 27 August 2001
Concluding observations on Guyana (CCPR/CO/79/Add.121)	Concluding observations on Guyana (CCPR/CO/79/Add.121) of 25 April 2000
Concluding observations on Honduras (CCPR/C/HND/CO/1)	Concluding observations on Honduras (CCPR/C/HND/CO/1) of 13 December 2006
Concluding observations on Italy (CCPR/C/ITA/CO/5)	Concluding observations on Italy (CCPR/C/ITA/CO/5) of 24 April 2006
Concluding observations on Italy (CCPR/C/79/Add. 37)	Concluding observations on Italy (CCPR/C/79/Add. 37) of 3 August 1994
Concluding observations on Japan (CCPR/C/JPN/CO/5)	Concluding observations on Japan (CCPR/C/JPN/CO/5) of 18 December 2008
Concluding observations on Kyrgyzstan (CCPR/CO/69/KGZ)	Concluding observations on Kyrgyzstan (CCPR/CO/69/KGZ) of 24 July 2000
Concluding observations on Kuwait (CCPR/CO/69/KWT)	Concluding observations on Kuwait (CCPR/CO/69/KWT) of 27 July 2000
Concluding observations on Lebanon (CCPR/CO/79/Add.78)	Concluding observations on Lebanon (CCPR/CO/79/Add.78) of 5 May 1997

Short name	Reference
Concluding observations on Lesotho (CCPR/CO/79/Add. 106)	Concluding observations on Lesotho (CCPR/CO/79/Add. 106) of 8 April 1999
Concluding observations on Morocco (CCPR/CO/82/MAR)	Concluding observations on Morocco (CCPR/CO/82/MAR) of 1 December 2004
Concluding observations on Peru (CCPR/CO/70/PER)	Concluding observations on Peru (CCPR/CO/70/PER) of 15 November 2000
Concluding observations on the Republic of Moldova (CCPR/CO/75/MDA)	Concluding observations on the Republic of Moldova (CCPR/CO/75/MDA) of 5 August 2002
Concluding observations on the Russian Federation (CCPR/CO/79/RUS)	Concluding observations on the Russian Federation (CCPR/CO/79/RUS) of 1 December 2003
Concluding observations on Sri Lanka (CCPR/CO/79/LKA)	Concluding observations on Sri Lanka (CCPR/CO/79/LKA) of 1 December 2003
Concluding observations on Togo (CCPR/CO/76/TGO)	Concluding observations on Togo (CCPR/CO/76/TGO) of 28 November 2002
Concluding observations on Tunisia (CCPR/C/TUN/CO/5)	Concluding observations on Tunisia (CCPR/C/TUN/CO/5) of 23 April 2008
Concluding observations on Ukraine (CCPR/CO/73/UKR)	Concluding observations on Ukraine (CCPR/CO/73/UKR) of 12 November 2001
Concluding observations on the United Kingdom of Great Britain and Northern Ireland (CCPR/C/GBR/CO/6)	Concluding observations on the United Kingdom of Great Britain and Northern Ireland (CCPR/C/GBR/CO/6) of 30 July 2008
Concluding observations on Uzbekistan (CCPR/CO/83/UZB)	Concluding observations on Uzbekistan (CCPR/CO/83/UZB) of 26 April 2005
Concluding observations on Zambia (CCPR/ZMB/CO/3)	Concluding observations on Zambia (CCPR/ZMB/CO/3) of 9 August 2007

Human Rights Council

Decision 1/107: Incitement to Racial and Religious Hatred and the Promotion of Tolerance of 30 June 2006, A/HRC/DEC/1/107

Resolution 4/9: Combating Defamation of Religions of 30 March 2007, A/HRC/RES/4/9

Resolution 7/19: Combating Defamation of Religions of 27 March 2008, A/HRC/RES/7/19

Resolution 10/22: Combating Defamation of Religions of 26 March 2009, A/HRC/RES/10/22

International Law Commission

Articles on Responsibility of States for Internationally Wrongful Acts, Report of the International Law Commission on the Work of Its Fifty-third Session, 2001 (A/56/10)

Security Council

Resolution 1624 (2005) of 14 September 2005, S/RES/1624 (2005)

Special Rapporteur on Freedom of Opinion and Expression

Joint Declaration by the UN Special Rapporteur on Freedom of Opinion and Expression, the OSCE Representative on Freedom of the Media and the OAS Special Rapporteur on Freedom of Expression of 18 December 2003

African Commission on Human and Peoples' Rights

Short name	**Reference**
Declaration of Principles on Freedom of Expression in Africa	Declaration of Principles on Freedom of Expression in Africa, 32nd Session, 17–23 October 2002
Resolution on Repealing Criminal Defamation Laws in Africa	Resolution on Repealing Criminal Defamation Laws in Africa, 48th Session, 10–24 November 2010

Council of Europe

Committee of Ministers

Recommendation No. R (81) 19 on the Access to Information held by Public Authorities

Recommendation No. R (91) 10 on the Communication to Third Parties of Personal Data held by Public Bodies

Recommendation No. R (97) 18 concerning the Protection of Personal Data Collected and Processed for Statistical Purposes

Recommendation No. R (94) 13 on Measures to Promote Media Transparency

Recommendation No. R (96) 10 on the Guarantee of the Independence of Public Service Broadcasting

Recommendation No. R (97) 20 on 'Hate Speech'

Recommendation No. (97) 21 on the Media and the Promotion of a Culture of Tolerance

Recommendation No. R (2000) 7 on the Right of Journalists not to Disclose their Sources of Information

Recommendation No. R(2000) 12 on the Social Sciences and the Challenge of Transition

Recommendation No. R (2000) 13 on a European Policy on Access to Archives

Recommendation Rec(2000)23 on the Independence and Functions of Regulatory Authorities for the Broadcasting Sector

Recommendation Rec(2003)13 on the Provision of Information through the Media in relation to Criminal Proceedings
Recommendation Rec(2004)16 on the Right of Reply in the New Media Environment
Recommendation Rec(2002)2 on Access to Official Documents
Recommendation CM/Rec(2007)2 on Media Pluralism and Diversity of Media Content
Recommendation CM/Rec(2011)7 on a New Notion of Media
Recommendation CM/Rec(2012)7 on the Responsibility of Public Authorities for Academic Freedom and Institutional Autonomy
Resolution (74) 26 on the Right of Reply – Position of the Individual in relation to the Press

European Court of Human Rights

Research Report, Positive Obligations on Member States under Article 10 to Protect Journalists and Prevent Impunity (2011)

Parliamentary Assembly

Recommendation 1215 (1993) on the Ethics of Journalism
Resolution 1165 (1998) on the Right to Privacy
Resolution 1551 (2007): Fair Trial Issues in Criminal Cases concerning Espionage or Divulging State Secrets
Resolution 1577 (2007): Towards Decriminalisation of Defamation
Resolution 1636 (2008): Indicators for Media in a Democracy
Resolution 1729 (2010): Protection of 'Whistle-blowers'
Recommendation 1950 (2011): The Protection of Journalistic Sources

European Union

Commission Decision 94/19/EC of 21 December 1993 relating to a Proceeding pursuant to Article 86 of the EC Treaty (IV/34.689 – Sea Containers v. Stena Sealink), OJ 1994, L 15/8
Commission Decision 94/119/EC of 21 December 1993 concerning a Refusal to Grant Access to the Facilities of the Port of Rødby (Denmark), OJ 1993, L 55/52
Commission Proposal for a Regulation on the Protection of Individuals with regard to the Processing of Personal Data and on the Free Movement of Such Data (General Data Protection Regulation), COM(2012) 11 final
Joint Action 96/443/JHA of 15 July 1996 adopted by the Council on the basis of Article K.3 of the Treaty on European Union, concerning Action to Combat Racism and Xenophobia, OJ 1996, L 185/5

Recommendation of the European Parliament and of the Council of 20 December 2006 on the Protection of Minors and Human Dignity and on the Right of Reply in Relation to the Competitiveness of the European Audiovisual and On-line Information Services Industry (2006/952/EC), OJ 2006, L 378/72

Inter-American Commission on Human Rights

Office of the Special Rapporteur for Freedom of Expression with the Inter-American Commission on Human Rights, Inter-American Legal Framework Regarding the Right to Freedom of Expression, 2009, CIDH/RELE/INF. 2/09

United Kingdom

Lord Justice Leveson, An Inquiry into the Culture, Practices and Ethics of the Press, 2012

Master of the Rolls, Report of the Committee on Super-Injunctions: Super-Injunctions, Anonymised Injunctions and Open Justice, 2011

Introduction: aim, scope and method

Ever since Johannes Gutenberg invented mechanical movable type printing, the mass media has played an important role for human communication. Before the internet emerged as the first democratic mass medium, operators of mass communication infrastructures, such as newspapers, TV or radio broadcasting, had the unique ability to disseminate information and ideas to a mass audience without the recipients having to be present, and to issue such publications on a periodical basis. The professional media, by virtue of its possibilities of newsgathering, its manpower and its infrastructure, was better equipped than private individuals to disseminate publications to a mass audience. It was incumbent on the traditional media to impart information and ideas on matters of public concern, to investigate government action, expose fraud and corruption and to inform the public, thus playing an essential role as a 'watchdog' or 'fourth estate' in a democratic society.[1] Therefore, the mass media had the capacity to inform the public and shape public opinion, together with the opportunities to abuse this power. Many domestic constitutions[2] and courts applying international human rights conventions[3] thus acknowledge a special role of the mass media in the framework of freedom of expression not only by granting special

[1] Stewart (1975) 634; Nimmer (1975) 653; West (2011) 1069–70; Lord Justice Leveson, An Inquiry into the Culture, Practices and Ethics of the Press, 2012, pp. 63 ff.

[2] Such as the First Amendment to the US Constitution, Article 5(1)2 German Basic Law, Article 21(2) Italian Constitution, Article 25(1) Belgian Constitution or Article 17 Swiss Constitution.

[3] See, e.g., Human Rights Committee, *Bodrožić* v. *Serbia and Montenegro* [2005] Communication no. 1180/2003 [7.2]; *Toktakunov* v. *Kyrgyzstan* [2011] Communication no. 1470/2006 [6.3]; Concluding observations on Kuwait (CCPR/CO/69/KWT), para. 20; ECtHR, *Sunday Times* v. *United Kingdom (No. 1)* [1979] App. no. 6538/74 [65]; *Lingens* v. *Austria* [1986] App. no. 9815/82 [42]; *Goodwin* v. *United Kingdom* [1996] App. no. 17488/90 [39]; IACtHR, *Fontevecchia and D'Amico* v. *Argentina* [2011] Case 12.524 [44–5]; *Vélez Restrepo* v. *Colombia* [2012] Case 12.658 [140].

privileges, but also by imposing enhanced duties and responsibilities on journalists and media companies.

Today, media law faces three fundamental challenges. First, the phenomenon of technological and content-related media convergence complicates the traditional categorisation of media services into broadcasting and press. Second, due to the concentration of media ownership, fewer individuals and organisations control increasing shares of the mass media. Third, as the internet evolves, the ability to reach a mass audience is no longer the privilege of traditional media corporations, and, hence, not a clearly distinguishing element for the media–public divide anymore. Citizen-journalists and other actors in civil society, in light of economically plagued traditional journalism, increasingly play the role of watchdog, for instance by covering local matters or reporting from conflict areas which professional journalists have hardly any access to.[4] At the same time, an increasing number of newspapers, magazines and broadcasters do not engage in investigative, core public interest journalism, but prefer to report on people's private lives.[5]

These challenges lead to significant legal uncertainty. Should media privileges be maintained, and, if so, how is 'the media' to be defined? Does 'media freedom' as a legal concept also encompass bloggers who have not undertaken journalistic education? And should a legal distinction be drawn between investigative journalism, on the one hand, and reporting on purely private matters, on the other? This book seeks to answer these questions.

In methodological terms, this study combines doctrinal and conceptual comparative analysis with descriptive and normative theory. At the same time, this book is, in a positivistic way, restricted to the *law* of the media; hence it does not expand on media ethics. It aims to develop a theoretical and doctrinal framework for the scope, content and limitations of media freedom as a fundamental right. The book particularly builds on the work of Jürgen Habermas and Robert Post on public discourse. A Media Freedom Principle[6] should create incentives for the media to strive towards an ideal communication community: a public sphere where undistorted rational public discussion of matters of general concern is institutionalised.[7] Media freedom has to be

[4] See Anonymous author (2007) 1005; Calvert and Torres (2011) 344.

[5] See, e.g., Lord Justice Leveson, An Inquiry into the Culture, Practices and Ethics of the Press, 2012, pp. 539 ff.

[6] The term is based on Frederick Schauer's 'Free Speech Principle'; see Schauer (1982) p. 6.

[7] See Habermas (1962); Habermas (1981b) p. 2.

conceptualised as a liberty that protects institutional mass communication against both the state and private actors.

Since the study of fundamental rights is to a significant extent the study of fundamental rights adjudication,[8] the book compares the approaches to media freedom taken by international conventions and their interpretation by courts and tribunals. Therefore, the book refers to international adjudicators' jurisprudence, but wants to provide theoretical underpinning, and aims at developing legal doctrine further. It thereby seeks to highlight and consolidate international minimum standards of media freedom where they exist, and developing globally applicable legal principles where they do not yet exist. This book searches for international consensus among human rights adjudicators on the content of media freedom, on the need to restrict media activity to protect individual or public interests and on the limitations of those restrictions, particularly the principle of proportionality. The book is theoretical in the sense that it provides a justification for the existence of media freedom, and a view on the general character and normative goals thereof. It is also doctrinal by deducing a workable and rationally reviewable system for the judicial interpretation and application of media freedom from the theoretical analysis.

The book is based on the principle that the provisions of each international human rights document should be interpreted and applied in light of the evolution of international human rights law in general. The evolution of the body of international human rights law relevant to the interpretation and application of a particular convention can be extracted from other instruments on human rights and their interpretation.[9] Thus, when examining a petition lodged against a state alleging violation of human rights, a regional adjudicator must pay attention to the other relevant norms of international law that apply to this state, such as the International Covenant on Civil and Political Rights (ICCPR), and to the evolution of a '*corpus juris gentium* of international human rights law over the course of time'.[10] International human rights conventions are 'living instrument[s]' which must be 'interpreted in the light of present day conditions'.[11]

8 See Alexy (2002) p. 2.
9 Compare IAComHR, *Oscar Elías Biscet and others* v. *Cuba* [2006] Case 12.476 [42], with further references; IACtHR, *Olmedo Bustos and others* v. *Chile ('The Last Temptation of Christ')* [2001] Case 11.803 [69]; *Ricardo Canese* v. *Paraguay* [2004] Case 12.032 [83] and [84]; AfComHPR, *Law Offices of Ghazi Suleiman* v. *Sudan* [2003] App. no. 228/99 [48] and [50]; *Article 19* v. *Eritrea* [2007] App. no. 275/03 [94] and [108]; ECtHR, *Stoll* v. *Switzerland* [2007] App. no. 69698/01 [111].
10 IAComHR, *Oscar Elías Biscet and others* v. *Cuba* [2006] Case 12.476 [41].
11 See ECtHR, *Tyrer* v. *United Kingdom* [1978] App. no. 5856/72 [31].

Because of its aim to develop globally applicable minimum standards of media freedom, the book is confined to the international dimension of media freedom, largely to the exclusion of domestic constitutions and jurisprudence. Although international human rights catalogues are rooted in domestic human rights declarations and codifications of the late eighteenth and nineteenth century, international human rights have developed into a 'self-contained regime', possessing a logic of their own.[12] International human rights adjudicators draw inspiration from the interpretation of domestic constitutions by states' courts, but in the hierarchy of a multi-layered judicial system, decisions of international courts, *de facto* and sometimes even *de jure*, take precedence over judgments of domestic courts.[13] This does not exclude, and might even require, a certain margin of appreciation to domestic courts' judgments. In turn, principles that are developed in this study are only applicable to a limited degree to states that are not member to one of the human rights treaties covered by this book or that have made reservations to the relevant provisions. This applies, in particular, to the United States, which has made substantive reservations to Article 20 ICCPR. Furthermore, the US has – in strange concomitance with, among other states, Cuba – not ratified the American Convention on Human Rights (ACHR) yet (although it has at least adopted the American Declaration of the Rights and Duties of Man). The book therefore refers to US case-law in order to describe conformity and divergence between the international approaches and First Amendment doctrine.[14] In the US, First Amendment jurisprudence is based on the presumption that if communication is categorised as 'speech' within the meaning of this clause, then it deserves strong, albeit not absolute, protection. This understanding requires US courts to define certain 'well-defined and narrowly limited classes of speech',[15] which do *a priori* not receive First Amendment protection. By contrast, the 'duties and responsibilities' clauses in international conventions allow adjudicators to balance freedom of expression with conflicting rights and interests on an *ad hoc* basis. Hence the seminal question is whether an interference with speech may be justified for the protection of conflicting rights and interests.

[12] De Schutter (2010) pp. 1, 8.

[13] Compare German Federal Constitutional Court, '*Presumption of innocence*' [1987] Case 2 BvR 589/79; '*Görgülü*' [2004] Case 2 BvR 1481/04. In Austria, the European Convention of Human Rights even has constitutional status.

[14] However, Congress referred to the jurisprudence of the UN Human Rights Committee on the law of libel in Section 2(4) Securing the Protection of our Enduring and Established Constitutional Heritage (SPEECH) Act 2010.

[15] US Supreme Court, *Chaplinsky* v. *New Hampshire*, 315 US 568, 571 (1942).

In contrast to the First Amendment, international conventions do not afford dominance to freedom of speech, but treat freedom of speech as a right with equal value to human rights of others, especially the right to respect for private life and its sub-categories, privacy and reputation.

A book that aims at the development of globally applicable doctrines of media freedom is almost necessarily subject to the suspicion of an over-broad generalisation. Claims of universalism in human rights have been highly controversial, as they risk overriding cultural, historical and theoretical differences. For example, the European Court of Human Rights (ECtHR) mainly deals with human rights interferences in developed democracies. Cases brought to Strasbourg alleging violations of freedom of expression and media freedom often require a delicate balancing exercise between the right to criticise one's government or to be informed on the lives of public figures, on the one hand, and the right to reputation and privacy of politicians or other prominent figures, on the other hand. Cases involving arbitrary arrests or prosecutions of journalists are the exception, not the rule in Strasbourg. By contrast, many member states to the ICCPR, the ACHR and the African Charter on Human and Peoples' Rights (AfCHPR) are, at best, developing and consolidating democracies. The UN Human Rights Committee, the Inter-American Court of Human Rights (IACtHR) and the African Commission on Human and Peoples' Rights (AfComHPR) often have to deal with appalling violations of human rights. Their cases imply accusations of torture and the killing of journalists for the exercise of their profession. Such claims of extrajudicial executions of, or physical violence against, journalists do not require the same fine balancing exercises as defining the limits of acceptable criticism of politicians in newspaper articles would. Authoritarian regimes usually interfere with the rights of journalists through direct limitations, including arbitrary arrests, extraditions or even murder. However, the more a country develops towards a democracy, direct interferences are replaced by more refined forms of limiting journalistic freedom, including administrative regulations and judicial decisions in civil law cases.[16]

It is also true that the jurisprudence of the Human Rights Commitee on freedom of expression and media freedom under the ICCPR is less refined than the case-law of regional adjudicators, especially the ECtHR. The ambit of the Human Rights Committee's jurisprudence is global rather than restricted to a particular continent, and therefore it is even more difficult for the Committee to define common standards for

[16] Compare Schonsteiner, Beltran y Puga and Lovera (2011) 365; Grossman (2001) 621–2.

freedom of expression and its limitations. Furthermore, the United Nations comprises a larger body of human rights treaties, including, for instance, the International Covenant on Economic, Social and Cultural Rights (ICESCR) and the Convention on the Elimination of All Forms of Discrimination against Women (CEDAW), all of which have equal legal status. Thus, compared to the regional conventions, the ICCPR does not constitute the core of human rights protection at UN level, and the Human Rights Committee does not yield powers comparable to the regional human rights courts. Furthermore, an adjudicator's case-law can only be as doctrinally refined as the cases brought to this adjudicator allow: the Human Rights Committee has had fewer media-related cases to decide than, for instance, the ECtHR, and thus less opportunity to develop a coherent body of case-law in this area.

In addition, notwithstanding the guidelines of the Vienna Convention on the Law of Treaties, the jurisprudence of international courts and committees is not always coherent and sometimes appears under-theorised.[17] This deficit is caused by several factors. First, international jurisdiction is of a subsidiary, reinforcing and complementary nature.[18] International human rights catalogues only protect human rights at a basic level, and they cannot substitute a domestic constitution. International courts and tribunals are thus not able to replace a domestic constitutional court.[19] Furthermore, international adjudicators need to respect a certain margin of appreciation of the Member States on matters where an internationally agreed standard is lacking, such as in the interpretation of 'morals' or where significant domestic interests are concerned, as is the case with national security. Conceptual uncertainty hence favours Member States' discretion. Consequently, in marginal cases, the exact balance between media freedom and conflicting interests that each liberal democracy develops differs according to constitutional, historical and social settings.[20]

Finally, the EC/EU jurisprudence and legislation in media law is to a significant degree characterised by the EU's focus on the development of a common market, and therefore on the media's role as an economic factor, rather than by the pursuit of human rights standards. Under EU law, media goods and services had, in the first place, been perceived as economic commodities. In the seminal *Sacchi* decision, the then-European Court of Justice (ECJ)[21] held that broadcasting of television

[17] Compare Fenwick and Phillipson (2006) pp. 1 and 6.
[18] IACtHR, *Perozo and others* v. *Venezuela* [2009] Case 12.442 [64].
[19] Fenwick and Phillipson (2006) p. 7. [20] Compare Weaver and Partlett (2005–6) 60.
[21] Court of Justice of the European Union (CJEU) since the Lisbon Treaty.

signals, including those in the nature of advertisements, falls within the rules of the Treaty relating to services.[22] In *Procureur du Roi* v. *Debauve*, the ECJ included transnational transmission of broadcasting signals by cable television within the rules of the Treaty relating to services as well.[23] Thus Article 62 in conjunction with Article 53(1) of the Treaty on the Functioning of the EU (TFEU) and their predecessors authorised the EU to issue the Audiovisual Media Services Directive (AVMS Directive), which harmonises the rules on TV broadcasting and video-on-demand in the EU.[24]

Despite all these objections, a global approach to media freedom can nonetheless be built on three principles that run as common threads throughout all jurisdictions.

First, all human rights treaties have been inspired by the Universal Declaration of Human Rights (UDHR): they are similarly worded and they even require taking into consideration the interpretation of other human rights conventions. The human rights enshrined in the UDHR have been further developed in subsequent international treaties, regional human rights instruments and national constitutions, and have served as the foundation for the ICCPR, the ICESCR and other international treaties.[25] According to Article 53 of the European Convention for the Protection of Human Rights and Fundamental Freedoms (ECHR) and Article 29(b) ACHR, nothing in these conventions shall be interpreted as limiting or derogating from any of the human rights which may be ensured under any agreement to which the state concerned is a party – and this is in most cases the ICCPR. Similarly, Article 7 of the Court Protocol to the AfCHPR provides that '[t]he Court shall apply the provisions of the Charter *and any other relevant human rights instruments ratified by the States concerned*' (emphasis added).[26] International human

[22] *Sacchi* [1974] ECR 00409, Case C-155/73 [6].

[23] *Procureur du Roi* v. *Debauve and others* [1980] ECR 00833, Case C-52/79 [15]. See also *Coditel and others* v. *Ciné Vog Films and others* [1980] ECR 00881, Case C-62/79: assignment of copyright limited to the territory of a Member State is capable of constituting a restriction on freedom to provide services.

[24] See Directive 2010/13/EU of the European Parliament and of the Council of 10 March 2010 on the Coordination of Certain Provisions Laid Down by Law, Regulation or Administrative Action in Member States concerning the Provision of Audiovisual Media Services (Audiovisual Media Services Directive), OJ 2010, L95/1, and its predecessor Directives.

[25] For example, the International Convention on the Elimination of All Forms of Racial Discrimination, the International Convention on the Elimination of Discrimination Against Women, the UN Convention on the Rights of the Child, or the UN Convention Against Torture.

[26] A similar provision, Article 60, applies in the AfCHPR; see AfComHPR, *Media Rights Agenda* v. *Nigeria* [2000] App no. 224/98 [52]; *Law Offices of Ghazi Suleiman* v. *Sudan*

rights instruments, therefore, include or presuppose general principles of law.[27] These principles include, for instance, the concept of an 'interference' with human rights, the principle of proportionality and the principle that states are not only compelled to abstain from violations of human rights, but that they may also be under an obligation to actively protect human rights. By regularly referring to each other,[28] international adjudicators are in a constant judicial dialogue when interpreting the provisions of the human rights treaty they supervise. As the decisions of the IACtHR over the last decade show, cases requiring a more refined approach to media freedom and its limits will inevitably appear with the progressing consolidation of democracies. It is not surprising that the Inter-American Court, when deciding on privacy issues or on conflicts between freedom of the media and religious freedom, regularly refers to the European Court of Human Rights.[29] In turn, the Inter-American Court has a more generous approach to freedom of access to information, which should serve as role-model for the interpretation of Article 10 ECHR.[30] As regards Africa, the uprising in the Arab Spring in particular will hopefully lead to a transition towards a more refined body of case-law concerning political participation – and media reporting thereof.

Moreover, the EC/EU has also recognised the media as a factor of public interest with implications that go far beyond the market, such as cultural diversity, the right to information, diversity of opinion, media plurality, the protection of minors and consumer protection. According to Article 167(1) TFEU, the EU 'shall contribute to the flowering of the cultures of the Member States, while respecting their national and regional diversity and at the same time bringing the common cultural heritage to the fore'. Article 167(4) TFEU requires the Union to take cultural aspects into account in its action under other provisions of that Treaty, in particular in order to respect and promote the diversity of its cultures. A cultural policy, such as the safeguarding of a pluralist and

[2003] App. no. 228/99 [49]; *Zimbabwe Lawyers for Human Rights & Associated Newspapers of Zimbabwe* v. *Republic of Zimbabwe* [2009] App. no. 284/03 [123].

27 Beck (2008) p. 239.

28 See, for instance, IACtHR, *Olmedo Bustos and others* v. *Chile ('The Last Temptation of Christ')* [2001] Case 11.803 [69]; *Ricardo Canese* v. *Paraguay* [2004] Case 12.032 [83] and [84]; *Kimel* v. *Argentina* [2008] Case 12.450 [88]; IAComHR, *Stephen Schmidt* v. *Costa Rica* [1984] Case no. 9178 [6]; AfComHPR, *Huri-Laws* v. *Nigeria* [2000] App. no. 225/98 [41]. From scholarship, see Bertoni (2009).

29 See, for instance, IACtHR, *Ivcher-Bronstein* v. *Peru* [2001] Case 11.762 [152]; *Herrera-Ulloa* v. *Costa Rica* [2004] Case 12.367 [113] and [126].

30 See ECtHR, *Stoll* v. *Switzerland* [2007] App. no. 69698/01 [111], referring to the seminal IACtHR case on access to information *Claude Reyes and others* v. *Chile* [2006] Case 12.108.

cultural range of programmes available on television distribution networks, may therefore constitute an overriding requirement relating to the general interest which justifies a restriction on the freedom to provide services.[31] Furthermore, it was the ECJ which introduced human rights into the Community legal order.[32] Since then, fundamental rights have formed an integral part of the general principles of law which the Court observes.[33] The principles established by the Court's case-law are now reaffirmed in Article 6(3) of the Treaty on European Union (TEU). Finally, the Charter of Fundamental Rights of the European Union (EUChFR), which has the same legal value as the Treaties, has brought significant change with regard to human rights protection in the EU.

Second, as a normative argument, the internationalisation and globalisation of trade, mobility and, with particular relevance for this book, communication, necessitates the development of globally applicable legal principles. The internet will inevitably lead to a rise of transnational violations of reputation and privacy, resulting in an increasingly important role of private international law and internationally coordinated regulation.[34] By institutionalising globally applicable standards and limitations of media freedom, this book will contribute to the development of a global *ordre public* for torts committed by, or against, the media, and to a harmonisation of regulatory principles.

Third, all human rights instruments include general principles of media freedom, which can all be traced back to one fundamental tenet: a free media is essential for any functioning democracy and state governed by the rule of law. Based on this tenet, rules of media freedom need to be developed on a global scale. Such rules include how to define 'journalism' and 'the media', what the rights and privileges of journalists

[31] ECJ, *United Pan-Europe Communications Belgium SA and others* v. *Belgium and others* [2007] ECR I-11135, Case C-250/06 [41]. On media pluralism, see Chapter 14. See also Article 16 Directive 2004/18/EC of the European Parliament and of the Council of 31 March 2004 on the Coordination of Procedures for the Award of Public Works Contracts, Public Supply Contracts and Public Service Contracts OJ 2004, L 134/114, which excludes public service contracts for certain audiovisual services in the field of broadcasting from the scope of the Directive.

[32] The first decisions were *van Eick* v. *Commission* [1968] ECR 329, Case C-35/67; *Stauder* v. *City of Ulm* [1969] ECR 419, Case C-29/69.

[33] See, e.g., *ERT* v. *DEP and others* [1991] ECR I-02925, Case C-260/89, [41]; *Schmidberger* v. *Austria* [2003] ECR I-05659, Case C-112/00 [71].

[34] See, for instance, CJEU, *eDate Advertising and Olivier Martinez, Robert Martinez* v. *MGN Ltd.* [2011] ECR I-10269, Cases C-509/10 and C-161/10; *Google Spain SL and others* v. *AEPD and others* [2014] (not yet reported), Case C-131/12; German Federal Court of Justice, '*Google*' [2013] Case VI ZR 269/12 [7]. See also ECJ, *Shevill* v. *Presse Alliance* [1995] ECR I-415, Case C-68/93, for a case involving a newspaper article.

are, what constitutes an 'interference' with the media's freedom and how such an interference can be justified. This does of course not exclude divergences at the margins and 'hard cases' in a Dworkinian sense.[35] However, while there might not yet be an international consensus on the *conceptions* of media freedom, it will be shown that media freedom is an internationally accepted *concept*.[36]

This book, therefore, positions itself in the movement towards the development of a transnational, transcontinental and international *jus commune* of human rights. There is no place for a specific 'African media freedom' or 'European freedom of expression'. A time where publications are being disseminated worldwide calls for universally applicable principles, providing legal certainty for those who generate, impart and receive information and ideas transnationally.

The book is divided into three parts: Part I develops a theory of media freedom, especially in its relationship with freedom of expression. Part II analyses the scope of media freedom and develops general principles for the examination of an interference with media freedom. Part III then provides specific rules on limitations to media freedom, divided into several sub-chapters concerning legitimate aims justifying an interference (Chapters 7 to 10), particular content-based limitations (Chapters 11 to 13) and the relationship between media freedom and media pluralism (Chapter 14). These examples are not exhaustive and necessarily limited to the core elements of the issues concerned. This book does not attempt to provide all-encompassing frameworks for these concepts, such as 'privacy' or 'morals', but rather to make them operable under a Media Freedom Principle. Reference to in-depth academic literature will be provided.

35 See Dworkin (1977) Chapter 4.
36 On the difference between a concept and conceptions, see Dworkin (1977) p. 134.

Part I

The theoretical foundations of media freedom

This Part builds on and further develops the ideas of Oster (2013).

1 The rationales for freedom of expression

'The media' is a differentiated system of human communication.[1] It holds a special role in the framework of human communication because of its ability to disseminate information and ideas to a mass audience at a distance, and to issue such publications on a periodical basis. By means of mass communication, such as the printing press, broadcasting and now also the internet, the media liberates speech acts from spatiotemporal limitations and makes them available for an indefinite, general public.[2] A theory that explains media freedom as a distinct fundamental right must thus have recourse to the rationales of freedom of expression as the general freedom to communicate. Two fundamental questions need to be distinguished: *Why* should speech be protected, and *how* should it be protected?

1.1 Why is speech protected?

According to well-rehearsed scholarship, freedom of expression may largely be based on three main conceptions: the argument from democracy, the argument from truth, including its sub-category, the 'marketplace of ideas', and the argument from individual autonomy or 'self-fulfilment'.[3] Yet upon closer examination, it becomes clear that these well-known labels do not provide clear-cut answers to all phenomena of speech alike. Therefore, in order to achieve full understanding of freedom of expression theory, and consequently of media freedom, two antithetical free speech philosophies can be distinguished along the following lines: the approaches tend to stress

[1] Luhmann (1996) p. 2. [2] Compare Habermas (1981b) p. 184.

[3] There are further rationales and interests to explain freedom of expression, which are related to the conceptions mentioned before, such as suspicion of government intrusion (see Chapter 2, Section 2.1), social interaction and community, or balance between stability and change; see Scanlon (1972); Wells (1997) 166; Emerson (1963) 884–6. For a general overview, see Barendt (2005) pp. 6–30.

- either the individual or the social interest of freedom of expression;
- that freedom of expression is either an end in itself or merely a means to an end; and
- that either the interest of the speaker alone or the effects of speech on society in general determine the moral value of speech.

For the purposes of presentation, these approaches are stylised as the 'deontological' versus the 'consequentialist' approach to freedom of expression.

A consequentialist understanding explains freedom of speech because of its instrumental value, not because of its intrinsic one. As a result, a consequentialist theory of freedom of expression

- emphasises the social interest of freedom of expression rather than the individual;
- regards freedom of expression as a means to an end rather than an end in itself; and
- focuses on the effects of speech on society in general, rather than on the interest of the speaker alone.

This finds its roots in the idea of civic republicanism, which can be traced back to the works of Plato and Aristotle, and which later had its most influential (and extreme) advocate in Jean-Jacques Rousseau.[4] In essence, the civic republican concept refers to citizens who understand themselves as free and equal members of a co-operative, self-governing community and who are primarily oriented to the *res publica*, the 'public affair' or public good.[5] Society is, in this context, understood not as merely the sum of all individuals, but rather as a subject in its own right, a 'collective body'.[6] Civic republicanism emphasises the 'value of civic self-organisation, so that human rights have a binding character for a political community only as elements of their own consciously appropriated tradition'.[7] Rousseau expressed this with the words: 'each giving himself to all, gives himself to nobody. . . . Each of us puts in common his person and his whole power under the supreme direction of the general will; and in return we receive every member as an indivisible part of the whole'.[8] Civic republicanism does not emphasise the individual autonomy of human beings (*hommes*), but the political autonomy of citizens (*citoyens*). Consequently, under a civic republican approach,

[4] On civic republicanism as a political theory, see Bassani (2002); Habermas (1992) pp. 267 ff.
[5] Habermas (1992) p. 268; see also Post (1991) 285–6. [6] Rousseau (1762) p. 15.
[7] Habermas (1992) p. 100. [8] Rousseau (1762) p. 15.

freedom of expression would be perceived as serving to carry out popular sovereignty and to contribute to the common good.

The free speech rationale that can most plainly be characterised as being based on a consequentialist understanding of freedom of expression is the argument from democracy. This argument follows the idea that, in order for an electorate to be appropriately knowledgeable, there must be no constraints on democratic deliberation and the free flow of information and ideas on matters of political concern.[9] Freedom of political debate lies at the heart of democracy and must therefore be afforded very strong protection. In a democratic society 'the actions or omissions of the Government must be subject to the close scrutiny not only of the legislative and judicial authorities but also of the press and public opinion'.[10] The right to scrutinise and to criticise one's government and its representatives is thus a fundamental principle prevailing throughout the application of any human rights convention.[11]

The connection between the argument from democracy and Rousseau's general will as a prominent expression of civic republicanism has been succinctly formulated by Hans Kelsen: 'A subject is politically free insofar as his individual will is in harmony with the "collective" (or "general") will expressed in the social order.'[12] Accordingly, '[t]he will of the community, in a democracy, is always created through a running discussion between majority and minority, through a free consideration of arguments for and against a certain regulation of a subject matter. This discussion takes place not only in parliament, but also, and foremost, at political meetings, in newspapers, books, and other vehicles of public opinion.'[13]

The argument from democracy has been developed further into an argument from 'public discourse' in order to appreciate the positive effect of free speech on the discussion of matters of public interest beyond the casting of votes. Focusing on explicitly political speech to the exclusion of other matters of public interest would perpetuate an 'old-fashioned distinction between public and private power'.[14] Freedom of speech thus protects the public discussion on all matters of public interest. These activities include all discussions of public issues such as education, philosophy and science, literature and the arts, and, in particular, speech

[9] See in particular Meiklejohn (1948); Meiklejohn (1961); Bork (1971) 20; Sunstein (1992) 263; Weinstein (2011a).

[10] ECtHR, *Castells* v. *Spain* [1992] App. no. 11798/85 [46]; see also *Kaperzyński* v. *Poland* [2012] App. no. 43206/07 [64]; High Court of Australia, *Lange* v. *Australian Broadcasting Corporation* [1997] HCA 25.

[11] See Chapter 7, Section 7.3.2.1.

[12] Kelsen (1928) p. 285.

[13] Kelsen (1928) pp. 287–8.

[14] See Chesterman (2000) p. 48.

related to figures and institutions exercising influence over the lives of people and in the formation of public opinion.[15] The ECtHR in particular has reiterated that 'there is no warrant in its case-law for distinguishing between political discussion and discussion of other matters of public concern'.[16] It is indeed accurate to say that the influence held by private actors, such as international corporations, sometimes presents a more immediate danger to individuals than the power of governments. In a democratic society the freedom to scrutinise and criticise those institutions may be at least as important as the freedom to scrutinise and criticise the government.[17]

There is a close link between the argument from democracy/public discourse and another consequentialist rationale for free speech, the argument from truth. Accordingly, freedom of expression serves the advancement of knowledge and the search for truth.[18] The argument from truth traces back to John Milton, who pleaded for the abolition of licensing restrictions for books. In *Areopagitica*, Milton wrote: 'And though all the windes of doctrine were let loose to play upon the earth, so Truth be in the field, we do injuriously by licensing and prohibiting to misdoubt her strength. Let her and Falsehood grapple; who ever knew Truth put to the wors, in a free and open encounter.'[19] Some two hundred years later, John Stuart Mill re-emphasised that the conventional wisdom of society is never complete. Rather, conflicting doctrines 'share the truth between them; and the nonconforming opinion is needed to supply the remainder of the truth, of which the received doctrine embodies only a part.'[20] The argument from truth thus protects freedom of expression because truth is best achieved, and falsehood best suppressed, when they face each other through free expression. In this context, truth should not be understood literally – only factual information can be proven true or false, but not opinions. Rather, the argument from truth can also refer to value judgments in terms of the 'most convincing idea'.

[15] Meiklejohn (1961) 257; Emerson (1963) 907; Blasi (1977) 559; Schauer (1983) 1303–4; Post (1993) 1116; Post (2000) 2363; House of Lords, *Reynolds* v. *Times Newspapers Ltd* [2001] 2 AC 127, 220 (Lord Cooke).

[16] ECtHR, *Thorgeir Thorgeirson* v. *Iceland* [1992] App. no. 13778/88 [64].

[17] See House of Lords, *Jameel* v. *Wall Street Journal Europe Sprl* [2006] UKHL 44 [158] (Baroness Hale); see also US Supreme Court, *Curtis Pub Co* v. *Butts*, 388 US 130, 164 f. (1967) (Warren CJ, concurring): 'the distinctions between governmental and private sectors are blurred. ... In many situations, policy determinations which traditionally were channeled through formal political institutions are now originated and implemented through a complex array of boards, committees, commissions, corporations, and associations, some only loosely connected with the Government'.

[18] Emerson (1963) 881; Schauer (1982) p. 15.

[19] Milton (1644) p. 35.

[20] Mill (1869) p. 85

Deriving from this conception, the theory of the 'marketplace of ideas' provides that a society will best arrive at truth or 'the best idea' by allowing everyone a voice in the public debate, and that ultimately market forces will select the ideas most beneficial to society.[21] As Justice Holmes explained:

> [W]hen men have realized that time has upset many fighting faiths, they may come to believe even more than they believe the very foundations of their own conduct that the ultimate good desired is better reached by free trade in ideas – that the best test of truth is the power of the thought to get itself accepted in the competition of the market.[22]

As a consequence, the arguments from democracy, from public discourse and from truth, including the 'marketplace of ideas' rationale, share the focus on the societal effect of speech, that is, the progress of a democratic society, contributions to discourses on matters of importance for society in general and the pursuit of truth.

These consequentialist approaches from civic republicanism stand in contrast to the deontological concept of liberal individualism, which largely can be ascribed to John Locke[23] and (to a certain degree) Immanuel Kant.[24] While civic republicanism is focused on collective and political autonomy, that is, the self-realisation of the political community, liberalism privileges individual or private autonomy, that is, individual self-determination.[25] Accordingly, liberalism regards individual liberties not as a means to an end, but an end in themselves.[26] Consequently, freedom of speech has to be regarded as valuable not because of its consequences, but because of its intrinsic value as an essential feature of a person's individual autonomy. It is based on the paradigm that individuals must *as such* be able to express themselves.[27] Communicative activities are perceived as crucial to dignity, self-fulfilment and self-realisation.[28]

21 See Baker (1978) 967; Ingber (1984); Garry (1989) 191; Pugh (1995) 1751; Volokh (2011a) 596.

22 US Supreme Court, *Abrams* v. *United States*, 250 US 616, 630 (1919) (Holmes J, dissenting). See also *Whitney* v. *California*, 274 US 357, 375–8 (1927) (Brandeis J, concurring); *Gertz* v. *Robert Welch, Inc.*, 418 US 323, 339–40 (1974); House of Lords, *R* v. *Secretary of State for the Home Department, ex p Simms* [2000] 2 AC 115.

23 Russell (1946) p. 548; see esp. Locke (1689) Book II.

24 See, in particular, Kant (1785).

25 Habermas (1992) pp. 99, 267 ff.; Berlin (1969) pp. 139–41.

26 See Kant (1785) p. 45; Schauer (1982) p. 60.

27 Compare Blasi (1977) 545; Baker (1978) 996; Scanlon (1979) 533 ff.; Redish (1982) 593; Richards (1986) p. 169; Baker (1989) p. 59; Post (1993); Richards (1999) p. 23; Nestler (2005) 211; Moore (2005).

28 Although self-fulfilment and self-realisation are also seen as freedom of expression rationales in their own right; see, e.g., Redish (1982) 593; Wragg (2013) 363 footnote 5.

The argument from individual autonomy is thus focused on the speaker, not on the speaker's impact on society.[29] It is not tied to the idea that speech should promote any goal for society at large, such as the attainment of truth. Rather, freedom of expression is a goal in itself. Nor does it serve collective self-determination, as the civic republican approach suggests, but mere individual self-fulfilment. As a consequence, freedom of expression is only an individual, and not a social, good.

However, it should be emphasised that neither in theory nor in practice may any of these freedom of expression arguments claim absolute prevalence. Rather, they are intertwined, encompass different aspects of freedom of expression and even complement each other.[30] The arguments from truth and from democracy are not exclusively audience-interest based, they are also speaker-interest based. Mill, who can be considered one of the main proponents of the argument from truth, emphasised that one of the main advantages of freedom of speech lies in enabling average human beings to attain the mental state which they are capable of.[31] Moreover, Robert Post, who significantly contributed to the development of Meiklejohn's more audience-based argument from democracy towards an argument of public discourse, indicated that democratic legitimacy is based on the notion that all of those to whom a law applies should be able to believe that they have an equal opportunity to become authors of the law through their participation in public discourse.[32] Thus the argument from democracy, or public discourse, is not purely community interest-based either, but also refers to the speakers' interest in becoming 'co-author' of the law.

Moving from the theoretical to the practical perspective, it becomes clear that international adjudicators do not avow themselves to one particular theory of freedom of expression. In *Handyside* v. *United Kingdom*, the ECtHR established, and has since then reiterated: 'Freedom of expression constitutes one of the essential foundations of [a democratic] society, one of the basic conditions for its progress and for the development of every man.'[33] In cases following *Handyside*, the

[29] Blasi (1977) 553.
[30] See Blasi (1977) 554; Barendt (2005) pp. 6–7; Milo (2008) p. 55; Marshall (1992) 44; Wragg (2013).
[31] Mill (1869) pp. 127–8. [32] Post (1991) 316.
[33] ECtHR, *Handyside* v. *United Kingdom* [1976] App. no. 5493/72 [49]; reiterated in, amongst many other decisions, *Sunday Times* v. *United Kingdom (No. 1)* [1979] App. no. 6538/74 [65]; *Lingens* v. *Austria* [1986] App. no. 9815/82 [41]; *Axel Springer AG* v. *Germany (No. 1)* [2012] App. no. 39954/08 [78].

Court replaced the term 'the development of every man' with 'each individual's self-fulfilment'.[34] The Human Rights Committee, the Inter-American Court of Human Rights, the Court of Justice of the EU and the African Commission on Human and Peoples' Rights established similar principles, and, in doing so, regularly refer to the ECtHR and to each other.[35] The Inter-American Commission rightly observed 'a convergence among the different regional systems for protecting human rights and the universal system, with respect to the essential role that [freedom of expression] plays in the exercise of democracy.'[36]

To begin with, the Human Rights Committee acknowledges that freedom of opinion and freedom of expression 'are indispensable conditions for the full development of the person'[37] and constitute the 'cornerstones in any free and democratic society. It is the essence of such societies that citizens must be allowed to inform themselves about alternatives to the political system/parties in power, and that they may criticize or openly and publicly evaluate their Governments without fear of interference or punishment by the Government, subject to certain restrictions set out in [Article 19(3) ICCPR].'[38] Furthermore, the Committee regularly reiterates that 'the right to freedom of expression is of paramount importance in any democratic society, and that any restrictions on its exercise must meet strict tests of justification.'[39]

The IACtHR frequently emphasises that freedom of expression

> is a cornerstone upon which the very existence of a democratic society rests. It is indispensable for the formation of public opinion. It is also a *conditio sine qua non* for the development of political parties, trade unions, scientific and cultural societies and, in general, those who wish to influence the public. It represents, in short, the means that enable the community, when exercising

[34] See, e.g., ECtHR, *Lindon, Otchakovsky-Laurens and July* v. *France* [2007] App. nos. 21279/02 and 36448/02 [45]; *Frankowicz* v. *Poland* [2008] App. no. 53025/99 [38].

[35] See, e.g., IACtHR, *Olmedo Bustos and others* v. *Chile ('The Last Temptation of Christ')* [2001] Case 11.803 [69]; *Ivcher-Bronstein* v. *Peru* [2001] Case 11.762 [152]; *Herrera-Ulloa* v. *Costa Rica* [2004] Case 12.367 [113] and [126]; AfComHPR, *Law Offices of Ghazi Suleiman* v. *Sudan* [2003] App. no. 228/99 [48] (to the ECtHR) and [50] (to the IACtHR); *Kenneth Good* v. *Republic of Botswana* [2010] App. no. 313/05 [197]; ECJ , *Familiapress* v. *Heinrich Bauer Verlag* [1997] ECR I-03689, Case C-368/95 [26].

[36] IAComHR, *Eduardo Kimel* v. *Argentina* [2007] Case 12.450 [71].

[37] General Comment no. 34, para. 2.

[38] Human Rights Committee, *Benhadj* v. *Algeria* [2007] Communication no. 1173/2003 [8.10]; see also *Aduayom and others* v. *Togo* [1996] Communication nos. 422–424/1990 [7.4]; *Gryb* v. *Belarus* [2011] Communication no. 1316/2004 [13.3]; General Comment no. 34, para. 2.

[39] See, e.g., Human Rights Committee, *Park* v. *Republic of Korea* [1998] Communication no. 628/1995 [10.3]; *Shchetko and others* v. *Belarus* [2001] Communication no. 1009/2001 [7.3]; *Velichkin* v. *Belarus* [2001] Communication no. 1022/2001 [7.3].

its options, to be sufficiently informed. Consequently, it can be said that a society that is not well informed is not truly free.[40]

The Court regards freedom of expression as having both

an individual dimension and a social dimension: It requires, on the one hand, that no one be arbitrarily limited or impeded in expressing his own thoughts. In that sense, it is a right that belongs to each individual. Its second aspect, on the other hand, implies a collective right to receive any information whatsoever and to have access to the thoughts expressed by others.[41]

Without effective freedom of expression protection, according to the Court, 'democracy is enervated, pluralism and tolerance start to deteriorate, the mechanisms for control and complaint by the individual become ineffectual and, above all, a fertile ground is created for authoritarian systems to take root in society.'[42]

The Court of Justice of the EU observed that '[t]he safeguarding of the freedoms protected under Article 11 of the Charter undoubtedly constitutes a legitimate aim in the general interest, the importance of which in a democratic and pluralistic society must be stressed in particular.'[43] Finally, the AfComHPR has regularly indicated that Article 9(2) AfCHPR 'reflects the fact that freedom of expression is a basic human right, vital to an individual's personal development, his political consciousness, and participation in the conduct of public affairs in his country'.[44] Accordingly, freedom of expression and information is of 'fundamental importance ... as an individual human right, as a cornerstone of democracy and as a means of ensuring respect for all human rights and freedoms.'[45]

[40] IACtHR, Advisory Opinion OC-5/85 [70]; reiterated in, for example, *Herrera-Ulloa* v. *Costa Rica* [2004] Case 12.367 [112]; *Ricardo Canese* v. *Paraguay* [2004] Case 12.032 [82]; *Vélez Restrepo* v. *Colombia* [2012] Case 12.658 [141]; IAComHR, *Francisco Martorell* v. *Chile* [1996] Case 11.230 [57]; *Víctor Manuel Oropeza* v. *Mexico* [1999] Case 11.740 [48].

[41] IACtHR, *Ricardo Canese* v. *Paraguay* [2004] Case 12.032 [77]; *Vélez Restrepo* v. *Colombia* [2012] Case 12.658 [137]. See also IAComHR, *Víctor Manuel Oropeza* v. *Mexico* [1999] Case 11.740 [51]; *Oscar Elías Biscet and others* v. *Cuba* [2006] Case 12.476 [196].

[42] IAComHR, *Perozo and others* v. *Venezuela* [2009] Case 12.442 [116]; see also IACtHR, *Vélez Restrepo* v. *Colombia* [2012] Case 12.658 [141].

[43] CJEU, *Sky Österreich* v. *Österreichischer Rundfunk* [2013] (not yet reported), Case C-283/11 [52] with further references.

[44] AfComHPR, *Media Rights Agenda, Constitutional Rights Project, Media Rights Agenda and Constitutional Rights Project* v. *Nigeria* [1998] App. nos. 105/93, 128/94, 130/94 and 152/96 [54]; reiterated in, e.g., *Amnesty International* v. *Zambia* [1999] App. no. 212/98 [54]; *Interights, Institute for Human Rights and Development in Africa, and Association mauritanienne des droits de l'Homme* v. *Mauritania* [2004] App. no. 242/01 [77].

[45] AfComHPR, *Law Offices of Ghazi Suleiman* v. *Sudan* [2003] App. no. 228/99 [40].

1.2 How is speech protected?

The examination of the theoretical question *why* speech is protected leads inevitably to the doctrinal question of *how* speech, and what forms of speech, should be protected. Although the reasons for protecting speech influence the acceptance or rejection of legal doctrine to a certain degree, these are nonetheless two distinct questions. Unfortunately, this distinction is not always observed in the academic debate, and courts provide hardly any insight into their theoretical foundations anyway.[46] Yet this distinction will become significant for the shape of the Media Freedom Principle.

The question of how speech has to be protected is in fact much older than the theoretical search for the normative foundations of free speech. It leads back to the controversy between Plato and the Rhetoricians (or Sophists) about knowledge and perception, and thus about the purpose of speech. The Sophists argued that there is no objective truth and no antecedent knowledge. One of the leading Sophists, Protagoras, is believed to have coined the dictum 'Man is the measure of all things, of things that are that they are, and of things that are not that they are not'.[47] He thus expressed his belief that there is no such thing as objective truth and objectively right or wrong conduct, but rather a relativity of convictions and values.[48] By contrast, Plato advocated an objective approach, judging doctrines by their social impact.[49] The Platonic Socrates was convinced that some people do have more knowledge than others, and that some opinions are better than others.[50]

This controversy laid the ground for a debate that is still discussed today: the purpose of free speech, and consequently the extent to which speech should be protected. According to the Sophists, the factual claim or opinion should prevail, that has been presented with the most convincing rhetorical and argumentative means. Here one can discern a lineage between the Sophists and the 'marketplace of ideas' theory. The marketplace of ideas theory rests on the scepticism that there is no absolute truth, or at least one can never be certain that the truth has been found.[51] This resembles Protagoras' claim that there was no objective truth or objectively right or wrong conduct, but simply conduct that was

[46] One notable exception is Justice Holmes' influential dissent in US Supreme Court, *Abrams* v. *United States*, 250 US 616 (1919); see Post (2000) 2361.

[47] Diogenes Laërtius (200) para. 51. The original source is supposed to be Protagoras' lost book 'Truth'.

[48] Dillon and Gergel (2003) Introduction p. xvi.

[49] See Russell (1946) p. 84.

[50] See Plato (369 BC) para. 161c ff.

[51] Schauer (1982) pp. 24–5, rightly highlights the distinction between truth and certainty.

'profitable' or 'useful'.[52] Accordingly, truth is determined solely by the value of the ideas or opinions in the intellectual marketplace.[53] Consequently, expression of opposition to the majoritarian belief in truth and certainty must always be possible.

Justice Oliver Wendell Holmes Jr, who wrote the influential dissent to *Abrams* v. *United States* establishing the 'marketplace of ideas rationale', was a legal pragmatist, and the *Abrams* dissent can be properly understood as an expression of American pragmatism.[54] Notably, one of the founders of the American philosophy of pragmatism, F. C. S. Schiller, called himself a disciple of Protagoras.[55]

By contrast, an objectivist Platonic approach to free speech doctrine judges speech by its impact on society. Speech is not protected *because* it contributes to a democratic society, to the marketplace of ideas or to finding the truth. Rather, speech is protected only *if* and *insofar* as it contributes to finding the truth or the 'best ideas' for society in general. An objectivist freedom of speech doctrine thus presupposes the possibility of objective knowledge and certainty.

Placing adjudicators' jurisprudence under the microscope, it becomes clear that US case-law has a strong tendency towards a sceptical Protagorean approach, while European and international adjudicators reveal a more objectivist Platonic conception of speech. The doctrinal divide between these approaches becomes particularly relevant with regard to the following questions, which will be further elaborated in this book:

- Should the intensity of protection afforded to speech vary according to the content of the speech? The argument from democracy purports that free speech contributes to effective self-government. Yet, one can also reverse this argument by requiring that in order to be protected 'speech', a communication objectively *has* to contribute to effective self-government (or at least to a matter of public concern). If, however, the speech does not contribute to such a matter, then it should not be protected as 'free speech'.[56]
- Should certain speech disseminators, such as the media, be afforded more protection than others? This claim is reflected in international adjudicators' jurisprudence, but widely rejected by the US Supreme Court.[57]
- What should be the limits to the dissemination of false statements of fact? While a sceptical conception of speech would allow false speech

[52] Compare Dillon and Gergel (2003) Introduction p. xvi.
[53] See Schauer (1982) p. 20.
[54] Schauer (1982) p. 20 including fn. 6; Post (2000) 2360.
[55] Russell (1946) p. 83.
[56] See Chapter 2, Section 2.2.3.1.
[57] See Chapter 2, Section 2.1.

to be disseminated, an objectivist approach would permit restrictions at least to intentionally false speech. This debate has its most relevant practical arena in the question of whether the denial of clearly established historical facts deserves protection.[58]

- Should there be restrictions on hate speech or religiously offensive speech?[59] A sceptical doctrine would not authorise limitations on speech because of their harmful effect on society (arguably unless it causes identifiable harm on a particular individual), while an objectivist understanding would interfere with speech if this is necessary to protect the interests of society in general.

[58] See Chapter 11. [59] See Chapters 11 and 12.

2 Theory of media freedom

While the debate on the theoretical explanation of freedom of expression has been led for several decades, a theory of media freedom has, it seems, not been subject to a distinct scrutiny so far.[1] First, a theory of media freedom has to rebut the objections against media freedom as a distinct fundamental right (see 2.1). Second, it is argued that the rationale for media freedom is the media's significance for public discourse (see 2.2.). Third, a theory of media freedom has to clarify the relationship between freedom of the media and freedom of expression (see 2.3).

2.1 General objections

The inference of a privileged protection of the media from freedom of expression is not uncontroversial. Even more, many legal scholars outrightly reject the notion that the media should enjoy any privileges or be subject to any special duties. This point of view is particularly widespread – and equally controversial – in US scholarship.[2] Different terms have been coined for this approach: the 'equivalence model', since the protection of the media should be equivalent to that of other individuals invoking freedom of expression,[3] the 'neutrality doctrine', because the absence of special media rights follows from the state's obligation to be neutral in granting such rights,[4] or the 'press-as-technology model', as freedom of the press should be conceptualised as the mere right of every person to use communications technology, and not as a right belonging exclusively to

[1] Freedom of the media or of media speech has usually been an implicit subject of freedom of speech analysis in general; see, in particular, Barendt (2005) Chapter XII.

[2] See, e.g., Lange (1975); Van Alstyne (1977) 768–9; Lewis (1979); Amar (1999) 714; Carter (1992) 874; Anderson (2002) 528; Baker (2007) 958; Baker (2011) 230; Volokh (2012) 538–9.

[3] Compare Fenwick and Phillipson (2006) p. 20. In addition, Fenwick and Phillipson identify the 'special privileges model', the 'differentiated privileges model', and 'a variable geometry of media freedom'.

[4] Compare Bezanson (1977) 755; Rooney (1983) 54.

members of the publishing industry.[5] Support in favour of this interpretation can be found in the US Supreme Court's approach to the First Amendment, where the words 'or of the press' are used. Although the Supreme Court has acknowledged the role of the press 'as a powerful antidote to any abuses of power by governmental officials',[6] it has 'consistently rejected the proposition that the institutional press has any constitutional privilege beyond that of other speakers'.[7]

The arguments for this approach, which is largely based on an originalist interpretation of the First Amendment,[8] are evident. The First Amendment, Justice Scalia noted, protects 'speech', not speakers.[9] Similarly, the Inter-American Court once indicated that '[t]he professional exercise of journalism cannot be differentiated from freedom of expression, but rather, to the contrary, both are evidently interrelated, since the professional journalist is not, and cannot be, anyone other than a person who has decided to exercise freedom of expression in a continuous, regular and paid manner'.[10] Affording privileged protection to the media would require defining 'the media' based on certain 'expert knowledge' and 'disciplinary methods'.[11] This, it is argued, would entail that the state could 'police' journalists in a similar way as it polices commercial or professional speech, namely to ensure that they are fulfilling the functions that entitle them to privileged protection.[12] Eventually, one could even argue that privileged protection for a particular group of 'experts' is elitist.

These arguments rightly reflect the notion that media freedom is a right that is not natural and inherent. Unlike freedom of expression,[13] it has to be 'earned' in the first place. Whether this is called 'elitist' is

[5] Volokh (2012) 463.

[6] US Supreme Court, *Mills* v. *Alabama*, 384 US 214, 219 (1966); see also *Estes* v. *Texas*, 381 US 532, 539 (1965): 'The free press has been a mighty catalyst in awakening public interest in governmental affairs, exposing corruption among public officers and employees and generally informing the citizenry of public events and occurrences.'

[7] US Supreme Court, *Citizens United* v. *FEC*, 130 S Ct 876, 905 (2010) (citations omitted). See, for instance, *Associated Press* v. *United States*, 326 US 1, 7 (1945); *Curtis Publishing Co.* v. *Butts*, 388 US 130, 150 (1967); *Branzburg* v. *Hayes*, 408 US 665, 704 (1972); *Pell* v. *Procunier*, 417 US 817, 834 (1974); *Saxbe* v. *Washington Post Co.*, 417 US 843, 848–9 (1974). The Supreme Court's approach stands in contrast to several judgments of District Courts; see, for instance, *New York Times Co.* v. *Gonzales*, 382 F. Supp. 2d 457, 501–3 (SDNY 2005); *O'Grady* v. *Superior Court*, 44 Cal. Rptr. 3d 72 (Cal Ct App 2006). Furthermore, forty States and the District of Columbia have adopted shield laws, that is, legislation providing a journalist with the right to refuse to testify as to information and/or sources of information obtained during the news gathering and dissemination process.

[8] See the elaborate works of Anderson (1983); Volokh (2012); see also Lange (1975) pp. 88–99; Lewis (1979) 600; Anderson (2002) 446–7.

[9] US Supreme Court, *Citizens United* v. *FEC*, 130 S Ct 876, 905 (2010) (Scalia J, concurring).

[10] IACtHR, *Vélez Restrepo* v. *Colombia* [2012] Case 12.658 [140].

[11] Blocher (2012) 442. [12] Blocher (2012) 442. [13] See Schauer (1982) p. 160.

a mere terminological issue. However, the counter-arguments do not fully embrace the idea of the personal and substantive scope of media freedom, especially in its relationship with freedom of expression. Whether a person abides by the 'disciplinary methods' of the media does not define whether he *is* 'media', that is, a journalist. The 'disciplinary methods', which, in accordance with international human rights provisions, will later be named 'duties and responsibilities' of the media, are not constitutive for being 'media'. Rather, the observance of certain rules is an aspect of the balancing exercise when media activity interferes with rights of others and social norms of civility. Consequently, it is not for the state to 'police' media activity; rather, it is for the courts to decide on a case-by-case basis whether the significance attributed to the exercise of media freedom outweighs the public or private interest in having the conflicting norm protected. How this can be translated into legal doctrine will be shown in Part II and III. For example, if a newspaper gets the results of last weekend's football match wrong, then it violates the requirement of accuracy, which certainly belongs to the 'disciplinary methods' of journalism. But since it does not violate individual or social legal norms, this 'transgression' will not be 'policed'. If, however, a newspaper publishes an inaccurate report alleging abusive behaviour of a football player after the match that may be considered defamatory, it may, under certain circumstances, be successfully sued if it did not attempt to verify the information before publication.[14]

But this argument implies another important objection to 'media freedom' as a legal concept. Whoever engages in the difficult task of defining what 'the media' actually is, risks an either over-exclusive or over-inclusive interpretation.[15] While an over-inclusive definition of the terms 'media' or 'journalist' might create a danger of misuse, an over-exclusive definition could be perceived as discriminatory because other regular contributors to matters of public importance, such as scientists and artists, would be deprived of additional protection by singling out the media for separate treatment.[16]

Yet this reasoning is circular. Protecting the media would not deprive those others of the rights they already possess, or should possess. Articles 13 EUChFR and several constitutional provisions[17] expressly protect freedom of science and freedom of the arts. A privileged protection of

[14] See Chapter 7, Section 7.3.4.

[15] US Supreme Court, *Branzburg* v. *Hayes*, 408 US 665, 704 (1972); compare Lange (1975) 106; Amar (1999) 714; Anderson (2002) 510; Alonzo (2006) 759; Baker (2007) 1015; Blocher (2012) 428–9.

[16] Lewis (1979) 602–3.

[17] Such as Articles 20 and 21 Swiss Constitution, Article 33 Italian Constitution or Article 5(3) German Basic Law.

the media should therefore not work to the detriment of artists and scientists. Rather, there is good reason to furnish those contributors and 'truth seekers' with privileges similar to those afforded to the media – *de lege lata* or *de lege ferenda*.

Moreover, the argument that a distinction between the media and non-media actors may be *difficult* to draw is not convincing either. It is certainly difficult to decide whether the 'lonely pamphleteer', omnipresent in US scholarship, does indeed constitute press.[18] However, line-drawing problems are an essential part of legal work. The difficulty of defining or identifying the media does not justify ignoring media protection clauses: press clauses, as provided in the First Amendment to the US Constitution, Article 21(2) of the Italian Constitution, Article 5(1)2 of the German Basic Law or Article 25(1) of the Belgian Constitution, and the media clauses in Article 17 Swiss Constitution or in Article 11(2) EUChFR. These clauses must mean something beyond free speech, otherwise they would be redundant.[19] Freedom of the media identifies, in the first place, the rights-holder, and not subject-matter of a freedom of expression right. It is freedom *of the* press and *of the* media, and not the freedom to publish something 'with' certain media. When constitutions, statutes and, as will be further analysed in this book, normative theory require privileged protection of the media, courts have to cope with the difficult task of line-drawing, although controversial judgments will inevitably occur.[20] Further legal terms which are difficult to define include: 'religion', 'association' and 'assembly'.[21] With equally vague textual guidance, courts regularly have to delineate which group is or is not a religion and what constitutes religious activity, or under what circumstances a group of people make an association or assembly, and so

[18] The example originates from Justice White in the US Supreme Court decision *Branzburg* v. *Hayes*, 408 US 665, 704 (1972); see, e.g., Lange (1975) 106; Lewis (1979) 606–7; Anderson (2002) 435; Ugland (2008) 127; Fargo and Alexander (2009) 1096. The ECtHR has rejected the notion that pamphleteers enjoy press freedom; see *Chorherr* v. *Austria* [1993] App. no. 13308/87 [24]; *Tolstoy Miloslavsky* v. *United Kingdom* [1993] App. no. 18139/91 [35]. By contrast, the German Federal Constitutional Court has held that leaflets constitute 'press' within the meaning of Article 5(1)2 of the German Basic Law; see '*Leaflet*' [1976] Case 1 BvR 460/72.

[19] Fundamentally Stewart (1975) 633. See also Nimmer (1975) 640; Pasich (1978) 385; Schauer (2005a) 1263–4; Ugland (2008) 136; West (2011) 1030–1; Bezanson (2012) 1261.

[20] See Dworkin (1996) p. 204; Schauer (2005a) 1260; Baker (2007) 1016; West (2011) 1048.

[21] See, e.g., the First Amendment to the US Constitution ('Congress shall make no law respecting an establishment of religion, or prohibiting the free exercise thereof; . . . or the right of the people peaceably to assemble'), Articles 4, 8 and 9 German Basic Law, Articles 17 to 19 Italian Constitution, Articles 9 and 11 ECHR, or Articles 10 and 12 EUChFR.

far they have been fairly successful in doing so.[22] Against this background, there is no compelling reason to refrain from conceptualising media freedom as a fundamental right. And the starting point for this analysis is freedom of expression theory and doctrine.

It has been shown in the previous sections that neither freedom of expression theory, nor doctrine, may claim absolute prevalence regarding the protection of speech in general. Some theories focus on the role of the speaker; others on the effect of the speech on society in general. International adjudicators apply a more consequentialist and objectivist approach to freedom of expression, while the US Supreme Court's jurisprudence reveals an individualist and sceptical stance.

However, it is argued here that a Media Freedom Principle should be conceptualised across these antithetical positions based on a *discourse theory* of media freedom. Such a discourse theory includes normative connotations of media freedom stronger than those of the liberal model, but weaker than those found in the civic republican model. It recognises the importance of the media for society as a whole, but does not neglect media freedom as an individual liberty. Whereas a purely liberal view of freedom of expression would ignore the importance of the media for the public good, an objectivist expression of the civic republican view tends towards paternalism by prescribing what to publish – and even worse, what *not* to publish. Paternalism, as Kant argued, 'would be the greatest conceivable *Despotism*' (emphasis original).[23] And even under the rule of a Platonic elite of wise men, despotism remains despotism.

2.2 Public discourse theory as the rationale for media freedom

A Media Freedom Principle states the legal conditions under which mass communication necessary for public discourse is institutionalised.

[22] Compare Rooney (1983) 55. With regard to religion, see, e.g., US Supreme Court, *Sherbert* v. *Verner*, 374 US 398 (1963); *Thomas* v. *Review Board of the Indiana Employment Security Division*, 450 US 707 (1981); *Church of the Lukumi Babalu Aye, Inc.* v. *City of Hialeah*, 508 US 520 (1993); EComHR, *Swami Omkarananda and the Divine Light Zentrum* v. *Switzerland* [1981] App. no. 8118/77; ECtHR, *Buscarini and others* v. *San Marino* [1999] App. no. 24645/94; *Pretty* v. *United Kingdom* [2002] App no. 2346/02; German Federal Constitutional Court, '*Bahai*' [1991] Case 2 BvR 263/86. With regard to assemblies, see, e.g., Human Rights Committee, *Kungurov* v. *Uzbekistan* [2011] Communication no. 1478/2006 [8.2]; ECtHR, *United Communist Party of Turkey and others* v. *Turkey* [1998] App. no. 133/1996/752/951 [24–34]; ECJ, *Schmidberger* v. *Austria* [2003] ECR I-05659, Case C-112/00; German Federal Constitutional Court, '*Fuckparade*' and '*Love Parade*' [2001] Case 1 BvQ 28/01 and 1 BvQ 30/01; '*Distinction Assembly – Crowd*' [2010] Case 1 BvR 1402/06.

[23] Kant (1793) p. 36.

The relation between the individual autonomy of journalists, on the one hand, and the importance of the media for the common good, on the other hand, requires a set of rules that the state, the media and affected people must recognise. A discourse theory of media freedom is based on the following tenets:

1. Media freedom is justified not only because of the individual liberty of the publisher, but because of the media's importance for public discourse.
2. Media freedom may be interfered with in order to prevent harm to individuals and to enforce civility rules to protect the public discourse.
3. The weight afforded to media freedom in the balancing exercise with conflicting rights and interests depends on whether the media has abided by its 'duties and responsibilities', especially the extent to which it contributes to public discourse.

2.2.1 *The media's significance for public discourse*

The importance attached to media freedom is not only justified by the individual liberty of the publisher, but in particular by the role that the media plays for public discourse in a democratic society. Ideal public discourse means that all relevant questions, issues and contributions are brought up and processed in debates on the basis of the best available information and arguments.[24] The mass media is regularly, and on a grand scale, concerned with contributions to such public debates. The expression of opinion and the dissemination of information by the institutional mass media are, in their sheer quantity and influence, distinct from speech of private individuals.

'Public discourse' shall be defined as an open, free and argumentative communicative process aimed at reaching understanding and forming public opinion on matters of public concern.[25] First, public discourse shall be 'open' in the sense that it is non-exclusive. Whoever wishes to participate in this discourse shall be entitled to do so – either as a private individual, based on freedom of expression, or as a journalist invoking media freedom. The 'openness' of the public discourse thus absorbs the

[24] Compare Habermas (1992) pp. 170, 228.

[25] The concept of public discourse largely builds on the works of Jürgen Habermas and Robert Post on communicative action and freedom of expression in general. Habermas' concept of 'discourse' is not merely a synonym for speech, but a technical term for a reflective form of speech that aims at reaching a rationally motivated consensus. Habermas' discourse theory thus rests on the assumption of the prevalence of reason, which, at the same time, is one its main points of criticism. Yet it is argued here that this reason can be expected from those who claim the privileges of the media.

'press-as-technology' approach: media freedom includes – among other rights – the right of every person to use mass communications technology. In addition, media freedom, as conceptualised in this book, does not distinguish between the medium used for publication or the prior education of those who claim to be journalists.[26] Eventually, the openness of public discourse prohibits a compulsory registration duty for journalists.[27]

Second, public discourse shall be 'free' in that it is non-coercive. No person or institution shall be forced to participate in the discourse, and whoever participates may – within the limits presupposed by public discourse itself – communicate whatever he wishes.

Third, the notion of 'argumentativeness' resembles Justice Holmes' 'marketplace of ideas' rationale. Public discourse shall be 'argumentative' in that the authority of the better argument is the only authority.[28] In turn, argumentative public discourse prohibits any recourse to hatred, violence or disparagement.

Fourth, public discourse shall be aimed at reaching understanding. This presupposes that a speaker raises at least three validity claims with his utterance, namely that a factual statement made is true (truthfulness); that the speech act is right with regard to the existing normative context (belief in the normative validity); and that the manifest intention of the speaker is meant as expressed (sincerity).[29] In short, public discourse does not aim at reaching understanding if communication is based on intentional deception and insincerity.

Fifth, public discourse shall be aimed at the formation of public opinion on matters of public concern. Public discourse depends on the maintenance of a public sphere, which is a sociological structure that is a prerequisite to the formation of public opinion.[30] The mass media is the institutional core of this public sphere.[31] It is essential to communicate information and ideas about political, cultural and other public issues. This normative concept of public discourse is not identical with, and partly even opposed to, the notion of public discourse as applied by the US Supreme Court,[32] which widely *suspends* public discourse from

[26] See Chapter 4. [27] See Chapter 6, Section 6.3.3.1.2.1.

[28] See Arendt (1958) p. 200; Habermas (1981a) p. 25; Schauer (1982) p. 78.

[29] See Habermas (1981a) pp. 39, 99; Habermas (1981b) p. 120. [30] Post (2011) 486.

[31] Habermas (1981b) p. 319. The 'public sphere' as a sociological concept has been broadly developed by Habermas in his early work on *The Structural Transformation of the Public Sphere*; see Habermas (1962). It does not need to be subject to further analysis here. However, the concept of 'public concern' in its *legal* implications will be developed below (Section 2.2.1).

[32] See US Supreme Court, *Cornelius* v. *NAACP Legal Defense & Educ. Fund*, 473 US 788, 802 (1985); *Bethel School Dist. No. 403* v. *Fraser*, 478 US 675, 682–3 (1986); *Hustler Magazine* v. *Falwell*, 485 US 46, 50 (1988).

the application of restrictive 'norms of civility'.[33] This reflects the fact that the Supreme Court's jurisprudence is primarily based on the individual autonomy rationale: individual autonomy protects the choice *not* to conform to behavioural norms of public discourse.[34]

To accomplish its purpose as an institution of public discourse, the media must be guaranteed an effective, privileged means to gather and disseminate the news.[35] In addition, a functioning and diverse marketplace of ideas requires that as many viewpoints as possible are represented.[36] Being the most powerful and ubiquitous channels of communication, the media therefore require particular protection or, conversely, as little restriction as possible. A privileged protection of journalists encourages the dissemination of more information and, consequently, of more valuable, truthful information.[37]

The practice of international adjudicators confirms this theoretical assumption. As the Strasbourg Court regularly emphasises,

> Although the press[38] must not overstep certain bounds, in particular in respect of the reputation and rights of others, its duty is nevertheless to impart – in a manner consistent with its obligations and responsibilities – information and ideas on all matters of public interest. Not only does the press have the task of imparting such information and ideas; the public also has a right to receive them. Were it otherwise, the press would be unable to play its vital role of 'public watchdog'.[39]

Freedom of the media 'affords the public one of the best means of discovering and forming an opinion of the ideas and attitudes of political leaders. It is incumbent on the press to impart information and ideas on political issues and on other subjects of public interest.'[40] Similarly, the Inter-American Court explained that the media plays an essential role

[33] See Post (1990) 604; Post (1991) 286; Post (1995) 1276. On the concept of 'norms of civility' see below (Section 2.2.2).

[34] Post (1987) 555.

[35] See Rooney (1983) 58; Garry (1989) 199.

[36] See US Supreme Court, *Dennis* v. *United States*, 341 US 494, 584 (1951) (Douglas J, dissenting); Alonzo (2006) 762.

[37] Nestler (2005) 211.

[38] The Court extends the protection afforded to the press to audiovisual media; see ECtHR, *Jersild* v. *Denmark* [1994] App. no. 15890/89 [31]; *Radio France and others* v. *France* [2004] App. no. 53984/00 [33]. However, the Court imposes higher duties and responsibilities on audiovisual media; see Chapter 6, Section 6.3.3.1.2.

[39] ECtHR, *Axel Springer AG* v. *Germany (No. 1)* [2012] App. no. 39954/08 [79]; *Von Hannover* v. *Germany (No. 2)* [2012] App. nos. 40660/08 and 60641/08 [102]. See also, e.g., ECtHR, *Sunday Times* v. *United Kingdom (No. 1)* [1979] App. no. 6538/74 [65]; *Bladet Tromsø and Stensaas* v. *Norway* [1999] App. no. 21980/93 [62]; *Times Newspapers Ltd* v. *United Kingdom (Nos. 1 and 2)* [2009] App. nos. 3002/03 and 23676/03 [40].

[40] ECtHR, *Centro Europa 7 Srl and Di Stefano* v. *Italy* [2012] App. no. 38433/09 [131]; see, e.g., *Lingens* v. *Austria* [1986] App. no. 9815/82 [41–2]; *Sürek* v. *Turkey (No. 1)* [1999] App. no. 26682/95 [59]; *Thoma* v. *Luxembourg* [2001] App. no. 38432/97 [45].

as a vehicle for the exercise of the 'social dimension' of freedom of expression in a democratic society, which is why it is vital that the media is able to gather the most diverse information and opinions.[41] Consequently, it is essential that journalists 'should enjoy the necessary protection and independence to exercise their functions comprehensively, because it is they who keep society informed, and this is an indispensable requirement to enable society to enjoy full freedom'.[42] Journalism is, in sum, 'one of the most important manifestations of freedom of expression and information'.[43] With regard to political parties, in particular, the Strasbourg Court observed that 'with the help of the media' they make 'an irreplaceable contribution to political debate, which is at the very core of the concept of a democratic society'.[44]

The Human Rights Committee has also acknowledged the importance of journalists and the media for a democratic society. In *Bodrozic* v. *Serbia and Montenegro*, the Committee observed 'that in circumstances of public debate in a democratic society, *especially in the media*, concerning figures in the political domain, the value placed by the Covenant upon uninhibited expression is particularly high' (emphasis added).[45] In this context, the Committee has also referred to the right to take part in the conduct of public affairs, as laid down in Article 25 ICCPR.[46] In order to ensure the full enjoyment of this right, the free communication of information and ideas about public and political issues between citizens, candidates and elected representatives is essential. This implies a free press and other

[41] IACtHR, *Fontevecchia and D'Amico* v. *Argentina* [2011] Case 12.524 [44]. See also *Ivcher-Bronstein* v. *Peru* [2001] Case 11.762 [149]; *Herrera-Ulloa* v. *Costa Rica* [2004] Case 12.367 [117].

[42] IACtHR, *Ivcher-Bronstein* v. *Peru* [2001] Case 11.762 [150]; *Herrera-Ulloa* v. *Costa Rica* [2004] Case 12.367 [119].

[43] IACtHR, Advisory Opinion OC-5/85 [71]; IAComHR, *Hugo Bustios Saavedra* v. *Peru* [1997] Case 10.548 [71]; Office of the Special Rapporteur for Freedom of Expression with the Inter-American Commission on Human Rights, Inter-American Legal Framework Regarding the Right to Freedom of Expression, 2009, CIDH/RELE/INF. 2/09, para. 165.

[44] See ECtHR, *United Communist Party of Turkey and others* v. *Turkey* [1998] App. no. 133/1996/752/951 [44].

[45] Human Rights Committee, *Bodrožić* v. *Serbia and Montenegro* [2005] Communication no. 1180/2003 [7.2].

[46] Article 25 ICCPR reads: 'Every citizen shall have the right and the opportunity, without any of the distinctions mentioned in article 2 and without unreasonable restrictions:

(a) To take part in the conduct of public affairs, directly or through freely chosen representatives;
(b) To vote and to be elected at genuine periodic elections which shall be by universal and equal suffrage and shall be held by secret ballot, guaranteeing the free expression of the will of the electors;
(c) To have access, on general terms of equality, to public service in his country.'

media able to comment on public issues and to inform public opinion.[47] According to the Committee, Article 25 ICCPR, read together with Article 19, implies 'that citizens, *in particular through the media*, should have wide access to information and the opportunity to disseminate information and opinions about the activities of elected bodies and their members' (emphasis added).[48]

As a result, freedom of the media is, in the first place, an instrumental right rather than an inherent one. The media is protected for fulfilling a beneficial function for society in general, that is, informing the public about matters of general concern, and contributing to finding the truth or the best ideas by participating in the marketplace of ideas. Thus, media freedom is more than merely freedom of expression for journalists: affording particular protection to the media is based on a consequentialist and functional understanding of media activity.

By contrast, the deontological 'self-fulfilment' argument for freedom of expression may not, or may only marginally, be applied to the media. The media, through its informing and opinion-shaping functions, is more significant than individual speech for democratic dialogue and from the 'marketplace of ideas' perspective. But the media is much less significant from the point of view of the individual autonomy rationale.[49] One of the underlying rationales of the argument from individual autonomy is to allow people 'to let off steam' – this rationale can only be applied to acts of individuals as individuals, but not to journalists while acting in their professional capacity. To be sure, journalists may achieve personal self-fulfilment from their publications. However, this should not be the primary aim of their activities. In addition, this rationale does not apply to media companies. A non-human entity such as a media corporation cannot receive the same self-fulfilment from engaging in expression as a natural person does.[50]

2.2.2 *Rules of civility as limitations to media freedom*

The mass media may not only use its considerable power to inform the public on matters of general interest: it can also abuse its power by invading a person's privacy and destroying his or her reputation in a

[47] General Comment no. 25, para. 25; see also Human Rights Committee, *Marques de Morais* v. *Angola* [2005] Communication no. 1128/2002 [6.8].

[48] Human Rights Committee, *Gauthier* v. *Canada* [1999] Communication no. 633/95 [13.4].

[49] See Nimmer (1975) 654; Nestler (2005) 212; Fargo and Alexander (2009) 1097; Marshall (1992) 42.

[50] Compare Nestler (2005) 212.

way private individuals would not be able to, or by divulging state secrets to a mass audience.[51] Furthermore, the media has the power not only to shape, but also to mislead, public opinion. In the internet age the traditional professional media has not lost its function as a gatekeeper to the awareness of the broader public and the 'public agenda', quite the contrary: by journalistically researching, editing and publishing on internet sources, the traditional media influences the public attention that is paid to particular publications among the deluge of information on the internet.[52] In the complex and overwhelming information environment of the internet, individuals simply lack the resources to compile and assess the information that might be relevant for them. Therefore, the Strasbourg Court rightly stressed: 'In a world in which the individual is confronted with vast quantities of information circulated via traditional and electronic media and involving an ever-growing number of players, monitoring compliance with journalistic ethics takes on added importance.'[53]

Since media freedom serves open, free and rational public discourse, the limits to media freedom must be, and can only be, those norms that are necessary to make such discourse possible. These 'norms of civility'[54] can be distinguished into two categories: *individual* rights of others and indispensable *social* norms necessary for the public discourse. Only those norms can constitute legitimate aims capable of justifying an interference with media freedom.[55]

The theory of public discourse thus seems to be built on a paradox.[56] On the one hand, media freedom is to be conceptualised as a liberty *from* regulatory requirements. On the other hand, the enjoyment of media freedom shall *depend* on the fulfilment of certain standards of public discourse. Yet there are several doctrinal stages where these underlying principles come to practical application, such as the media privileges, on the one hand, and media's duties and responsibilities, on the other hand. The conflict between those principles is only superficial; if properly conceptualised, the media's privileges in, and its duties and responsibilities for, the public discourse are complementary. If the media enjoyed *identical* liberties to private individuals and were to be subject to *the same* duties and responsibilities, the privileges of the media would be obsolete.

[51] See, e.g., Pasich (1978) 359; Carter (1984); Curran and Seaton (2010); Baker (2011) 234; Lord Justice Leveson, An Inquiry into the Culture, Practices and Ethics of the Press, 2012, pp. 76–8.
[52] Curran and Seaton (2010) p. 286; Calvert and Torres (2011) 345.
[53] *Novaya Gazeta and Borodyanskiy* v. *Russia* [2013] App. no. 14087/08 [42].
[54] See Post (1990); Post (1991) 286; Post (2000) 2365.
[55] See Chapter 6, Section 6.1.2.
[56] See Post (1990) 643; Post (1991) 287.

Therefore, greater demands on the media's duties and responsibilities justify the media's privileges, and *vice versa*.

Free, inclusive and argumentative public deliberation on matters of public concern is based on certain presuppositions of civility rules. These rules of civility include rights of others and certain social norms. Rights of others as limitations on freedom of expression and media freedom find their philosophical underpinning in Kant's understanding of 'law' as the 'sum of the conditions under which the choice of one [person] can be united with the choice of another [person] in accordance with a universal law of freedom'.[57] Kant thus justifies limitations to one's freedom of action if this is necessary to reconcile it with everyone else's freedom. Similarly, Mill's harm principle (which had already been adumbrated by Locke[58]) provides that the actions of individuals should be limited to prevent harm to other individuals; where such harm is done – and, according to Mill, *only* where such harm is done – is society justified in imposing restrictions.[59] Rawls' first principle of justice takes the same line: accordingly, 'each person is to have an equal right to the most extensive basic liberty compatible with a similar liberty for others'.[60] Consequently, there is a general duty inherent in human rights not to violate the rights of others while exercising one's own liberties.[61] Such 'rights of others' as limitations on freedom of expression and media freedom are now widely recognised in international conventions, such as in Article 19(3) ICCPR and Article 10(2) ECHR.[62]

However, media freedom finds its limitations in more than merely the rights of others. If one sees the foundation of media freedom in the public discourse rationale, as argued in this book, then the media has to abide by the standards that such public discourse itself presupposes. To be sure, not any contravention of social norms renders media publications illegal: freedom of expression and media freedom are not only applicable to information or ideas 'that are favourably received or regarded as inoffensive or as a matter of indifference, but also to those that offend, shock or disturb the State or any sector of the population'.[63]

57 Kant (1797) p. 24. 58 Locke (1689) Book II, Chapter II Sect. 6.
59 Mill (1869) pp. 21–2. 60 Rawls (1971) p. 60.
61 See Article 4 of the Declaration of the Rights of Man and of the Citizen of 26 August 1789: 'Liberty consists in being able to do anything that does not harm others: thus, the exercise of the natural rights of every man has no bounds other than those that ensure to the other members of society the enjoyment of these same rights. These bounds may be determined only by Law.'
62 These will be further elaborated on in Chapter 7.
63 Compare ECtHR, *Handyside* v. *United Kingdom* [1976] App. no. 5493/72 [49]; reiterated in, amongst many other decisions, *Sunday Times* v. *United Kingdom (No. 1)* [1979] App. no. 6538/74 [65]; *Lingens* v. *Austria* [1986] App. no. 9815/82 [41]; *Thorgeir*

However, media publications do not contribute to a free, rational and argumentative public discourse, but rather undermine it, if they result in violence, affect national security interests, prejudice a fair trial, offend against religious convictions or moral standards of a community, cause needless panic or incite hatred. It is therefore the task of the following chapters to provide a single framework for the balancing between the liberty of the media and the interests of other individuals and the community.

2.2.3 The media's contribution to public discourse

If media freedom is engaged in a balancing exercise with conflicting rights and interests, the 'weight' afforded to media freedom depends on whether the media fulfils its function as a contributor to public discourse: the extent to which the media reports on matters of public concern, the media's conduct prior to publication and whether the media acted in good faith. While the argument from public discourse provides the *theoretical* justification, the *textual* references for imposing such standards on media content and conduct are the 'duties and responsibilities' clauses in Articles 19(3) ICCPR and 10(2) ECHR, the limitations in Article 13(2) and (5) and Article 14 ACHR, and the duties enshrined in Articles 27 to 29 AfCHPR. Articles 19(3) ICCPR and 10(2) ECHR expressly stipulate that the exercise of freedom of expression carries with it duties and responsibilities. No other Convention or Covenant right provides such a qualification. Although applicable to speech of both media and non-media actors, the main purpose of the 'duties and responsibilities' clause is to offer Member States a tool to prevent abuse of power by the modern mass media.[64] The IACtHR and the AfComHPR, whose conventions do not expressly include such a clause, do nonetheless emphasise the responsibilities of the media when they exercise their function.[65]

Thorgeirson v. *Iceland* [1992] App. no. 13778/88 [63]; also accepted by the IACtHR since *Herrera-Ulloa* v. *Costa Rica* [2004] Case 12.367 [113]. See also US Supreme Court, *Cohen* v. *California*, 403 US 15, 25 (1971): 'one man's vulgarity is another's lyric'.

64 Compare Bossuyt (1987) p. 386; Marauhn (2009) para. 30.

65 See IACtHR, *Herrera-Ulloa* v. *Costa Rica* [2004] Case 12.367 [117]; *Fontevecchia and D'Amico* v. *Argentina* [2011] Case 12.524 [44]; IAComHR, *Francisco Martorell* v. *Chile* [1996] Case 11.230 [58]; Office of the Special Rapporteur for Freedom of Expression with the Inter-American Commission on Human Rights, Inter-American Legal Framework Regarding the Right to Freedom of Expression, 2009, CIDH/RELE/INF. 2/09, para. 172; AfComHPR, *Scanlen & Holderness* v. *Zimbabwe* [2009] App. no. 297/05 [107].

2.2.3.1 The extent to which a publication pertains to a matter of public concern

The media should enjoy greater protection in relation to contributions to matters of public concern. If, however, publications are not of public concern, they tend to enjoy less protection, and they may even constitute an abuse of media freedom if relating to exclusively private or even intimate matters.[66] The term 'public concern' should be preferred to the more frequently used 'public interest', which can be too easily confused with 'interest to the public'. 'Interest' is a subjective term, whereas 'concern' is an objective concept. This emphasises the fact that 'public concern' is a qualitative and normative, rather than an empirical or quantitative, criterion.

To be sure, this approach is presumed to face strong opposition particularly in US academic scholarship, where it is a fundamental First Amendment principle that it is 'generally not the government's job to decide what subjects speakers and listeners should concern themselves with'.[67] The impermissibility of content discrimination by the government constitutes a bedrock principle of First Amendment doctrine.[68] This 'negative' freedom of speech rationale,[69] which has been particularly emphasised by Frederick Schauer, is also known as the 'suspicion of government' theory.[70] However, as Cass Sunstein observed, 'it would be difficult to imagine a sensible system of free expression that did not distinguish among categories of speech in accordance with their importance to the underlying purposes of the free speech guarantee'.[71] Courts, including the United States Supreme Court, base their freedom of expression jurisprudence on distinctions such as speech that is of 'public interest' or 'public concern',[72] speech 'of political, social or other concern to the community',[73] speech that 'influences social relations and politics on a grand scale', and that is part of a 'debate about public

[66] See Chapter 2, Section 2.2.3.1. [67] Volokh (2000) 1089.

[68] See Rubenfeld (2001) 787–8; Berger (2003) 1411; Baker (2007) 1015; Volokh (2011b) 594.

[69] 'Negative' as opposed to the 'positive' arguments from democracy, from truth, and from individual autonomy; see Chapter 1.

[70] Barendt (2005) pp. 21–3; Schauer (1982) pp. 81, 148, 162–3: 'distrust of government'.

[71] Sunstein (1986) 605; reiterated in Sunstein (1992) 302; see also Post (1991) 288; Dworkin (1996) p. 204; Post (2011) 486.

[72] See, e.g., US Supreme Court, *Gertz* v. *Robert Welch, Inc.*, 418 US 323, 346 (1974); *Dun & Bradstreet, Inc.* v. *Greenmoss Builders*, 472 US 749, 761 (1985); *Hustler Magazine* v. *Falwell*, 485 US 46, 50 (1988); *Bartnicki* v. *Vopper*, aka *Williams and others*, 532 US 514, 528, 533–4 (2001); *Snyder* v. *Phelps*, 562 US (2011), p. 8; from the UK, see *London Artists* v. *Littler* [1969] 2 QB 375, 391 (Lord Denning); *Reynolds* v. *Times Newspapers Ltd* [2001] 2 AC 127, 205 (Lord Nicholls); *Flood* v. *Times Newspapers Ltd* [2012] UKSC 11 [24] (Lord Phillips).

[73] US Supreme Court, *Connick* v. *Myers*, 461 US 138, 146 (1983).

affairs', makes a 'contribution to the public debate' or concerns ideas which may bring about 'political and social changes'.[74]

To respond to these objections, one has to clarify, first, the notion of 'government' in this context. It is argued here that it is only for the courts, and decidedly not for the administration or for parliament, to estimate the extent to which a matter is of public concern. This approach would also render controversial statutory regulation of the media obsolete. Media freedom is incommensurate with the idea that governments should define who benefits from its protection.[75] Governments are subject to a natural bias towards the media, as it is the media's role to scrutinise and to criticise governmental behaviour. By contrast, independent regulatory authorities are prone to the risk of 'agency capture', that is, of identification with the regulated industry to the disadvantage of the public interest they should represent.[76] An independent judiciary, however, is relatively immune from political or popular pressure.

Second, one has to ask for a better alternative. To rephrase Winston Churchill's famous quote, courts are the least suitable institutions to determine what is of public concern, except for all the others. If 'the public' (or parts of the public? And if yes, how many people?) or even the media itself rather than courts had to determine whether, for example, private information is relevant or irrelevant, this would not only conceptually confuse 'public interest' with 'interest of the public', but it would also inevitably lead to the 'tyranny of the majority' and the 'tyranny of the prevailing opinion and feeling' John Adams and John Stuart Mill warned of.[77] Public demand for information, for example, on the private or even intimate lives of people, does not *per se* justify its supply. With the same argument, one could also justify the poaching of elephants, since there is a demand for ivory. The damage inflicted by paparazzi intruding into, and reporting on, people's private lives outweighs the interest in the satiation of public appetite for such entertainment. In addition, one may even question the relationship between cause and effect. It appears that media companies kindle the appetite for the private lives of certain people in the first place in order to create the demand, rather than the public

[74] See US Supreme Court, *Roth* v. *United States*, 354 US 476, 484 (1957); *New York Times Co.* v. *Sullivan*, 376 US 254, 269 (1964); *Hustler Magazine* v. *Falwell*, 485 US 46, 53 (1988); House of Lords, *Lion Laboratories Ltd* v. *Evans* [1984] 1 WLR 526, 530; *Francome* v. *Mirror Group Newspapers Ltd* [1984] 1 WLR 892, 897; *Reynolds* v. *Times Newspapers Ltd* [2001] 2 AC 127, 205 (Lord Nicholls); ECtHR, *Von Hannover* v. *Germany (No. 1)* [2004] App. no. 59320/00 [65].

[75] On compulsory registration requirements for journalists, see Chapter 6, Section 6.3.3.1.2.

[76] The idea of 'captured agencies' was first developed by Bernstein (1955).

[77] Adams (1856) p. 63; Mill (1869) p. 8.

demand creating itself and the media merely satiating it. Any attempt to establish 'public concern' by merely quantitative criteria would thus run the risk of being over- or under-inclusive.[78] It might be over-inclusive, because it considers trivial matters which are of interest for parts of the public; and it might be under-inclusive, if it excludes matters that most people have not yet heard of, although it affects them, such as state secrets. The question of how many people are interested in a matter should thus serve as just one indicator to whether something is of public concern.

Similar objections have to be raised to the idea that it should be for journalists themselves to decide what is of public concern. Journalistic privileges may not be based on the assumption that journalists can be trusted to decide for themselves what circumstances are sufficiently newsworthy, and to regulate themselves according to self-imposed standards. The media has too often misused its power and latitude, as the Leveson inquiry revealed.[79]

Because of its vagueness and inherent dynamics, any effort to exhaustively define 'public concern' is presumably doomed to fail. Recall Justice Potter Stewart's gallant refusal to define hard-core pornography with the famous phrase 'I know it when I see it'.[80] However, what is more important than to deliver an exhaustive and – if at all achievable – inevitably very abstract definition is to provide guidance for both journalists and courts as to what 'public concern' actually is, in order to provide legal certainty and thus reduce the risk of self-censorship. In order to accomplish this task, three factors should be considered.

First, rather than asking the binary question if or if not a matter is of public concern, it has to be established *to what extent* it is of public concern. Speech can be of both public and private concern. An example of this are alleged marital difficulties of the president of the Republic.[81] On the one hand, such matters may pertain to the most intimate aspects of the president's private life. On the other hand, they may also affect the exercise of his office. The seminal question is, therefore, to what extent it is a matter of public concern, and thus to what extent the media may report details about it. This corresponds to the idea that human rights are optimising requirements that require balancing conflicting interests, rather than binary rules of 'appropriateness' or 'inappropriateness'.[82] The more a publication pertains to a matter of public concern, the stronger the protection it deserves in the balancing exercise is. For instance, the alcohol

[78] Post (1990) 673.
[79] Inquiry into the Culture, Practices and Ethics of the Press, published in November 2012.
[80] US, *Jacobellis* v. *Ohio*, 378 US 184 (1964) (Stewart J, concurring).
[81] See Chapter 7, Section 7.3.4.1.1. [82] See Chapter 6, Section 6.3.3.

problems of a famous actor are *to a certain degree* of public concern, because they may affect the public's awareness of, and attitude towards, consumption of alcoholic beverages. However, this issue is at the same time a significantly private matter, as it relates to a person's health. By contrast, the alcohol problems of a politician are to an even higher degree of public concern, because they do not only raise the same questions as regarding the actor, but they may also affect the way the politician performs his mandate – which is directly related to democracy itself.

Second, case-law and international resolutions provide a variety of examples for publications that have been recognised as 'matters of public concern' or 'matters of public or general interest', which may serve as indicators for further cases. The examples can be categorised as follows:

- political reporting, on both a local and the national level: for example, information about locally elected representatives and public officials,[83] politicians in the exercise of their official functions[84] and in the exercise of functions after their resignation,[85] the management of state assets and the manner in which politicians fulfil their mandate,[86] a candidate's suitability for the office of mayor in the run-up to mayoral elections,[87] submission of an application for an *a posteriori* abstract review of legislation, especially by a Member of Parliament,[88] a serious illness of the Head of State,[89] the unsolved murder of a former prime minister,[90] any opinions and information pertinent to elections, both local and national, which are disseminated during the electoral campaign,[91] questions of

83 ECtHR, *Cumpănă and Mazăre* v. *Romania* [2004] App. no. 33348/96 [101]; IACtHR, *Palamara-Iribarne* v. *Chile* [2005] Case 11.571 [82]; IAComHR, *Rodolfo Robles Espinoza* v. *Peru* [1999] Case 11.317 [153]; *Tomás Eduardo Cirio* v. *Uruguay* [2006] Case 11.500 [72]; *Dudley Stokes* v. *Jamaica* [2008] Case 12.468 [75].

84 See, amongst many further decisions, ECtHR, *Lingens* v. *Austria* [1986] App. no. 9815/82 [42]; *Feldek* v. *Slovakia* [2001] App. no. 29032/95 [74]; *Brasilier* v. *France* [2006] App. no. 71343/01 [41]; *Gutiérrez Suárez* v. *Spain* [2010] App. no. 16023/07 [26]; IACtHR, *Fontevecchia and D'Amico* v. *Argentina* [2011] Case 12.524 [47].

85 ECtHR, *Axel Springer AG* v. *Germany (No. 2)* [2014] App. no. 48311/10 [58].

86 ECtHR, *Dalban* v. *Romania* [1999] App. no. 28114/95 [48].

87 ECtHR, *Brosa* v. *Germany* [2014] App. no. 5709/09 [42].

88 ECtHR, *Társaság a Szabadságjogokért* v. *Hungary* [2009] App. no. 37374/05 [28].

89 ECtHR, *Éditions Plon* v. *France* [2004] App. no. 58148/00 [44]; *Von Hannover* v. *Germany (No. 2)* [2012] App. nos. 40660/08 and 60641/08 [118].

90 ECtHR, *White* v. *Sweden* [2006] App. no. 42435/02.

91 See, e.g., ECtHR, *Bowman* v. *United Kingdom* [1998] App. no. 141/1996/760/961 [42]; *Incal* v. *Turkey* [1998] App. no. 41/1997/825/1031 [46]; *TV Vest AS & Rogaland Pensjonistparti* v. *Norway* [2008] App. no. 21132/05 [61]; IACtHR, *Ricardo Canese* v. *Paraguay* [2004] Case 12.032 [88]. If political speech stands in immediate context with elections, the Strasbourg Court considers the right to freedom of expression under Article 10 in the light of the right to free elections protected by Article 3 of Protocol No. 1 to the Convention.

abuse of power by a politician,[92] the attitude of political parties towards racism,[93] the promotion and protection of human rights and reports on violations thereof,[94] the protection of the environment,[95] the use of the death penalty,[96] debates on granting of subsidies to an association which assisted parents whose children had become involved in sects,[97] alleged use of the legislative powers to offer tax incentives promoting anti-competitive advantages to some businesses and plans for further amendments to the law leading to losses for ordinary workers,[98] preservation of land for agricultural and forestry use and avoiding the proliferation of second homes[99] and the development and functioning of the sewage system in the municipality.[100]

- reportings on public administration: for example, abuse of power by the police,[101] an illegal system of telephone tapping and recording directed against many prominent figures from civil society organised by the state,[102] alleged irregularities and corrupt practices in the admission of students to secondary schools,[103] and the administration of justice[104], although there are limits with regard to criticism of judges.[105]

[92] ECtHR, *Kuliś* v. *Poland* [2008] App. no. 15601/02 [46].
[93] ECtHR, *Lindon, Otchakovsky-Laurens and July* v. *France* [2007] App. nos. 21279/02 and 36448/02 [48].
[94] UN General Assembly, Resolution 53/144: Declaration on the right and responsibility of individuals, groups and organs of society to promote and protect universally recognized human rights and fundamental freedoms of 8 March 1999, A/RES/53/144, Article 6; Human Rights Committee, *Kivenmaa* v. *Finland* [1994] Communication no. 412/1990 [9.3]; AfComHPR, *Law Offices of Ghazi Suleiman* v. *Sudan* [2003] App. no. 228/99 [52]; IAComHR, *Rodolfo Robles Espinoza* v. *Peru* [1999] Case 11.317 [148].
[95] IACtHR, *Claude Reyes and others* v. *Chile* [2006] Case 12.108 [99]; ECtHR, *Tănăsoaica* v. *Romania* [2012] App. no. 3490/03 [44].
[96] Human Rights Committee, *Toktakunov* v. *Kyrgyzstan* [2011] Communication no. 1470/2006 [6.3].
[97] ECtHR, *Jerusalem* v. *Austria* [2001] App. no. 26958/95 [41].
[98] ECtHR, *Flux* v. *Moldova (No. 1)* [2006] App. no. 28702/03 [33].
[99] ECtHR, *Österreichische Vereinigung zur Erhaltung, Stärkung und Schaffung eines wirtschaftlich gesunden land-und forstwirtschaftlichen Grundbesitzes* v. *Austria* [2013] App. no. 39534/07 [35].
[100] ECtHR, *Kaperzyński* v. *Poland* [2012] App. no. 43206/07 [64].
[101] ECtHR, *Thorgeir Thorgeirson* v. *Iceland* [1992] App. no. 13778/88; *Nilsen and Johnsen* v. *Norway* [1999] App. no. 23118/93 [44]; *Sürek* v. *Turkey (No. 2)* [1999] App. no. 24122/94 [37].
[102] ECtHR, *Dupuis and others* v. *France* [2007] App. no. 1914/02 [41].
[103] ECtHR, *Kasabova* v. *Bulgaria* [2011] App. no. 22385/03 [56].
[104] See, e.g., ECtHR, *Prager and Oberschlick* v. *Austria* [1995] App. no. 15974/90 [34]; *De Haes and Gijsels* v. *Belgium* [1997] App. no. 19983/92 [37]; *Mustafa Erdoğan and others* v. *Turkey* [2014] App. nos. 346/04 and 39779/04 [40]; AfComHPR, *Zimbabwe Lawyers for Human Rights & Associated Newspapers of Zimbabwe* v. *Republic of Zimbabwe* [2009] App. no. 284/03 [90].
[105] See Chapter 7, Section 7.3.2.2.

- reportings on businesses and the economy in general: for example, the fact that a company chairman had received large pay increases while at the same time opposing his employees' claims for a rise in an industrial dispute,[106] the behaviour of multi-national companies[107] and allegations of corruption.[108]
- the search for historical truth and debates between historians that shape public opinion as to the events which took place and their interpretation.[109]
- violations of the law, especially crimes and acts of terrorism,[110] and their prevention, investigation and prosecution.[111]
- publications on further matters of public concern: for example, the Thalidomide scandal and the law relating to compensation by drug companies,[112] seal hunting and alleged actions of seal hunters in Norway,[113] a debate concerning the intentions of a country, with episodes of totalitarianism in its history, to come to terms with its past,[114] apparently failed cosmetic surgery provided at a private cosmetic surgery clinic by a specific physician,[115] the problem of alcohol consumption while working,[116] protection of animals and the manner in which they are reared,[117] the programming policy of public media[118] and sport issues.[119]

Third, the attempt to establish the extent to which a publication contributes to a matter of 'public concern' might be facilitated by contrasting the

106 ECtHR, *Fressoz and Roire* v. *France* [1999] App. no. 29183/95 [50].
107 ECtHR, *Steel and Morris* v. *United Kingdom* [2005] App. no. 68416/01; Oster (2011).
108 IACtHR, *Ricardo Canese* v. *Paraguay* [2004] Case 12.032 [92].
109 See, e.g., ECtHR, *Monnat* v. *Switzerland* [2006] App. no. 73604/01 [59]; *Radio France and others* v. *France* [2004] App. no. 53984/00 [34]; *Chauvy and others* v. *France* [2004] App. no. 64915/01 [69]; *Perinçek* v. *Switzerland* [2013] App. no. 27510/08 [103].
110 ECtHR, *Leroy* v. *France* [2009] App. no. 36109/03 [41]; *Brunet Lecomte et Lyon Mag* v. *France* [2010] App. no. 17265/05 [41].
111 See ECtHR, *White* v. *Sweden* [2006] App. no. 42435/02 [29]; *Egeland and Hanseid* v. *Norway* [2009] App. no. 34438/04 [58]; *Salumäki* v. *Finland* [2014] App. no. 23605/09 [54].
112 ECtHR, *Sunday Times* v. *United Kingdom (No. 1)* [1979] App. no. 6538/74.
113 ECtHR, *Bladet Tromsø and Stensaas* v. *Norway* [1999] App. no. 21980/93.
114 See, e.g., ECtHR, *Feldek* v. *Slovakia* [2001] App. no. 29032/95 [80]; *Karsai* v. *Hungary* [2009] App. no. 5380/07 [35].
115 ECtHR, *Bergens Tidende and others* v. *Norway* [2000] App. no. 26132/95 [51].
116 ECtHR, *Selistö* v. *Finland* [2004] App. no. 56767/00 [52].
117 ECtHR, *VgT Verein gegen Tierfabriken* v. *Switzerland (No. 1)* [2001] App. no. 24699/94 [70]; *PETA Deutschland* v. *Germany* [2012] App. no. 43481/09 [47]; *Animal Defenders International* v. *United Kingdom* [2013] App. no. 48876/08 [102].
118 ECtHR, *Wojtas-Kaleta* v. *Poland* [2009] App. no. 20436/02 [46].
119 ECtHR, *Société de Conception de Presse et d'Edition et Ponson* v. *France* [2009] App. no. 26935/05 [55].

concept of public concern to its counterpart: the degree to which a matter is of private concern. The concepts of 'public concern' and 'private concern' are not hermetically sealed off, but merge into one another. The crucial question, therefore, is to what degree a matter is of public concern, and to what degree it is of private concern. Just as the term public concern, 'private concern' is not susceptible to an exhaustive definition. A matter is of private concern if it concerns a person's privacy. Privacy describes the legitimate expectation of absence of others, the right to hide from the public realm and the right to be left alone.[120] Although a precise definition is lacking, Conventions and adjudicators' jurisprudence provide indicators as to what is covered by this term. Privacy encompasses the institutions mentioned in Article 8 ECHR and Article 17 ICCPR: family, home and correspondence; furthermore, a person's name[121] or picture,[122] a person's physical intimacy, such as nakedness, illness or injury,[123] a person's sexuality, sexual life and orientation,[124] the personality of each individual in his relations with other human beings,[125] and personal data.[126]

Privacy thus contradicts the idea of a general right to know everything about everybody. Yet privacy is a relative term, which is in the first place defined by the rights-holder himself. While some people voluntarily abandon their privacy, for instance, by exhibiting their intimate life on social internet networks, others wish to protect their private sphere, and have a right to have it respected.

However, private 'sphere' should not be understood as a purely spatial notion. While a legitimate expectation of privacy may also exist in public

[120] Warren and Brandeis (1890); Arendt (1958) pp. 38, 58 and 71. For a more detailed analysis of privacy, see Hughes (2012); Prosser (1960); Gavison (1980); Richardson (2002); Richardson (2013); Lusky (1972); Wacks (2013); Westin (1967); Whitman (2004); Mills (2008); Fried (1968).

[121] See Article 24(2) ICCPR, Article 18 ACHR and Articles 7 and 8 Convention on the Rights of the Child; ECtHR, *Burghartz* v. *Switzerland* [1994] App. no. 16213/90 [24]; *Standard Verlags GmbH* v. *Austria (No. 3)* [2012] App. no. 34702/07 [36].

[122] ECtHR, *Schüssel* v. *Austria* [2002] App. no. 42409/98; *Von Hannover* v. *Germany (No. 1)* [2004] App. no. 59320/00 [50 ff.]; *Eerikäinen and others* v. *Finland* [2009] App. no. 3514/02 [61].

[123] ECtHR, *X and Y* v. *Netherlands* [1985] App. no. 8978/80 [22]; *Raninen* v. *Finland* [1997] App. no. 152/1996/771/972 [63]; *Biriuk* v. *Lithuania* [2008] App. no. 23373/03 [43].

[124] ECtHR, *Peck* v. *United Kingdom* [2003] App. no. 44647/98 [57]; *Biriuk* v. *Lithuania* [2008] App. no. 23373/03 [34]; *Ruusunen* v. *Finland* [2014] App. no. 73579/10 [50].

[125] ECtHR, *Botta* v. *Italy* [1998] App. no. 153/1996/772/973 [32]; *Von Hannover* v. *Germany (No. 1)* [2004] App. no. 59320/00 [50].

[126] ECtHR, *S and Marper* v. *United Kingdom* [2008] App. nos. 30562/04 and 30566/04 [41].

spaces,[127] certain incidents that occur in the private domain are nonetheless of public concern. This includes, for example, marital difficulties or personal affairs that may affect the way a politician exercises his office. But in particular, as has been most powerfully brought forward by feminist theory, privacy must not be abused to hide domestic violence from public view.[128] On the contrary, the use of violence and the commission of crimes is always, everywhere, and *per se*, a matter of public concern. The right to respect for privacy is a shield, not a sword. Therefore, the public–private divide of media law cannot be compared with the ancient Greek dichotomy of the political realm of the *polis*, which happened in the market place (*agora*), and the private realm of the *oikos* (home). While the *polis* knew only equals, the household was based on inequality.[129]

The media itself is a part of the public sphere. However, it is not in the media's vocation to make public what is private, and thus create a 'pseudo-public sphere'[130] comprised of sensational and lurid news 'intended to titillate and entertain, which are aimed at satisfying the curiosity of a particular readership regarding aspects of a person's strictly private life',[131] serving only to 'entertain' and not to 'educate'.[132] By publishing certain issues, the mass media can confer public *status* on this information. However, this 'status conferral function' of the mass media as a concept of communication theory[133] is not identical with 'public concern' as a normative concept.

2.2.3.2 The media's conduct

Ideal public discourse presupposes the best available information and arguments. As a result, the integrity of public discourse depends upon factual accuracy.[134] Due to the mass media's ability to reach a large audience, false information disseminated by the mass media usually has a worse impact than false statements issued by private individuals. Public discourse as the rationale for media freedom therefore justifies requiring the media to abide by certain *standards of conduct* when gathering, editing and disseminating information and ideas, especially where the media

[127] See Chapter 7, Section 7.3.4.1.1. [128] See Fraser (1992) p. 129.
[129] Arendt (1958) p. 32. [130] Habermas (1962) p. 162.
[131] ECtHR, *Mosley* v. *United Kingdom* [2011] App. no. 48009/08 [114]; see also, e.g., *Von Hannover* v. *Germany (No. 1)* [2004] App. no. 59320/00 [65]; *Hachette Filipacchi Associés ("Ici Paris")* v. *France* [2009] App. no. 12268/03 [40]; *MGN Ltd* v. *United Kingdom* [2011] App. no. 39401/04 [143]; *Alkaya* v. *Turkey* [2012] App. no. 42811/06 [35].
[132] ECtHR, *Mosley* v. *United Kingdom* [2011] App. no. 48009/08 [131].
[133] See Lazarsfeld and Merton (1948) p. 20. [134] Post (1990) 659.

discloses factual information that is harmful to another person. In such cases, the media's privileged protection is subject to the proviso that it is acting on an accurate factual basis.[135]

However, to require a journalist to ensure that each factual statement he publishes is correct would have an intolerable chilling effect on the media to the detriment of public discourse itself. Consequently, the media may, under certain circumstances, deviate from the obligation to verify factual information it discloses. Whether such grounds exist depends on the gravity of the allegations, in particular where a defamatory statement is involved. However, the media must have taken all reasonable steps to verify the accuracy of its statements prior to publication, if rights of others are affected by this publication. *Which* steps are considered to be reasonable differs significantly between international courts and the US Supreme Court's First Amendment jurisprudence.[136]

2.2.3.3 The media's good faith

Another conduct-related duty is that journalists must always act in good faith.[137] Where a journalist lacks such good faith, there is no need for an examination of whether he can be exempted from his ordinary obligation to verify factual statements. Rather, civil liability for a false, defamatory statement made in bad faith is always justified.[138] Yet the question is what actually constitutes 'good faith'. The requirement of good faith may relate to two components: first, the veracity of the statement and, second, the integrity of the motivation of the publisher. These components

[135] Among many authorities, see ECtHR, *Bladet Tromsø and Stensaas* v. *Norway* [1999] App. no. 21980/93 [65]; *Fressoz and Roire* v. *France* [1999] App. no. 29183/95 [54]; *Bergens Tidende and others* v. *Norway* [2000] App. no. 26132/95 [53]; Council of Europe, Parliamentary Assembly, Recommendation 1215 (1993) on the ethics of journalism; IACtHR, *Kimel* v. *Argentina* [2008] Case 12.450 [79]; *Ríos and others* v. *Venezuela* [2009] Case 12.441 [106]; AfComHPR, *Scanlen & Holderness* v. *Zimbabwe* [2009] App. no. 297/05 [107]. From legal scholarship, see Mitchell (2011); Nowak (2005) Article 19 paras. 44–5

[136] This will be further elaborated on with regard to defamation; see Chapter 7, Section 7.3.4.1.3.

[137] Among many authorities, see ECtHR, *Bladet Tromsø and Stensaas* v. *Norway* [1999] App. no. 21980/93 [65]; *Fressoz and Roire* v. *France* [1999] App. no. 29183/95 [54]; *Bergens Tidende and others* v. *Norway* [2000] App. no. 26132/95 [53]; *Novaya Gazeta and Borodyankiy* v. *Russia* [2013] App. no. 14087/08 [37]; see also Council of Europe, Parliamentary Assembly, Recommendation 1215 (1993) on the ethics of journalism; IACtHR, *Kimel* v. *Argentina* [2008] Case 12.450 [79]; *Ríos and others* v. *Venezuela* [2009] Case 12.441 [106]; AfComHPR, *Scanlen & Holderness* v. *Zimbabwe* [2009] App. no. 297/05 [107]. From legal scholarship, see Nowak (2005) Article 19 paras. 44–5; Mitchell (2011).

[138] ECtHR, *Alithia Publishing Company Ltd and Constantinides* v. *Cyprus* [2008] App. no. 17550/03 [67]; see also *Pedersen and Baadsgaard* v. *Denmark* [2004] App. no. 49017/99 [78].

should be strictly distinguished. As regards the first point, it seems uncontroversial that journalists must not intentionally disseminate false, harmful information or act with a grossly negligent disregard for the truth.[139] This veracity component of good faith has its functional equivalence in the 'absent malice' standard applied by the US Supreme Court in defamation lawsuits by public figures since *New York Times Co.* v. *Sullivan.*[140]

Second, however, international adjudicators also require that the media must not publish a statement with improper motives or intentions, for instance, to stigmatise someone or to stir up violence and hatred.[141] This requirement is more critical, because it measures the value of speech according to the integrity of the speaker's intention. By considering the intentions of the publisher where factual statements are concerned, international adjudicators scrutinise whether media publications are *in moral terms* acceptable or unacceptable. However, such a moral appreciation should be rejected where factual contributions to matters of public concern are the subject of the dispute, as it is not the task of courts to impose their own moral standards on the media. This corresponds to the tenets of discourse theory, according to which validity claims raised by descriptive sentences, which serve to ascertain facts, can be accepted or rejected from the standpoint of the truth of the proposition; by contrast, only evaluative sentences or value judgments can be accepted or rejected because of the sincerity of the speaker's expressed intentions or feelings.[142]

The US Supreme Court thus rightly decided that even false defamatory speech published 'from personal spite, ill will or a desire to injure' does not amount to malice under *New York Times* v. *Sullivan*, if the publisher believed the statement to be true and was not reckless concerning their untruthfulness.[143] As a consequence, the US Supreme Court applies the 'malice' standard only as an instrument pertaining to the factual veracity of a statement and so as a policy to minimise the

[139] Compare ECtHR, *Alithia Publishing Company Ltd and Constantinides* v. *Cyprus* [2008] App. no. 17550/03 [66]; *Gutiérrez Suárez* v. *Spain* [2010] App. no. 16023/07 [38]; IAComHR, *Eduardo Kimel* v. *Argentina* [2007] Case 12.450 [122]; AfComHPR, *Scanlen & Holderness* v. *Zimbabwe* [2009] App. no. 297/05 [120].

[140] US Supreme Court, *New York Times Co.* v. *Sullivan*, 376 US 254 (1964).

[141] ECtHR, *Nilsen and Johnsen* v. *Norway* [1999] App. no. 23118/93 [50]; *Selistö* v. *Finland* [2004] App. no. 56767/00 [68]; *Lindon, Otchakovsky-Laurens and July* v. *France* [2007] App. nos. 21279/02 and 36448/02 [57]; *mutatis mutandis*, *Falakaoğlu* v. *Turkey* [2005] App. no. 77365/01 [35]; see also, *mutatis mutandis*, IACtHR, *Usón Ramírez* v. *Venezuela* [2009] Case 12.554 [86].

[142] See Habermas (1981a) pp. 39, 99; Habermas (1981b) p. 120.

[143] US Supreme Court, *Beckley Newspapers* v. *Hanks Corp.*, 389 US 81, 82 (1967).

chilling effect of the law of defamation on speech on public figures,[144] but not as a moral sincerity test.

International adjudicators, especially the Strasbourg Court, impose another 'duty and responsibility' on the media: the media has to act according to the 'ethics of journalism' and the principles of 'responsible journalism', which does not only refer to the content of a publication, but also to journalistic information gathering and the way in which material is presented. Such ethical restraints are often included in codes of conduct of media self-regulation. Although these codes are not laws in a formal sense, they nonetheless reflect the standards of care the journalistic profession sees itself as obliged to adhere to. A violation of the 'ethics of journalism' would be sufficient for the Strasbourg Court to tip the balance against the freedom of the media.[145]

However, the consideration of the 'ethics of journalism' or 'responsible journalism' as a legal factor meets objections similar to the consideration of the integrity of the publisher's motivation, and should thus be rejected. The law determines what the media may *legally* do and what it is *legally* prohibited from doing, but not what the media should or should not do in journalistic-ethical terms. Media law and 'responsible journalism' or 'ethical journalism' are overlapping, but not identical, concepts: a violation of media ethics can only be vindicated in a court if the ethical command has been absorbed into a *legal* obligation. In turn, a merely ethical obligation without legal underpinning can only be vindicated under media self-regulation or in the court of public opinion, but not in a court of law. For example: to provide the victim with an opportunity to reply to inaccuracies is not only an ethical standard for journalists,[146] but may, under certain circumstances, be legally relevant.[147] On the other hand, keeping sources confidential is only an ethical obligation for the media,[148] which is usually not legally enforceable.[149] Unfortunately, the Strasbourg Court considers 'responsible journalism' indistinctively as one aspect of its balancing exercise in the proportionality analysis, and thus blurs the boundaries between law and ethics.

144 Post (1987) 553.

145 Compare ECtHR, *Ricci* v. *Italy* [2013] App. no. 30210/06 [57]; but see also *Pipi* v. *Turkey* [2009] App. no. 4020/03, p. 8.

146 See, e.g., No. 2 of the PCC Editors' Code of Practice.

147 See Chapter 4, Section 4.1.4 and Chapter 7.

148 See, e.g., No. 14 of the PCC Editors' Code of Practice; Guideline 5.1 of the German Press Council's Press Code.

149 See Chapter 4, Section 4.2.1.3.

2.3 The relationship between media freedom and freedom of expression

Freedom of expression and media freedom are overlapping concepts, but they are not coextensive. In subjective terms, freedom of expression applies to everyone, while media freedom only protects 'the media'.[150] In objective terms, media freedom is partly a derivative right from freedom of expression, and partly a self-standing right. For adhering to its duties and responsibilities, media freedom affords particular privileges to the media, which do not apply to freedom of expression in general: the media speech privilege and the protection of the media as an institution.

2.3.1 Media freedom as a derivative right: the 'media speech privilege'

As a derivative right, media freedom is *lex specialis* to freedom of expression.[151] This explains why human rights legislators codify freedom of the media (or press or broadcasting) together with freedom of expression, as is the case with Article 11 EUChFR, Article 5(1) German Basic Law, Article 17 Swiss Constitution or the First Amendment to the US Constitution. It also clarifies why courts glean privileged protection of the media from general freedom of expression provisions if no express provision concerning the media is available, as the ECtHR does with regard to Article 10 ECHR or the UN Human Rights Committee concerning Article 19 ICCPR.

Freedom of the media is special in the sense that a person or institution, by virtue of being media and acting as media, is governed by a different set of factors concerning the intensity of protection when issuing a publication, compared to freedom of expression afforded to private individuals or non-media entities. The fact that an impugned statement is 'media speech', rather than speech by any other individual or institution, adds to the burden of justifying its restrictions. The protection of 'media speech' will be the subject of a distinct chapter.[152] However, three decisions of the ECtHR should already serve as illustrations.

In *Busuioc* v. *Moldova*, the applicant had been ordered to pay damages for the publication of a newspaper article containing allegations of favouritism against civil servants.[153] The respondent state referred to the Strasbourg Court's decision *Janowski* v. *Poland (No. 1)*, according to which 'civil

[150] See Chapter 3.
[151] Stewart (1975) 633. See also, amongst many other works, Bezanson (1977) 733; West (2011) 1032.
[152] See Chapter 4, Section 4.1.
[153] ECtHR, *Busuioc* v. *Moldova* [2004] App. no. 61513/00.

servants must enjoy public confidence in conditions free of undue perturbation if they are to be successful in performing their tasks and it may therefore prove necessary to protect them from offensive and abusive verbal attacks when on duty'.[154] However, the Strasbourg Court highlighted that, in contrast to the statements made by the applicant as a private individual in the case of *Janowski*, the impugned article in *Busuioc* v. *Moldova* was written by the applicant in his capacity as a journalist, and thus fell within the scope of freedom of the press. Therefore the Court held that the Moldovan authorities enjoyed a less extensive margin of appreciation when deciding whether there was a 'pressing social need' to interfere with the applicant's freedom of expression.[155] By contrast, in the cited *Janowski* decision, the Court observed that the applicant's critical remarks did not involve the issue of freedom of the press, since the applicant, 'although a journalist by profession, clearly acted as a private individual on this occasion'.[156]

The second example for the media speech privilege is *Wojtas-Kaleta* v. *Poland*.[157] The applicant was a journalist employed by a public television company. She was reprimanded for publicly complaining about the lack of support for classical music, and the fact that the quality of public television programmes was negatively affected as a result of fierce competition from private broadcasters. The Strasbourg Court, 'having regard to the role played by journalists in society and to their responsibilities to contribute to and encourage public debate', considered that the obligation of discretion and constraint under general employment law 'cannot be said to apply with equal force to journalists, given that it is in the nature of their functions to impart information and ideas'.[158]

Finally, in his concurring opinion to the ECtHR's decision in *Vejdeland and others* v. *Sweden*, Judge Zupančič pointedly summarised the effect of the media speech privilege. The applicants, private citizens, were convicted for distributing homophobic leaflets in an upper secondary school. The ECtHR upheld this conviction, but Judge Zupančič observed: '[I]f exactly the same words and phrases were to be used in public newspapers such as Svenska Dagbladet, they would probably not be considered as a matter for criminal prosecution and condemnation.'[159]

[154] ECtHR, *Janowski* v. *Poland (No. 1)* [1999] App. no. 25716/94. On the criticism of civil servants, see Chapter 7, Section 7.3.2.1.

[155] ECtHR, *Busuioc* v. *Moldova* [2004] App. no. 61513/00 [64] and [65]. On the margin of appreciation, see Chapter 6, Section 6.2.

[156] ECtHR, *Janowski* v. *Poland (No. 1)* [1999] App. no. 25716/94 [32].

[157] ECtHR, *Wojtas-Kaleta* v. *Poland* [2009] App. no. 20436/02.

[158] ECtHR, *Wojtas-Kaleta* v. *Poland* [2009] App. no. 20436/02 [46]; *Matúz* v. *Hungary* [2014] App. no. 73571/10 [39].

[159] ECtHR, *Vejdeland and others* v. *Sweden* [2012] App. no. 1813/07, concurring opinion by Judge Boštjan M. Zupančič [12]; see also *Barthold* v. *Germany* [1985] App. no. 8734/79

These examples explain how the Strasbourg Court distinguishes between journalists and private individuals (*Busuioc*), and how this distinction affects the application of both private law (*Wojtas-Kaleta*) and criminal law (*Vejdeland*). They also raise the question of whether this distinction is justified.

It is the media's obligation to inform the public and to shape public discourse. Consequently, the risk of being sued is the sword of Damocles that always looms over the media. The media is subject to considerable duties and responsibilities regarding the accuracy of their publications; and rightly so, given the power the media wields on public opinion. Yet in order to fulfil its function, the media must be afforded leeway regarding both the way in which journalistic material is presented and the content of its publications.

First, journalistic freedom protects both the substance of the ideas and information expressed and the form in which they are conveyed, including a certain degree of provocation and exaggeration,[160] immoderate statements,[161] the use of strong terms,[162] or polemic formulation,[163] vulgar phrases or a satirical style.[164] It is for journalists, and not for courts, to decide on the methods and techniques of their reporting.[165]

Second, if the media adheres to its duties and responsibilities, then media freedom also includes the right to make mistakes. There can be no absolute obligation to establish the truth of any publication, even if defamatory.[166] Such a duty would have a chilling effect on reporting on matters of public concern.

[42]: 'This is especially so since the publication prompting the restriction was an article written by a journalist and not a commercial advertisement.'

160 ECtHR, *Prager and Oberschlick* v. *Austria* [1995] App. no. 15974/90 [38]; *De Haes and Gijsels* v. *Belgium* [1997] App. no. 19983/92 [46]; *Bladet Tromsø and Stensaas* v. *Norway* [1999] App. no. 21980/93 [59]; *Fressoz and Roire* v. *France* [1999] App. no. 29183/95 [45]; *Thoma* v. *Luxembourg* [2001] App. no. 38432/97 [46]; *Radio France and others* v. *France* [2004] App. no. 53984/00 [37].

161 ECtHR, *Mladina d.d. Ljubljana* v. *Slovenia* [2014] App. no. 20981/10 [40].

162 ECtHR, *Thorgeir Thorgeirson* v. *Iceland* [1992] App. no. 13778/88 [67]; *July and SARL Liberation* v. *France* [2008] App. no. 20893/03 [75]. Compare US Supreme Court, *Cohen* v. *California*, 403 US 15 (1971), where the appellant wore a jacket bearing the words 'Fuck the Draft' in a county courthouse.

163 ECtHR, *Oberschlick* v. *Austria (No. 2)* [1997] App. no. 20834/92 [33]; *Unabhängige Initiative Informationsvielfalt* v. *Austria* [2002] App. no. 28525/95 [43].

164 ECtHR, *Tuşalp* v. *Turkey* [2012] App. nos. 32131/08 and 41617/08 [48].

165 See ECtHR, *Jersild* v. *Denmark* [1994] App. no. 15890/89 [31]; *Bladet Tromsø and Stensaas* v. *Norway* [1999] App. no. 21980/93 [63]; *Bergens Tidende and others* v. *Norway* [2000] App. no. 26132/95 [57]; *Stoll* v. *Switzerland* [2007] App. no. 69698/01 [146]; *Schweizerische Radio-und Fernsehgesellschaft SRG* v. *Switzerland* [2012] App. no. 34124/06 [64].

166 See Chapter 7, Section 7.3.4.1.3.

Third, freedom of the media does not only protect the dissemination of a newspaper's or broadcaster's own opinions; it also includes the publication of opinions of a third party, irrespective of whether the publisher associates himself with the content of the publication.[167]

2.3.2 Media freedom as an independent right: the institutional protection of the media

Media freedom provides privileged protection to the media that goes beyond the protection of media publications. It encompasses certain rights that are not available under freedom of expression at all. Here, freedom of the media differs from freedom of expression not only concerning the *intensity* of protection, as is the case with media speech, but also regarding the *scope* of protected action. As a self-standing fundamental right, media freedom protects the media as an institution. This institutional protection of the media guarantees rights that are not directly related to the content of a publication or the way in which it is presented, but are related to the media in its newsgathering, editorial or distribution process, or even to the mere existence of an independent media. The institutional protection of the media includes, for example, a journalist's protection from being compelled to give testimony of confidential information or sources, or protection against search and seizure.[168] These rights are not articulations of freedom of expression, like the right to publish, but an implementation of a legal right of journalists *as* journalists and *acting as* journalists only.[169] By contrast, a private individual has a right to freedom of expression and therefore also a right to publish, for instance, via a social network account. However, he does not have a right to protect his sources of information. Hence, the right to protect one's sources has to be a right that is independent from freedom of expression. This right is protected by freedom of the media, and applicable to the media, only.

[167] ECtHR, *Jersild* v. *Denmark* [1994] App. no. 15890/89 [36]; *Thoma* v. *Luxembourg* [2001] App. no. 38432/97 [62]; *Pedersen and Baadsgaard* v. *Denmark* [2004] App. no. 49017/99 [77]; *July and SARL Liberation* v. *France* [2008] App. no. 20893/03 [70]; as opposed to *Vejdeland and others* v. *Sweden* [2012] App. no. 1813/07; *mutatis mutandis, Sürek* v. *Turkey (No. 1)* [1999] App. no. 26682/95 [63]; *Éditions Plon* v. *France* [2004] App. no. 58148/00 [22].

[168] See Chapter 4, Section 4.2

[169] Therefore, freedom of expression is *not* a content-dependent justification for the protection of journalistic sources; see, however, Raz (1984) 7.

2.4 Freedom of the media as a fundamental right

The questions that necessarily follow the rationales for media freedom are: (i) why is it necessary to protect media freedom as a *fundamental* right, (ii) where is 'media freedom' codified as a fundamental right, and (iii) what are the consequences of media freedom being a fundamental right?

It is necessary to protect media freedom as a fundamental right (alternatively, one could also name it a human right or a constitutional right[170]) rather than as a statutory right. Media freedom should not be made subject to legislation, that is, to the will of temporary political majorities which may impose their values on society. Rather, legislation itself has to be justified in light of media freedom.

As regards the second question, except for the EUChFR in Article 11 (2), no international human rights catalogue includes an express provision protecting the media. Article 10(1)3 ECHR mentions broadcasting, television and cinema enterprises, but only with a view to the authorisation of Member States to license these entities, not by affording special protection to them. Similarly, Article 14 ACHR provides a right to reply to those who have been injured by a 'legally regulated medium of communication'. And although Article 19(2) ICCPR and Article 13(1) ACHR confer the right to impart information and ideas through any media of one's choice, the term 'media' in this context refers to the form of communication, not to the media as a legal institution.

However, the fact that media freedom has not been codified is not a compelling argument against accepting media freedom as a legal concept. Where media freedom is not expressly codified, as in the case of Article 11(2) EUChFR, media freedom is a derivative right, to be deduced from freedom of expression. The inference of new, second-generation human rights out of expressly codified human rights is not an uncommon procedure in human rights adjudication. For example, the German Federal Constitutional Court developed the general right of personality out of the general right to liberty (Article 2 German Basic Law) in conjunction with human dignity (Article 1). The ECtHR speaks of 'freedom of the press' when applying Article 10 ECHR to journalists

[170] The term 'fundamental right' is preferred to 'human right', as it expresses more adequately that media freedom is not only applicable to human beings, but also to juristic entities, such as media corporations. It is also preferred to 'constitutional right', because this book primarily deals with rights enshrined in international conventions rather than domestic constitutions.

and newspaper corporations.[171] And although neither freedom of speech nor freedom of the press was expressly codified in the UK prior to the Human Rights Act 1998, there was no doubt that these rights nonetheless existed in the UK.[172]

This leads to the third question: what are the consequences of media freedom being a *fundamental* right? Within the concepts of fundamental rights – dignity, liberty and equality[173] – media freedom is a liberty.[174] As a liberty, media freedom is to be conceptualised within the general framework of liberty doctrine: (i) the personal and substantive scope of that liberty, that is, the rights protected by the liberty ('what is protected?') and the beneficiary of the liberty ('who is protected?'), (ii) the notion of 'interference' with the liberty by an obligated addressee, and (iii) the justification of that interference.[175]

As a fundamental right, media freedom is a principle, as opposed to a rule. In contrast to principles, rules are norms which are always either fulfilled or not. Fundamental rights are principles which require that the right 'be realised to the greatest extent possible given the legal and factual possibilities'.[176] The distinction between rights and principles, which is drawn by Dworkin,[177] should not be confused with the distinction between rights and principles under the EU Charter of Fundamental Rights. While the rights in the Charter are 'principles' in a Dworkinian sense, the principles within the meaning of the Charter would be perceived as 'policies' according to Dworkin. This distinction between

[171] See, e.g., ECtHR, *Lingens* v. *Austria* [1986] App. no. 9815/82 [42]; *Oberschlick* v. *Austria (No. 1)* [1991] App. no. 11662/85 [58]; *Thoma* v. *Luxembourg* [2001] App. no. 38432/97 [45]; *Cumpănă and Mazăre* v. *Romania* [2004] App. no. 33348/96 [93]; *Rumyana Ivanova* v. *Bulgaria* [2008] App. no. 36207/03 [58].

[172] See Dicey (1889) pp. 233–4; House of Lords, *R* v. *Shayler* [2002] UKHL 11 [21–2] (per Lord Bingham), providing further references; Bradley and Ewing (2011) pp. 398, 502.

[173] See Alexy (2002) p. 2.

[174] Albeit with an equality dimension; see Chapter 4, Section 4.2.4.

[175] The beneficiary of media freedom, the media, will be the subject of the first paragraph of the following Chapter 3. The rights protected by media freedom will be analysed in Chapter 4. Chapter 5 then examines the notion of an interference as well as the obligated addressee of media freedom. Finally, Chapter 6 defines the general rules on justification of an interference with media freedom, followed by more specific elaborations in Part III.

[176] This definition is drawn from Alexy (2002) p. 47. Alexy seems to go even further by arguing that the optimisation requirement applies to all principles, and not just to constitutional rights. Yet it is doubtful whether the optimisation requirement also applies to a principle that is of lower legal status than the principle it stands in conflict with (such as regulations *vis-à-vis* a constitutional norms). Furthermore, it is not clear if the optimisation requirement applies if the norm the principle stands in conflict with is a rule, especially if the rule is of higher legal status than the principle. However, these questions do not need to be answered for the purposes of this book.

[177] Dworkin (1977) pp. 22 ff.

rights, on the one hand, and policies (Dworkin) or principles (EUChFR), on the other hand, becomes relevant with a view to media pluralism, which, as is argued here, is a policy in the Dworkinian sense and principle within the meaning of the Charter, but not a right.[178]

The distinction between rights as rules or as principles is significant where norms compete. Where two rules are conflicting, only one of them may apply. This is decided either by an express conflict rule or through the application of general tools of statutory interpretation, such as the *lex specialis* or the *lex posterior* rule. By contrast, the conflict of intersecting principles needs to be resolved through an estimation of the relative weight of each on a case-by-case basis: a 'balancing exercise'.[179] This balancing exercise is obsolete where one of the conflicting principles is of absolute value, such as the prohibition of torture or the prohibition of slavery. Media freedom, however, is not a right with absolute value. Rather, media freedom often needs to be balanced against conflicting principles, such as safeguarding public order, or the protection of privacy or reputation. The instrument rationalising the balancing exercise is the 'principle of proportionality'.[180]

This consequentialist approach to media freedom, and to freedom of expression in general, stands in conflict with the more deontological First Amendment doctrine of the United States Supreme Court. According to the Supreme Court's approach, there are not three categories of liberty doctrine – a right, an interference with this right and the justification of the interference – but just one category, a right which has a certain content. The idea of interference and justification is thus replaced by that of the extent of the right and its limits.[181] Hence the US Supreme Court grants significant protection to the right to free speech, but imposes certain restrictions by identifying categories of speech which are deemed not to fall within the scope of the First Amendment. Thus the US Supreme Court essentially undertakes a more abstract, categorical 'balancing exercise'. However, the case-to-case approach preferred here – and applied by all international human rights courts and tribunals – takes the burden from the court to *a priori* exclude certain categories of expression from protection. The arguments against this case-by-case balancing approach, especially the argument of incommensurability of conflicting rights, can be refuted through the establishment of rules that rationalise media freedom and make it practically operable, especially the balancing exercise between media freedom and competing principles.

178 See Chapter 14. 179 Dworkin (1977) p. 26; Alexy (2002) pp. 50 ff.
180 The principle of proportionality will be explained in detail in Chapter 6.
181 Compare Alexy (2002) p. 179.

Part II

General rules on media freedom

3 Beneficiaries of media freedom: who is 'the media'?

As with any other fundamental right, media freedom requires defining those who benefit from its protection. Beneficiaries of media freedom are 'the media'. Marshall McLuhan defined 'media' as extensions of human senses, including, for example, the spoken and the written word, radio and television broadcasting, but also clothing, housing and money.[1] Yet this is not the concept underlying media freedom. Rather, the kinship of media freedom and freedom of expression suggests that media freedom is related to communication media based on journalistically gathered and edited content. Within the framework of human communication – author, content, medium and one or more recipients[2] – 'the media' is to be characterised as 'authors', or more specifically, as persons or institutions generating information and ideas on a journalistic basis and disseminating them via facilities of mass communication to an undefined number of recipients.

3.1 The media as 'authors' of information and ideas

A message originates from a creator or author, and it is transmitted by a medium. Insofar as they create and publish information and ideas, journalists and media entities are such authors. By contrast, a mere medium only transmits or disseminates a third-party statement. The main difference between 'the media' as a legal concept and 'media' as the plural of medium is that 'the media' are content providers, whereas a medium is a mere speech facilitator, particularly a transmitter. Examples of mere speech intermediaries are newspaper vendors, communication network and service providers, search engines, news aggregators, social networks and website operators, insofar as they host unredacted comments from users. These mere facilitators of communication provide a

[1] See McLuhan (1964).
[2] See Shannon (1948) 379–423, 623–56. See also Shannon and Weaver (1949); Rogers (1994) pp. 434 ff.

platform for the possibility of media publications, but are not part of the fabrication of the publication themselves.[3] It is conceivable that the media, as a creator of messages, also operates the facilities for their dissemination. But this is not necessarily the case. Electronic communication services or broadcasting networks are often run by operators other than the content providers. In turn, media content providers may, under certain circumstances, also act as mere intermediaries, for instance, when they have to publish a reply.

The crucial difference between the media as 'author' or content provider, and a medium as a mere facilitator of communication, lies in the exercise of editorial control.[4] Editorial control describes the creation, selection or redaction of content before its publication.[5] Whoever exercises editorial control is fully liable for the published content. The author or creator of a statement has to abide by certain legal standards of conduct, or, in the words of Article 19(2) ICCPR and Article 10(2) ECHR, 'duties and responsibilities'. By the same token, the author or creator of a statement enjoys particularly strong freedom of expression protection. This is reflected, for example, in certain defences to defamation claims that are available to an author only, such as 'honest opinion' and 'publication on a matter of public interest'.[6]

By contrast, whoever transmits a third-party statement without editing it acts as a mere intermediary.[7] An intermediary cannot be considered an 'author', and, consequently, does not enjoy media freedom. Yet this does not mean that speech intermediaries are not protected at all. Freedom of expression includes the right to disseminate information and ideas of others. Speech intermediaries thus enjoy the right to impart information, but not the privileges afforded to the media. In turn, those intermediaries do not have to abide by the traditional medias' strict duties and responsibilities either. Speech intermediaries cannot be held fully liable for a transmitted statement, because they may not even be aware of its

[3] Compare Luhmann (1996) p. 3.

[4] Compare the following acts of legislation and judicial decisions requiring editorial control to distinguish between author and mere disseminator: Article 1(1)(c) and Recital 25 AVMS Directive; Section 1(2) UK Defamation Act 1996; *Bunt* v. *Tilley* [2006] EWHC 407 (QB) [22]; *Kaschke* v. *Gray* [2010] EWHC 690 (QB) [77]; *Tamiz* v. *Google* [2012] EWHC 449 (QB) [35].

[5] For more details on the concept of 'editorial control', see Council of Europe, Committee of Ministers, Recommendation CM/Rec(2011)7 on a new notion of media, Appendix, paras. 30–6.

[6] On honest opinion, see *Flood* v. *Times Newspapers* [2012] UKSC 12, now codified in Section 3 Defamation Act 2013; on publication on a matter of public interest, see *Reynolds* v. *Times Newspapers Ltd* [1999] 2 AC 127, now codified in Section 4 Defamation Act 2013.

[7] On the liability of speech intermediaries, see Oster (2015).

content. The law therefore provides limited liability or even immunity to those speech facilitators, such as under Articles 12 to 15 e-commerce Directive,[8] Section 230(c)(1) US Communications Decency Act 1996 or Section 5 UK Defamation Act 2013. Yet the limited or excluded liability of speech intermediaries is based on the principle of innocent dissemination[9] rather than freedom of expression concerns. The principle of innocent dissemination implies that no one may be liable for unlawful content that they merely distribute, but of which they are not the author, do not otherwise endorse and of which they do not have knowledge and the absence of knowledge was not due to any negligence on their part.[10] Thus the principle of innocent dissemination is a principle expressing lack of accountability.

Media freedom and its connected duties and responsibilities may thus only apply to content providers and not to mere disseminators of third-party speech. 'The media' are only those persons and entities who themselves produce content. Media freedom is therefore identical with journalistic freedom. Intermediaries who merely provide platforms for other people's speech are not to be categorised as 'media' according to the concept of media freedom. This is relevant, for example, with regard to the question whether these intermediaries are obliged to identify subscribers who allegedly committed unlawful acts on the internet, such as copyright infringement or defamation. If intermediaries were considered institutional media, and thus enjoyed media privileges, they would be entitled to refuse to reveal the subscriber's identity because they would have the same privilege like journalists not to disclose their 'sources'.[11] However, since they cannot be categorised as media, internet intermediaries cannot rely on the rights deriving from media freedom.

The CJEU indirectly confirmed this conclusion in two decisions on the liability of internet service providers (ISPs). In *Scarlet Extended* v. *SABAM and others* and *SABAM* v. *Netlog*, the Société belge des auteurs, compositeurs et éditeurs SCRL (SABAM), a management company representing authors, composers and publishers of musical works, ordered the access provider *Scarlet Extended* and the social network platform *Netlog*

[8] Directive 2000/31/EC of 8 June 2000 on Certain Legal Aspects of Information Society Services, in particular Electronic Commerce, in the Internal Market (Directive on Electronic Commerce), OJ 2000, L178/1.

[9] The defence of 'innocent dissemination' emerged under common law (see *Bromage* v. *Prosser* [1825] 4 B & C 247; *Chubb* v. *Flannagan* [1834] 6 Car & P 431; *Emmens* v. *Pottle* [1885] 16 QBD 354) and has been codified by legislative intervention in Section 10 Defamation Act 2013 and Section 1 Defamation Act 1996.

[10] *Emmes* v. *Pottle* [1885] 16 QBD 354; *Vizetelly* v. *Mudie's Select Library, Ltd* [1900] 2 QB 170; compare Collins (2010) para. 17.01, Oster (2015).

[11] See Chapter 4, Section 4.2.1.3.

to install a system for filtering electronic communications which use file-sharing software ('peer-to-peer') with the purpose of preventing the copyright infringing practice of file sharing. In both cases, the Court held that national authorities and courts have to strike a fair balance between the protection of the intellectual property right enjoyed by copyright holders, and of the freedom to conduct a business enjoyed by ISPs pursuant to Article 16 EUChFR.[12] The CJEU applied Article 11 EUChFR only to the freedom to receive and impart information of the ISPs' customers, but not to the ISPs themselves.[13] In addition, in his opinion on *Scarlet Extended*, Advocate-General Cruz Villalón referred to Scarlet Extended's right to impart information according to Article 11(1) EUChFR, but did not mention the possibility that they could also be violated in their 'freedom of the media' according to Article 11(2) EUChFR.[14]

This supports the view that the legal concept of 'media' includes the requirement of editorial control, which the ISPs did not exercise in these cases. Although media freedom also covers the dissemination of third-party speech,[15] this only applies to interviews or reports that have been journalistically edited. Hence, in the ambit of EU law, ISPs can only invoke Article 16 EUChFR and EU secondary law, in particular Articles 12 to 15 e-commerce Directive, but not media freedom according to Article 11(2) EUChFR.

3.2 The media as mass media

Having identified 'the media' as a legal concept for a particular type of author of information and ideas, as opposed to a mere speech intermediary, it is now necessary to distinguish the media from other authors. Based on the principles of human communication, the distinction between the media and other authors follows from the nature of the recipients of the information.

The main distinction between media publications and expression by other actors, such as private individuals, is the media's ability to disseminate information and ideas to a mass audience. Thus the media as a legal concept encompasses mass media, which can be defined as any author able to communicate to an undefined and non-exclusive number of

[12] CJEU, *Scarlet Extended* v. *SABAM and others* [2011] ECR I-11959, Case C-70/10 [47–9]; *SABAM* v. *Netlog* [2012] (not yet reported), Case C-360/10, [44–7].
[13] CJEU, *Scarlet Extended* v. *SABAM and others* [2011] ECR I-11959, Case C-70/10 [50]; *SABAM* v. *Netlog* [2012] (not yet reported), Case C-360/10 [48].
[14] CJEU, *Scarlet Extended* v. *SABAM and others* [2011] ECR I-11959, Case C-70/10, Opinion of AG Cruz Villalón [85].
[15] See Chapter 4, Section 4.1.2.

recipients.[16] Mass media is therefore not to be determined by the number of recipients, but by the openness of the communication itself or the subscription to it. An e-mail or a newsletter sent to 1,000 recipients does not constitute mass communication if the target group is exclusive, such as the staff members of a particular company. By contrast, an e-mail or a newspaper open to general subscription constitutes mass media, even if only twenty people actually sign up. A telephone connection between individual participants does not constitute mass media, because the target group is determined and closed. A telephone conversation broadcast by radio, however, is mass communication.

The concept of 'mass communication' should not be confused with the distinction between point-to-point and point-to-multipoint communication. Prior to the emergence of the internet and the phenomenon of media convergence, mass communication and point-to-multipoint communication were identical, and so were individual communication and point-to-point communication. Any communication via the internet, however, is point-to-point communication and may nonetheless be mass communication. Internet communication is carried out through the exchange of data packages between computers. Unlike traditional broadcasting, the internet is not based on the unilateral sending of signals without a back channel, but on the interaction between two computers. Despite this technological categorisation of internet communication as point-to-point communication, providing information to the general public on a website or making video on demand available nonetheless constitute mass communication. The difference between point-to-point communication and point-to-multipoint communication is significant for the application of rules in various regulatory regimes pertaining to the dissemination of ideas in a digital format, especially where the blocking of access to websites is concerned.[17] In any case, this distinction is irrelevant nowadays for the categorisation as mass communication or individual communication.

3.3 Media freedom as journalistic freedom

Before the emergence of the internet, the ability to reach a mass audience was a sufficiently decisive criterion to distinguish between journalistic

[16] Compare Anderson (2002) 469–70; Barendt (2005) p. 417; Keller (2011) p. 12; ECJ, *Mediakabel* v. *Commissariaat voor de Media* [2005] ECR I-04891, Case C-89/04 [30]; *Lagardère* v. *SPRE and others* [2005] ECR I-07199, Case C-192/04 [31]; CJEU, *Svensson and others* v. *Retriever Sverige AB* [2014] (not yet reported), Case C-466/12 [21]. From a systems-theoretic point of view, see Luhmann (1996) p. 2.

[17] See Frey, Rudolph and Oster (2012).

work and communications of private individuals. The traditional professional media had a monopoly and a gatekeeper role on addressing the general public. Only the traditional mass media had the opportunity to disseminate information and ideas to a mass audience, or to enable the dissemination of such publications. In the past decades, the mass media, especially the press, has played an essential role in informing the public by investigating and publishing stories that influenced public opinion, for instance, the Pentagon papers and the Watergate scandal in the US,[18] or the German *Spiegel* affair in 1962.[19] In his 2012 report, Lord Leveson lists many further recent examples from the UK.[20]

In the course of the evolution of the internet, the ability to reach a mass audience is no longer the privilege of traditional media corporations, and, hence, not a clearly distinguishing element for the media–public divide anymore. The internet enables individuals to reach a global audience in a way that is not comparable to the distribution of leaflets or to shouting in a megaphone, and has thus become an increasingly important source of news.[21] Some amateur journalists conduct 'old-fashioned, shoe-leather investigative reporting' once associated with the mainstream news media[22] or have even gained official recognition as 'press',[23] and thus enrich public discourse by contributing to debates of general interest. It is appropriate to say that the relationship between citizen-journalists and the traditional media is often symbiotic: by researching and covering citizen-journalists' findings, the traditional media lends credibility to their publications and allows their research to reach a much wider audience due to the readership and circulation of newspapers/broadcasts exceeding that of the daily readership of citizen-journalists' websites.[24] As a consequence, the boundaries between the traditional media, especially the press, and non-media actors, become more and more blurred, thus causing significant legal uncertainty.

One could therefore argue that anyone reaching a mass audience should be considered to be a journalist, and should enjoy journalists' privileges.[25]

[18] For the former, see US Supreme Court, *New York Times Co.* v. *United States*, 403 US 713 (1971).

[19] See German Federal Constitutional Court, '*Der Spiegel*' [1966] Case 1 BvR 586/62, 610/63 and 512/64.

[20] Lord Justice Leveson, An Inquiry into the Culture, Practices and Ethics of the Press, 2012, pp. 455 ff.

[21] See Durity (2006); Alonzo (2006) 754; Anonymous author (2007) 996–8; Anonymous author (2011) 4.

[22] Compare Calvert and Torres (2011) 341 and 344, with further references.

[23] See High Court of Ireland, *Cornec* v. *Morrice and others* [2012] IEHC 376; Seelye (2005) at C5.

[24] Curran and Seaton (2010) p. 286; Calvert and Torres (2011) 345.

[25] See Human Rights Committee, General Comment no. 34, para. 44.

This approach, which focuses on the technological ability to address the general public rather than the content of publications, would facilitate the distinction between media speech and non-media expression. Yet such an interpretation would be over-inclusive, as it encompasses virtually every internet publication. Internet publications do not only vary in their quality, but also in their appearance, ranging from political blogs to hotel evaluations. This variety suggests that any notion of 'internet publication' is sweeping. A meaningless 'tweet' would, in the first place, be legally indistinguishable from a blog reporting on uprisings in the Middle East. It is therefore imprecise to speak of 'an internet publication', or even of 'a blog', as such, and to protect all those publications *per se* as press publications.[26] The internet is abundant with meaningless postings on social networks, personal diaries and obscure or salacious blogs.[27] But even serious citizen-journalists often lack the education, the experience and the credentials that distinguish most professional journalists from private individuals.[28] Many bloggers post information despite uncertainty about its reliability and depend on their readers' judgment about its accuracy.[29]

An over-inclusive definition of 'journalism' would also be prone to abuse. Privileges granted to a particular group, such as the right not to reveal journalistic sources, usually convey a benefit to that group.[30] However, those privileges may also impose costs on society at large. The confidentiality of journalistic sources, for instance, deprives courts of testimonial evidence. It renders prosecutions and discovery in civil litigation less efficient because the public prosecutor or the claimant will have to perform their own investigations, rather than obtaining the information from the reporter as a witness.[31] In extreme cases, crimes may not be prosecuted at all, due to the loss of evidence only a journalist could have provided.[32]

The journalistic media's right not to reveal sources is therefore conceptualised as an exceptional privilege. If everyone with internet access and a blog or a social media account were considered to be a journalist, the exception would become the rule, which would severely impede the course of justice. As a result, the legal concept of 'journalism' should not be interpreted too extensively without further consideration. The fact that a statement has been published online and so can be accessed by a mass audience does not *per se* make the publication a journalistic publication:

[26] However, see Alonzo (2006) 753.
[27] See Lord Justice Leveson, An Inquiry into the Culture, Practices and Ethics of the Press, 2012, pp. 168–9.
[28] Compare Calvert and Torres (2011) 344. [29] Alonzo (2006) 755.
[30] Alonzo (2006) 774. [31] Alonzo (2006) 775. [32] Alonzo (2006) 775.

the 'medium' internet must not be confused with 'the media' as a legal concept, just as the medium 'paper' does not automatically constitute the press. It is necessary to distinguish the diligent journalist engaged in informing the public from someone who seeks a privilege in media disguise.

One could thus attempt to uphold the traditional media–public divide by establishing a requirement of professionalism, for example, that a publisher must be associated with a traditional media company or needs to undergo a journalistic education.[33] A requirement of professionalism for privileged protection of the media under Article 10 ECHR is supported by the fact that the Strasbourg Court and the Committee of Ministers of the Council of Europe regularly refer to 'media professionals'.[34] The ECtHR did not grant similarly strong protection to private internet publications.[35] Similarly, the Inter-American Court once indicated that 'the profession of journalism ... specifically involves seeking, receiving and imparting information'.[36]

Yet a requirement of 'professionalism' eliminates freelancers and anyone supplying news who does not receive remuneration, that is, most bloggers who do contribute to matters of general interest.[37] Private blogs are at times the only sources to receive news from conflict areas, as happened in the Arab Spring. Hence, it is unconvincing to establish the presumption that a tabloid newspaper paparazzo should *a priori* enjoy more protection than a private, diligently acting citizen-journalist reporting from Tahrir Square in the midst of turmoil, only because the latter does not receive remuneration or lacks previous journalistic

[33] See EComHR, *Loersch and Nouvelle Association du Courrier* v. *Switzerland* [1995] App. nos. 23868/94 and 23869/94 [3]; Council of Europe, Committee of Ministers, Recommendation No. R (97) 20 on 'Hate Speech', Principle 2; Recommendation Rec (2003)13 on the Provision of Information through the Media in relation to Criminal Proceedings, para. 3; Parliamentary Assembly, Resolution 1636 (2008): Indicators for Media in a Democracy', No. 10.

[34] See ECtHR, *Sürek and Özdemir* v. *Turkey* [1999] App. nos. 23927/94 and 24277/94 [63]; *Şener* v. *Turkey* [2000] App. no. 26680/95 [42]; *Wizerkaniuk* v. *Poland* [2011] App. no. 18990/05 [68]; *Kaperzyński* v. *Poland* [2012] App. no. 43206/07 [70]; Council of Europe, Committee of Ministers, Recommendation No. R (2000) 7 on the Right of Journalists not to Disclose their Sources of Information, Appendix: 'For the purposes of this Recommendation ... the term "journalist" means any natural or legal person who is regularly or professionally engaged in the collection and dissemination of information to the public via any means of mass communication'; Recommendation CM/Rec(2011)7 on a New Notion of Media, Appendix, para. 38.

[35] See ECtHR, *Perrin* v. *United Kingdom* [2005] App. no. 5446/03; *Willem* v. *France* [2009] App. no. 10883/05.

[36] IACtHR, *Vélez Restrepo* v. *Colombia* [2012] Case 12.658 [140]; see also Advisory Opinion OC-5/85 [72]; *Fontevecchia and D'Amico* v. *Argentina* [2011] Case 12.524 [45].

[37] See Ugland (2008) 137; West (2011) 1068; Blocher (2012) 429.

education. Therefore, journalism 'cannot be equated with the mere delivery of a public service through the practice of university-acquired knowledge or training'.[38]

The journalistic privilege should thus extend to contributions to the discussion of public affairs by actors of civil society other than traditional media undertakings if they act according to certain standards of conduct. The protection an actor of civil society ultimately receives will thus depend on his or her ability to act with a level of diligence comparable to that of traditional news media organisations.[39] Such actors may include, for instance, citizen-journalists, NGOs,[40] interest groups or credit rating agencies, especially when issuing sovereign ratings.[41] Even small and informal campaign groups 'must be able to carry on their activities effectively' and there exists 'a strong public interest in enabling such groups and individuals outside the mainstream to contribute to the public debate by disseminating information and ideas on matters of general public interest'.[42] While in the pre-internet age those groups depended on the traditional mass media to pick up their stories, they may now draw attention to the problems they are particularly sensitive to.

In the ECtHR case *Fatullayev* v. *Azerbaijan*, for instance, it was not clear whether the applicant posted the impugned statements online in his capacity as a journalist or whether he expressed his personal opinions as an 'ordinary citizen'. However, for the Court, it was more important that the applicant did not hide his identity when posting the statements and that 'he publicly disseminated his statements by posting them on a freely accessible popular internet forum, a medium which in modern times has

[38] IACtHR, *Herrera-Ulloa* v. *Costa Rica* [2004] Case 12.367 [118].

[39] Anonymous author (2007) 998; Oster (2013) 78; Appendix to Recommendation CM/Rec(2011)7 of the Committee of Ministers of the Council of Europe to Member States on a New Notion of Media, para. 41; compare Mitchell (2011) 19: 'Compliance with the standards of responsible journalism is a prerequisite for any defendant (*whether a journalist or not*)' (emphasis added).

[40] See Human Rights Committee, *Toktakunov* v. *Kyrgyzstan* [2011] Communication no. 1470/2006 [6.3]; Special Court for Sierra Leone, *Prosecutor* v. *Alex Tamba Brima and others*, Decision on Prosecution appeal against decision on oral application for witness TF1–150 to testify without being compelled to answer questions on grounds of confidentiality, Case No. SCSL-2004–16-AR73 [2006] SCSL 2 [33]. The Special Court acknowledged a privileged relationship between a human rights officer and his informants, as well as a public interest attached to the work of human rights officers gathering confidential information, and therefore protected researchers for NGOs similar to journalistic sources.

[41] See Oster (2012a) 211.

[42] ECtHR, *Steel and Morris* v. *United Kingdom* [2005] App. no. 68416/01 [89]; see also *Társaság a Szabadságjogokért* v. *Hungary* [2009] App. no. 37374/05 [27].

no less powerful an effect than the print media'.[43] Thus the applicant enjoyed significant free speech protection. Similarly, in the recent decision *Braun* v. *Poland*, the ECtHR held that the question of whether the applicant was a journalist within the meaning of the *domestic* law was not of particular relevance, since the Convention offers protection to all participants in debates on matters of legitimate public concern.[44] It was more relevant that the applicant, a film director, historian and author of press articles 'who actively and publicly commented on current affairs', had 'clearly been involved in a public debate on an important issue', namely a radio and a television debate on communist-era security services. Consequently, it was not justified to require the applicant to fulfil a standard of diligence more demanding than that applicable to journalists.[45]

Furthermore, being categorised as media requires that the publications should occur on a periodical basis. The media's privilege is based on the fact that a publisher is committed to regular and public dissemination of contributions to public discourse, which may be evidenced by a track record of gathering and disseminating information.[46] An exception to be made might be single publications of non-fictional books contributing to matters of public concern.

3.4 Conclusion

Due to the phenomenon of media convergence and the development of new forms of media, 'the media' as a legal term should be broadly conceptualised. It should include both professional and non-professional press, whether printed,[47] internet-based[48] or disseminated in other form,

[43] ECtHR, *Fatullayev* v. *Azerbaijan* [2010] App. no. 40984/07 [95]; see also *Editorial Board of Pravoye Delo and Shtekel* v. *Ukraine* [2011] App. no. 33014/05 [63]; *Yıldırım* v. *Turkey* [2012] App. no. 3111/10 [54].

[44] *Braun* v. *Poland* [2014] App. no. 30162/10 [47] (emphasis added).

[45] *Braun* v. *Poland* [2014] App. no. 30162/10 [50].

[46] Compare US Supreme Court, *O'Grady* v. *Superior Court*, 44 Cal. Rptr. 3d 72, 105 (2006); Berger (2003) 1412; Flanagan (2005) 415; West (2011) 1067; Council of Europe, Committee of Ministers, Recommendation CM/Rec(2011)7 on a New Notion of Media, Appendix, para. 28.

[47] See, e.g., ECtHR, *Sunday Times* v. *United Kingdom (No. 1)* [1979] App. no. 6538/74 [66]; *Bergens Tidende and others* v. *Norway* [2000] App. no. 26132/95 [60]; *Perna* v. *Italy* [2003] App. no. 48898/99 [39]; ECJ, *Familiapress* v. *Heinrich Bauer Verlag* [1997] ECR I-03689, Case C-368/95 [25].

[48] Human Rights Committee, General Comment no. 34, paras. 12, 43; ECtHR, *Times Newspapers Ltd* v. *United Kingdom (Nos. 1 and 2)* [2009] App. nos. 3002/03 and 23676/03 [27]; AfComHPR, *Zimbabwe Lawyers for Human Rights and Institute for Human Rights and Development in Africa (on behalf of Andrew Barclay Meldrum)* v. *Zimbabwe* [2009] App. no. 294/04 [112].

such as via e-mail or text messages,[49] audiovisual media,[50] radio broadcasting,[51] non-fictional books and periodicals[52].

'The media' as a legal concept encompasses media organisations and their owners, executive directors, editors, publishers and journalists, employed and self-employed, as well as their auxiliary persons.[53] The traditional dichotomy of professional newspaper/broadcasting journalism enjoying media privileges, on the one hand, and non-professional 'freedom of expression only' citizens who do not enjoy these privileges, on the other hand, should be replaced with a functional, content-based approach to media freedom. Rather than arguing that *because* a person or institution is to be categorised as a 'journalist' or 'media' they enjoy certain privileges and have to abide by standards of conduct, it is suggested that *if* a person or institution contributes to public discourse, then they are to be conceived of as journalists and should enjoy special privileges.[54] Only such a functional approach is capable of setting the right incentives for journalists

[49] Compare ECJ, *Tietosuojavaltuutettu* v. *Satakunnan Markkinapörssi Oy and Satamedia Oy* [2008] ECR I-09831, Case C-73/07 [29].

[50] See, e.g., EComHR, *Purcell and others* v. *Ireland* [1991] App. no. 15404/89; ECtHR, *Jersild* v. *Denmark* [1994] App. no. 15890/89 [31]; *Centro Europa 7 Srl and Di Stefano* v. *Italy* [2012] App. no. 38433/09 [131]; ECJ, *Stichting Collectieve Antennevoorziening Gouda and others* v. *Commissariaat voor de Media* [1991] ECR I-04007, Case C-288/89; *Commission* v. *Netherlands* [1991] ECR I-04069, Case C-353/89; *Veronica Omroep* v. *Commissariaat voor de Media* [1993] ECR I-00487, Case C-148/91; *TV 10 SA* v. *Commissariaat voor de Media* [1994] ECR I-04795, Case C-23/93.

[51] ECtHR, *Radio France and others* v. *France* [2004] App. no. 53984/00 [33].

[52] See, e.g. Human Rights Committee, Concluding observations on Kuwait (CCPR/CO/69/KWT), para. 20; ECtHR, *Chauvy and others* v. *France* [2004] App. no. 64915/01 [68]; *Éditions Plon* v. *France* [2004] App. no. 58148/00 [43]; *Lindon, Otchakovsky-Laurens and July* v. *France* [2007] App. nos. 21279/02 and 36448/02 [47]; ECJ, *VBVB and VBBB* v. *Commission* [1984] ECR 00019, Joined Cases 43/82 and 63/82; IAComHR, *Francisco Martorell* v. *Chile* [1996] Case 11.230 [53]; *Steve Clark and others* v. *Grenada* [1996] Case 10.325 [3].

[53] See, e.g., ECtHR, *Öztürk* v. *Turkey* [1999] App. no. 22479/93 [49]: publisher; *Manole and others* v. *Moldova* [2009] App. no. 13936/02: media employees; *Editorial Board of Pravoye Delo and Shtekel* v. *Ukraine* [2011] App. no. 33014/05 [48] and *OOO 'Vesti' and Ukhov* v. *Russia* [2013] App. no. 21724/03 [52]: editorial board; IACtHR, *Vélez Restrepo* v. *Colombia* [2012] Case 12.658: cameraman; ECJ, *Tietosuojavaltuutettu* v. *Satakunnan Markkinapörssi Oy and Satamedia Oy* [2008] ECR I-09831, Case C-73/07 [58]: media undertakings and 'every person engaged in journalism'; see generally Council of Europe, Committee of Ministers, Recommendation CM/Rec(2011)7 on a New Notion of Media, Appendix, para. 15. Notably, juristic entities, such as media companies, may not claim to be the victim of a violation of the ICCPR. Article 1 of the Optional First Protocol to the ICCPR states that the Committee may receive and consider communications from *individuals* who claim to be victims of a violation by that State Party. However, if an interference with a media company's right is at stake under the ICCPR, individual journalists may claim a violation of their own rights due to the impairment of the media enterprise they are working for; see Human Rights Committee, *Mavlonov et al* v. *Uzbekistan* [2009] Communication no. 1334/2004 [8.4].

[54] See Oster (2013).

and media entities, as well as non-professional bloggers, to behave in a prudent and diligent manner. It provides legal certainty for those bloggers who *de facto* conduct journalistic work, moves beyond the outdated distinction between methods of distribution and incentivises any publisher to contribute to matters of general concern. It also considers that media entities are under increasing market pressure to deliver what a part of the public *wants* to know: celebrity trivia, details on the private lives of public figures, etc. The tabloid media is free, within the boundaries of the law, to publish whatever it wants. However, it is not entitled to particular media freedom protection if they does not deliver what the public *needs* to know. The loss of media freedom privileges is therefore the price a magazine has to pay if it succumbs to easily marketable gossip rather than investigative journalism on matters of public interest.

4 The content of media freedom: media speech privileges and institutional protection of the media

As examined in Chapter 2, media freedom encompasses the media speech privilege and the protection of the media as an institution. The media speech privilege includes that a person or institution, by virtue of being media and acting as media, is governed by a different set of factors concerning the intensity of protection when issuing a publication, compared to freedom of expression afforded to private individuals or non-media entities. The media speech privilege therefore both covers and extends beyond the rights provided under freedom of expression in general (see Section 4.1). The institutional protection of the media encompasses certain rights that are not available under freedom of expression at all and are related to the media in its newsgathering, editorial and distribution process and to the existence of an independent media (see Section 4.2).

4.1 The protection of 'media speech'

Freedom of expression generally, and thus also media freedom, includes the freedom to receive and impart information and ideas without interference by public authorities and regardless of frontiers, as Articles 19(2) ICCPR, Article 13(1)2 ACHR and Article 10(1)2 ECHR almost identically stipulate. Furthermore, Article 19(1) ICCPR and Article 10(1)2 ECHR protect the freedom to hold opinions and Article 13(1)1 ACHR protects the freedom of thought. Article 9 AfCHPR protects the right to receive information and to express and disseminate one's opinions.

Therefore, freedom of expression can be sub-categorised into freedom to hold opinions and impart and receive ideas on the one hand, and to receive and impart information on the other hand. The clause 'regardless of frontiers' within the meaning of Article 19(2) ICCPR, Article 13(1)2 ACHR and Article 10(1)2 ECHR guarantees that cross-border speech, such as publications transmitted via broadcasting or the internet, enjoys the same freedom of expression protection as domestic speech.[1] Furthermore, freedom of expression prohibits any distinction between the protected freedom of expression of nationals and that of foreigners, and thus the preclusion of a foreigner from re-entering on grounds of his past opinions.[2] The African Charter does not expressly include a 'regardless of frontiers' clause. However, the African Commission highlighted that freedom of expression under Article 9 AfCHPR includes speech 'across frontiers'.[3]

4.1.1 Freedom to hold opinions

Freedom of expression comprises, as a necessary pre-condition of the right to express oneself freely, the right to hold opinions without interference, or, in the words of the ACHR, freedom of thought. With regard to the freedom of the media, this means that a journalist may freely have an opinion and may change this opinion, or *not* have an opinion at all, all of which must not be subject to any interference or punishment.[4] Article 19 (1) ICCPR, Article 10(1)2 ECHR, Article 13(1)1 ACHR and Article 9 (2) AfCHPR protect all forms of opinions, including opinions of a political, scientific, historic, moral or religious nature.[5]

The ICCPR does not permit any exception or restriction to the right to hold opinions according to Article 19(1) ICCPR; the qualifications of paragraph 3 apply only to paragraph 2. In addition, a reservation of a State Party to Article 19(1) would be incompatible with the object and purpose of the Covenant,[6] and freedom of opinion cannot be made subject to lawful derogation under Article 4 ICCPR, because it can never become necessary to derogate from it during a state of emergency.[7]

[1] Compare ECtHR, *Association Ekin* v. *France* [2001] App. no. 39288/98 [62]; Nowak (2005) Article 19 para. 16 fn. 37; Council of Europe, European Convention on Transfrontier Television (1989).

[2] ECtHR, *Cox* v. *Turkey* [2010] App. no. 2933/03 [31].

[3] Declaration of Principles on Freedom of Expression in Africa, Section I.

[4] See Human Rights Committee, *Mpaka-Nsusu* v. *Zaire* [1986] Communication no. 157/1983 [10]; *Primo Jose Essono Mika Miha* v. *Equatorial Guinea* [1994] Communication no. 414/1990 [6.8]; *Faurisson* v. *France* [1996] Communication no. 550/93; *Kang* v. *Republic of Korea* [2003] Communication no. 878/1999 [7.2]; General Comment no. 34, para. 9.

[5] See Human Rights Committee, General Comment no. 34, para. 9.

[6] See Human Rights Committee, General Comment no. 24; General Comment no. 34, para. 5.

[7] Human Rights Committee, General Comment no. 29, para. 11; General Comment no. 34, para. 5. Article 4 ICCPR states:

1. In time of public emergency which threatens the life of the nation and the existence of which is officially proclaimed, the States Parties to the present Covenant may take measures derogating from their obligations under the present Covenant to the extent strictly required by the exigencies of the situation, provided that such measures are not

Similarly, the derogations in Article 15 ECHR and Article 27 ACHR should not be applied to the freedom to hold opinions, because an exception to this right can never be required according to Article 15(1) ECHR and Article 27(1) ACHR.

Unlike Article 19(1) ICCPR or the right to freedom of thought, as protected by Article 9(1) ECHR, the right to hold an opinion under Article 10(1)2 ECHR and the freedom of thought under Article 13(1)1 ACHR are not unqualified rights, since Article 10(2) ECHR and Article 13(2) ACHR refer to the entire first paragraphs. Yet it is suggested here that, corresponding to Article 19(1) ICCPR and Article 9(1) ECHR, the freedom to hold an opinion and the freedom of thought, as part of the inner conviction or *forum internum*, should be unrestricted as opposed to the freedom to express oneself (external manifestation or *forum externum*). Therefore, measures that coercively manipulate one's opinion, such as indoctrination or brainwashing, should not be justifiable under any circumstances.[8]

4.1.2 Right to impart information and ideas

Freedom of expression and media freedom include the freedom not only to have information and ideas, but, of course, to impart them. In this context, the media's freedom to publish goes beyond the mere dissemination of factual information. The task of the media is not to merely impart information, the interpretation of which must be left to the reader: 'Freedom of the press ... affords the public one of the best means of discovering and forming an opinion of the ideas and attitudes of political leaders and on other matters of general interest.'[9]

inconsistent with their other obligations under international law and do not involve discrimination solely on the ground of race, colour, sex, language, religion or social origin.

2. No derogation from articles 6, 7, 8 (paragraphs I and 2), 11, 15, 16 and 18 may be made under this provision.
3. Any State Party to the present Covenant availing itself of the right of derogation shall immediately inform the other States Parties to the present Covenant, through the intermediary of the Secretary-General of the United Nations, of the provisions from which it has derogated and of the reasons by which it was actuated. A further communication shall be made, through the same intermediary, on the date on which it terminates such derogation.

[8] Compare ECtHR, *Kjeldsen, Busk Madsen and Pedersen* [1976] App. nos. 5095/71, 5920/72 and 5926/72 [53] with regard to Article 2 of Protocol No. 1.

[9] ECtHR, *Lingens* v. *Austria* [1986] App. no. 9815/82 [42]; reiterated in, e.g., *Oberschlick* v. *Austria (No. 1)* [1991] App. no. 11662/85 [58]; *Thoma* v. *Luxembourg* [2001] App. no. 38432/97 [45]; *Scharsach and News Verlagsgesellschaft mbH* v. *Austria* [2003] App. no. 39394/98 [30]; *Cumpănă and Mazăre* v. *Romania* [2004] App. no. 33348/96 [93].

Article 19(2) ICCPR, Article 10(1)2 ECHR and Article 13(1)2 ACHR distinguish between the freedom to hold opinions and to impart and receive *ideas*, on the one hand, and to receive and impart *information*, on the other hand, as sub-categories of freedom of expression. The provisions thus protect both statements of fact ('information'), and value judgments (opinions, comments or 'ideas'). The distinction between statements of fact and value judgments gains particular significance in defamation cases.[10] The difference lies in the susceptibility to proof: while the existence of facts can be demonstrated, value judgments are not susceptible to proof.[11] This corresponds to Habermas' theory of communicative action, which distinguishes between validity claims to propositional truth (assertoric sentences), normative rightness ('ought' sentences) and subjective truthfulness (evaluative sentences).[12] While validity claims to truth are raised by statements of fact, normative rightness and subjective truthfulness claims constitute value judgments. The dictum of the US Supreme Court, according to which under the First Amendment 'there is no such thing as a false idea',[13] is thus not only doctrinally but also semantically correct.

So far there have not been any convincing objections to the fact/opinion distinction. To be sure, the line between facts and opinion can be *difficult* to draw, for example, if factual statements serve to support value judgments or if someone ventures a guess on the inner motivations of a third person.[14] However, it has not been convincingly established that the line is *impossible* to draw. Furthermore, the categorisation of speech as a statement of fact has to be distinguished from the question as to whether the facts are theoretically *susceptible* to proof. That a statement of fact cannot be proven due to lack of data does not change the fact that it could be proved if the data were available. Thus, the question of whether a statement is susceptible to proof has to be distinguished from the question *if* it can be proven.[15] The latter is merely a question of the burden of proof.

There are additional categories of speech that are of interest here which do not seamlessly fit into the fact–opinion dichotomy. These include, for

[10] See Chapter 7, Section 7.3.4.

[11] See, for instance, ECtHR, *Lingens* v. *Austria* [1986] App. no. 9815/82 [46]; *De Haes and Gijsels* v. *Belgium* [1997] App. no. 19983/92 [42]; *Jerusalem* v. *Austria* [2001] App. no. 26958/95 [42]; *Steel and Morris* v. *United Kingdom* [2005] App. no. 68416/01 [87]; IACtHR, *Kimel* v. *Argentina* [2008] Case 12.450 [93].

[12] See Habermas (1981a) pp. 39, 99; Habermas (1981b) p. 120.

[13] US Supreme Court, *Gertz* v. *Robert Welch, Inc.*, 418 US 323, 339 (1974).

[14] See, e.g., ECtHR, *Axel Springer AG* v. *Germany (No. 2)* [2014] App. no. 48311/10 [63].

[15] See Post (1990) 656.

instance, fictional works, which may be relevant for copyright law,[16] and statements of religious belief that are not subject to empirical proof.[17] Further sub-categorisations of value judgments into 'preference expressions' (reports on the inner condition of the speaker) and 'judgments' (which do not simply make known the private feelings or attitudes of a speaker but rather make claims about the world that are independent of the speaker),[18] may be of linguistic and philosophical interest, but are not conducive to the law.

Article 9(2) AfCHPR only protects freedom to utter 'opinions' expressly. One could therefore conclude that the provision does not, *e contrario*, protect factual statements. Yet this is unconvincing, because facts are a necessary prerequisite to form an opinion. The AfComHPR thus correctly found that Article 9(2) also protects factual information.[19]

Freedom of expression is content-neutral regarding the information and ideas imparted or received. It is applicable not only to information or ideas 'that are favourably received or regarded as inoffensive or as a matter of indifference, but also to those that offend, shock or disturb. Such are the demands of that pluralism, tolerance and broadmindedness without which there is no "democratic society"'.[20] Even false and defamatory statements[21] and pornography[22] are *basically* protected by freedom of expression as well. The focal point of the analysis thus lies in the question whether a restriction of the expression concerned is justified, in particular regarding the proper balancing of conflicting rights and interests. Here lies a significant difference between the international adjudicators' jurisprudence and the more categorical approach of the US Supreme Court, where the argument is focused on the question of whether a certain expression is protected as 'speech' or not.

The media speech privilege does not only protect the publication of the media's own information and ideas. It also protects the publication of

[16] See Chapter 7, Section 7.4. [17] See Chapter 11. [18] See Post (1990) 653.

[19] See AfComHPR, *International PEN, Constitutional Rights Project, Civil Liberties Organisation and Interights (on behalf of Ken Saro-Wiwa Jnr.)* v. *Nigeria* [1995] App. nos. 137/94, 139/94, 154/96 and 161/97 [110]; *Scanlen & Holderness* v. *Zimbabwe* [2009] App. no. 297/05 [108].

[20] ECtHR, *Handyside* v. *United Kingdom* [1976] App. no. 5493/72 [49]; reiterated in, amongst many other decisions, *Sunday Times* v. *United Kingdom (No. 1)* [1979] App. no. 6538/74 [65]; *Lingens* v. *Austria* [1986] App. no. 9815/82 [41]; *Thorgeir Thorgeirson* v. *Iceland* [1992] App. no. 13778/88 [63]; *Axel Springer AG* v. *Germany (No. 1)* [2012] App. no. 39954/08 [78]. See also US Supreme Court, *Cohen* v. *California*, 403 US 15, 25 (1971): 'one man's vulgarity is another's lyric'.

[21] See Chapter 7.

[22] ECtHR, *Wingrove* v. *United Kingdom* [1996] App. no. 17419/90 [36]; EComHR, *Hoare* v. *United Kingdom* [1997] App. no. 31211/96 [1]. See also Dworkin (1981); Sunstein (1986).

third-party statements, such as those expressed in interviews, which is a core exercise of the journalistic profession. Such reporting constitutes one of the most important means whereby the media is able to play its vital role of 'public watchdog'.[23] There is also no general requirement for journalists to distance themselves from a quotation that might insult or provoke others, or damage their reputation.[24] The punishment of a journalist disseminating statements made by other persons would inhibit the contribution of the media to discussions of matters of public concern.[25] It should be considered only under narrow circumstances, for instance, if the newspaper provides a platform for incitement to violence and hatred, especially in situations of conflict and tension.[26]

Journalists or editors may basically also quote anonymous statements.[27] However, in those cases the Strasbourg Court applies stricter scrutiny to the veracity of the anonymous statement and whether value judgments had a sufficient factual basis. In *Print Zeitungsverlag GmbH* v. *Austria*, a newspaper had published an article quoting an anonymous letter with defamatory content that had been sent to members of the supervisory board of a tourism association. Although the applicant newspaper duly distanced itself from the contents of the letter, the Court held that by reproducing the anonymous letter the newspaper had disseminated it to a far larger public than the restricted circle of initial recipients. Thus the publication of the anonymous letter transgressed the limits of permissible reporting.[28]

Yet this approach confuses the obligation of the media to verify its facts with the obligations of the anonymous writer not to send a letter including false and defamatory allegations. If the media duly provides the victim with an opportunity to comment before publication and if it does not claim that the allegations made in the anonymous statement are true, then it adheres to the general rules of reporting.[29] Consequently, it should be entitled to publish an anonymous letter even if it might be

[23] See, e.g., ECtHR, *Selistö* v. *Finland* [2004] App. no. 56767/00 [59]; *Axel Springer AG* v. *Germany (No. 2)* [2014] App. no. 48311/10 [69].

[24] See, e.g., ECtHR, *Radio France and others* v. *France* [2004] App. no. 53984/00 [37]; *July and SARL Liberation* v. *France* [2008] App. no. 20893/03 [71]; *Orban and others* v. *France* [2009] App. no. 20985/05 [52]; *mutatis mutandis*, *Pedersen and Baadsgaard* v. *Denmark* [2004] App. no. 49017/99 [77].

[25] ECtHR, *Jersild* v. *Denmark* [1994] App. no. 15890/89 [35]; see also *July and SARL Liberation* v. *France* [2008] App. no. 20893/03 [69]; IACtHR, *Herrera-Ulloa* v. *Costa Rica* [2004] Case 12.367 [134].

[26] ECtHR, *Sürek* v. *Turkey (No. 1)* [1999] App. no. 26682/95 [63]; *Sürek* v. *Turkey (No. 2)* [1999] App. no. 24122/94 [36]. See Chapter 11, Section 11.3.2.

[27] ECtHR, *Albert-Engelmann-Gesellschaft mbH* v. *Austria* [2006] App. no. 46389/99 [32].

[28] *Print Zeitungsverlag GmbH* v. *Austria* [2013] App. no. 26547/07 [40–1].

[29] See Chapter 7, Section 7.3.4.1.3.

defamatory, if and as far as the content of the letter pertains to a matter of public concern. Therefore, the seminal question is whether it is necessary to quote the anonymous statement *verbatim*, or whether a (for the victim) less intrusive means of reporting was available to inform the public.[30] However, the decisive question is not whether the media verified the content of the third-party statement.

Print Zeitungsverlag GmbH v. *Austria* can therefore be distinguished from *Lavric* v. *Romania*. In this case a newspaper reproduced defamatory content of a complaint lodged by a defendant against a public prosecutor and presented it as the objective truth rather than as the statements of a party. Here the Strasbourg Court rightly held that the publisher lacked the professional care required of journalists.[31]

Moreover, journalists should not be under a general obligation to seek and obtain the authorisation of an interviewed person before publishing an interview. Such an obligation may inhibit journalistic work, and the quality of the entire public debate, in several ways: journalists may either be deterred from asking provocative questions lest their interviewees prevent the publication of the interview by refusing to grant the authorisation, or they choose their interlocutors according to their reputation as being co-operative.[32] Furthermore, an interviewee is not entitled to be interviewed in a particular manner. It is 'in the interest of freedom of political debate that the interviewing journalist may also express critical and provocative points of view and not merely give neutral cues for the statements of the interviewed person, since the latter can reply immediately.'[33]

The right to impart third-party speech also includes the publication of readers' comments. However, as the first ECtHR judgment on liability of news portals for its readers' comments section has shown, this right is a double-edged sword. *Delfi AS* v. *Estonia*[34] involved a company that had integrated a comment section into its news portal, and invited users to post comments. In 2006, the applicant company published an article on its portal accusing the company SLK of destroying public roads over the frozen sea. The article attracted many comments, several of which

[30] See Chapter 6, Section 6.3.3.3.1.
[31] ECtHR, *Lavric* v. *Romania* [2014] App. no. 22231/05 [47–8].
[32] ECtHR, *Wizerkaniuk* v. *Poland* [2011] App. no. 18990/05 [82].
[33] EComHR, *Haider* v. *Austria* [1995] App. no. 25060/94. See also ECtHR, *Filatenko* v. *Russia* [2007] App. no. 73219/01 [41]: 'The punishment of a journalist for having worded his questions in a specific manner would seriously hamper the contribution of the press to discussion of matters of public interest and should not be envisaged unless there are particularly strong reasons for doing so.'
[34] ECtHR, *Delfi AS* v. *Estonia* [2013] App. no. 64569/09.

contained personal threats and offensive language against L., SLK's majority shareholder. The applicant removed these comments immediately upon notification by L. Estonian courts nonetheless awarded L. EUR 320 in non-pecuniary damages.

The Strasbourg Court did not find that the award of damages against the applicant violated Article 10 ECHR. The Court conceded that the news article published on the applicant's news portal addressed a topic of public interest in a balanced manner. However, since the article dealt with activities that negatively affected a large number of people, the Court considered that the applicant company could have realised that the publication of the article might cause negative reactions to SLK's managers. The Court held that the applicant company 'was expected to exercise a degree of caution in the circumstances of the present case in order to avoid being held liable for an infringement of other persons' reputations'.[35]

Given the fact that the applicant's news portal has had a notorious reputation of publishing defamatory and degrading comments and that the awarded damages were rather low, the Court's judgment can be accepted. Furthermore, it should be noted that the publication of readers' comments is part of news portals' professional activity. It is therefore reasonable to impose obligations on such website operators to safeguard the rights and interests of third parties. This applies even more as the actual authors of the comments often hide behind pseudonyms and are therefore out of reach for an affected person. However, the Court's reasoning is precarious at one point, namely that the applicant company could have realised that the publication of the article might cause negative reactions. Matters of general interest are usually controversial. Holding that the publication of an article on a matter of public interest *increases* the publisher's obligation to monitor derogatory comments sets an incentive for news portals not to publish on matters of public interest, which is, however, the core discipline of journalism.

4.1.3 Means and form of expression

Article 19(2) ICCPR and Article 13(1) ACHR expressly protect all forms of expression and their means of dissemination. In addition, the Strasbourg Court decided that Article 10 ECHR does not only protect the substance of the ideas and information expressed, but also the form in

[35] ECtHR, *Delfi AS* v. *Estonia* [2013] App. no. 64569/09 [86].

which they are conveyed and the means of dissemination.[36] Similarly, the Inter-American Court stressed that freedom of expression 'encompasses the right to use any appropriate medium to disseminate opinions, ideas and information and allow them to reach the greatest number of persons'.[37]

'Means of expression' may thus include any publication medium, such as books, the printed press, radio or TV broadcasting and electronic and internet-based modes of expression, as well as means that do not constitute 'media speech', such as leaflets,[38] posters[39] or banners[40]. 'Forms of expression' may include spoken, written and sign language, and non-verbal expression, such as images and objects of art.[41] Freedom of expression also includes the speaker's right to use the language of their choice to express themselves.[42] Finally, freedom of expression protects not only speech in a literal sense, but also symbolic expression, such as wearing a badge[43] or actions impeding the activities of which the actors disapprove[44].

[36] See, e.g., ECtHR, *Autronic AG* v. *Switzerland* [1990] App. no. 12726/87 [47]; *Jersild* v. *Denmark* [1994] App. no. 15890/89 [31]; *De Haes and Gijsels* v. *Belgium* [1997] App. no. 19983/92 [48]; *Murphy* v. *Ireland* [2003] App. no. 44179/98 [61]; *Radio France and others* v. *France* [2004] App. no. 53984/00 [39].

[37] IACtHR, *Vélez Restrepo* v. *Colombia* [2012] Case 12.658 [138]; see also *Olmedo Bustos and others* v. *Chile ('The Last Temptation of Christ')* [2001] Case 11.803 [65]; *Ivcher-Bronstein* v. *Peru* [2001] Case 11.762 [147]; *Herrera-Ulloa* v. *Costa Rica* [2004] Case 12.367 [109]; *Ricardo Canese* v. *Paraguay* [2004] Case 12.032 [78]; based on IACtHR, Advisory Opinion OC-5/85 [31].

[38] See, *mutatis mutandis*, Human Rights Committee, *Kim* v. *Republic of Korea* [1999] Communication no. 574/1994 [12.4]; *Zalesskaya* v. *Belarus* [2011] Communication no. 1604/2007 [10.2]; Concluding observations on Japan (CCPR/C/JPN/CO/5), para. 26; ECtHR, *Chorherr* v. *Austria* [1993] App. no. 13308/87; *Tolstoy Miloslavsky* v. *United Kingdom* [1995] App. no. 18139/91; *Incal* v. *Turkey* [1998] App. no. 41/1997/825/1031 [46]; *Appleby and others* v. *United Kingdom* [2003] App. no. 44306/98 [41].

[39] ECtHR, *PETA Deutschland* v. *Germany* [2012] App. no. 43481/09 [42]; *Mouvement raëlien suisse* v. *Switzerland* [2012] App. no. 16354/06 [49].

[40] See Human Rights Committee, *Kivenmaa* v. *Finland* [1994] Communication no. 412/1990 [9.3].

[41] See Human Rights Committee, *Shin* v. *Republic of Korea* [2004] Communication no. 926/2000 [7.2].

[42] Human Rights Committee, *Ballantyne and others* v. *Canada* [1993] Communication no. 359, 385/89 [11.3]; IACtHR, *López-Álvarez* v. *Honduras* [2006] Case 12.387 [164]; Office of the Special Rapporteur for Freedom of Expression with the Inter-American Commission on Human Rights, Inter-American Legal Framework Regarding the Right to Freedom of Expression, 2009, CIDH/RELE/INF. 2/09, para. 23; ECJ, *United Pan-Europe Communications Belgium SA and others* v. *Belgium and others* [2007] ECR I-11135, Case C-250/06 [42]; De Varennes (1993) 163.

[43] ECtHR, *Vajnai* v. *Hungary* [2008] App. no. 33629/06 [47].

[44] Such as blowing a hunting horn and engagement in hallooing with the intention of disrupting the activities of a hunt; see ECtHR, *Hashman and Harrup* v. *United Kingdom* [1999] App. no. 25594/94 [28].

Yet media freedom goes beyond the mere choice of means and form of publication. Journalistic freedom also includes the right to decide upon the methods and techniques of reporting and the way in which journalistic material is presented.[45] Offensive language may, however, not be protected by freedom of expression if it amounts to wanton denigration, for example 'where the sole intent of the offensive statement is to insult'.[46]

One important method of expressing information and ideas is via the form of arts. This becomes relevant for the media where the publication of satires, caricatures or poems is concerned. In contrast to Article 19(2) ICCPR, Article 13(1) ACHR and Article 13 EUChFR, the ECHR and the AfCHPR do not contain an express provision protecting the arts or artistic speech. The Strasbourg Court thus refused to afford protection to artistic expression *as such*, as was called for by Judges Spielmann and Jebens in their joint dissenting opinion in *Vereinigung Bildender Künstler* v. *Austria*.[47] Freedom of expression nonetheless protects the arts as a *form* of expression.[48] As the ECtHR noted in *Müller* v. *Switzerland*: 'Those who create, perform, distribute or exhibit works of art contribute to the exchange of ideas and opinions which is essential for a democratic society.'[49]

Although in the case of *Müller* the Court eventually rejected the claim of the applicants that the seizure of their allegedly obscene paintings constituted a violation of Article 10 ECHR, this is not to be perceived as a *categorically* lesser protection of 'artistic speech'. Rather, it is owed to the fact that, first, the paintings in *Müller* did not specifically contribute to a public debate, and second, the interfering state invoked the protection

[45] See, e.g., ECtHR, *Jersild* v. *Denmark* [1994] App. no. 15890/89 [31]; *De Haes and Gijsels* v. *Belgium* [1997] App. no. 19983/92 [48]; *Bergens Tidende and others* v. *Norway* [2000] App. no. 26132/95 [57]; *Radio France and others* v. *France* [2004] App. no. 53984/00 [39].

[46] ECtHR, *Tuşalp* v. *Turkey* [2012] App. nos. 32131/08 and 41617/08 [48]; see also *Skałka* v. *Poland* [2003] App. no. 43425/98 [34].

[47] ECtHR, *Vereinigung Bildender Künstler* v. *Austria* [2007] App. no. 68354/01, joint dissenting opinion of Judges Spielman and Jebens [6]. Judges Spielman and Jebens nevertheless voted against finding a violation of Article 10, because they found the impugned painting in violation of human dignity.

[48] See ECtHR, *Müller and others* v. *Switzerland* [1988] App. no. 10737/84 [33]; *Vereinigung Bildender Künstler* v. *Austria* [2007] App. no. 68354/01 [26]; *Leroy* v. *France* [2009] App. no. 36109/03 [39]; *Société de Conception de Presse et d'Edition et Ponson* v. *France* [2009] App. no. 26935/05 [34]; Office of the Special Rapporteur for Freedom of Expression with the Inter-American Commission on Human Rights, Inter-American Legal Framework Regarding the Right to Freedom of Expression, 2009, CIDH/RELE/INF. 2/09, para. 23

[49] ECtHR, *Müller and others* v. *Switzerland* [1988] App. no. 10737/84 [33]; see also *Vereinigung Bildender Künstler* v. *Austria* [2007] App. no. 68354/01 [26]; *Leroy* v. *France* [2009] App. no. 36109/03 [44].

of morals as the reason for seizing the paintings.[50] However, this is not related to the chosen form of 'artistic expression'. If speech on a debate of public concern is expressed in the form of arts, all courts and tribunals grant extensive freedom of expression protection in favour of the artist.[51]

4.1.4 The right not to publish

Like any other liberty, freedom of the media consists of two concepts of freedom: negative and positive freedom. Positive freedom describes the freedom *to do* something. With regard to the media, the media's positive freedom encompasses its right to gather and to publish information, as developed in the previous paragraphs. Negative freedom protects the right of *not* having to do something. This is the media's right not to have to publish certain information. The media is, in principle, free to exercise editorial discretion in deciding what to publish, including articles, comments and letters submitted by private individuals.[52] Furthermore, the media must not be compelled to carry messages from specified political figures, such as the president of the Republic.[53]

The media's freedom from forced speech is interfered with where the media is being ordered to publish a reply or an apology or where the incumbent of a 'bottleneck infrastructure' is required to enable certain groups to disseminate their information and ideas via this infrastructure.

4.1.4.1 Obligation to publish a reply or an apology

A judicial order to publish a reply constitutes an interference with media freedom. For example, in the EU audiovisual media framework, such an order can be required by Article 28 AVMS Directive.[54] Most notably,

[50] See Chapter 9, Section 9.2.

[51] Compare ECtHR, *Karataş* v. *Turkey* [1999] App. no. 23168/94; *Vereinigung Bildender Künstler* v. *Austria* [2007] App. no. 68354/01. See, however, Cooper and Williams (1999) 603 and Fenwick and Phillipson (2006) p. 38 fn. 3 and pp. 51 ff., who argue that the Strasbourg Court grants less protection to 'artistic speech' than to political speech. Yet 'artistic speech' is not a *content* of expression as political speech, but a mere *form* of expression, which may also constitute political speech and as such deserves strong protection.

[52] See, e.g., ECtHR, *Melnychuk* v. *Ukraine* [2005] App. no. 28743/03, p. 6. By contrast, see IACtHR, *Urrutia* v. *Guatemala* [2003] Case 11.043 [103], but without further explanation; this has been convincingly criticised by Pasqualucci (2006) 388–9.

[53] See Joint Declaration by the UN Special Rapporteur on Freedom of Opinion and Expression, the OSCE Representative on Freedom of the Media and the OAS Special Rapporteur on Freedom of Expression of 18 December 2003, p. 2.

[54] See also Article 8 of the European Convention on Transfrontier Television (1989); Council of Europe, Committee of Ministers, Resolution (74) 26 on the Right of Reply – Position of the Individual in relation to the Press; Recommendation Rec (2004)16 on the Right of Reply in the New Media Environment; European Parliament

Article 14 ACHR expressly provides a right of reply to '[a]nyone injured by inaccurate or offensive statements or ideas disseminated to the public in general by a legally regulated medium of communication' even on Convention level. Article 14 ACHR is therefore a remarkable human right, in that it has direct horizontal effect between private individuals.[55]

However, there may be circumstances in which the media may legitimately be required to publish a retraction, a counterstatement, an apology or a judgment in a defamation case. In the seminal decision *Ediciones Tiempo SA* v. *Spain*, the European Commission of Human Rights observed that the aim of the right of reply is 'to afford everyone the possibility of protecting himself against certain statements or opinions disseminated by the mass media which are likely to be injurious to his private life, his honour or his dignity.'[56] The Commission further noted that the order to publish a reply was justified in the given case 'since the applicant company was not obliged to amend the content of the article and had the opportunity to insert its own version of the facts once more when it published the reply of the person criticised'.[57] The Commission also rejected the applicant's claim that Article 10 ECHR had been violated because the courts did not examine the veracity of the version of the facts contained in the reply before ordering its publication. The Commission considered that the purpose of the right of reply 'is to safeguard the interest of the public in receiving information from a variety of sources and thereby to guarantee the fullest possible access to information'.[58] However, Article 10 ECHR does not guarantee the right of communication companies to publish only information which they consider to reflect the truth. Furthermore, in order to be effective, a reply has to be distributed immediately. Consequently, a newspaper is not under an obligation to check the veracity of the facts asserted in the reply,[59] and may also add a comment that it does not guarantee that the reply reflects the truth.

and Council, Recommendation of 20 December 2006 on the Protection of Minors and Human Dignity and on the Right of Reply in relation to the Competitiveness of the European Audiovisual and On-line Information Services Industry (2006/952/EC), OJ 2006, L378/72. From the US, see *Red Lion Broadcasting* v. *FCC*, 395 US 367 (1969), on the right of reply to personal attacks on radio and television; however, see also *Miami Herald* v. *Tornillo*, 418 US 241 (1974), where the Supreme Court invalidated a statute providing a mandatory right of reply against a newspaper.

[55] See Chapter 5, Section 5.2.3.

[56] EComHR, *Ediciones Tiempo SA* v. *Spain* [1989] App. no. 13010/87, p. 253; see also ECtHR, *Kaperzyński* v. *Poland* [2012] App. no. 43206/07 [66].

[57] EComHR, *Ediciones Tiempo SA* v. *Spain* [1989] App. no. 13010/87, p. 253.

[58] EComHR, *Ediciones Tiempo SA* v. *Spain* [1989] App. no. 13010/87, p. 254.

[59] EComHR, *Ediciones Tiempo SA* v. *Spain* [1989] App. no. 13010/87, p. 254.

The European Court of Human Rights later emphasised that the right of reply of an aggrieved person is itself protected by Article 10 ECHR, and may as such give rise to a positive obligation on the state to enforce this right through its courts.[60] As the Court held in *Kaperzynski* v. *Poland*, 'a legal obligation to publish a rectification or a reply may be seen as a normal element of the legal framework governing the exercise of the freedom of expression by the print media. It cannot, as such, be regarded as excessive or unreasonable.'[61] The Court has recognised a 'need not only to be able to contest untruthful information, but also to ensure a plurality of opinions, especially in matters of general interest such as literary and political debate'.[62] In addition, the media may be under a professional obligation to inform the party concerned about the reasons why it refused to publish a reply or rectification.[63]

Yet the Court's approach, according to which a right of reply is based on freedom of expression, is not convincing. Rather, the right of reply is derived from the right to protection of one's reputation as a sub-category of the right to respect for private life and, hence, as a 'right of others' within the meaning of Article 19(3) ICCPR, Article 10(2) ECHR, Article 13(2) ACHR and Article 27(2) AfCHPR.[64] This also follows from a comparative reading of Article 14(3) ACHR, which states that '*[f]or the effective protection of honor and reputation*, every publisher, and every newspaper, motion picture, radio, and television company, shall have a person responsible who is not protected by immunities or special privileges' (emphasis added). The ACHR thus indicates that the right of reply is based on honour and reputation and not on the victim's freedom of expression.

4.1.4.2 Obligation of speech intermediaries to grant access to media infrastructure

Broadcasting channels, broadcasting frequencies and other forms of electronic communication enable a mass audience to be reached. Because of its character as a monopoly or 'bottleneck', operators of such infrastructure may be under an obligation to grant access. The 'bottleneck' rationale applies to the justification of 'must carry' obligations, that is, the obligation of an infrastructure provider to

60 ECtHR, *Kaperzyński* v. *Poland* [2012] App. no. 43206/07 [66]; *Melnychuk* v. *Ukraine* [2005] App. no. 28743/03, p. 6.

61 ECtHR, *Kaperzyński* v. *Poland* [2012] App. no. 43206/07 [66].

62 See also ECtHR, *Melnychuk* v. *Ukraine* [2005] App. no. 28743/03, p. 6.

63 ECtHR, *Kaperzyński* v. *Poland* [2012] App. no. 43206/07 [67].

64 Compare Marauhn (2009) para. 19.

transmit specified radio and television broadcast channels, as may be imposed according to Article 31 Universal Services Directive.[65] 'Must carry' obligations aim to preserve a pluralist range of programmes available on television distribution networks, and thus ensure that all television viewers have access to a wide range of programmes.[66] In addition, the 'bottleneck' rationale applies to the right of access to, and use of, specific electronic communications network facilities, in accordance with Article 12 Access Directive.[67] Finally, providers of broadcasting services may be under an obligation to grant time slots to campaign groups or political parties in order to safeguard a high level of plurality of ideas in the media.[68] If and insofar as the infrastructure providers and the broadcasters do not have the ability to edit content they are obliged to carry or to publish, they are mere disseminators and not responsible for the content.[69]

By contrast, where the monopoly or 'bottleneck' rationale does not apply, a right against an infrastructure provider to support the exercise of the petitioner's freedom of expression is hardly conceivable, given the fact that freedom of expression and media freedom include the right *not* to disseminate certain information and ideas. Therefore, the Strasbourg Court's decision in *Appleby and others* v. *United Kingdom,*[70] where the Court upheld the domestic authority's decision to restrict the applicants' ability to communicate their views in a private shopping mall, is correct.

4.1.5 *The right to receive information and ideas*

According to all freedom of expression provisions in international human rights catalogues, the right to freedom of expression includes not only the right to impart but also the freedom to *receive* information and ideas. Of all international adjudicators, the IACtHR has analysed this aspect of

65 Directive 2002/22/EC of the European Parliament and of the Council of 7 March 2002 on Universal Service and Users' Rights relating to Electronic Communications Networks and Services (Universal Service Directive), OJ 2002, L108/51.

66 ECJ, *United Pan-Europe Communications Belgium SA and others* v. *Belgium and others* [2007] ECR I-11135, Case C-250/06 [40]; *Kabel Deutschland* v. *Niedersächsische Landesmedienanstalt für privaten Rundfunk* [2008] ECR I-10889, Case C-336/07 [37].

67 Directive 2002/19/EC of the European Parliament and of the Council of 7 March 2002 on Access to, and Interconnection of, Electronic Communications Networks and Associated Facilities (Access Directive), OJ 2002, L108/7.

68 See Chapter 14.

69 Oster (2015); see, *mutatis mutandis*, Australia, *Thompson* v. *Australian Capital TV Ltd* [1996] HCA 38; Hong Kong, *Oriental Press Group Ltd and others* v. *Fevaworks Solutions Ltd and others* [2013] HKCFA 47 [57].

70 ECtHR, *Appleby and others* v. *United Kingdom* [2003] App. no. 44306/98.

freedom of expression in the most detail. In its 'social dimension', the Court explains, freedom of expression 'is a way of exchanging ideas and information between persons; it includes the right to try to communicate one's point of view to others, but it also implies everyone's right to receive other people's opinions, information and news. For the ordinary citizen, awareness of other people's opinions and information is as important as the right to impart their own'.[71] As a result, 'it is based on both [the individual and the social] dimensions that freedom of expression requires that no one may be arbitrarily impaired or impeded from expressing his own thoughts and, therefore, represents a right of each individual, but also entails a collective right to receive any information and to know the expression of the thought of others'.[72] Both dimensions, individual and social, are 'of equal importance and should be guaranteed simultaneously in order to give total effect to the right to freedom of expression in the terms of Article 13 of the Convention'.[73]

The right to receive information is a corollary of the right to freedom of expression. It is an original right to receive a speaker's expression alongside a speaker's right to express himself, and not a mere derivative right.[74] As a consequence, the right to receive information imposes on states the duty not to restrict a person from receiving information that others wish, or may be willing, to impart on him.[75] Therefore, the media does not only have the right to impart information and ideas; the public also has a right to receive them.[76]

[71] IACtHR, *Olmedo Bustos and others* v. *Chile ('The Last Temptation of Christ')* [2001] Case 11.803 [65]; *Ivcher-Bronstein* v. *Peru* [2001] Case 11.762 [148]; *Herrera-Ulloa* v. *Costa Rica* [2004] Case 12.367 [110]; *Ricardo Canese* v. *Paraguay* [2004] Case 12.032 [79]; based on Advisory Opinion OC-5/85 [32].

[72] IACtHR, *Vélez Restrepo* v. *Colombia* [2012] Case 12.658 [138].

[73] See, e.g., IACtHR, *Olmedo Bustos and others* v. *Chile ('The Last Temptation of Christ')* [2001] Case 11.803 [67]; *Ivcher-Bronstein* v. *Peru* [2001] Case 11.762 [149]; *Vélez Restrepo* v. *Colombia* [2012] Case 12.658 [137]. See also Grossman (2001) 629–31.

[74] See the analysis of Ramsay (2012), providing further references.

[75] Human Rights Committee, *Mavlonov et al* v. *Uzbekistan* [2009] Communication no. 1334/2004 [8.4]; EComHR, *Loersch and Nouvelle Association du Courrier* v. *Switzerland* [1995] App. nos. 23868/94 and 23869/94 [3]; ECtHR, *Faccio* v. *Italy* [2003] App. no. 33/04.

[76] See, amongst many other authorities, Human Rights Committee, *Mavlonov et al.* v. *Uzbekistan* [2009] Communication no. 1334/2004 [8.4]; ECtHR, *Sunday Times* v. *United Kingdom (No. 1)* [1979] App. no. 6538/74 [65]; *Observer and Guardian* v. *United Kingdom* [1991] App. no. 13585/88 [59]; *Bladet Tromsø and Stensaas* v. *Norway* [1999] App. no. 21980/93 [62]; IACtHR, Advisory Opinion OC-5/85 [30]; *Ivcher-Bronstein* v. *Peru* [2001] Case 11.762 [153]; IAComHR, *Francisco Martorell* v. *Chile* [1996] Case 11.230 [53]; *Steve Clark and others* v. *Grenada* [1996] Case 10.325 [4]; AfComHPR, *Media Rights Agenda, Constitutional Rights Project, Media Rights Agenda and Constitutional Rights Project* v. *Nigeria* [1998] App. nos. 105/93, 128/94, 130/94 and 152/96 [57]; *Constitutional Rights Project, Civil Liberties Organisation and Media Rights Agenda*

Article 9 AfCHPR even locates a right to receive information in a paragraph prior to freedom of expression. This highlights that the right to receive information is not only a derivative of freedom of expression, but a human right in its own right. The AfComHPR therefore scrutinises interferences with freedom of expression not only under Article 9(2) AfCHPR but also under Article 9(1) AfCHPR. The Commission has held, for instance, that the proscription of a newspaper or the imprisonment of a journalist violates not only the publisher's right, but also the rights of the public to receive information protected by Article 9(1) AfCHPR.[77]

The right to receive information is infringed even when measures merely make receiving information more cumbersome.[78] For example, the prohibition to receive television programmes by means of a dish or other aerial thus inhibits the right to receive information.[79] In *Faccio* v. *Italy*, the Strasbourg Court decided that sealing off the applicant's television amounted to an interference with Article 10(1) ECHR, which, however, was justified because the applicant refused to pay his licence fee.[80] The Inter-American Commission held in *Tarciso Medina Charry* v. *Colombia* that the detainment of a person for merely carrying a Communist newspaper violated his right to seek, receive and impart information and ideas.[81]

4.2 Media freedom beyond 'media speech': the institutional protection of the media

Media freedom goes beyond the mere protection of 'media speech'. Media companies and journalists are also protected against undue state interference that is not directly publication-related, that is, as *institutions* fulfilling their role as 'public watchdog' and 'fourth estate'. Here,

v. *Nigeria* [1999] App. nos. 140/94, 141/94 and 145/95 [38]; *Scanlen & Holderness* v. *Zimbabwe* [2009] App. no. 297/05 [118].

77 AfComHPR, *Media Rights Agenda, Constitutional Rights Project, Media Rights Agenda and Constitutional Rights Project* v. *Nigeria* [1998] App. nos. 105/93, 128/94, 130/94 and 152/96 [57]; *Constitutional Rights Project, Civil Liberties Organisation and Media Rights Agenda* v. *Nigeria* [1999] App. nos. 140/94, 141/94 and 145/95 [38]; *Scanlen & Holderness* v. *Zimbabwe* [2009] App. no. 297/05 [108].

78 ECtHR, *Társaság a Szabadságjogokért* v. *Hungary* [2009] App. no. 37374/05 [26].

79 ECtHR, *Autronic AG* v. *Switzerland* [1990] App. no. 12726/87 [47]; *Khurshid Mustafa and Tarzibachi* v. *Sweden* [2008] App. no. 23883/06 [36]; German Federal Constitutional Court, '*Parabolic antenna I*' [1994] Case 1 BvR 1687/92; '*Parabolic antenna II*' [2013] Case 1 BvR 1314/11.

80 ECtHR, *Faccio* v. *Italy* [2003] App. no. 33/04.

81 IAComHR, *Tarciso Medina Charry* v. *Colombia* [1998] Case 11.221 [77].

freedom of the media differs from general freedom of expression not only in terms of the *intensity* of protection, as is the case with media speech, but also in terms of the *scope* of protected action. This 'institutional protection' of the media guarantees rights that are not directly speech-related, but related to the media in its newsgathering, editorial and distribution process and to independence of the media in general.

These rights can be furcated into two categories: defensive rights of the media against state action and positive entitlements of the media against the state, in particular protection by the state.

4.2.1 Defensive rights

According to the classic liberal understanding, liberties are, in the first place, defensive rights of the citizen against state action, or, in the words of John Stuart Mill, 'limits to the power which the ruler should be suffered to exercise over the community'.[82] As a defensive right, media freedom involves, for instance, the protection of newspaper distribution infrastructure against state interference.[83] Four particular defensive rights encompassed by media freedom will be outlined in the following paragraphs: journalistic independence, protection of journalistic research and investigation, a journalist's immunity from being compelled to testify about confidential information or sources and protection of the media against arbitrary search warrants.

4.2.1.1 Independence of the media

Democracy is based on the tenet that all state authority is derived from the people.[84] Since the media has the power to significantly shape and influence public opinion, independence of the media from state institutions is thus a requirement of democracy itself. The media, as an institution, must not be unduly influenced by the government. If a powerful political group obtained a dominant position over the media and curtailed their editorial freedom, the fundamental role of the media in a democratic society would be undermined.[85]

[82] Mill (1869) p. 5.

[83] IACtHR, *Palamara-Iribarne* v. *Chile* [2005] Case 11.571 [73]; see also ECtHR, *VgT Verein gegen Tierfabriken* v. *Switzerland (No. 1)* [2001] App. no. 24699/94 [48].

[84] Compare Article 20(2) German Basic Law.

[85] ECtHR, *Manole and others* v. *Moldova* [2009] App. no. 13936/02 [98]; *Centro Europa 7 Srl and Di Stefano* v. *Italy* [2012] App. no. 38433/09 [133]; AfComHPR, Declaration of Principles on Freedom of Expression in Africa, Sections VIII(2) and XIV; Bezanson (1977) 734.

The independence of the media is particularly relevant with regard to public broadcasting. States that have established public broadcasters, such as the BBC in the UK, ARD and ZDF in Germany, or RAI in Italy, must observe the principle of separation of state and society. Public broadcasters must not be abused by the government and forced to translate governmental power into social influence and thus to back political power. Because of their special role in disseminating information and ideas, and precisely because they do not – and must not be used to – exercise governmental powers, media freedom also applies to public broadcasters. These are not comparable with governmental organisations established for purposes of public administration, and therefore qualify as 'non-governmental organisations' within the meaning of human rights law.[86] Where a state decides to create a public broadcasting system, 'the domestic law and practice must guarantee that the system provides a pluralistic audiovisual service'.[87]

In Section VI of its Declaration of Principles on Freedom of Expression in Africa, the African Commission outlined its understanding of public broadcasting. It explained that state-controlled broadcasters should be transformed into public service broadcasters, accountable to the public through the legislature rather than the government, in accordance with several principles. These principles include that public broadcasters should be adequately funded, governed by an independent board and editorially independent. Furthermore, the public service ambit of public broadcasters 'should be clearly defined and include an obligation to ensure that the public receive adequate, politically balanced information, particularly during election periods'.[88]

As regards the private media, governments must neither directly nor indirectly influence the editorial process in media undertakings, for example, by exerting pressure on board members or journalists, or by arbitrarily granting and withdrawing public subsidies or privileges.

4.2.1.2 Protection of journalistic research and investigation

The freedom of the media to publish would be worthless if journalists were subject to arbitrary obstacles in the preparatory process of information gathering. Consequently, media freedom also prevents unjustified interferences with the media's newsgathering activities. Journalists

[86] See, e.g., EComHR, *British Broadcasting Corporation* v. *United Kingdom* [1996] App. no. 25798/94; ECtHR, *Radio France and others* v. *France* [2004] App. no. 53984/00; *Österreichischer Rundfunk* v. *Austria* [2006] App. no. 35841/02 [49]; compare *The Holy Monasteries* v. *Greece* [1994] App. nos. 13092/87 and 13984/88 [49].

[87] ECtHR, *Wojtas-Kaleta* v. *Poland* [2009] App. no. 20436/02 [47].

[88] AfComHPR, Declaration of Principles on Freedom of Expression in Africa.

enjoy the right to seek information, including the freedom to decide on the method to obtain the information, such as by means of investigative journalism.[89] The Strasbourg Court stated that 'the law cannot allow arbitrary restrictions which may become a form of indirect censorship should the authorities create obstacles to the gathering of information[, which] is an essential preparatory step in journalism and ... an inherent, protected part of press freedom'.[90] Two particularly important aspects of the media's right to gather news will be dealt with in separate sections: the protection of journalistic sources and a right of access to public information.[91]

Media freedom protects all forms of newsgathering, such as undercover work.[92] Even measures that are indistinctly applicable to journalists and the general public may violate media freedom if they disproportionately hamper the exercise of the journalist's profession.[93] However, media freedom does not give licence to illegal activity or violations of public safety rules that apply to everyone.[94] Yet media freedom protects the media's right to publish information, even if it has been obtained unlawfully, if the public interest in receiving the information supersedes the state's or an individual's interest in confidentiality.[95]

4.2.1.3 Protection of journalistic sources

The right of journalists not to disclose information identifying a source is one of the most important rights deriving from media freedom and is widely recognised under domestic law[96] and in several international

[89] ECtHR, *Cumpănă and Mazăre* v. *Romania* [2004] App. no. 33348/96 [96]; *Dammann* v. *Switzerland* [2006] App. no. 77551/01 [52]; *Társaság a Szabadságjogokért* v. *Hungary* [2009] App. no. 37374/05 [27]. See also EComHR, *Loersch and Nouvelle Association du Courrier* v. *Switzerland* [1995] App. nos. 23868/94 and 23869/94 [3].

[90] ECtHR, *Társaság a Szabadságjogokért* v. *Hungary* [2009] App. no. 37374/05 [27]; see also *Kenedi* v. *Hungary* [2009] App. no. 31475/05 [43]: access to original documentary sources for historical research.

[91] See below Section 4.2.1.3 and 4.2.3.

[92] See ECtHR, *Nordisk Film & TV A/S* v. *Denmark* [2005] App. no. 40485/02.

[93] ECtHR, *Gsell* v. *Switzerland* [2009] App. no. 12675/05 [49]: restrictions on road access to the World Economic Forum in Davos.

[94] Compare ECtHR, *Pentikäinen* v. *Finland* [2014] App. no. 11882/10 [47].

[95] US Supreme Court, *New York Times Co.* v. *United States*, 403 US 713 (1971); *Bartnicki* v. *Vopper*, aka *Williams and others*, 532 US 514 (2001); ECtHR, *Radio Twist AS* v. *Slovakia* [2006] App. no. 62202/00 [62]; *Nagla* v. *Latvia* [2013] App. no. 73469/10 [97]; German Federal Constitutional Court, '*Springer/Wallraff*' [1984] Case 1 BvR 272/81. On the protection of whistle-blowers, see Chapter 8, Section 8.3.3.2.

[96] See, e.g. Section 10 UK Contempt of Court Act 1981; Section 53(1) no. 5 German Criminal Procedure Code; Section 383(1) no. 5 German Civil Procedure Code. Under Swiss law, the protection of sources even has constitutional status; see Article 17(3) Swiss Federal Constitution 1999.

documents.[97] In addition, there is a considerable body of case-law[98] and legal scholarship[99] concerning the protection of journalistic sources. Based on the seminal decision *Goodwin* v. *United Kingdom*, the ECtHR has consistently emphasised the right of journalists to protect their sources as an important safeguard of media freedom. The ECtHR explained that protection of journalistic sources 'is one of the basic conditions for press freedom. Without such protection, sources may be deterred from assisting the press in informing the public on matters of public interest.'[100] As a result, the ability of the press to provide accurate and reliable information, and thus its public-watchdog role, may be undermined. Therefore, an order for the disclosure of the identity of an anonymous source of information already constitutes an interference with a journalist's rights under Article 10 ECHR, even though the order had not been enforced.[101]

The protection of journalistic sources does not only apply to domestic court proceedings but also to international courts and tribunals. In 2002, the Appeals Chamber of the International Criminal Tribunal for former Yugoslavia (ICTY) decided on a subpoena issued by a Trial Chamber. The subpoena compelled the testimony of a *Washington Post* war

[97] UN Commission on Human Rights, Report of the Special Rapporteur on the Promotion and Protection of the Right to Freedom of Opinion and Expression, Mr Abid Hussain, submitted pursuant to Commission Resolution 1997/27, E/CN.4/1998/40/Add.1, paras. 17 and 22; Human Rights Resolution 2005/38: The Right to Freedom of Opinion and Expression, E/CN.4/RES/2005/38; Council of Europe, Committee of Ministers, Recommendation No. R(2000) 7 on the Right of Journalists not to Disclose their Sources of Information; Parliamentary Assembly, Recommendation 1950 (2011): The Protection of Journalistic Sources; AfComHPR, Declaration of Principles on Freedom of Expression in Africa, Section XV.

[98] See, e.g., ECtHR, *Goodwin* v. *United Kingdom* [1996] App. no. 17488/90 [39]; *Roemen and Schmit* v. *Luxembourg* [2003] App. no. 51772/99 [57]; *Cumpǎnǎ and Mazǎre* v. *Romania* [2004] App. no. 33348/96 [106]; *Radio Twist AS* v. *Slovakia* [2006] App. no. 62202/00 [62]; *Voskuil* v. *Netherlands* [2007] App. no. 64752/01 [65]; *Tillack* v. *Belgium* [2007] App. no. 20477/05 [53]; *Financial Times Ltd and others* v. *United Kingdom* [2009] App. no. 821/03 [59]; *Sanoma Uitgevers BV* v. *Netherlands* [2010] App. no. 38224/03 [50]; *Nagla* v. *Latvia* [2013] App. no. 73469/10; ICTY, *Prosecutor* v. *Brdjanin and Talic*, Case no. IT-99–36-AR73.9, Decision on interlocutory appeal of Jonathan Randal (11 December 2002) [50]. See also Human Rights Committee, Concluding observations on Kuwait (CCPR/CO/69/KWT), para. 20.

[99] See Helle (1982) 27–8; Monk (1986) 4–5; Chemerinsky (2000); Nestler (2005); Ugland (2008); Abramowicz (2009) 101; Carney (2009); Barendt (2009) 146.

[100] ECtHR, *Goodwin* v. *United Kingdom* [1996] App. no. 17488/90 [39].

[101] ECtHR, *Financial Times Ltd and others* v. *United Kingdom* [2009] App. no. 821/03 [56], reiterated in *Sanoma Uitgevers BV* v. *Netherlands* [2010] App. no. 38224/03 [50]; *Roemen and Schmit* v. *Luxembourg* [2003] App. no. 51772/99 [57]; *Telegraaf Media Nederland Landelijke Media BV and others* v. *Netherlands* [2012] App. no. 39315/06 [127]. Under domestic law, see *British Steel Corporation* v. *Granada Television Ltd* [1981] 1 All ER 417.

correspondent concerning an interview he conducted while reporting on the conflict in former Yugoslavia. The Appeals Chamber had to decide whether the International Tribunal should recognise a qualified testimonial privilege for war correspondents and, if so, whether the privilege requires the quashing of the subpoena. The Appeals Chamber held that a two-pronged test must be satisfied in order for the Trial Chamber to issue a subpoena to the war correspondent: 'First, the petitioning party must demonstrate that the evidence sought is of direct and important value in determining a core issue in the case. Second, it must demonstrate that the evidence sought cannot reasonably be obtained elsewhere.'[102] Based on this observation, the Appeals Chamber reversed the impugned decision and set aside the subpoena.

The right to protect a journalistic source is based on two rationales. First, it protects the journalist, whose reputation may be negatively affected by the disclosure in the eyes of future potential sources.[103] Therefore, a journalist does not only have the right but is also under an ethical obligation to protect his sources.[104] Second, it serves to protect the source who assists the media in informing the public about matters of public concern.

Consequently, a 'source' can only be a person who freely assists the media to inform the public. People who are unaware that they reveal information to a journalist, as in cases where journalists work undercover, cannot be regarded as sources of journalistic information deserving protection.[105] A further requirement for being a 'journalistic source' is that the media receives the information on a confidential and unattributable basis. If the information consists of recordings of events that had taken place in public and were not secret or confidential, or if the informant sought publicity and not confidentiality, it does not fulfil the prerequisites for being a 'journalistic source'. In these cases the degree of protection does not reach the same level as that afforded to journalists when it comes to their right to keep their sources confidential.[106]

[102] ICTY, *Prosecutor* v. *Brdjanin and Talic*, Case No.: IT-99–36-AR73.9, Decision on interlocutory appeal of Jonathan Randal (11 December 2002) [50].

[103] ECtHR, *Sanoma Uitgevers BV* v. *Netherlands* [2010] App. no. 38224/03 [89]; see also *Financial Times Ltd and others* v. *United Kingdom* [2009] App. no. 821/03 [63].

[104] Compare Clause 14 of the PCC Editors' Code of Practice.

[105] ECtHR, *Nordisk Film & TV A/S* v. *Denmark* [2005] App. no. 40485/02, p. 11.

[106] See ECtHR, *Goodwin* v. *United Kingdom* [1996] App. no. 17488/90; *Cumpănă and Mazăre* v. *Romania* [2004] App. no. 33348/96 [106]; *Stichting Ostade Blade* v. *Netherlands* [2014] App. no. 8406/06 [65]; see also, *mutatis mutandis*, EComHR, *British Broadcasting Corporation* v. *United Kingdom* [1996] App. no. 25798/94.

Yet, the protection of journalistic sources is not absolute.[107] When assessing whether a legitimate interest in a disclosure outweighs the media freedom right not to disclose information identifying a source, the following factors are relevant for the proportionality analysis:[108]

- The nature of the interest in a disclosure: the public interest in preventing and punishing offences, especially where serious crimes are at issue, usually overrides the interest in keeping sources confidential.[109] Where private interests of a victim of leaked information in identifying a source are concerned, it has to be examined whether the interest in bringing proceedings to prevent further dissemination of confidential information and to recover damages for any loss already sustained supersede the public interest in keeping journalistic sources confidential.[110] However, the interest of an employer in identifying the source of a leak of confidential material in order to terminate an employee's employment is in itself insufficient to justify the disclosure of a source.[111]
- The authenticity of the information:[112] where the information appears to be false, the claimant's right in knowing the source may supersede in order to be able to rectify the information.
- The conduct of the source: if the source has been acting in bad faith with a harmful purpose and disclosed intentionally falsified information, this might tip the balance in favour of a disclosure order.[113]
- Whether the journalist acted in good faith.[114]
- The availability of alternative, less intrusive means: whether the information or similar information leading to the same result can be obtained elsewhere, and whether such alternative measures to the

[107] ECtHR, *Goodwin* v. *United Kingdom* [1996] App. no. 17488/90 [39]. See, e.g., Section 10 UK Contempt of Court Act 1981 *in fine*; Section 53(2) German Criminal Procedure Code; AfComHPR, Declaration of Principles on Freedom of Expression in Africa, Section XV.

[108] On the balancing exercise in the proportionality test in general, see Chapter 6, Section 6.3.3.

[109] See, *mutatis mutandis*, ECtHR, *Roemen and Schmit* v. *Luxembourg* [2003] App. no. 51772/99 [58]; AfComHPR, Declaration of Principles on Freedom of Expression in Africa, Section XV.

[110] ECtHR, *Goodwin* v. *United Kingdom* [1996] App. no. 17488/90 [45]; *Financial Times Ltd and others* v. *United Kingdom* [2009] App. no. 821/03 [68]; see also *Cumpănă and Mazăre* v. *Romania* [2004] App. no. 33348/96 [106].

[111] ECtHR, *Financial Times Ltd and others* v. *United Kingdom* [2009] App. no. 821/03 [64–6].

[112] See, *mutatis mutandis*, ECtHR, *Financial Times Ltd and others* v. *United Kingdom* [2009] App. no. 821/03 [67].

[113] See, *mutatis mutandis*, ECtHR, *Financial Times Ltd and others* v. *United Kingdom* [2009] App. no. 821/03 [63]; *Telegraaf Media Nederland Landelijke Media BV and others* v. *Netherlands* [2012] App. no. 39315/06 [128].

[114] ECtHR, *Financial Times Ltd and others* v. *United Kingdom* [2009] App. no. 821/03 [67].

disclosure have been exhausted by the persons or public authorities that seek the disclosure.[115] Where journalists have to respond to an order to disclose information identifying a source, the disclosure must be limited to the necessary information and, with due respect to judicial guarantees, under exclusion of the public from the disclosure.[116]

4.2.1.4 Protection against interception of communication, surveillance, search and seizure, and arrests

Searches and seizures interfere with the right to respect one's home as an aspect of a person's privacy, even if conducted on business premises,[117] and the entitlement to the enjoyment of property according to Article 1 of the First Protocol to the ECHR, Article 21 ACHR, Article 14 AfCHPR and Article 17(1) EUChFR.[118] The arrest of a person interferes with his right to liberty and security of person under Article 9 ICCPR, Article 5 ECHR, Article 6 AfCHPR, Article 7 ACHR and Article 6 EUChFR. Finally, the interception of communication and the surveillance of persons interfere with the right to privacy and secrecy of correspondence under Article 17(1) ICCPR, Article 8 ECHR, Article 11(2) ACHR and Article 7 EUChFR.

However, searching journalists' homes and workplaces, the interception of journalistic communication, seizures of journalistic material, and the surveillance or the arrest of journalists, constitute an *additional* interference with media freedom. Investigators 'who raid a journalist's workplace unannounced and armed with search warrants have very wide investigative powers as, by definition, they have access to all the documentation held by the journalist'.[119] Unjustified searches of a journalist's home and workplace therefore constitute a violation of media freedom in addition to a violation of the right to respect for one's home and correspondence. In this context, one has to distinguish between searches and seizures of media premises with the aim of disclosure of journalistic sources, on the one hand, and of other journalistic information, on the other hand.

[115] AfComHPR, Declaration of Principles on Freedom of Expression in Africa, Section XV; Council of Europe, Committee of Ministers, Recommendation No. R(2000) 7 on the Right of Journalists not to Disclose their Sources of Information, Principle 3(b)(i).

[116] Compare Council of Europe, Committee of Ministers, Recommendation No. R(2000) 7 on the Right of Journalists not to Disclose their Sources of Information, Principle 5(e).

[117] On the protection of business premises as 'home', ECtHR, *Niemietz* v. *Germany* [1992] App. no. 13710/88 [30]; *Saint-Paul Luxembourg SA* v. *Luxembourg* [2013] App. no. 26419/10 [37].

[118] See EComHR, *Noviflora Sweden AB* v. *Sweden* [1993] App. no. 14369/88.

[119] ECtHR, *Roemen and Schmit* v. *Luxembourg* [2003] App. no. 51772/99 [57]; *Nagla* v. *Latvia* [2013] App. no. 73469/10 [95].

Searches and seizures of media premises are irreconcilable with media freedom if their sole or predominant purpose is the disclosure of journalistic sources. Such searches and seizures have an intolerable chilling effect on journalistic work and may also deter informants from providing information that they are only willing to provide confidentially.[120] An order for search and seizure in the journalist's home or workplace is thus an even more drastic measure than an order to disclose the source's identity. The searches of a journalist's home and workplace undermine the protection of sources to an even greater extent than disclosure orders.

By contrast, the order and the search and seizure that merely serve to gain material which does not relate to a journalistic source is not *per se* contrary to media freedom. In these cases, the rationale 'protection of the source'[121] is not applicable. However, there must be an overriding public or private interest in obtaining the information, and regard must be had to whether the public authorities have pursued alternative means of gathering the information. In *Roemen and Schmit* v. *Luxembourg*, the authorities had searched the premises of journalists to discover the identity of a leak without asking individuals responsible for investigating the matter beforehand. The Strasbourg Court therefore concluded that a proper balance between the competing interests had not been struck.[122]

Even if searches prove unproductive, it does not deprive them of their purpose, namely to establish the identity of a journalist's source or the discovery of other journalistic information.[123] Therefore, the mere threat to carry out a search of journalistic premises already causes a 'chilling effect' and thus constitutes an interference with media freedom.[124]

4.2.2 Entitlements of the media

One of the main characteristics distinguishing media freedom from freedom of expression is that media freedom not only includes more

[120] German Federal Constitutional Court, '*Cicero*' [2007] Cases 1 BvR 538/06 and 1 BvR 2045/06 [44].
[121] See above Section 4.2.1.3.
[122] ECtHR, *Roemen and Schmit* v. *Luxembourg* [2003] App. no. 51772/99 [60].
[123] ECtHR, *Roemen and Schmit* v. *Luxembourg* [2003] App. no. 51772/99 [57]; *Tillack* v. *Belgium* [2007] App. no. 20477/05 [64].
[124] ECtHR, *Sanoma Uitgevers BV* v. *Netherlands* [2010] App. no. 38224/03 [71]; German Federal Constitutional Court, '*Cicero*' [2007] Cases 1 BvR 538/06 and 1 BvR 2045/06 [44].

defensive rights against the state, but also more positive entitlements to state action. Those entitlements serve to provide the preconditions for the opportunity to utilise media freedom. Remarkably, as regards media entitlements, the Strasbourg Court grants even stronger protection than the US Supreme Court. In *Schweizerische Radio-und Fernsehgesellschaft SRG* v. *Switzerland*, the ECtHR held that the domestic authority's refusal of permission to film inside a prison and to conduct an interview there was disproportionate.[125] By contrast, in *Pell* v. *Procunier*[126] and in *Saxbe* v. *Washington Post*,[127] the Washington Court held that the First Amendment does not confer upon the press rights to special access or immunities, and thus rejected claims of newspapers to enter prisons and interview prisoners. This juxtaposition reflects the instrumental and objectivist approach of the ECtHR, which grants privileged protection of the media, on the one hand, and the mere 'press-as-technology' freedom advocated by the US Supreme Court, which affords no privileged constitutional protection of the media, on the other hand.

Article 2 ICCPR provides that each State Party undertakes to respect *and ensure* the rights recognised in the Covenant. In the same vein, Article 1 ECHR requires each Contracting State to '*secure* to everyone within [its] jurisdiction the rights and freedoms' defined in the ECHR (emphasis added). According to Article 1 AfCHPR, the Member States shall recognise 'the rights, duties and freedoms enshrined in this Chapter and shall undertake to adopt legislative or other measures to give effect to them'. Eventually, Article 1 ACHR requests the State Parties to the American Convention to 'undertake to respect the rights and freedoms recognized herein and to ensure to all persons subject to their jurisdiction the free and full exercise of those rights and freedoms'. Article 2 ACHR adds that '[w]here the exercise of any of the rights or freedoms ... is not already ensured by legislative or other provisions, the States Parties undertake to adopt ... such legislative or other measures as may be necessary to give effect to those rights or freedoms'.

It follows from these provisions that the state must not only negatively abstain from interfering with Convention and Covenant guarantees; the beneficiaries of these guarantees may also be entitled to positive action in order to secure the rights and freedoms. Georg Jellinek named this dimension of liberty as the *status civitatis* or *status positivus*.[128] Because of the *status positivus*, states are under an obligation to ensure the

[125] ECtHR, *Schweizerische Radio-und Fernsehgesellschaft SRG* v. *Switzerland* [2012] App. no. 34124/06 [65].

[126] 417 US 817 (1974). [127] 417 US 843 (1974). [128] Jellinek (1892) p. 109.

protection of human rights and are required to take positive action to protect individuals from interference by other parties, corresponding to an entitlement of the beneficiary of that human right.[129]

Media freedom thus involves not only defensive rights against the state, but also entitlements to state actions, where these are necessary for the media to fulfil its role as 'public watchdog' and to inform the public on matters of general interest. These entitlements include the right to enable a publisher to distribute his publications by any appropriate means,[130] including the possibility to introduce a newspaper in a certain region,[131] privileged access to government information,[132] press conferences,[133] or court trials,[134] and special obligations of the state to protect the media, especially to protect journalists from acts of violence as they exercise their journalistic work.[135]

The obligation to protect the lives and personal integrity of reporters follows not only from media freedom, but also from the right to life (Article 6 ICCPR, Article 2 ECHR, Article 4 AfCHPR and Article 4 ACHR) in general, and thus applies to everybody. However, threats and attacks against journalists in particular, or a state's refusal to conduct a full investigation into such acts, is especially serious because of its detrimental impact on society as a whole. State omissions to protect journalists or impunity for the commitment of acts of aggression against journalists have a dissuasive effect on other journalists and deter them from doing their work for the benefit of society. Therefore, the state obligation to protect reporters follows not only from their right to life and personal integrity but also autonomously from media freedom itself.[136]

[129] See; e.g., Kay (2005); see also ECtHR, Research Report, Positive Obligations on Member States under Article 10 to Protect Journalists and Prevent Impunity (2011).

[130] IACtHR, *Palamara-Iribarne* v. *Chile* [2005] Case 11.571 [73]; ECtHR, *VgT Verein gegen Tierfabriken* v. *Switzerland (No. 1)* [2001] App. no. 24699/94 [48].

[131] See ECtHR, *Halis Doğan and others* v. *Turkey* [2006] App. no. 50693/99 [24]; AfComHPR, Declaration of Principles on Freedom of Expression in Africa, Section VIII(3).

[132] See, e.g., Section (4)(A)(ii)(II) US Freedom of Information Act 1966, providing for the limitation of fees for FOIA requests by 'a representative of the news media'; compare Helle (1982) 3–4; McDonald (2004) 354; Friedman (2006) 300.

[133] Human Rights Committee, *Gauthier* v. *Canada* [1999] Communication no. 633/95 [13.4]; Anderson (2002) 432.

[134] See German Federal Constitutional Court, '*NSU trial*' [2013] Case 1 BvR 990/13: reservation of seats for media correspondents in a criminal trial.

[135] See, e.g., ECtHR, *Özgür Gündem* v. *Turkey* [2000] App. no. 23144/93 [38 ff.]

[136] IAComHR, *Héctor Félix Miranda* v. *Mexico* [1999] Case 11.739 [52]; *Rafael Ignacio Cuesta Caputi* v. *Ecuador* [2008] Case 12.487 [98]; *Manoel Leal de Oliveira* v. *Brasil* [2010] Case 12.308 [100]; *mutatis mutandis*, IACtHR, *González Medina and family* v. *Dominican Republic* [2012] Case 11.324 [192].

A further state obligation is to protect the media from undue influence by financially powerful groups.[137] The state has a duty to ensure 'that the public has access to impartial and accurate information through television and radio and a range of opinion and comment, reflecting *inter alia* the diversity of political outlook within the country'.[138] Hence the state has to protect an independent media in order to safeguard media pluralism.[139] Article 13(3) ACHR expressly stipulates that freedom of expression may not be restricted, *inter alia*, by private controls over newsprint, radio broadcasting frequencies or equipment used in the dissemination of information.

4.2.3 Right of access to information?

Access to public information is one of the most important sources for investigative journalism. However, access to state-held information should not only be conceptualised as a privilege of the media but as a generally applicable right. The right of access to information, also known as freedom of information, is based on the principles of openness and transparency of public authority.[140] 'Openness enables citizens to participate more closely in the decision-making process and guarantees that the administration enjoys greater legitimacy and is more effective and more accountable to the citizen in a democratic system. Openness contributes to strengthening the principles of democracy and respect for fundamental rights.'[141] There is, therefore, a strong link between freedom of expression and freedom of information, in a way that only well-informed citizens may discuss matters of public interest and contribute to the marketplace of ideas.[142]

The first international human rights court to declare access to information an aspect of freedom of expression was the Inter-American Court in its seminal judgment *Claude Reyes and others* v. *Chile*.[143] In this case, an NGO unsuccessfully requested information from the Chilean Committee on Foreign Investment on a deforestation project. The NGO wished to evaluate the commercial factors and also the environmental impact of this

[137] See ECtHR, *VgT Verein gegen Tierfabriken* v. *Switzerland (No. 1)* [2001] App. no. 24699/94 [72]; *Animal Defenders International* v. *United Kingdom* [2013] App. no. 48876/08 [112].

[138] ECtHR, *Manole and others* v. *Moldova* [2009] App. no. 13936/02 [100].

[139] See Chapter 14.

[140] See Goldberg (2009); Oswald (2012).

[141] Recital 2 of Regulation (EC) No. 1049/2001 of the European Parliament and of the Council of 30 May 2001 regarding Public Access to European Parliament, Council and Commission Documents, OJ 2001, L145/43.

[142] Compare Barendt (2005) p. 110; Knight (2013) 474.

[143] IACtHR, *Claude Reyes and others* v. *Chile* [2006] Case 12.108.

activity. In its decision, the Inter-American Commission on Human Rights held that the divulgence of state-held information plays a very important role in a democratic society, because it enables citizens to control the actions of the government to which it has entrusted the protection of its interests.[144] The Inter-American Court of Human Rights then observed that 'access to public information is an essential requisite for the exercise of democracy, greater transparency and responsible public administration and that, in a representative and participative democratic system, the citizenry exercises its constitutional rights through a broad freedom of expression and free access to information'.[145] The Court therefore acknowledged access to information as a fundamental right, but it is subject to certain exceptions. In the instant case, the Court held that the restriction applied to the access to information was not based on a law, since there had been no legislation in Chile that regulated the issue of restrictions to access to state-held information.[146] Furthermore, the respondent state 'did not prove that the restriction responded to a purpose allowed by the American Convention, or that it was necessary in a democratic society, because the authority responsible for responding to the request for information did not adopt a justified decision in writing, communicating the reasons for restricting access to this information in the specific case'.[147]

Similarly, the Human Rights Committee interprets the right to seek and receive information rather broadly as a right of (media) access to information.[148] In its General Comment on Article 19, the Committee stated that Article 19(2) ICCPR 'embraces a right of access to information held by public bodies. Such information includes records held by a public body, regardless of the form in which the information is stored, its source and the date of production'.[149] Yet the Committee's finding in the earlier decision *Gauthier* v. *Canada* contradicts the apparently absolute approach in the General Comment. The Committee held in this decision that Article 19, taken together with Article 25 ICCPR, grants a right of access to information on public affairs to the citizens, 'in particular through the media'.[150] However, the Committee qualified this right of

[144] See IACtHR, *Claude Reyes and others* v. *Chile* [2006] Case 12.108 [58].
[145] IACtHR, *Claude Reyes and others* v. *Chile* [2006] Case 12.108 [84].
[146] IACtHR, *Claude Reyes and others* v. *Chile* [2006] Case 12.108 [94]. On the principle of legality, see Chapter 6, Section 6.1.1.
[147] IACtHR, *Claude Reyes and others* v. *Chile* [2006] Case 12.108 [95].
[148] See Human Rights Committee, *Gauthier* v. *Canada* [1999] Communication no. 633/95 [13.4]; *Toktakunov* v. *Kyrgyzstan* [2011] Communication no. 1470/2006 [6.3].
[149] General Comment no. 34, para. 18.
[150] Human Rights Committee, *Gauthier* v. *Canada* [1999] Communication no. 633/95 [13.4].

access, recognising that 'such access should not interfere with or obstruct the carrying out of the functions of elected bodies and that a State party is thus entitled to limit access' in accordance with the provisions of the Covenant.[151] As a consequence, the right of access to information or to 'seek' information within the meaning of Article 19(2) ICCPR is limited to *generally accessible* information.

In contrast to the Inter-American Court of Human Rights and similar to the Human Rights Committee's decision *Gauthier* v. *Canada*, the ECtHR has long refused to accept a general right of access to information, although documents of the Council of Europe and international recommendations encourage Member States to establish such freedom of information acts.[152] An additional protocol that was discussed in the late 1970s failed to gain sufficient support. The Strasbourg Court found in a number of cases that the authorities had an obligation under Article 8 ECHR to disclose certain data that was relevant for the applicant, such as information about risks to one's health and well-being resulting from environmental pollution,[153] information which would permit them to assess any risk resulting from their participation in nuclear tests,[154] tests involving exposure to toxic chemicals,[155] access to social service records containing information about their childhood and personal history[156] and access to copies of their medical records.[157] However, the Court had been reluctant to recognise that Article 10 ECHR guarantees a general and independent right of access to state-held information, and thus saw no obligation on governments to provide such data to the public.[158]

[151] Human Rights Committee, *Gauthier* v. *Canada* [1999] Communication no. 633/95 [13.4].

[152] See Council of Europe, Convention on Access to Official Documents, adopted on 27 November 2008; Council of Europe, Committee of Ministers, Recommendation No. R (81) 19 on the Access to Information held by Public Authorities; Council of Europe, Committee of Ministers, Recommendation No. R (91) 10 on the Communication to Third Parties of Personal Data held by Public Bodies; Council of Europe, Committee of Ministers, Recommendation No. R (97) 18 concerning the Protection of Personal Data Collected and Processed for Statistical Purposes; Council of Europe, Committee of Ministers, Recommendation No. R (2000) 13 on a European Policy on Access to Archives; Council of Europe, Committee of Ministers, Recommendation Rec(2002)2 on Access to Official Documents.

[153] ECtHR, *Guerra and others* v. *Italy* [1998] App. no. 116/1996/735/932 [60].

[154] ECtHR, *McGinley and Egan* v. *United Kingdom* [1998] App. no. 10/1997/794/995–996 [101].

[155] ECtHR, *Roche* v. *United Kingdom* [2005] App. no. 32555/96 [167].

[156] ECtHR, *M.G.* v. *United Kingdom* [2002] App. no. 39393/98 [27].

[157] ECtHR, *K.H. and others* v. *Slovakia* [2009] App. no. 32881/04 [50].

[158] See ECtHR, *Leander* v. *Sweden* [1987] App. no. 9248/81 [74]; *Matky* v. *Czech Republic* [2006] App. no. 19101/03, p. 10; *Társaság a Szabadságjogokért* v. *Hungary* [2009] App. no. 37374/05 [35].

The right to receive information and ideas in Article 10(1)2 ECHR has thus been restricted to publicly available information disseminated by others, in particular media companies.

Yet since 2006[159] the Court has progressed towards a broader interpretation of the notion of 'freedom to receive information' and thereby towards the recognition of a general right of access to information. In *Társaság a Szabadságjogokért* v. *Hungary*, the Court stated that 'the State's obligations in matters of freedom of the press include the elimination of barriers to the exercise of press functions where, in issues of public interest, such barriers exist solely because of an information monopoly held by the authorities'.[160] The Court considered that 'obstacles created in order to hinder access to information of public interest may discourage those working in the media or related fields from pursuing such matters'.[161] As a consequence, 'they may no longer be able to play their vital role as "public watchdogs" and their ability to provide accurate and reliable information may be adversely affected'.[162] Similarly, in the context of historical research, the Strasbourg Court has found in *Kenedi* v. *Hungary* that access to original documentary sources in the state archives is an essential element of the exercise of Article 10 ECHR rights.[163]

In *Gillberg* v. *Sweden*, the Court had the opportunity to analyse the right of access to information from a different perpective, namely from the perspective of the information-holder. The applicant, a professor specialising in child and adolescent psychiatry at the University of Gothenburg, refused to provide access to his research material. The Strasbourg Court decided in favour of the right of the petitioners to receive the information, and against the applicant.[164] The disputed research material was considered to belong to the University of Gothenburg. Therefore, it was part of the public domain, and thus subject to the principle of freedom of information as codified in Swedish law.

In the case of *Youth Initiative for Human Rights* v. *Serbia*, the Strasbourg Court held that the refusal of an intelligence agency to provide the applicant NGO with information as to the use of electronic surveillance measures constituted an interference with the applicant's right to freedom of

[159] The first decision in which the ECtHR considered (but eventually rejected) to derive a right to access to public documents from Article 10 ECHR was *Matky* v. *Czech Republic* [2006] App. no. 19101/03.

[160] ECtHR, *Társaság a Szabadságjogokért* v. *Hungary* [2009] App. no. 37374/05 [35].

[161] ECtHR, *Társaság a Szabadságjogokért* v. *Hungary* [2009] App. no. 37374/05 [38].

[162] ECtHR, *Társaság a Szabadságjogokért* v. *Hungary* [2009] App. no. 37374/05 [38].

[163] ECtHR, *Kenedi* v. *Hungary* [2009] App. no. 31475/05 [43].

[164] ECtHR, *Gillberg* v. *Sweden* [2012] App. no. 41723/06 [93].

expression, as 'the applicant was obviously involved in the legitimate gathering of information of public interest with the intention of imparting that information to the public and thereby contributing to the public debate'.[165] Because of the factual peculiarities of the case the precedential character of the decision for a general right of access to information should not be overrated: the intelligence agency first refused the request, and then, after an order by the Information Commissioner that the information at issue be nevertheless disclosed, the intelligence agency notified the applicant that it did not hold that information. After very brief reasoning, the Court concluded that 'the obstinate reluctance of the intelligence agency of Serbia to comply with the order of the Information Commissioner was in defiance of domestic law [i.e. the Serbian Freedom of Information Act 2004] and tantamount to arbitrariness'.[166] However, *Youth Initiative for Human Rights* v. *Serbia* may be seen as a further step of the ECtHR to accept a general right of access to information out of Article 10 ECHR. Judges Sajó and Vučinić highlighted 'the general need to interpret Article 10 in conformity with developments in international law regarding freedom of information' in their concurring opinion.[167]

The Strasbourg Court then moved a step closer towards a general right of access to information, at least for the media and other associations involved in the legitimate gathering of information of public interest, in the case of *Österreichische Vereinigung zur Erhaltung, Stärkung und Schaffung eines wirtschaftlich gesunden land-und forstwirtschaftlichen Grundbesitzes* v. *Austria*.[168] In this case the applicant association requested paper copies of all decisions issued by a public Real Property Transactions Commission from 1 January 2000 to mid-2005. It argued that the state had an obligation either to publish all decisions of the Commission in an electronic database, or to provide it with anonymised paper copies upon request, which the Commission refused. Although the Strasbourg Court did 'not consider that a general obligation of this scope can be inferred from its case-law under Article 10', it nonetheless saw its task in the present case 'to examine whether the reasons given by the domestic authorities for refusing the applicant association's request were "relevant and sufficient" in the specific circumstances of the case and whether the

[165] ECtHR, *Youth Initiative for Human Rights* v. *Serbia* [2013] App. no. 48135/06 [24].
[166] ECtHR, *Youth Initiative for Human Rights* v. *Serbia* [2013] App. no. 48135/06 [26].
[167] ECtHR, *Youth Initiative for Human Rights* v. *Serbia* [2013] App. no. 48135/06, concurring opinion of Judges Sajó and Vučinić.
[168] EctHR, *Österreichische Vereinigung zur Erhaltung, Stärkung und Schaffung eines wirtschaftlich gesunden land-und forstwirtschaftlichen Grundbesitzes* v. *Austria* [2013] App. no. 39534/07 [34–6] and [41].

interference was proportionate to the legitimate aim pursued'.[169] Yet this reasoning seems paradoxical: if a general obligation to provide access to information cannot be inferred from Article 10 ECHR, then there has been no interference with that right in the present case. To scrutinise whether the reasons given by the domestic authorities to justify 'the interference' were 'relevant and sufficient' is illogical, if there has been no such interference. An examination of the justification of the refusal to grant access to information would only be necessary if access to information is a right encompassed by Article 10(1) ECHR.

The Court eventually found that the reasons relied on by the domestic authorities in refusing the applicant association's request were 'relevant', but not 'sufficient'. It decided that a complete refusal to give it access to any of its decisions was disproportionate, since the Commission held an information monopoly in respect of its decisions. This made it impossible for the applicant association to carry out its research and to participate in a meaningful manner in the legislative process concerning amendments of real estate transaction law. Much of the difficulty brought forward by the Commission were caused by its own choice not to publish any of its decisions.[170]

EU primary and secondary law grant relatively generous rights of access to information. Article 42 EUChFR and – with some reservations – Article 15(3) TFEU stipulate that '[a]ny citizen of the Union, and any natural or legal person residing or having its registered office in a Member State, has a right of access to documents of the institutions, bodies, offices and agencies of the Union, whatever their medium'. Several pieces of secondary legislation further expatiate on this right.[171]

Jurisprudence on freedom of information under the African Charter is not available thus far. However, in its Declaration of Principles on Freedom of Expression in Africa, the African Commission stated that

[169] ECtHR, *Österreichische Vereinigung zur Erhaltung, Stärkung und Schaffung eines wirtschaftlich gesunden land-und forstwirtschaftlichen Grundbesitzes* v. *Austria* [2013] App. no. 39534/07 [42].

[170] ECtHR, *Österreichische Vereinigung zur Erhaltung, Stärkung und Schaffung eines wirtschaftlich gesunden land-und forstwirtschaftlichen Grundbesitzes* v. *Austria* [2013] App. no. 39534/07 [46–7].

[171] Regulation (EC) No. 1049/2001 of the European Parliament and of the Council of 30 May 2001 regarding Public Access to European Parliament, Council and Commission documents, OJ 2001, L145/43; Decision of the European Central Bank of 4 March 2004 on Public Access to European Central Bank Documents (2004/258/EC), OJ 2004, L80/42; Directive 2003/4/EC of the European Parliament and of the Council of 28 January 2003 on Public Access to Environmental Information and Repealing Council Directive 90/313/EEC, OJ 2003, L41/26; Directive 2003/98/EC of the European Parliament and of the Council of 17 November 2003 on the Re-use of Public Sector Information, OJ 2003, L345/90.

'[p]ublic bodies hold information not for themselves but as custodians of the public good and everyone has a right to access this information, subject only to clearly defined rules established by law'.[172]

4.2.4 Non-discrimination

Media freedom also has an equality dimension. It includes a right to non-discrimination in addition to the general right to equal protection under Article 2 ICCPR, Article 14 ECHR, Article 3 AfCHPR, Article 24 ACHR and Article 20 EUChFR. Media freedom as an equality right is at stake when allocation of state resources among journalists and media companies is at issue. In order to deal with such situations, a distinction needs to be made between 'necessary choice situations' and 'unnecessary choice situations'.[173] A necessary choice situation exists when the resources to be allocated are scarce, such as broadcasting frequencies, places in a press conference or seats reserved for media representatives in a court trial.[174] In these situations, the state has to act on a transparent and non-discriminatory basis. This may be implemented, for example, by drawing lots or on a first come-first served principle. In particular, the state must abstain from making decisions based on content-related or personal preferences, and it must ensure that all representatives have equal access to the distribution mechanism. By contrast, if resources are not scarce, such as information, it is not necessary to make choices, and states must not artificially and arbitrarily make such resources scarce in order to discriminate between media undertakings.[175]

In the case of *Vereinigung demokratischer Soldaten Österreichs and Gubi* v. *Austria*, the Strasbourg Court thus correctly held that if a Convention State supports the dissemination of certain materials, it must not discriminate between types of publication based on the publication's content.[176] Therefore the applicant company was entitled to distribute their magazine on military life, 'Der Igel' ('The Hedgehog'), which often contained critical information and articles, in the military barracks in the same way as the only other two military magazines published by private associations.

172 AfComHPR, Declaration of Principles on Freedom of Expression in Africa, Section IV.
173 Schauer (1982) p. 118.
174 Schauer (1982) p. 118. On the latter situation, see German Federal Constitutional Court, '*NSU trial*' [2013] Case 1 BvR 990/13.
175 Compare German Federal Constitutional Court, '*Newspaper mail service*' [1989] Case 1 BvR 727/84 [1989]: delivery of newspapers by the then-governmental mail service at a discount rate.
176 Nicol, Millar and Sharland (2009) para. 2.32.

5 The notion of an 'interference' with media freedom

The concept of liberty is intrinsically tied to the notion of interference. The notion of 'interference' with human rights and the need for its justification[1] are thus general themes common to all jurisdictions. In order to establish an interference with media freedom, two components of the notion of interference have to be distinguished: first, the obligated addressee of media freedom ('interference by whom?') and, second, the manifestation of an interference ('interference through what?').

5.1 The obligated addressee of media freedom

It is inherent in the concept of human rights that they run against the state, not against private persons. In international human rights law, this becomes clear with a view to the fact that states have signed up to international human rights treaties, not private companies or individuals. Article 10(1) ECHR thus provides that the right to freedom of expression 'shall include freedom to hold opinions and to receive and impart information and ideas without interference by *public* authority' (emphasis added). Article 2(1) ICCPR stipulates that '[e]ach *State Party*' undertakes to respect the rights recognised in the Covenant (emphasis added). In the same vein, Article 1 AfCHPR obligates the *Member States* of the AU to recognise the rights enshrined in the Chapter, and Article 1 (1) ACHR places the *States Parties* to the Convention under an obligation to respect the rights and freedoms recognised therein.

Freedom of expression and media freedom are therefore binding on all branches of the state (executive, legislative and judicial) and all parts of federal states. The state is accountable for acts of all its organs, agents and servants, irrespective of their rank.[2] This also includes private

[1] See Chapter 6.

[2] ECtHR, *Wille* v. *Liechtenstein* [1999] App. no. 28396/95 [46]. See, e.g., *Ageyevy* v. *Russia* [2013] App. no. 7075/10 [174]: hospital under the authority of the Department of Healthcare of the City of Moscow.

bodies, if a state holds a dominant stake in such an entity or if it exercises elements of governmental authority.[3] Important examples in media law are domestic non-governmental organisations under a statutory requirement to classify videos, DVDs or video games, such as the British Board of Film Classification.[4] Furthermore, human rights bind the state even when acting on the basis of private law.[5]

Being both media entities and part of the state, public broadcasters are not only beneficiaries of media freedom, but also addressees of human rights. Therefore, public broadcasting services should operate in an impartial, independent and non-discriminatory manner and with editorial freedom; competing views, including those of political parties opposed to government policy, must be appropriately reflected in the broadcaster's transmissions.[6] They also have to safeguard 'internal editorial freedom'. Employees of public broadcasters are therefore under a less strict obligation to observe their duties of loyalty and discretion when publicly criticising the programming policy of their employer.[7]

5.2 Manifestation of an interference

Fundamental rights, including freedom of the media, are in the first place defensive rights against actions by domestic authorities. However, human rights also include an obligation of states to protect those rights. Eventually, although human rights basically have no direct horizontal effect, they may influence the application of domestic law between private individuals.

*5.2.1 Interference with media freedom as a defensive right (*status negativus*)*

An interference with media freedom is any impairment through the exercise of official authority, pressure or force rather than civilised

[3] See International Law Commission, Articles on Responsibility of States for Internationally Wrongful Acts, Report of the International Law Commission on the Work of Its Fifty-third Session, 2001 (A/56/10), Articles 5 and 8.

[4] See ECtHR, *Wingrove* v. *United Kingdom* [1996] App. no. 17419/90 [36]; Human Rights Committee, *Hertzberg and others* v. *Finland* [1985] Communication no. 61/1979 [9.1].

[5] ECtHR, *Vereinigung demokratischer Soldaten Österreichs and Gubi* v. *Austria* [1994] App. no. 15153/89 [27].

[6] Human Rights Committee, Concluding observations on Republic of Moldova (CCPR/CO/75/MDA), para. 14; Concluding observations on Togo (CCPR/CO/76/TGO), para. 17; Concluding observations on Peru (CCPR/CO/70/PER), para. 17.

[7] ECtHR, *Wojtas-Kaleta* v. *Poland* [2009] App. no. 20436/02 [47]; *Matúz* v. *Hungary* [2014] App. no. 73571/10 [33].

discourse. In order to effectively guarantee the full thriving of the media, the notion of 'interference' has to be conceptualised broadly. First, an interference with media freedom may consist of any *legal* act against a particular publication, including administrative regulations or judicial decisions, such as prohibition of, or civil or criminal liability for, a publication. Article 10(2) ECHR mentions 'formalities, conditions, restrictions or penalties' as aspects of an interference within the meaning of paragraph 1. Furthermore, Article 10(1)3 ECHR stipulates that states may require the licensing of broadcasting, television or cinema enterprises. Such a licensing requirement also constitutes an interference and thus has to be justified under Article 10(2) ECHR.

Second, the notion of interference also covers more subtle restrictions of media freedom. Any direct or indirect *factual* restriction thus constitutes an interference, too. Examples from case-law are attempts to uncover journalistic sources by search or seizure,[8] abuse of control over equipment used in the dissemination of information,[9] arbitrary and discriminatory granting of public subsidies or privileges, such as the placement of advertisements,[10] travel constraints for journalists,[11] the blockage of internet sites,[12] confiscation of journalistic equipment,[13] reprimands or dismissals,[14] the revocation of the citizenship of the director of a media outlet as a consequence of its editorial point of view,[15] harassment and intimidation[16] and official statements creating a media-hostile environment.[17]

[8] See Chapter 4, Section 4.2.1.4. [9] See Article 13(3) ACHR.

[10] Office of the Special Rapporteur for Freedom of Expression with the Inter-American Commission on Human Rights, Inter-American Legal Framework Regarding the Right to Freedom of Expression, 2009, CIDH/RELE/INF. 2/09, para. 96.

[11] Human Rights Committee, *Marques de Morais* v. *Angola* [2005] Communication no. 1128/2002 [6.8]; Concluding observations on Democratic People's Republic of Korea (CCPR/CO/72/PRK), para. 23.

[12] ECtHR, *Yıldırım* v. *Turkey* [2012] App. no. 3111/10 [55].

[13] IAComHR, *Oscar Elías Biscet and others* v. *Cuba* [2006] Case 12.476 [211].

[14] See, e.g., ECtHR, *Wille* v. *Liechtenstein* [1999] App. no. 28396/95 [50]; *Fuentes Bobo* v. *Spain* [2000] App. no. 39293/98 [38]; *Steur* v. *Netherlands* [2003] App. no. 39657/98 [29]; *Frankowicz* v. *Poland* [2008] App. no. 53025/99 [44]; *Wojtas-Kaleta* v. *Poland* [2009] App. no. 20436/02 [44]; Voorhoof and Humblet (2014) 3.

[15] IACtHR, *Ivcher-Bronstein* v. *Peru* [2001] Case 11.762 [152].

[16] See, e.g., Human Rights Committee, Concluding observations on Uzbekistan (CCPR/CO/83/UZB), para. 20; Concluding observations on Morocco (CCPR/CO/82/MAR), para. 23; Concluding observations on the Russian Federation (CCPR/CO/79/RUS), para. 22; Concluding observations on Guyana (CCPR/CO/79/Add.121), para. 19; IACtHR, *Uzcátegui and others* v. *Venezuela* [2012] Case 12.661 [190]; *Vélez Restrepo* v. *Colombia* [2012] Case 12.658 [142].

[17] IACtHR, *Ríos and others* v. *Venezuela* [2009] Case 12.441 [122]; IAComHR, *Perozo and others* v. *Venezuela* [2009] Case 12.442 [160].

5.2.2 *Interference with media freedom as an entitlement (*status positivus*)*

As explained above,[18] a state must not only negatively abstain from interfering with the Convention and Covenant guarantees; the beneficiaries of these guarantees may also be entitled to positive state action in order to secure their rights and freedoms. Regrettably, international human rights adjudicators do not always clearly distinguish between the 'horizontal effect'[19] of human rights and the *status positivus*, especially the 'obligation to protect'. These are overlapping, but not fully congruent, concepts. Horizontal effect only applies where the exercise of two fundamental rights stand in conflict with each other. By contrast, the *status positivus* is engaged in the following three situations: first, where individuals need to be protected from harming themselves; second, where individuals need to be protected from being attacked by others; and third, where the state has to enable individuals to exercise their rights in the first place.[20] A state violates its obligation to secure media freedom, for instance, where it does not protect journalists from threats and acts of violence as they carry out their journalistic work, and if it does not duly, promptly and exhaustively investigate such acts if they occurred.[21]

5.2.3 *Horizontal effect of media freedom: the constitutionalisation of privacy and defamation law*

The primary addressee of human rights is the state. Consequently, human rights principally do not have a direct effect between individuals; they are not actionable *per se* between private parties. This is, as apparent, generally accepted today. Human rights are not rules stipulating conditions for actionable claims, such as the right to damages or injunctions. There is one exception to this principle, where a human rights catalogue

[18] See Chapter 4, Section 4.2.2. [19] See below Section 5.2.3.

[20] See, e.g., Human Rights Committee, Concluding observations on the Russian Federation (CCPR/CO/79/RUS), para. 22; Concluding observations on Sri Lanka (CCPR/CO/79/LKA), para. 18; General Comment no. 34, para. 32; General Comment no. 31, para. 8; IAComHR, *Carlos Ranferí Gómez López* v. *Guatemala* [1996] Case 11.303 [104]; *Francisco Martorell* v. *Chile* [1996] Case 11.230 [66].

[21] See, e.g., ECtHR, *Özgür Gündem* v. *Turkey* [2000] App. no. 23144/93 [38 ff.]; IACtHR, *Perozo and others* v. *Venezuela* [2009] Case 12.442 [120]; *Ríos and others* v. *Venezuela* [2009] Case 12.441 [109]; IAComHR, *Carlos Ranferí Gómez López* v. *Guatemala* [1996] Case 11.303 [105]; *Hugo Bustios Saavedra* v. *Peru* [1997] Case 10.548 [73]; UN Commission on Human Rights, Report of the Special Rapporteur on the Promotion and Protection of the Right to Freedom of Opinion and Expression, Mr Abid Hussain, submitted pursuant to Commission Resolution 1997/27, E/CN.4/1998/40/Add.1, para. 28; AfCtHPR, *Abdoulaye Nikiema and others* v. *Burkina Faso (case of the late Norbert Zongo)* [2014] App. no. 013/2011 [187].

itself provides that certain rights apply between private individuals. Articles 13(3) and 14 ACHR are such directly actionable private law claims. Article 13(3) ACHR provides that '[t]he right of expression may not be restricted by indirect methods or means, such as the abuse of government *or private controls* over newsprint, radio broadcasting frequencies, or equipment used in the dissemination of information, or by any other means tending to impede the communication and circulation of ideas and opinions' (emphasis added). Article 14 ACHR provides a right to reply to '[a]nyone injured by inaccurate or offensive statements or ideas disseminated to the public in general by a legally regulated medium of communication'. These provisions are, therefore, human rights directly applicable between private individuals.

However, in complex societies the protection afforded by human rights has to extend not just to the exercise of governmental power but also to the exercise of power by fellow citizens, and especially the social and economic power of large organisations. The intrusion of powerful and influential mass media on the privacy and reputation of individuals is a prime example. The gain of freedom on the one side corresponds to the loss of freedom on the other. Consequently, although human rights are, apart from the exceptions mentioned above, not directly applicable, they must nonetheless influence the interpretation and application of pre-existing law in a trial between private individuals.[22] This 'indirect horizontal effect' of human rights follows from the fact that human rights constitute objective principles that have to be realised also in the interpretation of private law through state institutions.[23] Both the legislator as creator of private law and the courts as adjudicators are obliged to protect individuals from fellow citizens within the private law order. Accordingly, the balancing of conflicting principles has to take place within the application of private law rules, and not independently thereof. This may be accomplished either by interpreting existing private law rules in light of fundamental rights, or even through the extension of existing private law rules. An example of the former is the interpretation of open statutory clauses, such as 'morality' or 'public policy', in a human rights-friendly way.[24] An example of the latter is the particularly

[22] See, e.g., Drzemczewski (1979); Alkema (1988); Clapham (1993); Barak (2001); Kay (2005) 475 ff.; Nowak (2005) Introduction para. 4; Fenwick and Phillipson (2006) p. 128.

[23] The theory of human rights influencing private law as 'objective principles' (*objektive Wertordnung*) originates from the German Federal Constitutional Court; see *'Lüth'* [1958] Case 1 BvR 400/51.

[24] See German Federal Constitutional Court, *'Lüth'* [1958] Case 1 BvR 400/51 with a view to the interpretation of Section 826 of the German Civil Law Code (Intentional damage

common law-based approach to extend or enrich existing rules with human rights-compatible components, such as the – now codified – '*Reynolds* defence' in the tort of defamation, or the considerable expansion of breach of confidence claims with a view to misuse of private information.[25] Although the US Supreme Court has never expressly acknowledged the doctrine of 'indirect horizontal effect', the Court achieved the same effect, albeit in a doctrinally different way,[26] in the seminal decision *New York Times Co.* v. *Sullivan*. There the Supreme Court stated:

> What a State may not constitutionally bring about by means of a criminal statute is likewise beyond the reach of its civil law of libel. . . . The fear of damage awards under a rule such as that invoked by the Alabama courts here may be markedly more inhibiting than the fear of prosecution under a criminal statute. . . . Whether or not a newspaper can survive a succession of such [libel] judgments, the pall of fear and timidity imposed upon those who would give voice to public criticism is an atmosphere in which the First Amendment freedoms cannot survive. Plainly the Alabama law of civil libel is 'a form of regulation that creates hazards to protected freedoms markedly greater than those that attend reliance upon the criminal law'.[27]

The Court thus recognised that the civil law of libel has to be applied in accordance with the First Amendment. As a consequence, it established the doctrine that a public official suing for defamation must prove that the statement in question was made with actual malice, which in this context refers to knowledge or reckless disregard for the truth.[28]

Where human rights are in conflict with other private interests, domestic courts have to apply the law, usually private law, taking into account the human rights in a balancing exercise. With regard to media freedom, the doctrine of horizontal effect becomes particularly relevant in cases where the freedom of the media needs to be balanced against the right to respect for one's private life as an aspect of the 'rights of others' within the meaning of Article 19(3) ICCPR, Article 27(2) AfCHPR, Article 32(2) ACHR and Article 10(2) ECHR. The doctrine of 'horizontal effect' therefore overlaps with the doctrine of 'obligation to protect' to the effect

contrary to public policy) in light of the fundamental right to freedom of opinion, Article 5 Basic Law.

[25] With regard to the '*Reynolds* defence', see *Reynolds* v. *Times Newspapers Ltd* [2001] 2 AC 127; *Jameel* v. *Wall Street Journal Europe Sprl* [2006] UKHL 44; now Section 4 Defamation Act 2013. On the extension of breach of confidence, see *Campbell* v. *MGN* [2004] UKHL 22; *OBG Ltd. and others* v. *Allan and others* [2007] UKHL 21.

[26] See the analysis of Barak (2001) pp. 13, 25 ff.: the 'judiciary model'; see also Volokh (2010); Sunstein (1992) 269–71; Weaver and Partlett (2005–6) 66.

[27] US Supreme Court, *New York Times Co.* v. *Sullivan*, 376 US 254, 277–8 (1964).

[28] On the requirement of good faith in general, see Chapter 2, Section 2.2.3.3.

that courts, as state institutions, need to protect the human right of a person who alleges they are the victim of the exercise of another individual's human right. Human rights charters emphasise this positive obligation to protect people's private lives by stating that everyone has the right to *respect* for their private life (Article 8(1) ECHR) or the right to the *protection* of the law against interferences with their privacy or attacks on their honour and reputation (Article 17(2) ICCPR and Article 11(3) ACHR).[29] Hence, in addition to the negative undertaking not to interfere with private life, there is a positive state obligation inherent in an effective 'respect for' and 'protection of' private life.[30] This obligation involves the adoption of measures securing respect for private life also in private law relations. As a consequence, courts must find a proper balance between the right to respect for one's private life and media freedom on a case-by-case basis.

The doctrine of indirect horizontal effect does not only apply in situations where a private individual claims to be the victim of the exercise of media freedom. It also applies, *vice versa*, where a media company or a journalist claims to be the victim of another party's, including another media company's, action. This has been the case, for instance, in the 1969 *Blinkfüer* decision of the German Federal Constitutional Court.[31] The powerful publishing house Springer had urged newspaper retailers to boycott the *Blinkfüer* magazine, because it had published the television programme listings of then-GDR channels. Springer combined the call for a boycott with the threat of trade sanctions against the retailers. Applying the doctrine of indirect horizontal effect, the Constitutional Court decided in favour of *Blinkfüer*'s press freedom and against Springer's freedom of expression, and thus declared the call for a boycott 'unlawful' within the meaning of German tort law.[32]

Furthermore, horizontal effect may also apply in cases where an employed journalist claims to be affected by a general rule or sanction

[29] The African Charter does not include a right to private life or privacy. However, Article 28 AfCHPR states that '[e]very individual shall have the duty to respect and consider his fellow beings without discrimination, and to maintain relations aimed at promoting, safeguarding and reinforcing mutual respect and tolerance'.

[30] Based on the seminal decision ECtHR, *Von Hannover* v. *Germany (No. 1)* [2004] App. no. 59320/00 [57], but see also *Marckx* v. *Belgium* [1979] App. no. 6833/74 [31]. From the IACtHR, see *Fontevecchia and D'Amico* v. *Argentina* [2011] Case 12.524 [49], referring to *Von Hannover* v. *Germany (No. 1)*.

[31] German Federal Constitutional Court, '*Blinkfüer*' [1969] Case 1 BvR 619/63.

[32] See Section 823(1) German Civil Law Code: 'A person who, intentionally or negligently, *unlawfully* injures the life, body, health, freedom, property or another right of another person is liable to make compensation to the other party for the damage arising from this' (Translation provided by the Langenscheidt Translation Service, juris GmbH, 2009; emphasis added).

applied by his employer that restricts his journalistic freedom, for instance, the dismissal of a journalist who publicly criticises his employer. This requires the courts, when applying domestic employment law, to balance the employees' duty of loyalty, reserve and discretion owed to his employer with the necessity of a public debate.[33] Another media-related case where the doctrine of horizontal effect applies is a situation where a landlord prohibits a tenant from installing a satellite dish to receive foreign TV channels.[34] Finally, the reconciliation of the conflict between the right to disseminate information and intellectual property rights also constitutes an application of the doctrine of horizontal effect.[35]

As previously stated, cases of horizontal effect usually involve a person alleging they are the victim of another individual's *action*. Yet, especially in the area of media law, another situation of horizontal effect of human rights is conceivable, and this is where an individual person does not claim to be the victim of the media's action, but of the media's *omission*. These are the cases where the media's right *not* to disseminate information competes with an individual's claim against the media to publish certain information, such as a reply or an apology.[36] These cases also have to be solved by recourse to the doctrine of indirect horizontal effect, and therefore have to be decided in light of media freedom and the right to respect for one's privacy or reputation.

[33] See, e.g., ECtHR, *Fuentes Bobo* v. *Spain* [2000] App. no. 39293/98 [38]; *Manole and others* v. *Moldova* [2009] App. no. 13936/02 [103]; *Wojtas-Kaleta* v. *Poland* [2009] App. no. 20436/02; *Heinisch* v. *Germany* [2011] App. no. 28274/08 [65]; Voorhoof and Humblet (2014) 29.

[34] ECtHR, *Khurshid Mustafa and Tarzibachi* v. *Sweden* [2008] App. no. 23883/06 [36]; German Federal Constitutional Court, '*Parabolic antenna I*' [1994] Case 1 BvR 1687/92; '*Parabolic antenna II*' [2013] Case 1 BvR 1314/11.

[35] See Chapter 7, Section 7.4.

[36] See Chapter 4, Section 4.1.4.1.

6 Justification of an interference with media freedom

A common principle that runs through all international human rights catalogues is that freedom of expression and media freedom are not absolute. The exercise and enjoyment of freedom of expression and/or media freedom can be restricted under the conditions mentioned in Article 19(3) ICCPR, Article 13(2) ACHR, Article 10(2) ECHR and Article 52 EUChFR.

Unfortunately, the African Charter provides a confusing system of limitations. Article 9(2) AfCHPR does not stipulate examples of limitations, but states in rather general terms that '[e]very individual shall have the right to express and disseminate his opinions within the law'. Article 9 (2) AfCHPR thus includes the caveat 'within the law'. This contradicts two basic ideas of international human rights: first, legislation must operate within the framework of human rights, and not *vice versa*. Second, international human rights standards should prevail over national law. Consequently, State Parties must not be enabled to negate the rights conferred upon individuals by the Charter. Accordingly, the AfComHPR rightly held that national law cannot set aside the right to express and disseminate one's opinions, because this would make the protection of this right ineffective.[1] If national law had precedence over the Charter, this would defeat the purpose of its protection. Rather, any interference with the rights enshrined in the Charter must be in conformity with the Charter. As a consequence, 'within the law' means that the interference itself must be lawful – especially with a view to international human rights law.

[1] See, e.g., AfComHPR, *Media Rights Agenda, Constitutional Rights Project, Media Rights Agenda and Constitutional Rights Project* v. *Nigeria* [1998] App. nos. 105/93, 128/94, 130/94 and 152/96 [66]; *John D. Ouko* v. *Kenya* [2000] App. no. 232/99 [28]; *Malawi Africa Association, Amnesty International, Ms Sarr Diop, Union interafricaine des droits de l'Homme and RADDHO, Collectif des veuves et ayants-Droit, Association mauritanienne des droits de l'Homme* v. *Mauritania* [2000] App. nos. 54/91, 61/91, 96/93, 98/93, 164/97, 196/97 and 210/98 [102]; *Interights, Institute for Human Rights and Development in Africa, and Association mauritanienne des droits de l'Homme* v. *Mauritania* [2004] App. no. 242/01 [77]; *Kenneth Good* v. *Republic of Botswana* [2010] App. no. 313/05 [188].

However, this leaves open the question what the requirements of a limitation are, and, in particular, what aims an interference has to pursue. For this purpose, Part I Chapter II of the African Charter provides duties every individual has to fulfil under the Charter, which bears a close resemblance to the 'duties and responsibilities' clauses in Article 19(3) ICCPR and Article 10(2) ECHR. Article 27(2) AfCHPR provides that '[t]he rights and freedoms of each individual shall be exercised with due regard to the rights of others, collective security, morality and common interest'. Article 28 AfCHPR adds that '[e]very individual shall have the duty to respect and consider his fellow beings without discrimination, and to maintain relations aimed at promoting, safeguarding and reinforcing mutual respect and tolerance'. Finally, under Article 29 AfCHPR, the individual shall also have the duty, *inter alia*,

3. Not to compromise the security of the State whose national or resident he is;
4. To preserve and strengthen social and national solidarity, particularly when the latter is threatened;
5. To preserve and strengthen the national independence and the territorial integrity of his country and to contribute to its defense in accordance with the law; ...
7. To preserve and strengthen positive African cultural values in his relations with other members of the society, in the spirit of tolerance, dialogue and consultation and, in general, to contribute to the promotion of the moral well being of society;
8. To contribute to the best of his abilities, at all times and at all levels, to the promotion and achievement of African unity.

The notion of individual responsibility to the community thus expressed is ingrained in African tradition and the values of African civilization.[2] Defendant State Parties may therefore invoke these clauses, especially Article 27(2) AfCHPR, to justify restrictions on freedom of expression and freedom of the media.[3]

[2] Gittleman (1982) 676.

[3] AfComHPR, *Media Rights Agenda, Constitutional Rights Project, Media Rights Agenda and Constitutional Rights Project* v. *Nigeria* [1998] App. nos. 105/93, 128/94, 130/94 and 152/96 [68]; *Interights, Institute for Human Rights and Development in Africa, and Association mauritanienne des droits de l'Homme* v. *Mauritania* [2004] App. no. 242/01 [77]; *Scanlen & Holderness* v. *Zimbabwe* [2009] App. no. 297/05 [108]; *Kenneth Good* v. *Republic of Botswana* [2010] App. no. 313/05 [189].

6.1 The requirements for a justification

Interferences with fundamental rights, and thus also with freedom of expression and media freedom, are allowed if such limitations are prescribed by law (principle of legality), pursue a legitimate aim (principle of legitimacy) and are necessary in pursuit of this aim (principle of proportionality).[4] The onus to demonstrate that the restriction on the applicant's fundamental right is justified is on the interfering state.[5]

6.1.1 Prescribed, or provided, by law (principle of legality)

Restrictions on freedom of expression and media freedom must be prescribed, or provided, by law. The requirements for the condition of legality can be summarised as follows: first, the law must be both adequately accessible and foreseeable. Foreseeability includes that the law is formulated with sufficient precision to enable the individual to anticipate the consequences which a given action may entail, and thus to regulate their conduct accordingly.[6] For example, in *Hashman and Harrup* v. *United Kingdom*, the Strasbourg Court found that an order by which applicants were bound to keep the peace and not to behave *contra bonos mores* did not comply with the requirement of Article 10(2) ECHR

[4] See, amongst many other authorities, ECtHR, *Novaya Gazeta and Borodyanskiy* v. *Russia* [2013] App. no. 14087/08 [32]; IACtHR, *Ricardo Canese* v. *Paraguay* [2004] Case 12.032 [95]; *Herrera-Ulloa* v. *Costa Rica* [2004] Case 12.367 [120]; AfComHPR, *Scanlen & Holderness* v. *Zimbabwe* [2009] App. no. 297/05 [107]; see generally UN Economic and Social Council, Siracusa Principles on the Limitation and Derogation Provisions in the International Covenant on Civil and Political Rights, UN Doc. E/CN.4/1985/4, Annex (1985); De Schutter (2010) p. 288.

[5] See, e.g., UN Economic and Social Council, Siracusa Principles on the Limitation and Derogation Provisions in the International Covenant on Civil and Political Rights, UN Doc. E/CN.4/1985/4, Annex (1985), no. 12; Human Rights Committee, *Coleman* v. *Australia* [2006] Communication no. 1157/2003 [7.3]; Office of the Special Rapporteur for Freedom of Expression with the Inter-American Commission on Human Rights, Inter-American Legal Framework Regarding the Right to Freedom of Expression, 2009, CIDH/RELE/INF. 2/09, para. 83.

[6] See ECtHR, *Sanoma Uitgevers BV* v. *Netherlands* [2010] App. no. 38224/03 [81]; Human Rights Committee, General Comment no. 34, para. 25; IACtHR, *Usón Ramírez* v. *Venezuela* [2009] Case 12.554 [55]; IAComHR, *Tomás Eduardo Cirio* v. *Uruguay* [2006] Case 11.500 [64]; Office of the Special Rapporteur for Freedom of Expression with the Inter-American Commission on Human Rights, Inter-American Legal Framework Regarding the Right to Freedom of Expression, 2009, CIDH/RELE/INF. 2/09, para. 69; ECJ, *Association Église de Scientologie and others* v. *The Prime Minister* [2000] ECR I-01335, Case C-54/99 [21–2]. On legal certainty as a general principle of EU law, see Craig and de Búrca (2011) pp. 533–8.

that it be 'prescribed by law'.[7] Yet foreseeability does not require absolute certainty; many laws are inevitably drafted in vague terms, the interpretation of which is a matter of judicial practice.[8] The degree of foreseeability depends on the content of the law, its area of application, and the number and status of those to whom it is addressed.[9] The consequences of a law may still be sufficiently foreseeable if the person concerned has to take appropriate legal advice.[10] Persons carrying on a professional activity, such as journalists, are expected to take special care in assessing the legal risks that their activity entails.[11]

Second, the law must provide legal protection against arbitrary interferences by public authorities. It must indicate with sufficient clarity the scope of any discretion conferred on the authorities entrusted with the application of the law, and it must not grant unfettered power.[12]

Third, the law must meet certain formal requirements. It must either be enshrined in a statute or another legally binding document, or it can be judge-made law.[13] Customary law based on tradition or religion is not sufficient.[14]

[7] ECtHR, *Hashman and Harrup* v. *United Kingdom* [1999] App. no. 25594/94 [41]. See also *Kenedi* v. *Hungary* [2009] App. no. 31475/05; *Sanoma Uitgevers BV* v. *Netherlands* [2010] App. no. 38224/03; *Yıldırım* v. *Turkey* [2012] App. no. 3111/10.

[8] See, e.g., ECtHR, *Sunday Times* v. *United Kingdom (No. 1)* [1979] App. no. 6538/74 [49]; *Hertel* v. *Switzerland* [1998] App. no. 59/1997/843/1049 [35]; *Glas Nadezhda EOOD and Elenkov* v. *Bulgaria* [2007] App. no. 14134/02 [45]; IACtHR, *Usón Ramírez* v. *Venezuela* [2009] Case 12.554 [55]; IAComHR, *Tomás Eduardo Cirio* v. *Uruguay* [2006] Case 11.500 [64].

[9] See ECtHR, *Cantoni* v. *France* [1996] App. no. 17862/91 [35].

[10] See, among other authorities, ECtHR, *Tolstoy Miloslavsky* v. *United Kingdom* [1995] App. no. 18139/91 [37]; *Chauvy and others* v. *France* [2004] App. no. 64915/01 [44]; *Lindon, Otchakovsky-Laurens and July* v. *France* [2007] App. nos. 21279/02 and 36448/02 [41].

[11] ECtHR, *Chauvy and others* v. *France* [2004] App. no. 64915/01 [48]; *Lindon, Otchakovsky-Laurens and July* v. *France* [2007] App. nos. 21279/02 and 36448/02 [41].

[12] Compare Human Rights Committee, *Pinkney* v. *Canada* [1981] Communication no. 27/1978 [34]; General Comment no. 27, para. 13. See also UN Economic and Social Council, Siracusa Principles on the Limitation and Derogation Provisions in the International Covenant on Civil and Political Rights, UN Doc. E/CN.4/1985/4, Annex (1985), nos. 15–18. From the ECtHR, see, e.g., *Sanoma Uitgevers BV* v. *Netherlands* [2010] App. no. 38224/03 [82]; *Telegraaf Media Nederland Landelijke Media BV and others* v. *Netherlands* [2012] App. no. 39315/06 [102]; see also IACtHR, *Claude Reyes and others* v. *Chile* [2006] Case 12.108 [89]; Office of the Special Rapporteur for Freedom of Expression with the Inter-American Commission on Human Rights, Inter-American Legal Framework Regarding the Right to Freedom of Expression, 2009, CIDH/RELE/INF. 2/09, para. 70.

[13] See the seminal decision of the EComHR, *X. Ltd and Y.* v. *United Kingdom* [1982] App. no. 8710/79 [5 ff.]; furthermore ECtHR, *Sunday Times* v. *United Kingdom (No. 1)* [1979] App. no. 6538/74; *Tolstoy Miloslavsky* v. *United Kingdom* [1995] App. no. 18139/91 [37]; *Sanoma Uitgevers BV* v. *Netherlands* [2010] App. no. 38224/03 [83].

[14] See Human Rights Committee, General Comment no. 32.

Fourth, criminal laws in particular must satisfy the principle of strict legality, *nullum crimen, nulla poena sine lege* according to Article 15 ICCPR, Article 7 ECHR, Article 7(2) AfCHPR and Article 9 ACHR.[15]

In addition, the Strasbourg Court and the Inter-American Court require that the adoption of the law must comply with the legislative procedural rules under the domestic constitution.[16] However, since international courts do not review the observance of domestic law, their supervision of the domestic legislative procedure is restricted to cases of 'clear non-observance' of fundamental rules on law-making.[17]

An area of media law where courts find particularly often that an interference has not been 'prescribed by law' is media licensing or compulsory registration of media companies. For such a licensing regime to be 'prescribed by law', the applicant for a licence must be made aware on what basis the national authority exercises its discretion to deny such a licence. Domestic law must also afford a measure of legal protection against an arbitrary refusal to grant a licence. The Council of Europe Recommendation Rec(2000)23 on the Independence and Functions of Regulatory Authorities for the Broadcasting Sector provides further guidance for the Convention States and, finally, the Strasbourg Court. Against this background the ECtHR found a violation of Article 10 ECHR in *Glas Nadezhda EOOD and Elenkov* v. *Bulgaria* and *Meltex Ltd and Mesrop Movsesyan* v. *Armenia*, because the process in which the licence had been denied was not sufficiently transparent.[18] Similarly, in *Centro Europa 7 Srl and Di Stefano* v. *Italy*, the Court decided that the Italian legislative framework on the allocation of broadcasting frequencies 'lacked clarity and precision and did not enable the applicant company to foresee, with sufficient certainty, the point at which it might be allocated the frequencies and be able to start performing the activity for which it had been granted a licence'.[19] Furthermore, the Italian authorities did not observe the deadlines set in the licence, thereby frustrating the applicant

[15] On the interpretation of these provisions, see, e.g., ECtHR, *Khodorkovskiy and Lebedev* v. *Russia* [2013] App. no. 11082/06 and 13772/05 [778–85], providing further references; IACtHR, *Usón Ramírez* v. *Venezuela* [2009] Case 12.554 [55]; *Fontevecchia and D'Amico* v. *Argentina* [2011] Case 12.524 [89]; Office of the Special Rapporteur for Freedom of Expression with the Inter-American Commission on Human Rights, Inter-American Legal Framework Regarding the Right to Freedom of Expression, 2009, CIDH/RELE/INF. 2/09, para. 72.

[16] ECtHR, *Barthold* v. *Germany* [1985] App. no. 8734/79 [48]; IACtHR, Advisory Opinion OC-6/86 [22–4].

[17] See ECtHR, *Barthold* v. *Germany* [1985] App. no. 8734/79 [48].

[18] ECtHR, *Glas Nadezhda EOOD and Elenkov* v. *Bulgaria* [2007] App. no. 14134/02 [50]; *Meltex Ltd and Mesrop Movsesyan* v. *Armenia* [2008] App. no. 32283/04 [83].

[19] ECtHR, *Centro Europa 7 Srl and Di Stefano* v. *Italy* [2012] App. no. 38433/09 [154].

company's expectations. Since the company did not have effective legal means at its disposal to compel the authorities to abide by the law, it was not afforded sufficient protection against arbitrariness.[20] The Court thus found a violation of Article 10(1) ECHR in this case as well.

6.1.2 The pursuit of a legitimate aim (principle of legitimacy)

An interference with media freedom must pursue a legitimate aim: a civility rule that public discourse presupposes.[21] Such aims are, in the first place, the aims applicable to freedom of expression mentioned in Article 19(3) ICCPR, Article 10(2) ECHR, Article 13(2) ACHR and Article 27(2) AfCHPR. At first glance, Article 10(2) ECHR permits more restrictions than the other provisions. Belgium and France therefore submitted reservations to the effect that Article 19 ICCPR shall be applied in the context of the restrictions authorised in Article 10 ECHR. However, the interests enshrined in Article 10(2) ECHR are usually encompassed by the 'public order' purpose in Article 19(3) ICCPR and Article 13(2) ACHR, or by the 'common interest' in Article 27(2) AfCHPR, and a broad interpretation of the 'rights of others' in all of these provisions. For this reason, the different wordings of Article 10(2) ECHR and the other provisions hardly bear any practical consequences.

Although the Human Rights Committee in its General Comment on Article 19 ICCPR expressed otherwise,[22] aims which are not expressly provided in those paragraphs may under certain circumstances nonetheless justify an interference with freedom of expression. With regard to media law, this may in particular be the aim of achieving a high level of media pluralism.[23] Furthermore, the preservation of order in a particular group, such as the armed forces,[24] and the 'protection of effective democracy'[25] have been regarded as legitimate aims, too. Eventually, international adjudicators take a rather broad stance on what is encompassed by the notion of 'rights of others'. For example, the ECtHR decided that 'constitutional principles which underpin a democracy', such as the requirement for elected representatives in a state based on a monarchical model of government to take an oath of allegiance to the monarch,

[20] ECtHR, *Centro Europa 7 S.r.l. and Di Stefano* v. *Italy* [2012] App. no. 38433/09 [155].
[21] See Chapter 2, Section 2.2.2. [22] General Comment no. 34, para. 22.
[23] See Chapter 14.
[24] ECtHR, *Vereinigung demokratischer Soldaten Österreichs and Gubi* v. *Austria* [1994] App. no. 15153/89 [32]; IAComHR, *José Francisco Gallardo Rodríguez* v. *Mexico* [1996] Case 11.430 [85]; *Rodolfo Robles Espinoza* v. *Peru* [1999] Case 11.317 [148]; *Tomás Eduardo Cirio* v. *Uruguay* [2006] Case 11.500 [75].
[25] ECtHR, *Ahmed and others* v. *United Kingdom* [1998] App. no. 65/1997/849/1056 [52].

constitute 'rights of others'.[26] Similarly, 'the aim of preserving the impartiality of broadcasting on public interest matters and, thereby, of protecting the democratic process' has been held to correspond to the legitimate aim of protecting the 'rights of others'.[27]

Under the EUChFR, the aim must, according to Article 52(1), be a legitimate aim of EU law: limitations may be made only if they are necessary and genuinely meet objectives of general interest recognised by the Union or the need to protect the rights and freedoms of others. In this context, Articles 2 and 3 TEU and Title II of the TFEU warrant attention. As the EU is not a state, aims to protect national sovereignty, such as 'the interests of national security [or] territorial integrity', have less significance in the field of Article 11 EUChFR.

The civility rules to be enforced by states when interfering with media freedom may be divided into the preservation of public interests, on the one hand, and the protection of individual rights, on the other hand. Social norms of civility include national security, territorial integrity, public safety, the prevention of disorder and crime, the protection of health, the protection of morals and the maintenance of the authority and impartiality of the judiciary. A public interest may also be represented in cases where not an individual person, but an entire group of people or a community as a whole, is concerned, particularly in cases of 'hate speech' or attacks on religious feelings.[28] Individual rights are, for example, the right to respect for one's reputation or privacy, the right to respect for one's religious feelings and intellectual property rights.

By contrast to the principle of proportionality,[29] the establishment of the legitimate aim pursued is not subject to any state discretion. The requirement of legitimacy allows international adjudicators to investigate the motives behind the impugned restriction, and to screen out illegitimate motives.[30] Hence they have to review the 'legitimate aim' claimed by the state with strict scrutiny. For instance, whether public order concerns may serve as a *reason* for justification is not subject to any discretion of the state authorities. However, whether legitimately invoked public order interests do indeed *justify* the interference under the principle of proportionality is subject to a certain margin of appreciation.

[26] ECtHR, *McGuinness* v. *United Kingdom* [1999] App. no. 39511/98.

[27] ECtHR, *Animal Defenders International* v. *United Kingdom* [2013] App. no. 48876/08 [78].

[28] See Chapters 11 and 12; Human Rights Committee, *Faurisson* v. *France* [1996] Communication no. 550/93 [9.6]; *Ross* v. *Canada* [2000] Communication no. 736/97 [11.5]; ECtHR, *Jersild* v. *Denmark* [1994] App. no. 15890/89; *Otto-Preminger-Institut* v. *Austria* [1994] App. no. 13470/87; *Vejdeland and others* v. *Sweden* [2012] App. no. 1813/07.

[29] See below Section 6.3.

[30] De Schutter (2010) p. 307.

Finally, according to the principle *iura novit curia*, international courts and tribunals may add another legitimate aim to the ones asserted by the state, find that one or more asserted aims are not suitable or substitute the aim asserted by the state with another legitimate aim.[31]

6.1.3 The principle of proportionality

Fundamental rights principles are optimisation requirements.[32] They have to be 'realised to the greatest extent possible given the legal and factual possibilities'.[33] The instrument to resolve conflicts between competing principles is the principle of proportionality, the textual reference point of which is the requirement of 'necessity' of the interference in all human rights catalogues.

The proportionality test examines:

(1.) whether the interference was suitable to achieve the legitimate aim pursued (suitability);
(2.) whether the interference was the least intrusive instrument amongst those which might achieve the legitimate aim (necessity); and
(3.) whether the interference was strictly proportionate to the legitimate aim pursued (proportionality *sensu stricto*).[34]

The proportionality test establishes 'a conditional relation of precedents'[35] between conflicting principles. It realises conflicting principles in a rationalised way with a view to a concrete case, considering, as

[31] Compare ECtHR, *Observer and Guardian* v. *United Kingdom* [1991] App. no. 13585/88 [56]; *Erdoğdu* v. *Turkey* [2000] App. no. 25723/94 [84].
[32] See Chapter 2, Section 2.4. [33] Alexy (2002) p. 47.
[34] See, amongst many other authorities, Human Rights Commitee, *Ballantyne and others* v. *Canada* [1993] Communication no. 359, 385/89 [11.4]; *Coleman* v. *Australia* [2006] Communication no. 1157/2003 [7.3]; ECtHR, *Sunday Times* v. *United Kingdom (No. 1)* [1979] App. no. 6538/74 [62]; *Lingens* v. *Austria* [1986] App. no. 9815/82 [40]; *Observer and Guardian* v. *United Kingdom* [1991] App. no. 13585/88 [59]; IACtHR, *Ricardo Canese* v. *Paraguay* [2004] Case 12.032 [96]; *Herrera-Ulloa* v. *Costa Rica* [2004] Case 12.367 [121]; Office of the Special Rapporteur for Freedom of Expression with the Inter-American Commission on Human Rights, Inter-American Legal Framework Regarding the Right to Freedom of Expression, 2009, CIDH/RELE/INF. 2/09, paras. 85 to 88; IAComHR, *Tomás Eduardo Cirio* v. *Uruguay* [2006] Case 11.500 [65]; AfComHPR, *Media Rights Agenda, Constitutional Rights Project, Media Rights Agenda and Constitutional Rights Project* v. *Nigeria* [1998] App. nos. 105/93, 128/94, 130/94 and 152/96 [69]; *Scanlen & Holderness* v. *Zimbabwe* [2009] App. no. 297/05 [107]; ECJ, *R* v. *Minister for Agriculture, Fisheries and Food and the Secretary of State for Health ex p Fedesa* [1990] ECR I-04023, Case C-331/88 [13]; *R* v. *Secretary of State for Health, ex p British American Tobacco* [2002] ECR I-11453, Case C-491/01 [122]; CJEU, *Sky Österreich* v. *Österreichischer Rundfunk* [2013] (not yet reported), Case C-283/11 [48] and [50].
[35] See Alexy (2002) p. 52.

required by the nature of principles, the legal and factual possibilities: the suitability and necessity tests derive from the nature of principles as optimisation requirements with a view to what is *factually* possible, while the proportionality *sensu stricto* analysis follows from their relation to the *legally* possible.[36]

But before international adjudicators are able to examine whether the interference with media freedom has been justified under the principle of proportionality, they need to establish the margin of appreciation of the defendant state. The margin of appreciation plays a crucial role for the revision of the impugned measure. The greater the margin of appreciation afforded to the Member States, the less intense the scope of the adjudicator's judicial review. The margin of appreciation may be relevant for all three steps of the proportionality analysis.

6.2 The determination of the width of the margin of appreciation and the scope of judicial review

It is inherent in international human rights conventions that they are subsidiary to the national protection of human rights[37] or, as Lord Hoffman expressed it: 'human rights are universal in abstraction but national in application'.[38] Article 2 of the Optional First Protocol to the ICCPR, Article 46(1)(a) ACHR, Article 35(1) ECHR and Article 56(5) AfCHPR stipulate that international courts and tribunals become involved only when all domestic remedies have been exhausted. Hence the Member States are initially responsible for securing human rights.[39] An international adjudicator's task is not to take the place of the national authorities, but rather to *review* under the human rights convention the decisions they have taken.[40] Accordingly, the national authorities have to apply standards which were in conformity with the principles embodied in the human rights catalogue, and, moreover, they have to base their decisions on an acceptable assessment of the relevant facts.[41]

[36] Alexy (2002) p. 67.

[37] See ECtHR, Case 'relating to certain aspects of the laws on the use of languages in education in Belgium' [1968] App. nos. 1474/62, 1677/62, 1691/62, 1769/63, 1994/63 and 2126/64 [10].

[38] Hoffmann (2009) 422.

[39] ECtHR, *Handyside* v. *United Kingdom* [1976] App. no. 5493/72 [49]; *Sunday Times* v. *United Kingdom (No. 1)* [1979] App. no. 6538/74 [59].

[40] ECtHR, *Handyside* v. *United Kingdom* [1976] App. no. 5493/72 [50]; *Sunday Times* v. *United Kingdom (No. 1)* [1979] App. no. 6538/74 [59].

[41] See, amongst many other ECtHR judgments, *Dichand and others* v. *Austria* [2002] App no. 29271/95 [38]; *OOO Ivpress and others* v. *Russia* [2013] App. nos. 33501/04, 38608/04, 35258/05 and 35618/05 [68].

The more the margin of appreciation is limited, the stricter the scrutiny an international adjudicator applies regarding the legal and factual circumstances of an application. A narrow margin of appreciation therefore leads to a higher degree of harmonisation of domestic laws.

However, the margin of appreciation doctrine has been subject to strong objections in legal scholarship,[42] the discussion of which would go beyond the scope of this book. But even if one accepts the margin of appreciation doctrine, its use should be coherent and principled. Unfortunately, this has not always been the case in practice.

It is submitted that the crucial factors for the margin of appreciation should be, first, at which step of the proportionality test the margin of appreciation was relevant, and second, the intensity of the scrutiny. The first question is, unfortunately, not always observed by international adjudicators. Instead, they often seem to afford discretion to the Member States regarding the entire proportionality analysis. This, however, disregards the reasons *why* a margin of appreciation actually has to be afforded. As elaborated above, the proportionality test consists of three steps, the first two of which are factual, while only the third one – proportionality *sensu stricto* – is normative. The reason for granting a margin of appreciation must therefore be found in the objective of the respective step of the proportionality analysis, or, more precisely, in the epistemic, or knowledge-related, deficit of the supervising adjudicator regarding this particular step.[43] This means *in concreto* that a margin of appreciation on the suitability and necessity step is necessitated because of a factual, that is, empirical uncertainty, while a margin of appreciation on the proportionality *sensu stricto* step is required because of a normative uncertainty.

This leads to the second question: what is the decisive factor for the intensity of the scrutiny? This factor must imply either a factual or a normative knowledge-related deficit of the adjudicator. Where the uncertainty is *factual*, supervisory bodies have to grant a margin of appreciation only with regard to the factual determinants of the proportionality analysis, that is, the suitability and the necessity tests. The proportionality *sensu stricto*, which is an entirely normative analysis, then remains the province of the international courts. By contrast, international supervisors are subject to a *normative* deficit where the invoked interest in question lacks consensus amongst the Member States of a particular convention. These are situations where domestic authorities are better

[42] For a critical assessment of the margin of appreciation doctrine, see Greer (2004) 425; Fenwick and Phillipson (2006) pp. 82–6; De la Rasilla del Moral (2006).

[43] Alexy (2002) p. 414.

placed to make normative evaluations concerning issues that require knowledge of local sensitivities.

For example, while the aims of protecting national security or public safety may often imply an epistemic factual uncertainty, the protection of morals or of religious feelings of others involves an epistemic normative deficit for an international court. For domestic legislation or administration it is difficult to establish what the most suitable means to protect national security or public safety actually are. This requires careful analysis of the situation and a difficult prediction of further developments, that is, a high degree of factual uncertainty. International courts must therefore grant a means-selecting margin of appreciation to the Member States where national security or public safety interests should justify an interference with media freedom. In addition, states have considerable means-selective discretion where the *status positivus* of media freedom applies.[44] Where the media claims an entitlement to positive state action, the state would have discretion for the means it chooses to fulfil its obligation. Moreover, within the complex economic framework of the EU, the CJEU also allows a considerable margin of appreciation for both EU and national authorities when matters which raise complex political, economic or social issues are concerned. The Court of Justice has held that 'the legality of a measure adopted in that sphere can be affected only if the measure is *manifestly inappropriate* having regard to the objective which the competent institution is seeking to pursue' (emphasis added).[45] The rationales for the Court's self-restraint are, first, the political responsibility and accountability of the policy-makers, second, their superior expertise, and third, where national measures are concerned, the recognition of the diversity of regulatory systems and national values within the EU.[46] The effect of the discretion described by the expression 'manifestly inappropriate' is that the Court of Justice applies the necessity or 'least intrusive means' requirement

[44] Compare Alexy (2002) p. 308; see Chapter 4, Section 4.2.2.

[45] ECJ, *R* v. *Minister for Agriculture, Fisheries and Food and the Secretary of State for Health, ex p Fedesa* [1990] ECR I-04023, Case C-331/88 [14]; see also *SA Roquette Frères* v. *Council of the European Communities* [1980] ECR 03333, Case 138/79 [25]; *Aragonesa de Publicidad Exterior SA* v. *Departamento de Sanidad y Seguridad Social de la Generalitat de Cataluña* [1991] ECR I-04151, Joined Cases C-1/90 and C-179/90 [17–18]; *Federal Republic of Germany* v. *Council* [1994] ECR I-04973, Case C-280/93 [90]; *R* v. *Minister of Agriculture, Fisheries and food, ex p National Federation of Fishermen's Organisations and others and Federation of Highlands and Islands Fisherman and other* [1995] ECR I-3115, Case C-44/94 [123].

[46] Compare *Sinclair Collis Ltd* v. *Secretary of State for Health* [2011] EWCA Civ 437 [127].

with a lower level of scrutiny.[47] However, a measure would be considered manifestly inappropriate if it had the protection of domestic economic interests as its aim, such as the commercial interest of a national profession or some national public financial interest.[48] In addition, the Court of Justice allows for a certain margin of appreciation for domestic courts in the context of the public policy exceptions to fundamental freedoms where fundamental rights are concerned.[49]

In these cases of factual uncertainty international adjudicators have to grant a margin of appreciation only with regard to the suitability and the necessity tests. The Member States' margin of appreciation only applies to the choice of the means. International courts and commissions still have to scrutinise carefully and in detail whether the conflicting principles have been properly balanced under the proportionality *sensu stricto* test. Furthermore, the greater the interference with media freedom, the greater the certainty of its underlying factual premises must be.[50]

By contrast, the protection of morals often implies a normative deficit, because the invoked interest in question lacks consensus amongst the state members of a particular convention: '[I]t is not possible to find in the domestic law of the various Contracting States a uniform ... conception of morals'.[51] Similar considerations apply to speech on religious matters.[52] However, in these cases the epistemic deficit is usually *only* normative, *not* factual. Courts must therefore strictly scrutinise whether the measure has been suitable and necessary to achieve the aim, but allow for a margin of appreciation with regard to the proportionality *sensu stricto*. Unfortunately, the Strasbourg Court ignored this fine but important distinction in *Müller* v. *Switzerland*.[53]

In addition, the margin of appreciation on the proportionality *sensu stricto* level only applies to the weighting of the principle that the interference aims at justifying. But no margin of appreciation applies with regard to weight attached to the impugned publication.[54] As a consequence, where political speech is at issue, a margin of appreciation concerning the

[47] *Sinclair Collis Ltd* v. *Secretary of State for Health* [2011] EWCA Civ 437 [126].

[48] See ECJ, *Deutscher Apothekerverband eV* v. *0800 DocMorris NV* [2003] ECR I-14887, Case C-322/01 [122].

[49] Articles 36, 45(3), 52(1), 62 TFEU. See, e.g., ECJ, *Schmidberger* v. *Austria* [2003] ECR I-05659, Case C-112/00 [82]; *Omega Spielhallen-und Automatenaufstellungs-GmbH* v. *Oberbürgermeisterin der Bundesstadt Bonn* [2004] ECR I-09609, Case C-36/02 [31].

[50] See Alexy (2002) p. 418.

[51] ECtHR, *Handyside* v. *United Kingdom* [1976] App. no. 5493/72 [48]; EComHR, *Hoare* v. *United Kingdom* [1997] App. no. 31211/96 [1]; Human Rights Committee, *Hertzberg and others* v. *Finland* [1985] Communication no. 61/1979 [10.3].

[52] See Chapter 12. [53] This will be further examined in Chapter 9, Section 9.2.

[54] See below Section 6.3.

value a Member State attaches to morals or the religious feelings of others may hardly justify the interference, because the high value attached to political speech is not subject to the Member State's margin of appreciation. This is why the Strasbourg Court's decisions in *Handyside* v. *United Kingdom* and *Otto-Preminger-Institut* v. *Austria* have to be criticised as well.[55]

Conversely, a margin of appreciation on the proportionality *sensu stricto* test is not to be granted where a normative uncertainty does not exist. For example, this is the case with regard to interferences protecting the authority and impartiality of the judiciary, a term international adjudicators interpret autonomously.[56] Therefore, the concept of authority and impartiality of the judiciary does not involve any legal uncertainty and is therefore subject to strict scrutiny.

Finally, even where states enjoy a margin of appreciation, the exercise of their discretion goes 'hand in hand' with supervision by international human rights courts and tribunals.[57] In its decision *Sunday Times* v. *United Kingdom (No. 1)*, the Strasbourg Court explained that its supervision is not limited to ascertaining whether a respondent state exercised its discretion reasonably, carefully and in good faith. Even a state so acting 'remains subject to the Court's control as regards the compatibility of its conduct with the engagements it has undertaken under the Convention'.[58]

The Strasbourg Court's decision *Animal Defenders International* v. *United Kingdom* brought a new twist into the Court's margin of appreciation jurisprudence, as applied to freedom of expression. The case concerned a ban on political advertising under the UK Communications Act 2003. The Court distinguished between 'general measures' interfering with freedom of expression and prior restraints. According to the Court, 'general measures' are rules 'which apply to pre-defined situations regardless of the individual facts of each case even if this might result in individual hard cases'.[59] The Court then laid down a three-step test to determine the proportionality of a 'general measure': (a) the legislative choices underlying the general measure, (b) the quality of the parliamentary and judicial review of the necessity of the measure, and (c) the risk of

[55] See Chapter 9, Section 9.2. [56] See Chapter 10.

[57] ECtHR, *Éditions Plon* v. *France* [2004] App. no. 58148/00 [42]; *Egeland and Hanseid* v. *Norway* [2009] App. no. 34438/04 [48]; *Ringier Axel Springer Slovakia, as* v. *Slovakia* [2011] App. no. 41262/05 [98].

[58] ECtHR, *Sunday Times* v. *United Kingdom (No. 1)* [1979] App. no. 6538/74 [59]; see also, amongst many further decisions, *Observer and Guardian* v. *United Kingdom* [1991] App. no. 13585/88 [59]; *Chauvy and others* v. *France* [2004] App. no. 64915/01 [65]; *Cumpănă and Mazăre* v. *Romania* [2004] App. no. 33348/96 [89].

[59] ECtHR, *Animal Defenders International* v. *United Kingdom* [2013] App. no. 48876/08 [106], with further references.

abuse if a general measure is relaxed.[60] The more convincing the general justifications for the general measure are, the less importance the Court will attach to its impact in the particular case.[61]

The Court then held that the

> central question as regards such measures is not, as the applicant suggested, whether less restrictive rules should have been adopted or, indeed, whether the State could prove that, without the prohibition, the legitimate aim would not be achieved. Rather the core issue is whether, in adopting the general measure and striking the balance it did, the legislature acted within the margin of appreciation afforded to it.[62]

However, the 'general measure' doctrine is to be rejected with regard to freedom of expression and media freedom. It confuses the principle of legality with the principle of proportionality. While the principle of legality asks whether the interference has been prescribed by valid law, the principle of proportionality always examines the application of this law in the concrete case. In addition, the proportionality of the general measure itself is a question of legality of the underlying authorisation to act (the 'prescribing law'). The fact that a general measure was enacted after proper legislative debate by a domestic parliament does not alter the Court's duty to apply the established standards that serve for the protection of human rights.[63] Human rights protection does not allow a double standard of review based on the interfering domestic act: for a human right, it is irrelevant whether an interference with that right originates in legislation or in a judicial or administrative act.[64]

6.3 The application of the principle of proportionality

As stated above, the proportionality test consists of the following three steps:

(1.) whether the interference was suitable to achieve the legitimate aim pursued (suitability);

[60] ECtHR, *Animal Defenders International* v. *United Kingdom* [2013] App. no. 48876/08 [108].

[61] ECtHR, *Animal Defenders International* v. *United Kingdom* [2013] App. no. 48876/08 [109].

[62] ECtHR, *Animal Defenders International* v. *United Kingdom* [2013] App. no. 48876/08 [110].

[63] ECtHR, *Animal Defenders International* v. *United Kingdom* [2013] App. no. 48876/08, joint dissenting opinion of Judges Ziemele, Sajó, Kalaydjieva, Vučinić and De Gaetano [8].

[64] ECtHR, *Animal Defenders International* v. *United Kingdom* [2013] App. no. 48876/08, joint dissenting opinion of Judges Ziemele, Sajó, Kalaydjieva, Vučinić and De Gaetano [10].

(2.) whether the interference was the least intrusive instrument amongst those which might achieve the legitimate aim (necessity); and
(3.) whether the interference was strictly proportionate to the legitimate aim pursued (proportionaility *sensu stricto*).

6.3.1 *Suitability to achieve the aim*

As a first step in the proportionality analysis, it needs to be investigated whether the interference was appropriate to achieve its function, that is, the pursuit of the legitimate aim in question. This is the case if the measure taken is effectively conducive to achieving the legitimate objective. As stated in the previous paragraph, Member States enjoy a certain margin of appreciation if factual uncertainty as to the suitability of the measure taken remains. This is particularly the case with regard to national security and public safety as reasons for the interference.

6.3.2 *No less intrusive means available: necessity or 'pressing social need'*

The second step of the proportionality test probes whether the action taken by the domestic authorities was necessary or, in the words of the Inter-American and the Strasbourg Court, whether there was a 'pressing social need' for the measure.[65] This is not the case if there was another measure to pursue the legitimate aim that would have been less restrictive, but nonetheless equally effective. The necessity test is therefore the search for Pareto-efficiency, a situation in which it is impossible to make anyone better off without making another one worse off.[66]

The necessity test has to be distinguished from the above-mentioned 'legitimate aim': the 'legitimate aim' test establishes whether the aim pursued by the interfering measure was *generally* legitimate. By contrast, the 'necessity' test asks whether it was necessary to protect the right or interest in the way it has been done *in the particular case*. In other words, the 'legitimate aim' test asks for the ends, whereas the 'necessity' test explores the means. The width of margin of appreciation granted to the states' authorities by the Strasbourg Court because of factual uncertainty plays a crucial role at this stage of the inquiry, because it decides whether the adjudicator examines the suitability of the applied measure and

[65] See, e.g., ECtHR, *Handyside* v. *United Kingdom* [1976] App. no. 5493/72 [48]; IACtHR, *Fontevecchia and D'Amico* v. *Argentina* [2011] Case 12.524 [54].
[66] Compare Alexy (2002) p. 105 fn. 222.

alternative measures with strict scrutiny, or whether it leaves this estimation to the discretion of the Member States.

In addition, the 'necessity' needs to be distinguished from the balancing of the conflicting rights or 'proportionality *sensu stricto*'. The 'necessity' test estimates the factual possibility to achieve the aim pursued with less severe means, but does not engage in a means/end analysis. This is left to the 'proportionality *sensu stricto*' balancing test. As a consequence, the 'legitimate aim' test logically precedes the 'necessity' test and the latter necessarily antedates the balancing test.

6.3.3 *Balancing the conflicting rights and interests: 'proportionality* sensu stricto*' or 'proportionality in a narrower sense'*

The concept of 'proportionality *sensu stricto*' or 'proportionality in a narrower sense' strongly reflects a consequentialist perception of human rights, and in this case of media freedom. Like freedom of expression, media freedom is not an absolute right, as the demands of public discourse may justify an interference with these rights: when exercising its freedom, the media is subject to 'duties and responsibilities', the scope of which depends on the particular situation. Under the proportionality *sensu stricto* test, adjudicators have to ask whether the sacrifice of media freedom is appropriate in relation to the advantages obtained through the interference. It implies that the enforcement of the civility rule has to be 'balanced' against the value of media freedom in the particular case. In order to be proportionate, the importance of the aim pursued by the restriction must 'outweigh' the gravity of the interference, taking into account the nature and severity of the measures imposed on the media, the importance of the competing right or interest and the degree to which it is affected.

This 'balancing exercise' has been subject to considerable debate, a detailed discussion of which would go beyond the scope of this book.[67] However, three main points of criticism should be briefly outlined in order to clarify that the approach taken here is not uncontroversial, but nonetheless at least justifiable: the 'balancing exercise' has been criticised, first, with a view to the alleged incommensurability of conflicting principles, second, for including 'irrational rulings' and, third, for its lack of legal certainty.

67 See, in particular, Habermas (1992) pp. 259 ff.; Post (1995) 1279; Chang (1997); Alexy (2002) pp. 47–8; Greer (2004) 412–24; Alexy (2005) 572–81; Schauer (2005b); Alder (2006); Zucca (2007); De Schutter (2010) pp. 324–6; Weinstein (2011a) 510–11; Barak (2012) pp. 340 ff.; Webber (2013).

The first point of criticism, the incommensurability of fundamental rights and thus the impossibility of balancing, has been inimitably summarised by Justice Scalia: 'It is more like judging whether a particular line is longer than a particular rock is heavy'.[68] And, admittedly, 'balancing' is not a particularly felicitous metaphor. It reflects the symbol of the Roman goddess Justitia, suggesting that a particular weight can be attached to rights in conflict in a quantifiable way, so that one right 'outweighs' the other. This is, however, not the case. A succinct analysis of what 'balancing' conflicting rights and interests actually includes has been provided by the principle of 'practical concordance' (*praktische Konkordanz*), developed by the German legal scholar Konrad Hesse and applied by the German Federal Constitutional Court.[69] The principle of 'practical concordance' aims at avoiding, to the fullest extent possible, sacrificing one right for the other. Rather, it seeks an *optimising* compromise between the conflicting or 'colliding' rights.

The second point of criticism is related to the argument of incommensurability and has been raised in particular by Jürgen Habermas. Accordingly, the notion of balancing increases the 'danger of irrational rulings', since there are allegedly no standards for rational control of a balancing exercise.[70] Furthermore, Habermas fears that balancing reduces the debate about the relationship between rights, or between a right and collective interests, to policy arguments.[71] As a consequence, constitutional rights are being deprived of their nature as 'trump in the argumentation game'.[72]

This argument finds strong support in US jurisprudence and scholarship. Two influential First Amendment scholars, Justice Black and Alexander Meiklejohn,[73] took the words of the First Amendment ('Congress shall make *no law*') literally and argued that the First Amendment does indeed prohibit any restrictions on 'speech' within the meaning of this provision. This approach, however, requires a narrow interpretation of what constitutes speech: Meiklejohn himself had to concede that the First Amendment does not establish 'an unlimited license to talk'.[74] As a consequence, certain forms of communication, which are lexically defined 'speech', should not be considered protected 'speech' within the meaning of the First Amendment. This includes Justice Holmes' famous example of falsely shouting fire in a theatre and causing a panic,[75]

[68] US Supreme Court, *Bendix Autolite Corp.* v. *Midwesco Enterprises, Inc.*, 486 US 888, 897 (1988) (Scalia J, concurring).
[69] Hesse (1999) para. 72. [70] Habermas (1992) p. 259. [71] See Greer (2004) 414.
[72] Habermas (1992) p. 259.
[73] See Black (1960); Meiklejohn (1961); see also Jeffery (1986) 224–6.
[74] Meiklejohn (1961) 249.
[75] US Supreme Court, *Abrams* v. *United States*, 250 US 616, 627 (1919).

malicious libel, misrepresentation or perjury.[76] Only activities 'utilized for the governing of the nation' should be considered protected speech under the First Amendment.[77]

Similarly, even the non-absolute reading of the First Amendment that prevails today is based on the presumption that if communication is categorised as 'speech' within the meaning of this clause, then it deserves strong, but not absolute, protection. This understanding allows for a wider interpretation of what constitutes 'speech' under the First Amendment, but requires US courts to define what kind of speech should *not* be protected under this clause. Those 'well-defined and narrowly limited classes of speech'[78] do *a priori* not receive First Amendment protection. This includes, for instance, speech that is directed at inciting or producing imminent lawless action and is likely to incite or produce such action, obscene speech and child pornography.[79]

The *a priori* categorisation of certain forms of speech certainly has the advantage of providing predictability and thus more legal certainty for the speaker. It is true that the balancing exercise does not necessarily lead to one precise outcome in every case – the many diverging decisions on the same case, even between chambers of the same court, are proof of that. This is an intrinsic part of the legal profession, in contrast to natural sciences, and a 'Judge Hercules'[80] has not been found yet.

But in contrast to the First Amendment, international conventions do not afford dominance to freedom of speech, but treat freedom of speech as a right with equal value to rights of others, especially privacy and reputation. They themselves address Habermas' concern that balancing undermines the 'strict priority' of fundamental rights over competing interests by establishing the reasons for which a liberty may be interfered with, such as in Article 10(2) ECHR and in Article 19(3) ICCPR. This, in turn, is one of the main doctrinal difficulties for the application of the First Amendment of the US Constitution, which itself does not provide any exception to freedom of speech.

International conventions and covenants therefore require a 'balancing exercise' when rights and interests are in conflict. The following elaborations should refute the arguments against *ad hoc* balancing with a view to media freedom by establishing rationally reviewable *conditions of rules* according to which a conflict between media freedom and a competing

[76] Meiklejohn (1961) 258. [77] Meiklejohn (1961) 256–7.

[78] US Supreme Court, *Chaplinsky* v. *New Hampshire*, 315 US 568, 571 (1942).

[79] On the 'imminent lawless action' test, see US Supreme Court, *Brandenburg* v. *Ohio*, 395 US 444 (1969); on obscenity, see *Miller* v. *California*, 413 US 15 (1973); on child pornography, see *New York* v. *Ferber*, 458 US 747 (1982).

[80] See Dworkin (1977) pp. 105 ff.

principle has to be solved. By establishing such rationally reviewable conditions, the outcome of a balancing process may be reasonably predictable. These conditions will then be expatiated upon in Part III. The *ad hoc* balancing exercise should hence be preferred to its alternative, the categorisation of 'appropriate' and 'inappropriate' norms.[81] The latter requires carving out certain phenomena *a priori* from the scope of a human right, which would usually be encompassed by this right. In essence, such an approach is merely a more abstract and less fine-tuned categorical balancing exercise, a 'definitional balancing'.[82]

One important aspect that has already been indicated[83] must again be highlighted: the following test can be applied regardless of whether media freedom has been the right that has been interfered with, or whether someone claims an interference with his right, such as the right to respect for private life, by the media. As the Strasbourg Court rightly held, 'the outcome of the application should not, in theory, vary according to whether it has been lodged with the Court under Article 8 of the Convention, by the person who was the subject of the article, or under Article 10 by the publisher'.[84]

6.3.3.1 *Per se* disproportionate interferences

The starting point of the proportionality *sensu stricto* analysis is the *abstract* weighting of the conflicting principles. It has been stated before that media freedom is not an absolute right. However, certain types of interferences are fundamentally contrary to media freedom in a way that they destroy the essence of this right, and may thus under no circumstances be justified. Such interferences include attacks on journalists targeted at their profession, such as arbitrary arrest, torture, threats to life and killing.[85] These cases usually not only amount to a violation of media freedom, but also to a violation of the right to life, personal

[81] Compare Habermas (1992) p. 260.

[82] Nimmer (1968) 942 n.24; Weinstein (2011b) 638–9.

[83] See Chapter 5, Section 5.2.3.

[84] ECtHR, *Von Hannover* v. *Germany (No. 2)* [2012] App. nos. 40660/08 and 60641/08 [106]; *Von Hannover* v. *Germany (No. 3)* [2013] App. no. 8772/10 [43].

[85] See, e.g., Human Rights Committee, *Mukong* v. *Cameroon* [1994] Communication no. 458/91 [9.7]; *Marques de Morais* v. *Angola* [2005] Communication no. 1128/2002 [6.8]; *Njaru* v. *Cameroon* [2007] Communication no. 1353/2005 [6.4]; AfComHPR, *Constitutional Rights Project, Civil Liberties Organisation and Media Rights Agenda* v. *Nigeria* [1999] App. nos. 140/94, 141/94 and 145/95 [37]; *Media Rights Agenda* v. *Nigeria* [2000] App no. 224/98 [69]; *John D. Ouko* v. *Kenya* [2000] App. no. 232/99 [28]; IACtHR, *Uzcátegui and others* v. *Venezuela* [2012] Case 12.661 [190]; *Vélez Restrepo* v. *Colombia* [2012] Case 12.658 [144] and [209]; IAComHR, *Carlos Ranferí Gómez López* v. *Guatemala* [1996] Case 11.303 [92]; *Hugo Bustios Saavedra* v. *Peru* [1997] Case 10.548 [76].

liberty or humane treatment. Such measures have to be considered disproportionate *per se*, regardless of the aim they pursue.

6.3.3.1.1 Prior restraints

'Prior restraint' covers all state measures which seek to prevent rather than to punish.[86] It is unclear whether media freedom contradicts any form of prior restraint or whether certain forms of prior restraint can be justified. For the sake of conceptual clarity, a categorisation into two different forms of prior restraint is called for: licensing requirements and judicial or administrative injunctions.

First, prior restraints may consist of a requirement to submit a publication to a public authority in advance in order to obtain permission to publish. Such licensing requirements had already been the subject of Milton's vigorous attack in *Areopagitica*. And also the German Federal Constitutional Court regards such requirements as 'censorship' within the meaning of Article 5(1)3 German Basic Law, which this provision prohibits in absolute terms.[87] Licensing requirements for books and newspapers cannot be reconciled with media freedom, and should therefore never be subject to a balancing exercise.

Second, it is more problematic whether prior restraints other than licensing requirements may be justifiable. Such a prior restraint occurs if a publication is not subject to a submission and licensing requirement, but is banned from first or further distribution by an administrative or a court order. Article 13(2) ACHR expressly prohibits such 'prior censorship', except for the caveat in Article 13(4) ACHR. The Inter-American Court interprets Article 13(2) ACHR broadly as a prohibition of any form of prior restraint.[88] This approach is similar to the jurisprudence of the US Supreme Court on the First Amendment.[89] Furthermore, the *travaux préparatoires* to Article 19 ICCPR indicate that an absolute prohibition on prior restraints was intended under this provision as well.[90] Finally, the jurisprudence of the African Commission also allows the conclusion that the Commission prohibits any kind of prior restraint.[91]

[86] Schauer (1982) p. 150.
[87] German Federal Constitutional Court, '*Censorship*' [1972] Case 1 BvL 13/67.
[88] See, e.g., IACtHR, *Palamara-Iribarne* v. *Chile* [2005] Case 11.571 [78]; Office of the Special Rapporteur for Freedom of Expression with the Inter-American Commission on Human Rights, Inter-American Legal Framework Regarding the Right to Freedom of Expression, 2009, CIDH/RELE/INF. 2/09, para. 144 ff.
[89] US Supreme Court, *Near* v. *Minnesota*, 283 US 697, 713 (1931); *Bantam Books, Inc* v. *Sullivan*, 372 US 58, 70 (1963); *New York Times Co.* v. *United States*, 403 US 713, 714 (1971).
[90] See Bossuyt (1987) pp. 398 ff.
[91] See AfComHPR, *Media Rights Agenda, Constitutional Rights Project, Media Rights Agenda and Constitutional Rights Project* v. *Nigeria* [1998] App. nos. 105/93, 128/94, 130/94 and

By contrast, the Strasbourg Court has consistently held that Article 10 ECHR does not generally prohibit the imposition of prior restraints. This is, according to the Court, evidenced by the words 'conditions', 'restrictions', 'preventing' and 'prevention' in Article 10(2) ECHR.[92] Accordingly, prior restraints may be 'justified in cases which demonstrate no pressing need for immediate publication and in which there is no obvious contribution to a debate of general public interest'.[93] However, the Strasbourg Court also conceded that 'news is a perishable commodity', and even a short delay of its publication may deprive it of all its value.[94] As a consequence, 'the dangers inherent in prior restraints are such that they call for the most careful scrutiny on the part of the Court'.[95] Where preventive measures are applied, the requirements for the legal basis to be regarded as 'law' within the meaning of Article 10(2) ECHR are particularly high. The provision on which the preventive measure is based must be formulated with sufficient precision to clarify the type of restrictions authorised, their purpose, duration, scope and control, and to enable the citizen to foresee the consequences of a violation of the prior restraint.[96] Restraints that are not imposed on particular types of news reports or articles, but on the future publications of entire newspapers, are not 'necessary' in a democratic society.[97]

152/96 [57] ('Of more concern is the total discretion and finality of the decision of the registration board, which effectively gives the government the power to prohibit publication of any newspapers or magazines they choose. This invites censorship and seriously endangers the rights of the public to receive information, protected by Article 9.1. There has thus been a violation of Article 9.1.') and *Amnesty International, Comité Loosli Bachelard, Lawyers' Committee for Human Rights, Association of Members of the Episcopal Conference of East Africa* v. *Sudan* [1999] App. nos. 48/90, 50/91, 52/91 and 89/93 [80] ('The government concerned has imposed a blanket restriction on the freedom of expression. This constitutes a violation of the spirit of Article 9.2.').

[92] ECtHR, *Sunday Times* v. *United Kingdom (No. 2)* [1991] App. no. 13166/87 [51]; see also *Association Ekin* v. *France* [2001] App. no. 39288/98 [56]; *Chauvy and others* v. *France* [2004] App. no. 64915/01 [47]; *Mosley* v. *United Kingdom* [2011] App. no. 48009/08 [117]; *Wizerkaniuk* v. *Poland* [2011] App. no. 18990/05 [65]. However, see also the partly dissenting opinion of Judge De Meyer (concerning prior restraint), joined by Judges Pettiti, Russo, Foighel and Bigi in *Observer and Guardian* v. *United Kingdom* [1991] App. no. 13585/88.

[93] ECtHR, *Mosley* v. *United Kingdom* [2011] App. no. 48009/08 [117].

[94] ECtHR, *Mosley* v. *United Kingdom* [2011] App. no. 48009/08 [117].

[95] See, e.g., ECtHR, *Observer and Guardian* v. *United Kingdom* [1991] App. no. 13585/88 [60]; *Mosley* v. *United Kingdom* [2011] App. no. 48009/08 [117]; *Wizerkaniuk* v. *Poland* [2011] App. no. 18990/05 [81]; see also Luhmann (1996) p. 33.

[96] ECtHR, *RTBF* v. *Belgium* [2011] App. no. 50084/06 [107–15].

[97] See ECtHR, *Ürper and others* v. *Turkey* [2009] App. nos. 14526/07, 14747/07, 15022/07, 15737/07, 36137/07, 47245/07, 50371/07, 50372/07 and 54637/07 [42–4]; *Güdenoğlu and others* v. *Turkey* [2013] App. nos. 42599/08, 30873/09, 38775/09, 38778/09, 40899/09, 40905/09, 43404/09, 44024/09, 44025/09, 47858/09, 53653/09, 5431/10 and 8571/10 [19].

The question, therefore, is whether an absolute prohibition of prior restraint should likewise apply to the ECHR. With regard to violations of Article 8 ECHR rights, the Strasbourg Court has held that *ex post facto* damages usually provide an adequate remedy.[98] The Strasbourg Court should take the consequent step to accept the absolute prohibition of any form of prior restraint as a general principle of media freedom as well, as was already suggested by Judge De Meyer in his partly dissenting opinion to *Observer and Guardian* v. *United Kingdom*[99] and in his dissenting opinion in *Wingrove* v. *United Kingdom.*[100] To be sure, the threat of *ex post* measures may already exert a considerable chilling effect on journalists. One could even argue that prior restraints are to the benefit of a publisher who is protected from a costly lawsuit. However, this argument is based on a tenuous premise, as the chilling effect of *ex post* measures is in itself problematic. Moreover, it is paternalistic with a view to both the publisher, who should decide for himself whether he takes the risk of being sued, and to society at large, which is prescribed what not to read.

6.3.3.1.2 Licensing and regulation of journalists and media companies

Licensing and regulation of media companies and journalists belong to the more divergent areas of media human rights law. Yet before entering into the analysis, the term 'media regulation' needs clarification. 'Media regulation' within the meaning of the following passages only refers to a regulatory system

(1.) enforced by the government or an administrative agency
(2.) specifically targeted against the media, and thus
(3.) to the exclusion of generally applicable – that is, not media-specific – rules of criminal law, administrative law and private law.

Unfortunately, this distinction has not always been made clear, as the overheated debate accompanying the UK Royal Charter on self-regulation of the press has shown. It is beyond doubt that journalists should not violate generally applicable criminal laws, for example, by hacking other people's mobile phones, even in the exercise of their profession. Likewise, journalists buying pens and paper are subject to contract law, just as media companies should obtain a required building licence before erecting an office building. This is not 'media regulation'.

[98] ECtHR, *Wizerkaniuk* v. *Poland* [2011] App. no. 18990/05 [83].
[99] ECtHR, *Observer and Guardian* v. *United Kingdom* [1991] App. no. 13585/88, partly dissenting opinion of Judge De Meyer (concerning prior restraint), joined by Judges Pettiti, Russo, Foighel and Bigi.
[100] ECtHR, *Wingrove* v. *United Kingdom* [1996] App. no. 17419/90, dissenting opinion of Judge De Meyer [1].

Instead, media regulation refers to the enforcement of media-specific rules by the executive branch of the state (necessarily based on a parliamentary statute). Examples are the FCC in the US or Ofcom in the UK. Defamation or violation of privacy torts are therefore not 'regulation' within the meaning of this definition.

Media regulation can be furcated into three areas: mere formal regulation, such as registration and licensing regimes for journalists (see (6.3.3.1.2.1)) and broadcasters (see (6.3.3.1.2.2)), and substantive, content-based regulation (see (6.3.3.1.2.3)).

6.3.3.1.2.1 Registration of journalists or compulsory membership in a journalist association Obligations for journalists to sign up to an official register or compulsory membership of journalists in a journalist association are often based on a formal, rather than a functional, understanding of journalism: accordingly, a journalist is a person whose name is registered on an official list or in an association, and thus only those persons enjoy the media's privileges. However, the notion of 'journalism' should be based on a functional rather than formal understanding: a journalist is someone who does journalistic work, which is not dependent on having one's name on a particular list.[101] On the contrary, compulsory registration or membership requirements may seriously impede journalistic activity and may even amount to censorship. As a consequence, one has to distinguish carefully between the different forms of registration, and the penalties attached to trespasses.

First, a licensing requirement for journalists that is based on the fulfilment of particular external or internal prerequisites, such as quotas, qualifications or content, are *per se* a disproportionate interference with media freedom. Such requirements would impede access to public discourse, which is a non-exclusive concept. Based on the 'press-as-technology' argument,[102] everyone should be entitled to journalistic activity.

Second, contrary to the view of the Human Rights Committee and the Strasbourg Court,[103] it is submitted that compulsory official registration of journalists *per se* violates media freedom if the registration regime is

[101] See Chapter 3, Section 3.3. [102] See Chapter 2, Section 2.1 and Section 2.2.1.

[103] Human Rights Committee, Concluding observations on Lesotho (CCPR/CO/79/Add. 106), para. 23; compare *Mavlonov et al.* v. *Uzbekistan* [2009] Communication no. 1334/2004 [8.4]; General Comment no. 34, para. 39; Nicol, Millar and Sharland (2009) para. 11.19. In ECtHR, *Gawęda* v. *Poland* [2002] App. no. 26229/95 [48], the Strasbourg Court held that a Polish registration scheme for registration of periodicals was not 'prescribed by law'.

based on sanctions, even if the requirements for the registration are purely formal. Although the interference is less grave than a licensing requirement that is dependent on prerequisites, a registration regime based on sanctions allows the state or a journalist association to control journalistic activity, and would thus turn the 'public watchdog' function of the media upside down. This has been most convincingly established by the Inter-American Court in its Advisory Opinion on Compulsory Membership in an Association Prescribed by Law for the Practice of Journalism. Following the decision *Stephen Schmidt* v. *Costa Rica*, where the Inter-American Commission held that obligatory membership of journalists or the requirement of a professional card does not unjustifiably restrict freedom of expression,[104] the government of Costa Rica requested an Advisory Opinion by the IACtHR on compulsory membership of journalists in an association prescribed by law. In its Advisory Opinion, the Court distinguished journalists from the organisation of other professions. While the organisation of professions in general by means of professional '*colegios*' is not *per se* contrary to the Convention by reasons of public order, this rationale does not apply to the media. Such regulation 'would have the effect of permanently depriving those who are not members of the right to make full use of the rights that Article 13 of the Convention grants to each individual. Hence, it would violate the basic principles of a democratic public order on which the Convention itself is based.'[105] The compulsory licensing of journalists is unnecessary, because 'the establishment of a law that protects the freedom and independence of anyone who practices journalism is perfectly conceivable without the necessity of restricting that practice only to a limited group of the community'.[106]

The African Commission expressly followed the Inter-American Court's approach in *Scanlen & Holderness* v. *Zimbabwe*. Yet the Commission observed *obiter* that self-regulation by journalists through their professional organisations, as opposed to a regulatory body whose regulations are drawn up by the government, would be allowed, provided that the registration procedures 'are purely technical and administrative in nature and do not involve prohibitive fees, or do not impose onerous conditions'.[107] However, the African Commission came to a different

104 IAComHR, *Stephen Schmidt* v. *Costa Rica* [1984] Case no. 9178 [6]; however, see also the dissenting opinion by Dr Bruce McColm.

105 IACtHR, Advisory Opinion OC-5/85 [68–76]; reiterated in IAComHR, *Juan José López* v. *Argentina* [2011] Case 11.395 [43].

106 IACtHR, Advisory Opinion OC-5/85 [79].

107 AfComHPR, *Scanlen & Holderness* v. *Zimbabwe* [2009] App. no. 297/05 [90]; see also *Media Rights Agenda, Constitutional Rights Project, Media Rights Agenda and*

conclusion in its Declaration of Principles on Freedom of Expression in Africa, where it stated that '[a]ny registration system for the print media shall not impose substantive restrictions on the right to freedom of expression.'[108] This implies that registration systems for the print media are not entirely prohibited.

Third, a voluntary accreditation scheme is basically compatible with media freedom, if the registration merely serves practical purposes, such as the receipt of a press card. However, the receipt of a press card should not be constitutive for being a journalist and the disadvantages of not having been registered must not be arbitrary. In those cases where a state applies limited accreditation schemes to provide journalists with privileged access to certain places or events, these schemes must not be applied in a discriminatory manner and they must provide a legal remedy to determine the legality of denying certain journalists access.[109]

In its 2011 decision *López* v. *Argentina*, the Inter-American Commission distinguished a system of compulsory membership of journalists from a law that did not prevent people from working as journalists, but rather offered benefits to journalists who had obtained an ID card and signed up for a retirement and pension system. However, it appeared from the facts of the case that the system did not only offer benefits to journalists, but that the issuing of a professional journalist's ID card and enrolment in the National Journalists' Pensions and Retirements System was necessary in order to work as a professional journalist and be considered as such.[110] Such a system, the Commission held, would effectively violate the prohibition of compulsory registration of journalists.

In its 1995 decision *Loersch and Nouvelle Association du Courrier* v. *Switzerland*, the European Commission of Human Rights held that it does not amount to a violation of Article 10 ECHR if privileged access to Supreme Court hearings and judgments requires accreditation of journalists that is subject to particular conditions, including a requirement that the journalist must have had legal training.[111] While it is justifiable to require prior accreditation for administrative purposes, the requirement of legal training would have to be reassessed with regard to

Constitutional Rights Project v. *Nigeria* [1998] App. nos. 105/93, 128/94, 130/94 and 152/96 [56].

108 AfComHPR, Declaration of Principles on Freedom of Expression in Africa, Section VIII(1).

109 Human Rights Committee, *Gauthier* v. *Canada* [1999] Communication no. 633/95 [13.7]; see also General Comment no. 34, para. 44. On the right of the media not to be discriminated against, see Chapter 4, Section 4.2.4.

110 IAComHR, *Juan José López* v. *Argentina* [2011] Case 11.395 [35].

111 EComHR, *Loersch and Nouvelle Association du Courrier* v. *Switzerland* [1995] App. nos. 23868/94 and 23869/94 [3].

citizen-journalists who did not undergo a prior education, but who work with a diligence comparable to professional journalists.[112]

Fourth, registration requirements for journalists have to be distinguished from transparency requirements. As institutions exercising a privileged influence in the public realm, the media should itself be subject to transparency.[113] It is therefore not absolutely prohibited to legally require statements of the ownership or authorship on media publishers, as has been done, for instance, in Article 5 AVMS Directive and Article 5 e-commerce Directive. Such transparency requirements should enable victims of media publications to seek redress. Only under exceptional circumstances may media publications be anonymous, for instance, in countries where critical journalistic activity is as such subject to repression, fear and intimidation.

6.3.3.1.2.2 Licensing and regulation of broadcasting By contrast to journalists, compulsory licensing requirements for broadcasters do not *per se* violate media freedom. Such licensing may be justified by the need to manage scarce resources, such as the electromagnetic wavelength spectrum.[114] Sentence 3 of Article 10(1) ECHR states that freedom of expression shall not prevent states from requiring the licensing of broadcasting, television or cinema enterprises. This provision has not been expressly transferred to the EUChFR. However, the Explanations to Article 11 EUChFR elaborate that 'Article 11 corresponds to Article 10' ECHR. Under the EUChFR, media licensing requirements constitute an interference with Article 11(2) alt. 1 EUChFR. However, the practical significance of this question is rather small under the EUChFR, because broadcasting licensing does not fall within the competences of the EU, but the Member States. Furthermore, Article 14(1) ACHR implicitly provides a legitimisation of Member States to regulate communication media by stating that '[a]nyone injured by inaccurate or offensive statements or ideas disseminated to the public in general *by a legally regulated medium of communication* has the right to reply' (emphasis added). Article 19 ICCPR does not include a provision corresponding to Article 10(1)3 ECHR, nor does the African Charter. However, the UN General Assembly rejected the inclusion of such a provision in the ICCPR lest it might be applied to interfere with free expression. Somewhat inconsistently, the General Assembly also

[112] See Chapter 3, Section 3.3. [113] Habermas (1962) p. 209.

[114] Council of Europe, Committee of Ministers, Recommendation CM/Rec(2011)7 on a new notion of media, Appendix, para. 77.

decided that such a provision was not necessary because licensing in the sense intended was regarded as being encompassed by the reference to 'public order' in Article 19(3) ICCPR anyway.[115] State Parties may thus impose licensing conditions and fees on the broadcasting media under the ICCPR as well.

No human rights provision explicitly or implicitly allows states to require such licensing in absolute terms. Rather, licensing requirements constitute 'interferences' and are therefore subject to the requirements for the justification of an interference.[116] Hence media regulation must be 'prescribed by law' and necessary in a democratic society for one of the legitimate purposes mentioned in the human rights catalogues. In this context, the granting of a broadcasting licence may also be made conditional on certain considerations, 'such as the nature and objectives of a proposed channel, its potential audience at national, regional or local level, the rights and needs of a specific audience and the obligations deriving from international legal instruments'.[117] Furthermore, states may impose a fee for the reception of a licence.

However, the prerequisites for the application of such conditions and licence fees have to be reasonable and objective, clear, transparent, non-discriminatory and otherwise in compliance with human rights, especially with procedural safeguards; furthermore, the broadcasting licensing authority should be independent.[118] In the case of *Centro Europa 7 Srl and Di Stefano* v. *Italy*, the Strasbourg Court observed that the mere receipt of a licence does not satisfy the requirements of Article 10 ECHR; in addition, the applicant must also be able to transmit its programmes via broadcasting frequencies. Failure to allocate such frequencies deprives the licence of all practical purpose since the activity it authorised

[115] See General Assembly Document A/5000 of the sixteenth session, 5 December 1961, para. 23; see also ECtHR, *Groppera Radio AG and others* v. *Switzerland* [1990] App. no. 10890/84 [61].

[116] See, e.g., ECtHR, *Groppera Radio AG and others* v. *Switzerland* [1990] App. no. 10890/84 [61]; *Informationsverein Lentia and others* v. *Austria* [1993] App. nos. 13914/88, 15041/89, 15717/89, 15779/89 and 17207/90 [29]; *Demuth* v. *Switzerland* [2002] App. no. 38743/97 [33]; *Glas Nadezhda EOOD and Elenkov* v. *Bulgaria* [2007] App. no. 14134/02 [44].

[117] ECtHR, *Centro Europa 7 Srl and Di Stefano* v. *Italy* [2012] App. no. 38433/09 [139].

[118] Human Rights Committee, Concluding observations on Lebanon (CCPR/CO/79/Add.78), para. 24; Concluding observations on Kyrgyzstan (CCPR/CO/69/KGZ), para. 21; Concluding observations on Ukraine (CCPR/CO/73/UKR), para. 22; AfComHPR, Declaration of Principles on Freedom of Expression in Africa, Section V(2). See also the reservation to Article 19(3) ICCPR by Italy: 'The provisions of article 19, paragraph 3, are interpreted as being compatible with the existing licensing system for national radio and television and with the restrictions laid down by law for local radio and television companies and for stations relaying foreign programmes.'

would be *de facto* impossible to carry out. 'This accordingly', the Court held, 'constituted a substantial obstacle to, and hence an interference with, the applicant company's exercise of its right to impart information and ideas'.[119]

6.3.3.1.2.3 Regulation of content The compliance of media content regulation with media freedom is particularly problematic. In this context, one has to distinguish between audiovisual media and print media.

Press freedom contradicts any notion of regulation that is content-based and press-specific. However, generally applicable provisions of private law, such as the tort of defamation, and of criminal law, such as criminal disclosure of state secrets and espionage,[120] are not press-specific and may therefore be applied to the press, albeit only in the narrow circumstances media freedom permits.[121]

By contrast, while an article based on words can be contradicted by words, pictures can neither be contradicted by words nor by pictures.[122] Television broadcasting media have a more immediate and suggestive impact than print media because of their power to convey messages through sound and images. The television's position as a source of information and entertainment 'in the intimacy of the listener's or viewer's home further reinforces [its] impact.'[123] Marshall McLuhan described this phenomenon with the famous words 'the medium is the message'.[124] Consequently, enhanced duties and responsibilities apply to audiovisual media. States are therefore to a certain extent permitted to regulate audiovisual media content to ensure the protection of civility rules for public discourse and media pluralism.[125]

And although First Amendment doctrine imposes less duties and responsibilities on the media than international adjudicators, the US Supreme Court held that different First Amendment standards apply to

[119] *Centro Europa 7 Srl. and Di Stefano* v. *Italy* [2012] App. no. 38433/09 [138].

[120] See, e.g., Sections 96 and 97 German Criminal Law Code, Sections 253 and 254 Austrian Criminal Law Code, or the US Espionage Act 1917.

[121] See Chapters 7 and 8. [122] Compare Luhmann (1996) p. 40.

[123] ECtHR, *Manole and others* v. *Moldova* [2009] App. no. 13936/02 [97], citing ECtHR, *Jersild* v. *Denmark* [1994] App. no. 15890/89 [31]. See also, for example, *Monnat* v. *Switzerland* [2006] App. no. 73604/01 [68]; *TV Vest AS & Rogaland Pensjonistparti* v. *Norway* [2008] App. no. 21132/05 [60]; *Centro Europa 7 Srl and Di Stefano* v. *Italy* [2012] App. no. 38433/09 [132]; EComHR, *Purcell and others* v. *Ireland* [1991] App. no. 15404/89; Human Rights Committee, *Hertzberg and others* v. *Finland* [1985] Communication no. 61/1979 [10.4]; General Comment no. 34, para. 34.

[124] McLuhan (1964) p. 7. [125] See Chapter 14.

broadcasters: 'of all forms of communication, it is broadcasting that has received the most limited First Amendment protection.'[126] For example, in *Red Lion Broadcasting* v. *FCC*, the Supreme Court upheld an FCC policy requiring broadcasters to present discussions of public issues, and to give each side of those issues fair coverage (the so-called 'fairness doctrine').[127] This decision is quite remarkable, as the Supreme Court emphasised that '[i]t is the right of viewers and listeners, not the right of the broadcasters, which is paramount'.[128] The Court thus revealed an even more instrumentalist and consequentialist understanding of the role of broadcasting media than the European Court of Human Rights.

6.3.3.1.3 Criminal sanctions

So far, international courts have not considered criminal measures as a disproportionate response to an unlawful publication as such.[129] However, there is a strong and convincing international move towards the general abolition of criminal sanctions, in particular prison sentences,[130], for defamation.[131] Laws criminalising defamation are *per se* disproportionate to protect the reputation of others. They are unnecessary, because a civil court's judgment in favour of the victim would be a sufficient remedy to vindicate the victim's reputation by publicly establishing that the defendant was not entitled to issue the statement. They are also disproportionate because their mere existence has a dissuasive effect on anyone who intends to contribute to a matter of general interest, but has to consider the risk of criminal liability, even if the imposed fine is rather low.[132] The threat of civil liability is an adequate deterrence.

126 US Supreme Court, *FCC* v. *Pacifica Foundation*, 438 US 726 (1978).

127 US Supreme Court, *Red Lion Broadcasting* v. *FCC*, 395 US 367 (1969). However, the Federal Communications Commission (FCC) repealed the 'fairness doctrine' in 1987; see Weaver (2006) p. 707.

128 US Supreme Court, *Red Lion Broadcasting* v. *FCC*, 395 US 367, 390 (1969).

129 See, e.g., ECtHR, *Radio France and others* v. *France* [2004] App. no. 53984/00 [40]; *Lindon, Otchakovsky-Laurens and July* v. *France* [2007] App. nos. 21279/02 and 36448/02 [59]; *Rumyana Ivanova* v. *Bulgaria* [2008] App. no. 36207/03 [68]; *Saaristo and others* v. *Finland* [2010] App. no. 184/06 [69].

130 See ECtHR, *Cumpănă and Mazăre* v. *Romania* [2004] App. no. 33348/96 [116]; *Belpietro* v. *Italy* [2013] App. no. 43612/10 [61].

131 See, e.g., Human Rights Committee, Concluding observations on Algeria (CCPR/C/DZA/CO/3), para. 24; Concluding observations on Italy (CCPR/C/ITA/CO/5); Council of Europe, Parliamentary Assembly, Resolution 1577 (2007): Towards Decriminalisation of Defamation; AfComHPR, Resolution on Repealing Criminal Defamation Laws in Africa. From academic scholarship, see, e.g., Grossman (2001) 646; O'Fathaigh (2013); Pasqualucci (2006) 403–5.

132 See, for instance, ECtHR, *Brasilier* v. *France* [2006] App. no. 71343/01 [43]: one 'symbolic franc'; *Fatullayev* v. *Azerbaijan* [2010] App. no. 40984/07 [102].

Criminal defamation laws are also prone to abuse, as they enable states to stifle unpalatable expression.

Where criminal laws sanctioning media publications are still in place, international human rights courts and tribunals must carry out strict supervision if a criminal penalty, in particular a sentence of imprisonment, is at issue.[133] The imposition of a criminal sentence for a media-specific offence will be compatible with media freedom only in exceptional circumstances, notably where human rights of others or national security concerns have been seriously impaired.[134] In addition, the imposition of criminal penalties does not only have to be measured against media freedom, but also against the prohibition of deprivation of liberty (Article 9 ICCPR, Article 5 ECHR, Article 6 AfCHPR and Article 7 ACHR).[135] Similarly, an order prohibiting journalists from working as journalists calls for the most careful scrutiny and may be justified only in exceptional circumstances.[136]

6.3.3.2 Determination of the competing principles in relative terms

If the interference with media freedom is not unjustified in abstract terms, then, as a second step, the value attached to media freedom, on the one hand, and to the conflicting interest, on the other hand, must be estimated in *relative* terms with a view to the particular case. According to Robert Alexy, 'the greater the degree of non-satisfaction of, or detriment to, one principle, the greater must be the importance of satisfying the other'.[137] Neither media freedom nor any other norm – apart from rights protected in absolute terms, such as human dignity[138] – enjoys precedence *per se* over the other.

[133] Amongst many other authorities, see Human Rights Committee, General Comment no. 34, para. 47; ECtHR, *Wille* v. *Liechtenstein* [1999] App. no. 28396/95 [50]; *Nikula* v. *Finland* [2002] App. no. 31611/96 [54]; IACtHR, *Ricardo Canese* v. *Paraguay* [2004] Case 12.032 [106]; *Kimel* v. *Argentina* [2008] Case 12.450 [94].

[134] ECtHR, *Cumpǎnǎ and Mazǎre* v. *Romania* [2004] App. no. 33348/96 [115]; *Saaristo and others* v. *Finland* [2010] App. no. 184/06 [69]; *Fatullayev* v. *Azerbaijan* [2010] App. no. 40984/07 [103].

[135] See, amongst many other authorities, Human Rights Committee, *Fernando* v. *Sri Lanka* [2005] Communication no. 1189/2003 [9.2]; *Dissanayake* v. *Sri Lanka* [2005] Communication no. 1373/2005 [8.2].

[136] See, *mutatis mutandis*, ECtHR, *Cumpǎnǎ and Mazǎre* v. *Romania* [2004] App. no. 33348/96 [118]; see also German Federal Constitutional Court, '*Professional ban I*' [1959] Case 1 BvL 118/53; *mutatis mutandis*, '*Professional ban II*' [1969] Case 1 BvR 438/65: professional ban for journalists may be issued only by the Federal Constitutional Court.

[137] Alexy (2002) p. 102.

[138] See Article 1 EUChFR; Article 1(1) of the German Basic Law; McCrudden (2008).

6.3.3.2.1 The weight attached to the legitimate aim pursued

Article 19 ICCPR, Article 10 ECHR, Article 13 ACHR and Article 9 AfCHPR are founded on the – rebuttable – presumption that freedom of expression and media freedom prevail over the *public* interest rules of civility[139] that may justify an interference, unless there are pressing reasons why the public interest should supersede. This follows from the principle *in dubio pro libertate*. In *Sunday Times* v. *United Kingdom (No. 1)*, the ECtHR developed the relevant guidelines for the interpretation of Article 10(2) ECHR, which should apply to the other Conventions as well:

> The Court is faced not with a choice between two conflicting principles but with a principle of freedom of expression that is subject to a number of exceptions which must be narrowly interpreted. . . . It is not sufficient that the interference involved belongs to that class of the exceptions listed in Article 10(2) which has been invoked; neither is it sufficient that the interference was imposed because its subject-matter fell within a particular category or was caught by a legal rule formulated in general or absolute terms: the Court has to be satisfied that the interference was necessary having regard to the facts and circumstances prevailing in the specific case before it.[140]

Freedom of expression and media freedom thus enjoy *prima facie* precedence *vis-à-vis* the public interests protected by the limitation clauses. Therefore, the restrictions in Article 19(3) ICCPR, Article 13(2) ACHR, Article 10(2) ECHR and Article 27(2) AfCHPR must be construed strictly and the necessity for any restrictions must be convincingly established.[141]

However, the justification of an interference for the protection of another *individual's* human rights,[142] especially the right to respect for one's private life, differs significantly from the approach to a justification based on public interest. Cases in which the exercise of media freedom potentially violates the human rights of others require balancing of conflicting *equal* rights rather than presuming that media freedom prevails. Both media freedom and the right to respect for private life are qualified rights and neither has pre-eminence over the other.[143] International

[139] See Chapters 8 ff.

[140] ECtHR, *Sunday Times* v. *United Kingdom (No. 1)* [1979] App. no. 6538/74 [65] (references omitted).

[141] See, e.g., ECtHR, *Observer and Guardian* v. *United Kingdom* [1991] App. no. 13585/88 [59]; *Thorgeir Thorgeirson* v. *Iceland* [1992] App. no. 13778/88 [63]; *Tammer* v. *Estonia* [2001] App. no. 41205/98 [59]; UN Economic and Social Council, Siracusa Principles on the Limitation and Derogation Provisions in the International Covenant on Civil and Political Rights, UN Doc. E/CN.4/1985/4, Annex (1985).

[142] See Chapter 7 and also Chapter 12.

[143] See ECtHR, *Hachette Filipacchi Associés ("Ici Paris")* v. *France* [2009] App. no. 12268/03 [41]; *Mosley* v. *United Kingdom* [2011] App. no. 48009/08 [111]; *Von Hannover* v.

monitoring bodies must therefore scrutinise whether the domestic authorities struck a fair balance between the two equal conflicting values.

6.3.3.2.2 The weight attached to the exercise of media freedom: the media's contribution to public discourse

The media is protected not for its own sake or for its 'self-fulfilment', but for fulfilling a function to the benefit of a democratic society in general. As a consequence, the intensity of protection afforded to the media depends on whether it fulfils this function, or whether it abuses its position. The significance attached to the exercise of media freedom thus has to be determined with recourse to the question of whether the media observed its duties and responsibilities. Where the media does not act according to its duties and responsibilities, the relative importance of the protection of media freedom is significantly lowered. As a consequence, an interference with media freedom is then usually justified. The 'duties and responsibilities' clause is therefore, doctrinally, an aspect of the balancing exercise under the principle of proportionality.[144]

In order to determine what the media's duties and responsibilities are, recourse must be had to the rationale that explains the enhanced protection of the media: the argument from public discourse.[145] According to the public discourse rationale, the media should enjoy enhanced protection because of its ability to contribute to matters of public concern on a grand scale, provided that they act on an accurate factual basis, and, in cases of inaccuracies, in good faith.

Publications on matters of public concern are of utmost importance for any democratic society, and thus deserve strong protection.[146] In

Germany (No. 2) [2012] App. nos. 40660/08 and 60641/08 [106]; IACtHR, *Fontevecchia and D'Amico* v. *Argentina* [2011] Case 12.524 [50]; Office of the Special Rapporteur for Freedom of Expression with the Inter-American Commission on Human Rights, Inter-American Legal Framework Regarding the Right to Freedom of Expression, 2009, CIDH/RELE/INF. 2/09, para. 103; Fenwick and Phillipson (2006) p. 1070; Nicol, Millar and Sharland (2009) para. 5.21.

144 Grote and Wenzel (2013) para. 72.

145 See Chapter 2, Section 2.2.3.

146 See, e.g., Human Rights Committee, *Bodrožić* v. *Serbia and Montenegro* [2005] Communication no. 1180/2003 [7.2]; *Coleman* v. *Australia* [2006] Communication no. 1157/2003 [7.3]; *Benhadj* v. *Algeria* [2007] Communication no. 1173/2003 [8.10]; *Mavlonov and others* v. *Uzbekistan* [2009] Communication no. 1334/2004 [8.4]; Concluding observations on Japan (CCPR/C/JPN/CO/5), para. 26; ECtHR, *Lingens* v. *Austria* [1986] App. no. 9815/82; *Oberschlick* v. *Austria (No. 1)* [1991] App. no. 11662/85 [59]; *Castells* v. *Spain* [1992] App. no. 11798/85 [46]; *Flux* v. *Moldova (No. 1)* [2006] App. no. 28702/03 [32]; AfComHPR, *International PEN, Constitutional Rights Project, Civil Liberties Organisation and Interights (on behalf of Ken Saro-Wiwa Jnr.)* v. *Nigeria* [1995] App. nos. 137/94, 139/94, 154/96 and 161/97 [110]; *Kenneth Good* v. *Republic of Botswana* [2010] App. no. 313/05 [198]; IACtHR, *Ivcher-Bronstein* v. *Peru* [2001] Case 11.762 [155].

turn, rather weak protection should be granted to reporting on exclusively private matters. Where the private lives of individuals serve mere entertainment purposes, the media does not exercise its role as 'public watchdog' in a democracy and thus does not contribute to public discourse on matters of general concern. The media's protection may then have to yield to the requirements of Article 17 ICCPR, Article 11 ACHR, Article 8 ECHR or Article 27(2) AfCHPR. Moreover, publications that incite hatred or violence or are directed against a democratic society's underlying values enjoy very little protection.

In contrast to this content-based differentiation, the *form* in which certain material is presented lies, in the first place, in the speaker's or publisher's discretion.[147] Article 19(2) ICCPR and Article 13(1) ACHR congruently provide that freedom of expression includes freedom to impart information and ideas 'either orally, in writing, in print, in the form of art, or through any other medium of one's choice'. It is therefore submitted that the distinction of classes of speech that currently prevails in legal scholarship – the categories of political, commercial and artistic speech – should be rejected. Neither descriptive nor normative theory warrants 'artistic speech' as a distinct category of speech. Rather, 'artistic speech', such as satires, caricatures, poetry, films or novels, deserves the same protection as investigative newspaper articles if it contributes to a matter of general interest. Artistic speech should thus not be perceived as a category of speech *content*, but rather as a *form* of speech. It is not a coincidence that early classics of English literature were written by journalists and pamphleteers such as Daniel Defoe and Jonathan Swift. Moreover, William Hogarth is not only considered the first cartoonist in Western history, but also the first *political* cartoonist.[148] In today's leisure culture even entertainment may be used as a way of informing the public, so-called 'infotainment'.

6.3.3.3 Reconciliation of the conflicting interests through alternative means

Rather than one interest necessarily preceding the other, as is the case with rules, principles are norms which require the greatest possible realisation. This also applies to media freedom. Both media freedom and the principle conflicting with it should be optimised according to the principle of practical concordance. This requires considering the value attached to the exercise of media freedom, on the one hand, and the gravity of the interference in pursuit of the conflicting interest, on the

[147] See Chapter 4, Section 4.1.3.
[148] See Keane (2008) 850, providing further references.

other hand. As a consequence, a 'balancing exercise' is not a binary procedure. It is a consideration of alternatives that achieve only part of the aim, but interfere only partly with the protected right. It requires comparing the marginal benefit for the protected interest with the marginal damage inflicted upon the right that has been interfered with.[149] This examination should not be confused with the necessity test: the necessity test asks whether a less intrusive means is equally suitable to achieve the same aim, searching for legal Pareto-efficiency. Practical concordance, by contrast, looks for alternatives which are less intrusive to the right that has been interfered with, but which are also less suitable to achieve the aim. In Pareto terms, the principle of practical concordance makes the protection of one interest 'better off', while making the pursuit of another interest 'worse off'.

With regard to media freedom and freedom of expression, the application of the principle of practical concordance may have a significant impact in two ways: first, with regard to alternatives concerning an impugned media action, and second, with regard to alternatives concerning the severity of the interference. Only in cases where no such alternatives are conceivable, the relative weight attached to the interests concerned remains the decisive factor.

6.3.3.3.1 Alternative ways of publication

Rather than asking, for example, whether a newspaper or broadcasting report allegedly violating rights and interests of others may be published or not, the principle of practical concordance requires an analysis as to what can be done to *reconcile* the conflicting interests. As a consequence, the media itself, when publishing an article or a broadcast, is under an obligation to consider the rights and interests of others when conducting its work, and to accommodate them as prudently as possible. The search for less intrusive alternative ways of publication is part of the media's duties and responsibilities.

This may include, for example, that the report may be basically published, but has to omit certain expressive terms, or can only be published after a certain lapse of time.[150] Where the publication of a privacy-related photo in addition to an article is concerned, one has to ask whether the publication of this photo was necessary to ensure the credibility of the story.[151] The – newsworthy – fact that a famous actor has been the victim of a burglary does not need to be corroborated by the publication of her

[149] Barak (2012) pp. 129 ff.
[150] See ECtHR, *Éditions Plon* v. *France* [2004] App. no. 58148/00 [51].
[151] See Chapter 7, Section 7.3.4.1.1.2.

home address.[152] Finally, where a state claims that the publication of a secret document interferes with matters of national security and poses a threat to the lives of agents, the media has to examine whether a shortened version of the document may satisfy the public interest in its publication, but does not risk the lives of others.

However, the media's responsibility to resort to alternative means in order to get its message across should not be overstrained. Journalists should enjoy considerable leeway in the way they present their material, including room for exaggeration and provocation,[153] and courts should not try to take their place. Especially the argument that there has allegedly been a more 'ethical' way to gather or present material should not be applied.[154] As has been stated before, journalistic freedom should find its external boundaries in the *law*, especially in the rights of others, and not in the *ethics* of journalism.[155]

6.3.3.3.2 Alternative ways of interference

It is not only for the media to contemplate a less intrusive means of publication, but also for the interfering state to consider less intrusive interferences. Based on the observations made above a), state authorities should take into consideration:

(1.) *Ex post* rather than *ex ante* measures: although *ex post* measures are usually less effective to protect another person's reputation or privacy, they nonetheless have to be considered as a less intrusive, and thus more proportionate, invasion of media freedom.

(2.) Civil rather than criminal liability: where criminal sanctions for media wrongdoing are still enforced, they must be applied with the utmost reservation, and mere civil liability has to be considered as a less intrusive remedy.

(3.) Mere transparency requirements rather than voluntary membership in a journalistic organisation.

[152] ECtHR, *Alkaya* v. *Turkey* [2012] App. no. 42811/06 [36].
[153] See Chapter 4, Section 4.1.3.
[154] See, however, ECtHR, *Ricci* v. *Italy* [2013] App. no. 30210/06 [57].
[155] See Chapter 2, Section 2.2.3.3.

Part III

Specific limitations to media freedom

7 Personality rights and intellectual property as 'rights of others'

Article 19(3)(a) ICCPR, Article 10(2) ECHR, Article 27(2) AfCHPR and Article 13(2)(a) ACHR state that the exercise of freedom of expression may be subject to, *inter alia*, restrictions as are necessary for the protection of the rights of others. With regard to limitations on media freedom, the most relevant 'rights of others' are the rights relating to one's personality: the right to respect for honour, reputation and privacy according to Article 17 ICCPR and Article 11 ACHR, and the right to private life according to Article 8(1) ECHR and Article 7 EUChFR. A personality right in the broader sense is freedom of religion according to Article 18 ICCPR, Article 9(1) ECHR, Article 8 AfCHPR and Article 12 ACHR.[1] Further 'rights of others' are intellectual property rights and other exclusive rights.[2]

On a sidenote, neither privacy nor reputation is constitutionally protected in the United States. This accounts for many of the divergencies between the Supreme Court's and international adjudicators' case law.

7.1 The taxonomy of 'personality rights'

The wording of international conventions is not coherent regarding the protection of honour, reputation and privacy. Article 17 ICCPR is the only provision expressly protecting privacy, honour and reputation. Article 8 ECHR, Article 7 EUChFR and Article 11 ACHR use the term 'private life' instead of 'privacy', and Article 8 ECHR does not expressly protect honour and reputation at all. However, it is submitted that the ICCPR, the ACHR and the ECHR/EUChFR merely use different terms for the same legal concept. Together with the right to privacy,[3] honour and reputation are thus sub-categories of the concept of 'private life'.[4] For this reason, the reference to 'reputation' in Article 10(2) ECHR is redundant.

[1] See Chapter 12. [2] See below Section 7.4. [3] See Chapter 2, Section 2.2.3.1.
[4] On reputation, see, e.g., ECtHR, *Chauvy and others* v. *France* [2004] App. no. 64915/01 [70]; *Radio France and others* v. *France* [2004] App. no. 53984/00 [31]; *Pfeifer* v. *Austria* [2007] App. no. 12556/03 [35]; *Petrina* v. *Romania* [2008] App. no. 78060/01 [19]; *Print*

The distinction between reputation and privacy is based on the dichotomy of factual information and comment, and the further distinction between true and false factual information.[5] False statement of facts (which includes 'leaving out true facts which, had they been stated, could have significantly altered the perception of the matter'[6]) and defamatory comment may tarnish a person's honour. By contrast, privacy rights are usually engaged where true but private information is being gathered or disclosed.[7] Furthermore, the concept of 'honour' can be sub-categorised into a person's self-esteem and a person's esteem by others, that is, a person's reputation. As a consequence, reputation is itself a sub-category of honour. For instance, the tort of defamation protects a person's reputation and not just a person's honour, as it requires that at least one recipient of the defamatory statement is not identical to the defamed person. By contrast, the legal concept of 'insult'[8] also protects against a violation of a person's self-esteem by punishing derogatory statements made face-to-face.

Unlike Article 12 UDHR, Article 17 ICCPR and Article 11(3) ACHR, Article 8 ECHR does not expressly provide for a right to protection against attacks on a person's honour and reputation. However, the ECtHR has, in recent cases, recognised reputation and also honour as part of the right to respect for private life. As the Strasbourg Court established in *Radio France* v. *France*, the right to protection of one's reputation is one of the rights guaranteed by Article 8 ECHR as one element of the right to respect for private life.[9] The Court explained in *Pfeifer* v. *Austria* and reiterated in *Petrina* v. *Romania* that 'a person's reputation ... forms part of his or her personal identity and psychological

Zeitungsverlag GmbH v. *Austria* [2013] App. no. 26547/07 [31]. On honour, see, e.g., ECtHR, *Polanco Torres et Movilla Polanco* v. *Spain* [2010] App. no. 34147/06 [40]; *A.* v. *Norway* [2009] App. no. 28070/06 [64].

5 See Chapter 4, Section 4.1.2.

6 ECtHR, *Shabanov and Tren* v. *Russia* [2006] App. no. 5433/02 [36].

7 Compare Marshall (1992) 54; ECtHR, *Markt intern Verlag GmbH and Klaus Beermann* v. *Germany* [1989] App. no. 10572/83 [35]. But see also *John Terry (previously referred to as "LNS")* v. *Persons Unknown* [2010] EWHC 119 (QB) [96]: 'the law of privacy gives rise to an overlap with the law of defamation', albeit 'only in limited classes of cases'. For example, under US law, the publication of untrue facts that are not defamatory, but which portray a person in a 'false light', may give rise to a tort of invasion of privacy; see Prosser (1960) 400. In turn, under German Law, a violation of a person's reputation may occur despite proof of truth if the insult results from the circumstances under which the statement was made (Section 192 German Criminal Law Code).

8 See, e.g., Section 185 German Criminal Law Code.

9 ECtHR, *Radio France and others* v. *France* [2004] App. no. 53984/00 [31]; reiterated in, for example, *Pfeifer* v. *Austria* [2007] App. no. 12556/03 [35]; *Petrina* v. *Romania* [2008] App. no. 78060/01 [19]; *Alithia Publishing Company Ltd and Constantinides* v. *Cyprus* [2008] App. no. 17550/03 [53]. See also Fenwick and Phillipson (2006) p. 1069.

integrity and therefore also falls within the scope of his or her "private life"'.[10] An individual's reputation and honour[11] are thus not only protected as defensive rights against free speech, as Article 10(2) ECHR suggests.[12] Rather, they have their own value as fundamental rights, namely as characteristics of the right to respect for private life as guaranteed in Article 8(1) ECHR.

However, the ECtHR's case law has not been consistent in this respect. In *Karakó* v. *Hungary,*[13] the Second Section of the Court held that there was no conflict between Article 8 ECHR, which the applicant invoked because he claimed to be violated in his reputation, and Article 10 ECHR. Referring to the *von Hannover (No. 1)* decision, the judges distinguished between 'personal integrity and reputation, the two being protected in different legal ways', whereby 'reputation has traditionally been protected by the law of defamation as a matter related primarily to financial interests or social status'.[14] Different from matters of reputation, rights to personal integrity falling within the scope of Article 8 ECHR were unrelated to the external evaluation of an individual.[15] The external evaluation may harm a person's esteem by society, but not one's inalienable integrity. Reputation may only be deemed to be an independent right 'under exceptional circumstances', particularly when 'the factual allegations were of such a seriously offensive nature that their publication had an inevitable direct effect on the applicant's private life'.[16] The Court suggested that the 'inherent logic of Article 10, that is to say the special rule contained in its second paragraph, precludes the possibility of conflict with Article 8'.

In *Axel Springer AG* v. *Germany (No. 1)*, however, the Grand Chamber of the Court alleviated the strict *Karakó* requirements for reputation to fall under Article 8(1) ECHR – most notably: without even citing the *Karakó* decision.[17] In *Axel Springer AG (No. 1)*, the Court merely required that 'an attack on a person's reputation must attain a certain level of seriousness' in order for Article 8 ECHR to come into play, thus confirming that reputation is a sub-category of the notion of 'private life'.[18] This

[10] ECtHR, *Pfeifer* v. *Austria* [2007] App. no. 12556/03 [35]; *Petrina* v. *Romania* [2008] App. no. 78060/01 [29].
[11] ECtHR, *A.* v. *Norway* [2009] App. no. 28070/06 [64].
[12] For this approach, see *Douglas* v. *Hello!* [2001] QB 967, CA 1003 [136]; *Berezovski* v. *Forbes Inc (No. 2)* [2001] EWCA Civ 1251 [11].
[13] ECtHR, *Karakó* v. *Hungary* [2009] App. no. 39311/05 [25].
[14] ECtHR, *Karakó* v. *Hungary* [2009] App. no. 39311/05 [22].
[15] ECtHR, *Karakó* v. *Hungary* [2009] App. no. 39311/05 [23].
[16] ECtHR, *Karakó* v. *Hungary* [2009] App. no. 39311/05 [23].
[17] ECtHR, *Axel Springer AG* v. *Germany (No. 1)* [2012] App. no. 39954/08 [83].
[18] *Axel Springer AG* v. *Germany (No. 1)* [2012] App. no. 39954/08 [83] (emphasis added); confirmed in *Delfi AS* v. *Estonia* [2013] App. no. 64569/09 [80]; *Tănăsoaica* v. *Romania*

attenuation of *Karakó* is to be appreciated, since the Second Section's reasoning in *Karakó* is unconvincing. The fact that reputation is mentioned in Article 10(2) ECHR does not mean that it may not be protected by other provisions as well. Furthermore, a comparison between the ECHR and other international human rights catalogues suggests that both reputation and privacy should be perceived as a 'personality right' and thus be protected by Article 8(1) ECHR. Article 17(1) ICCPR and Article 11(3) ACHR expressly protect privacy/private life and reputation in the same paragraph.[19] Similarly, Article 12 UDHR, upon which Article 8(1) ECHR is patterned,[20] stipulates that: 'No one shall be subjected to arbitrary interference with his privacy ... nor to attacks upon his honour and reputation. Everyone has the right to the protection of the law against such interference or attacks.'

Remarkably, in recent decisions involving a balancing exercise between freedom of expression and reputation, Sections of the ECtHR neither referred to *Karakó* nor to *Axel Springer AG (No. 1)*. Rather, the Sections either based their decision only on pre-*Radio France* case-law[21] or they avoided the question entirely.[22] This reveals that the Court's jurisprudence in this respect is far from settled.

In addition to the 'rights of others', Article 10(2) ECHR also allows interferences in order to protect 'information received in confidence'. If this confidential information is private information rather than a state secret, it is in itself a sub-category of the right to privacy, so-called 'information privacy'.[23] As such, it is protected by the notion of 'private life' under Article 8 ECHR and also Article 17 ICCPR and Article 12 UDHR, where 'information received in confidence' has not been expressly mentioned as a legitimate aim justifying an interference.

Unlike the other international human rights catalogues, the African Charter recognises neither a right to privacy nor a right to honour. According to Article 5 sentence 1 of the Charter, '[e]very individual shall have the right to the respect of the dignity inherent in a human being and to the recognition of this legal status'. One might argue that the concept of human dignity under the Charter also includes a right to privacy and reputation. However, Article 5 sentence 1 AfCHPR has to be read in

[2012] App. no. 3490/03 [37] and *Lavric* v. *Romania* [2014] App. no. 22231/05 [31]: 'a certain level of gravity'.

19 'No one shall be subjected to arbitrary or unlawful interference with his privacy, family, home or correspondence, nor to unlawful attacks on his honour and reputation.'

20 Janis, Kay and Bradley (2008) p. 268.

21 See ECtHR, *Brosa* v. *Germany* [2014] App. no. 5709/09.

22 See ECtHR, *Soltész* v. *Slovakia* [2013] App. no. 11867/09.

23 See below Section 7.3.4.1.1.

context with the following sentence, which provides that '[a]ll forms of exploitation and degradation of man particularly slavery, slave trade, torture, cruel, inhuman or degrading punishment and treatment shall be prohibited'. Hence, an interference with a person's honour or privacy may only amount to a violation of human dignity if this interference equates to an action equivalent to those in sentence 2. Yet this arguably applies only to degrading humiliations and the most intimate exposures.

Privacy and honour are nevertheless encompassed by the notion of 'rights of others' in Article 27(2) AfCHPR and Article 28 AfCHPR,[24] according to which '[e]very individual shall have the duty to respect and consider his fellow beings without discrimination, and to maintain relations aimed at promoting, safeguarding and reinforcing mutual respect and tolerance'. This follows from Article 60 AfCHPR, whereupon the African Commission 'shall draw inspiration from international law on human and peoples' rights', particularly from the UDHR and other instruments adopted by the United Nations. The term 'rights' thus extends beyond the rights and freedoms recognised in the African Charter and covers any right accepted under international human rights law.[25] This includes in particular the rights enshrined in the UDHR and the ICCPR, where both Article 12 UDHR and Article 17 ICCPR protect a person's honour and privacy.

Upon closer examination, Article 17 ICCPR reveals remarkable idiosyncrasies. Article 17(1) ICCPR protects against any unlawful *interference* with privacy etc., but only against unlawful *attacks* on honour and reputation.[26] Therefore it seems that Article 17 ICCPR provides more comprehensive 'horizontal' protection for privacy than for honour, as the existence of an 'attack' sets higher standards than an interference; an attack requires intent on behalf of the trespasser, whereas an interference may occur involuntarily.[27] Article 17(2) ICCPR confirms the seemingly unequal protection of privacy and honour. By comparison, Article 19(3)(a) ICCPR allows interferences with freedom of expression for the 'respect of the ... reputations of others'; hence the provision does not require an 'attack' on someone's reputation, but it does not expressly

[24] See AfComHPR, *John D. Ouko* v. *Kenya* [2000] App. no. 232/99 [28]; *Scanlen & Holderness* v. *Zimbabwe* [2009] App. no. 297/05 [121].

[25] Compare Human Rights Committee, General Comment no. 34, para. 28; see also UN Economic and Social Council, Siracusa Principles on the Limitation and Derogation Provisions in the International Covenant on Civil and Political Rights, UN Doc. E/CN.4/1985/4, Annex (1985), no. 35.

[26] The term 'arbitrary' in Article 17(1) ICCPR, which is based on Article 12 UDHR, suggests a violation committed by state institutions only, but not by other private individuals; see Nowak (2005) Article 17 para. 12.

[27] Compare Nowak (2005) Article 17 para. 51.

refer to a person's honour either. As a consequence, any interference with another's reputation, even an involuntary one, suffices to engage the justification of Article 19(3) ICCPR. However, in order to prompt a Member State's positive obligation to protect a person's honour or reputation according to Article 17(2) ICCPR, an intentional attack is required. Hence, where the speaker intentionally attacks someone's honour or reputation, the State Party is *obliged to* act according to Article 17(2) ICCPR. By contrast, where the speaker involuntarily interferes with a person's reputation, the State Party *may* restrict the expression based on Article 19(3)(a) ICCPR. This distinction is of course not sustainable, as the elaborations on the concept of 'obligation to protect' have shown.[28]

7.2 Scope of the margin of appreciation

A margin of appreciation is justified because of either a factual or normative uncertainty on the adjudicator's side.[29] Normative uncertainty relates to the relative importance of the right or interest the media has interfered with, and the factual uncertainty is related to the best means of protecting this right or interest. Factual (or empirical) uncertainty necessitates a margin of appreciation on the suitability and necessity of the interference, while normative uncertainty requires a margin of appreciation on the proportionality *sensu stricto* step.

With regard to the margin of appreciation to be granted in cases of violations of personality rights, the Strasbourg Court has highlighted, first, that 'bearing in mind the diversity of the practices followed and the situations obtaining in the Contracting States' the requirements of the notion of 'respect' in Article 8 ECHR 'will vary considerably from case to case.'[30] Second, because of 'their direct and continuous contact with the vital forces of their countries', the ECtHR considers the state authorities 'in a better position than the international judge to give an opinion on how best to secure the right to respect for private life within the domestic legal order'.[31]

This observation is to be partly endorsed, but also to be partly criticised. It is to be endorsed in so far as the first part of the Court's statement is concerned: the value attached to privacy or honour may indeed be subject to different estimations depending on cultural attitudes. This affects the normative uncertainty of international

[28] See Chapter 5, Section 5.2.2. [29] See Chapter 6, Section 6.2.
[30] ECtHR, *Mosley* v. *United Kingdom* [2011] App. no. 48009/08 [108].
[31] ECtHR, *Mosley* v. *United Kingdom* [2011] App. no. 48009/08 [108].

adjudicators, and thus justifies a margin of appreciation. Yet in core areas of a person's strictly private life, 'where a particularly important facet of an individual's existence or identity is at stake' or 'where the activities at stake involve a most intimate aspect of private life',[32] the common standards among states are rather broad. As a consequence, the margin of appreciation allowed to states is narrowed. Furthermore, the estimation of the weight attached to the exercise of media freedom is entirely the courts' province.[33] The margin of appreciation, therefore, only applies where the media publication is not of public concern *and* where it does not include core areas of private life. If the publication pertains to a matter of public concern, media freedom calls for strict scrutiny, and if the publication is related to a person's strictly private life, the right to respect for private life requires strict scrutiny. In practice, the importance attached to media freedom is usually on the same scale as personality rights. The more a publication pertains to a person's private life, the less it is of public concern. The relative weight attached to the exercise of media freedom thus corresponds to the importance ascribed to the protection of the personality rights concerned, and *vice versa*.

However, it is not convincing to argue that the protection of personality rights also includes empirical uncertainty, that is, uncertainty with regard to the question what the 'best means' for protecting personality rights are. This relates to the second part of the Court's observation, namely that the state authorities are in a better position to estimate *how* best to secure the right to respect for private life. The question of whether a restriction imposed on the media is suitable and necessary to prevent or remedy a violation of a person's honour or privacy – that is, there are no less restrictive means available – is far from being a complex or prognostic assessment and can be fully scrutinised by an international court.

7.3 Principles of the balancing exercise between media freedom and personality rights

When reviewing the balancing exercise of domestic courts, international adjudicators have to scrutinise whether the national authorities applied standards which were in accordance with the Media Freedom Principle. For this purpose an international supervisor considers the impugned judicial decisions in the light of the case as a whole, including the following criteria: the position of the person or institution preparing, issuing or distributing the impugned reporting, the position of the

32 ECtHR, *Mosley* v. *United Kingdom* [2011] App. no. 48009/08 [109].
33 See Chapter 6, Section 6.3.3.2.

affected person or association and their activities and the content of the reporting. In addition, international adjudicators review the proportionality of any penalty imposed.

7.3.1 The position of the person or institution making the statement

If the person who has issued the statement was a journalist, the essential function the media fulfils in a democratic society has to be considered.[34] The exceptions to the media speech privilege[35] must be construed strictly and the need for any such restrictions must be established convincingly.[36] Similar to the protection afforded to the institutional media, international adjudicators grant strong protection to speech of politicians, even if this speech is not protected by parliamentary immunity,[37] to actors of civil society, such as NGOs,[38] and to professional groups, such as lawyers, when they exercise their functions.[39]

Except for Article 13 EUChFR, international human rights catalogues do not include an express provision protecting academic speech. However, freedom of expression also covers the publication of academic articles, teaching and speeches.[40] Yet, the freedom of academic speech is conceptually different from freedom of media speech. In determining whether speech is academic, it is necessary to establish: (a) whether the person making the speech can be considered an academic; (b) whether that

[34] ECtHR, *Chemodurov* v. *Russia* [2007] App. no. 72683/01 [19]; *Krasulya* v. *Russia* [2007] App. no. 12365/03 [36]; *Lombardo and others* v. *Malta* [2007] App. no. 7333/06 [53].

[35] See Chapter 4, Section 4.1.

[36] ECtHR, *Krasulya* v. *Russia* [2007] App. no. 12365/03 [36].

[37] ECtHR, *Castells* v. *Spain* [1992] App. no. 11798/85 [42]; *Brasilier* v. *France* [2006] App. no. 71343/01 [39]; *Filipović* v. *Serbia* [2007] App. no. 27935/05 [58]; *Kubaszewski* v. *Poland* [2010] App. no. 571/04 [38]; *Lombardo and others* v. *Malta* [2007] App. no. 7333/06 [53].

[38] See Human Rights Committee, *Toktakunov* v. *Kyrgyzstan* [2011] Communication no. 1470/2006 [6.3]; Special Court for Sierra Leone, *Prosecutor* v. *Alex Tamba Brima and others*, Decision on Prosecution appeal against decision on oral application for witness TF1–150 to testify without being compelled to answer questions on grounds of confidentiality, Case No. SCSL-2004–16-AR73 [2006] SCSL 2 [33]; ECtHR, *Steel and Morris* v. *United Kingdom* [2005] App. no. 68416/01; *Animal Defenders International* v. *United Kingdom* [2013] App. no. 48876/08; *Youth Initiative for Human Rights* v. *Serbia* [2013] App. no. 48135/06; IACtHR, *Claude Reyes and others* v. *Chile* [2006] Case 12.108.

[39] See ECtHR, *Steur* v. *Netherlands* [2003] App. no. 39657/98 [38]; see also *Nikula* v. *Finland* [2002] App. no. 31611/96 [45].

[40] See, e.g., ECtHR, *Hertel* v. *Switzerland* [1998] App. no. 59/1997/843/1049 [50]; *Wille* v. *Liechtenstein* [1999] App. no. 28396/95 [36 ff.]; *Lombardi Vallauri* v. *Italy* [2009] App. no. 39128/05 [30]; *Mustafa Erdoğan and others* v. *Turkey* [2014] App. nos. 346/04 and 39779/04 [40]; AfCHPR, *Kenneth Good* v. *Republic of Botswana* [2010] App. no. 313/05 [199]; IAComHR, *Ricardo Jacob Israel Zipper* v. *Chile* [2009] Case 12.470 [63].

person's public comments or utterances fall within the sphere of his or her research; and (c) whether that person's statements amount to conclusions or opinions based on his or her professional expertise and competence.[41] Thus, academic speech is to a larger degree based on the self-fulfilment of the academic scholar than newspaper articles are. But comparable to journalistic publications, academic articles, speeches and teaching are fact-and-research based and regularly contribute to discourses on matters of public concern – within the academic community and beyond. Similar to media freedom of news organisations and journalists, academic freedom of both universities as institutions and researchers as individuals is thus an institutional and instrumental freedom. Consequently, there is good reason to furnish academic 'truth seekers' with privileges similar to those afforded to the media.[42] The importance of both institutional academic freedom and individual freedom of researchers, scholars or academics in general has been expressed in several Recommendations of the Committee of Ministers to Member States.[43]

7.3.2 The position of the victim of the statement and their activities

With regard to the person who is the subject of the media reporting, a distinction has to be made between private individuals and persons acting in the public sphere. People who expose themselves by virtue of their role as a 'public figure', as a participant in a public debate on a matter of public concern or by otherwise entering the public scene, may claim weaker protection of their personality rights than a private person. Special considerations apply to reportings on judges and the judiciary.

7.3.2.1 'Public figures'

Unlike a private individual who does not exercise official functions, a 'public figure' who knowingly exposes himself to scrutiny by the general public has to display a greater degree of tolerance with regard to public criticism and intrusions into his private affairs.[44] 'Public figures' can be defined as 'persons holding public office and/or using public

[41] See ECtHR, *Mustafa Erdoğan and others* v. *Turkey* [2014] App. nos. 346/04 and 39779/04, joint concurring Opinion of Judges Sajó, Vučinič and Kūris [8].

[42] Oster (2013) 66; compare Dworkin (1996) p. 247; Post (2012) pp. 61 ff.; Blocher (2012) 440.

[43] Council of Europe, Committee of Ministers, Recommendation Rec(2012)7 on the Responsibility of Public Authorities for Academic Freedom and Institutional Autonomy; Recommendation No. R(2000) 12 on the Social Sciences and the Challenge of Transition.

[44] The case-law on public scrutiny of public figures is abundant. See, amongst many other authorities, Human Rights Committee, *Bodrožić* v. *Serbia and Montenegro* [2005]

resources and, more broadly speaking, all those who play a role in public life, whether in politics, the economy, the arts, the social sphere, sport or in any other domain.'[45]

The right to scrutinise one's government or anyone else who exercises power is one of the core elements of democracy itself. The limits of acceptable public scrutiny are thus wider in relation to professional politicians acting in their public capacity than in relation to private individuals.[46] Issues which would be of no public interest with regard to private individuals may be of interest if politicians are concerned.[47] In addition, the integrity of holders of high offices remains a matter of public concern even after their resignation.[48]

As a consequence, a special legal status for politicians or state institutions shielding them from scrutiny solely on account of their function or status is not reconcilable with the essential function freedom of expression and media freedom fulfil in a democratic society. Laws that serve to protect the state and its officials from public opinion or criticism based on the function of the person should therefore be abolished. Such laws include *lèse-majesté*,[49] defamation of a head of state, both domestic[50] and foreign,[51] the protection of the honour of public authorities as such,[52] and the prohibition of criticism of public institutions, such as,

Communication no. 1180/2003 [7.2]; *Marques de Morais* v. *Angola* [2005] Communication no. 1128/2002 [6.8]; ECtHR, *Lingens* v. *Austria* [1986] App. no. 9815/82 [42]; *Oberschlick* v. *Austria (No. 1)* [1991] App. no. 11662/85 [59]; *Lombardo and others* v. *Malta* [2007] App. no. 7333/06 [54]; AfComHPR, *Media Rights Agenda, Constitutional Rights Project, Media Rights Agenda and Constitutional Rights Project* v. *Nigeria* [1998] App. nos. 105/93, 128/94, 130/94 and 152/96 [74]; *Kenneth Good* v. *Republic of Botswana* [2010] App. no. 313/05 [198]; IACtHR, *Herrera-Ulloa* v. *Costa Rica* [2004] Case 12.367 [127]; *Ricardo Canese* v. *Paraguay* [2004] Case 12.032 [102]; *Fontevecchia and D'Amico* v. *Argentina* [2011] Case 12.524 [47].

45 Council of Europe, Parliamentary Assembly, Resolution 1165 (1998) on the Right to Privacy, para. 7.

46 See, e.g., ECtHR, *Lingens* v. *Austria* [1986] App. no. 9815/82; *Oberschlick* v. *Austria (No. 1)* [1991] App. no. 11662/85 [59]; IACtHR, *Ivcher-Bronstein* v. *Peru* [2001] Case 11.762 [155]; *Ricardo Canese* v. *Paraguay* [2004] Case 12.032 [98]; High Court of Australia, *Lange* v. *Australian Broadcasting Corporation* [1997] HCA 25.

47 See ECtHR, *Rumyana Ivanova* v. *Bulgaria* [2008] App. no. 36207/03 [60]: a person's financial integrity.

48 ECtHR, *Ungváry and Irodalom Kft* v. *Hungary* [2013] App. no. 64520/10 [64]; *Axel Springer AG* v. *Germany (No. 2)* [2014] App. no. 48311/10 [56].

49 Human Rights Committee, *Aduayom and others* v. *Togo* [1996] Communication nos. 422–424/1990 [7.4].

50 Human Rights Committee, Concluding observations on Zambia (CCPR/ZMB/CO/3), para. 25; ECtHR, *Eon* v. *France* [2013] App. no. 26118/10 [55].

51 ECtHR, *Colombani and others* v. *France* [2002] App. no. 51279/99 [68].

52 Human Rights Committee, Concluding observations on Costa Rica (CCPR/C/CRI/CO/5), para. 11; Concluding observations on Honduras (CCPR/C/HND/CO/1), para. 18; UN Economic and Social Council, Siracusa Principles on the Limitation and

for instance, 'the army' or 'the administration'.[53] When public officials or politicians are scrutinised or criticised in the media, media freedom has to be balanced against their *personal* right to privacy and reputation, as public figures benefit from its protection as well, but not against the 'honour' of the office they exercise. In this context, it must also be taken into account that such officials, particularly because of their exposed function, usually have access to means of communication available to reply to allegedly unjustified attacks.[54] They may therefore act within the public discourse without having to seek redress in court.

Trading companies are to be considered public figures *per se*.[55] It is the purpose of every trading corporation to participate in the broader economic sphere by producing and selling goods or services. Therefore, companies are, as such, subject to public interest,[56] even if they do not seek to appear on the public scene.[57]

Further examples of public figures are sport stars, functionaries or performing artists.[58] The communications officer for one of the two presidential candidates is, according to *Saaristo and others* v. *Finland*, to be considered a public figure, too.[59] In *Standard Verlags GmbH* v. *Austria (No. 3)*, the ECtHR held that a senior employee of a bank is not a 'public figure', and the fact that his father had been a politician does not make him a public figure either.[60]

Derogation Provisions in the International Covenant on Civil and Political Rights, UN Doc. E/CN.4/1985/4, Annex (1985), no. 37; Office of the Special Rapporteur for Freedom of Expression with the Inter-American Commission on Human Rights, Inter-American Legal Framework Regarding the Right to Freedom of Expression, 2009, CIDH/RELE/INF. 2/09, para. 134 ff.: *desacato* laws in Latin America.

53 Human Rights Committee, Concluding observations on Tunisia (CCPR/C/TUN/CO/5), para. 18.

54 See, e.g., ECtHR, *Axel Springer AG* v. *Germany (No. 2)* [2014] App. no. 48311/10 [66].

55 Oster (2011) 269.

56 See ECtHR, *Fayed* v. *United Kingdom* [1994] App. no. 17101/90 [75]; *Steel and Morris* v. *United Kingdom* [2005] App. no. 68416/01 [94]. From US case law and scholarship: *Martin Marietta Corp* v. *Evening Star Newspaper Co*, 417 F Supp 947, 956 (DDC 1976): 'It would be possible to hold ... that the malice standard applies to any libel action brought by a corporate plaintiff' (emphasis added); Jackson (2001) 508; Lee (1987) 347 f.

57 ECtHR, *Verlagsgruppe News GmbH* v. *Austria (No. 2)* [2006] App. no. 10520/02 [36].

58 See ECtHR, *Nikowitz and Verlagsgruppe News GmbH* v. *Austria* [2007] App. no. 5266/03 [25]; *Colaço Mestre and SIC – Sociedade Independente de Comunicação, SA* v. *Portugal* [2007] App. nos. 11182/03 and 11319/03 [28]; *Sapan* v. *Turkey* [2010] App. no. 44102/04 [34].

59 ECtHR, *Saaristo and others* v. *Finland* [2010] App. no. 184/06 [66].

60 ECtHR, *Standard Verlags GmbH* v. *Austria (No. 3)* [2012] App. no. 34702/07 [38]; see also *De Haes and Gijsels* v. *Belgium* [1997] App. no. 19983/92 [45]: 'One of the allusions

According to *Axel Springer AG* v. *Germany (No. 1)*, the fact that a TV actor plays the role of a police superintendent, 'whose mission is law enforcement and crime prevention', increases the public's interest in being informed of an arrest of this actor for a criminal offence.[61] This reasoning, however, is unconvincing: *mutatis mutandis*, one could conclude that there is less public interest in the arrest of an actor who usually plays the role of the 'bad guy'. Instead, the Court could have trusted the public's capability to distinguish between the actor and his role. What was most relevant here was the fact that the case concerned criminal prosecution, which – within the boundaries of the presumption of innocence – is *per se* of public concern.[62] Furthermore, the TV actor himself had divulged details about his private life in a number of interviews, which increased the public interest in his arrest.[63]

In the seminal case of *von Hannover* v. *Germany (No. 1)*, the Court emphasised that the applicant, a daughter of the then-ruling Prince of Monaco, president of certain humanitarian and cultural foundations and also representing the ruling family at public events, does not perform any function within or on behalf of the State of Monaco or any of its institutions.[64] This may have led to the conclusion that the Princess is not a public figure, but a mere private individual. In *von Hannover* v. *Germany (No. 2)*, however, the Court considered that 'irrespective of the question whether and to what extent the [Princess of Monaco] assumes official functions on behalf of the Principality of Monaco, it cannot be claimed that [she and her husband], who are undeniably very well known, are ordinary private individuals. They must, on the contrary, be regarded as public figures.'[65] The Court confirmed this finding in its *von Hannover* v. *Germany (No. 3)* decision.[66]

The *von Hannover* decisions reveal the intrinsic conflict between the rationales of media freedom and hereditary monarchies. Media freedom is based on the importance of the media for public discourse. Public discourse involves free public deliberation of matters of public concern, especially – but not only – the scrutiny of those who exercise power. Consequently, democratically elected politicians (or those who aim to be

to the alleged political sympathies was inadmissible – the one concerning the past history of the father of one of the judges criticised . . . It is unacceptable that someone should be exposed to opprobrium because of matters concerning a member of his family.'

61 ECtHR, *Axel Springer AG* v. *Germany (No. 1)* [2012] App. no. 39954/08 [99].

62 See Chapter 2, Section 2.2.3.1.

63 See below Section 7.3.3.2.

64 ECtHR, *Von Hannover* v. *Germany (No. 1)* [2004] App. no. 59320/00 [62]. See in this context the critical remarks of Sanderson (2004) 631 ff.

65 ECtHR, *Von Hannover* v. *Germany (No. 2)* [2012] App. nos. 40660/08 and 60641/08 [120].

66 ECtHR, *Von Hannover* v. *Germany (No. 3)* [2013] App. no. 8772/10 [53].

democratically elected) have at some point inevitably and knowingly laid themselves open to public scrutiny. By contrast, hereditary monarchs and their relatives never entered the public scene voluntarily; they were born into it.

At the same time, those who exercise public influence must be subject to public scrutiny, even if their office is only representative in nature, whether they have been democratically elected or not. One may even add that *especially* those who have not been democratically elected must be subject to public scrutiny. The media must therefore focus on reportings on the exercise of public office rather than obsequious palace journalism, on the one side, and intrusions into people's private lives with the aim to satisfy the yearnings and curiosity of a particular readership, on the other side.

Couderc et Hachette Filipacchi Associés v. *France* illustrates the problems involved in such a balancing exercise. A French tabloid magazine published an interview with a woman, who claimed that Prince Albert II of Monaco was the father of her son. She also revealed details about the relationship between her and Prince Albert, including photographs showing Prince Albert with the child, which had been taken with his consent. Later on, Prince Albert acknowledged his paternity of the child. French courts ordered the applicant magazine to pay damages for the invasion of Prince Albert's privacy.[67]

Under the Constitution of Monaco, the boy could not succeed to the throne. Therefore, he would never be in a position (at least by virtue of his birth) to exercise power and influence. However, the majority of the Chamber found that in a hereditary monarchy the birth of the monarch's child was *as such* a matter of legitimate public interest.[68] In addition, the interview revealed information about the Prince's personality and his ability to exercise his functions.[69] Therefore, the Strasbourg Court balanced the need to protect Prince Albert's private life against the debate on the future of the hereditary monarchy, which is an important political question.[70] Yet, the Court also distinguished between this central message of the article and the other details on the Prince's private life, the revelation of which was not of public concern.[71] With a narrow majority of four to three, the Court thus held that Article 10 ECHR had been violated. By contrast, the dissenting opinion found that the succession to

[67] ECtHR, *Couderc et Hachette Filipacchi Associés* v. *France* [2014] App. no. 40454/07.
[68] ECtHR, *Couderc et Hachette Filipacchi Associés* v. *France* [2014] App. no. 40454/07 [59].
[69] ECtHR, *Couderc et Hachette Filipacchi Associés* v. *France* [2014] App. no. 40454/07 [59].
[70] ECtHR, *Couderc et Hachette Filipacchi Associés* v. *France* [2014] App. no. 40454/07 [59].
[71] ECtHR, *Couderc et Hachette Filipacchi Associés* v. *France* [2014] App. no. 40454/07 [59] and [73].

the throne, and thus the central political question the majority emphasised, was not the issue of the interview.[72] Rather, the interview focused on the details of Prince Albert's private life, which violated Article 8 ECHR.

The dissenting opinion rightly emphasised that the question of whether the revelation of certain details, such as photographs, were necessary to ensure the credibility of the story, is a factor that has to be considered in the balancing exercise.[73] However, the question of whether a publication *contributes* to a matter of general concern does not require that the publication expressly *raises* this concern. To be sure, the interview in question arguably aimed at a readership which was more interested in the Prince's private affairs rather than constitutional questions of the Principality of Monaco. Yet, this closes the circle to the point that has been raised initially: the private life of the monarch *is* a matter of political and even constitutional relevance, if his conduct in private affairs can have an impact on his capability to exercise his office and how his personality is being perceived.

With regard to civil servants who are not politicians, the limits of acceptable scrutiny are wider than in relation to private individuals, because civil servants are entrusted with the execution of public authority. However, even when acting in an official capacity, civil servants do not lay themselves open to the same scrutiny as politicians, and should therefore not be treated equally with the latter when it comes to the criticism of their actions or investigations into their private conduct.[74]

The case-law provides illustrious examples of the Strasbourg Court's – unfortunately not always consistent – approach to criticism of civil servants. In *Janowski* v. *Poland (No. 1)* and in *Nikula* v. *Finland*, the Court emphasised that civil servants – in these cases: municipal guards and a public prosecutor, respectively – 'must enjoy public confidence in conditions free of undue perturbation if they are to be successful in performing their tasks and it may therefore prove necessary to protect them from offensive and abusive verbal attacks when on duty'.[75] These requirements have to be weighed against the interests of open discussion of

[72] ECtHR, *Couderc et Hachette Filipacchi Associés* v. *France* [2014] App. no. 40454/07, dissenting opinion of Judges Villger, Zupančič and Lemmens [3].

[73] See Chapter 6, Section 6.3.3.3.1.

[74] See ECtHR, *Nikula* v. *Finland* [2002] App. no. 31611/96 [48]; *Steur* v. *Netherlands* [2003] App. no. 39657/98 [40–1]; *Pedersen and Baadsgaard* v. *Denmark* [2004] App. no. 49017/99 [80]; *Saaristo and others* v. *Finland* [2010] App. no. 184/06 [60]; *mutatis mutandis*, *July and SARL Liberation* v. *France* [2008] App. no. 20893/03 [74]; *Haguenauer* v. *France* [2010] App. no. 34050/05 [48].

[75] ECtHR, *Janowski* v. *Poland (No. 1)* [1999] App. no. 25716/94 [33]; *Nikula* v. *Finland* [2002] App. no. 31611/96 [48].

matters of public concern, to which the exercise of official authority *per se* belongs. However, the Court qualified the public confidence rationale in *Busuioc* v. *Moldova*, where the judges indicated that the complainants in issue were neither law-enforcement officers nor prosecutors, as in *Janowski* and in *Nikula*, but airport administrators; it would 'go too far to extend the *Janowski* principle to all persons who are employed by the State or by State-owned companies'.[76]

7.3.2.2 Judges and the judiciary

One of the most critical problems of media freedom is the extent to which the media may criticise a judge or the judiciary.[77] Where judges or courts are being criticised, not only the reputation of the judges themselves is at stake but also the functioning of the judiciary. International adjudicators therefore apply particularly strict scrutiny where judges are the subject of a critical publication. The African Commission rightly observed that '[o]ver the years, the line to be drawn between genuine criticism of the judiciary and insulting language has grown thinner'.[78]

As an exercise of public authority, the administration of justice is *per se* a matter of public concern, and must therefore be subject to public scrutiny. This applies everywhere, but especially in countries where state institutions do not operate under the rule of law.[79] However, three reasons can be identified why judges have to be subject to enhanced protection against public scrutiny. First, the judiciary in general, as 'the guarantor of justice', must enjoy public confidence if it is to be successful in carrying out its duties.[80] This rationale is closely tied to the 'authority and impartiality of the judiciary' as a principle justifying an interference with media freedom.[81] Second, with its rules on procedure and especially the possibility to appeal judicial decisions, the judiciary itself provides an internal check on its proper functioning, which has to be exhausted in the first place. Third, because of the formality of the legal proceedings, the individual judges are subject to a duty of discretion that precludes them from replying to criticism, and hence, as opposed to politicians, they are

[76] ECtHR, *Busuioc* v. *Moldova* [2004] App. no. 61513/00 [64].
[77] See Addo (2000); Addo (1998) 425 ff.
[78] AfComHPR, *Zimbabwe Lawyers for Human Rights & Associated Newspapers of Zimbabwe* v. *Republic of Zimbabwe* [2009] App. no. 284/03 [93].
[79] See IAComHR, *Eduardo Kimel* v. *Argentina* [2007] Case 12.450 [111].
[80] See, e.g., ECtHR, *Prager and Oberschlick* v. *Austria* [1995] App. no. 15974/90 [34]; *De Haes and Gijsels* v. *Belgium* [1997] App. no. 19983/92 [37]; *Skałka* v. *Poland* [2003] App. no. 43425/98 [34]; AfComHPR, *Zimbabwe Lawyers for Human Rights & Associated Newspapers of Zimbabwe* v. *Republic of Zimbabwe* [2009] App. no. 284/03 [89].
[81] See Chapter 10.

not at liberty to discuss their decisions in public.[82] Consequently, although the actions of judges in their official capacity are matters of public concern and may thus be the subject of public discourse, the judges themselves are basically excluded from this discourse, apart from the delivery of their judgment. This imbalance has to be evened out by an enhanced protection of their professional reputation. While it is the media's obligation to scrutinise and criticise a court's judicial reasoning, in must refrain from personal attacks on the judges themselves or comments calculated to bring the judiciary into disrepute.[83]

Against this backdrop, the fact that media-savvy judges increasingly tend to express their personal views in public is a highly regrettable development. As a general concern, any extra-judicial public statement of a judge may substantiate a claim of bias in subsequent trials that include questions on which the judge expressed himself, thus jeopardising the functioning of the judiciary. With a view to the problem of criticism of judges in particular, if a judge makes a public statement in an interview, one of the main rationales that justifies limitations on criticism of judges becomes inapplicable: the fact that judges are subject to a duty of discretion that precludes them from replying. On the contrary, if judges express their point of view in interviews, they enter public debate beyond their judgments and thus make themselves personally subject to objection and criticism. This sets in motion a vicious circle. As a result, in order to further justify the limitations on criticism of judges, they should be encouraged to speak to the public exclusively through their judgments, and leave the media spotlight to their court's press officers.

An illustrative, non-media related case on the distinction between justified criticism of judicial decisions and personal attacks on judges is the African Commission's decision on the admissibility of *Zimbabwe Lawyers for Human Rights & Associated Newspapers of Zimbabwe* v. *Republic of Zimbabwe*. Article 56(3) AfCHPR requires that applications submitted to the African Commission are 'not written in disparaging or insulting language directed against the State concerned and its institutions or to the Organization of African Unity' (now the African Union).

82 See, e.g., ECtHR, *Prager and Oberschlick* v. *Austria* [1995] App. no. 15974/90 [34]; *De Haes and Gijsels* v. *Belgium* [1997] App. no. 19983/92 [37]; *Skałka* v. *Poland* [2003] App. no. 43425/98 [34]; *Kobenter and Standard Verlags GmbH* v. *Austria* [2006] App. no. 60899/00 [31]; AfComHPR, *Zimbabwe Lawyers for Human Rights & Associated Newspapers of Zimbabwe* v. *Republic of Zimbabwe* [2009] App. no. 284/03 [89].

83 Compare ECtHR, *Barfod* v. *Denmark* [1989] App. no. 11508/85 [35]; AfComHPR, *Zimbabwe Lawyers for Human Rights & Associated Newspapers of Zimbabwe* v. *Republic of Zimbabwe* [2009] App. no. 284/03 [90].

The respondent state, Zimbabwe, argued that the application was written in a language insulting to the judiciary of the state: the complainants had claimed that a judge of the Supreme Court was deliberately omitted from the domestic trial. Zimbabwe argued that the complainants were insinuating that the composition of the Supreme Court was manipulated, and thus their communication was written 'in disparaging language' within the meaning of Article 56(3) AfCHPR. The African Commission rightly rejected the state's argument, holding that Article 56(3) AfCHPR must be interpreted bearing in mind Article 9(2) of the African Charter.[84]

7.3.2.3 Private persons

In contrast to public figures and other persons on the public scene, private individuals unknown to the public may claim strong protection of their personality rights.[85] Despite the opportunities of the internet, private individuals do not have the instruments available to respond to media scrutiny in a public discourse. The media must be aware of its impact on society in general, especially the fact that their reporting on private individuals may cause public humiliation and exclusion from local society.[86]

7.3.3 The prior conduct of the person concerned

Another criterion for balancing media freedom against rights of others is the prior conduct of the person concerned. This criterion may cut both ways: public figures may receive stronger protection of their personality rights if they shield their private lives from public attention. On the other hand, the lives of private persons may become matters of public interest if those persons participated in a matter of public interest or otherwise entered the public scene.

7.3.3.1 Shielding private lives from public attention

Personality rights protect the right to decide *if* someone wants his private life to be known to the public. Even if persons are known to the public and had been in the media on account of their function, they may nonetheless claim strong protection of their personality rights if they had not disclosed details of their private life prior to a publication.[87] This applies especially

[84] AfComHPR, *Zimbabwe Lawyers for Human Rights & Associated Newspapers of Zimbabwe* v. *Republic of Zimbabwe* [2009] App. no. 284/03 [91].

[85] See, e.g., ECtHR, *Armonienė* v. *Lithuania* [2008] App. no. 36919/02 [47]; *Ageyevy* v. *Russia* [2013] App. no. 7075/10 [217].

[86] ECtHR, *Biriuk* v. *Lithuania* [2008] App. no. 23373/03 [41]; *Armonienė* v. *Lithuania* [2008] App. no. 36919/02 [47]; *Ageyevy* v. *Russia* [2013] App. no. 7075/10 [216].

[87] Compare ECtHR, *Print Zeitungsverlag GmbH* v. *Austria* [2013] App. no. 26547/07 [37].

where public figures expressly request that details of their private life should not be published, or if they have taken legal steps to prevent such publications.[88]

Yet, even if public figures sought to avoid public attention on a private matter, they may nonetheless provoke legitimate public scrutiny because of their prior behaviour. This may be the case where public figures voluntarily open aspects of their private life to a public audience, or if they publicly deny facts relating to their private life. In *MGN* v. *United Kingdom*, for example, the Court found that the core facts of well-known top model Naomi Campbell's drug addiction, and the fact that she was in treatment, were legitimately a matter of public interest and capable of being published, because Ms Campbell publicly denied the use of drugs beforehand.[89]

7.3.3.2 Entering the public scene

However, personality rights do not give licence to choose *how* someone wants to be seen in the eyes of the public. Persons who provoke in a public debate[90] or who seek the limelight of public attention by laying open details regarding private lives, even if they have not been known to the public before, expose themselves to scrutiny and must therefore bear the consequences.

Private individuals become subject to legitimate public interest 'when they enter the arena of public debate', although they do not fulfil official functions.[91] In the case of *Nilsen and Johnsen* v. *Norway*, for instance, the Strasbourg Court found that a government-appointed expert involved in a dispute with the applicants, two police officers, could not be compared to a politician. However, the Court held that his participation in a public debate and his publication of a book voicing harsh criticism of the working methods of the police were relevant factors in the balancing of his and the applicant's rights, who allegedly defamed him.[92] Similarly, in *Jerusalem* v. *Austria*, the Court found that since the criticised associations in this case participated in public discussions on drug policy and co-operated with a political party, 'they ought to have shown a higher degree of tolerance to criticism when opponents considered their aims as well as to the

[88] See ECtHR, *Von Hannover* v. *Germany (No. 3)* [2013] App. no. 8772/10 [55].

[89] ECtHR, *MGN Ltd* v. *United Kingdom* [2011] App. no. 39401/04 [147].

[90] See, e.g., ECtHR, *Oberschlick* v. *Austria (No. 2)* [1997] App. no. 20834/92 [33] and [34]; *Unabhängige Initiative Informationsvielfalt* v. *Austria* [2002] App. no. 28525/95 [43]; *Mladina d.d. Ljubljana* v. *Slovenia* [2014] App. no. 20981/10 [44].

[91] See, for instance, ECtHR, *Nilsen and Johnsen* v. *Norway* [1999] App. no. 23118/93 [52]; *Karsai* v. *Hungary* [2009] App. no. 5380/07 [35]; *Jerusalem* v. *Austria* [2001] App. no. 26958/95 [38].

[92] ECtHR, *Nilsen and Johnsen* v. *Norway* [1999] App. no. 23118/93 [52].

means employed in that debate'.[93] Moreover, persons who publicly express extremist views particularly lay themselves open to public scrutiny.[94]

Furthermore, private individuals may become subject to legitimate public interest if they have been involved in criminal investigations or proceedings, as crimes and criminal investigations are *per se* a matter of public concern.[95] However, the fact that a person has been the subject of criminal proceedings does not fully deprive him of his right to respect for private life.[96]

Eventually, private persons enter the public domain if their conduct pertains to a matter of public concern. In *Flinkkilä and others* v. *Finland*, for instance, the person concerned ('B') had developed a relationship with a married senior public figure. The Strasbourg Court thus found that the prohibition against disclosing B's identity in reports of the affair violated Article 10 ECHR.[97]

7.3.4 Subject-matter, form and veracity of the publication

The most important factor in the balancing exercise between freedom of the media and the rights to respect for privacy or honour is the extent to which the impugned reporting does contribute to a matter of public concern. The question of whether the person who is the subject of the reports being published is a public figure or otherwise entered the public scene may only serve as an indicator for a legitimate public interest. The freedom of the media is not absolute, and it does not extend as far as the protection afforded by the US Supreme Court on speech about public figures. For the US Supreme Court, criticism of the government is essentially indistinguishable from criticism of individual government officials or politicians.[98] Since *New York Times Co.* v. *Sullivan*,[99] a public figure has to prove actual malice on behalf of the defendant in order to succeed in a defamation lawsuit. The Washington Court's jurisprudence therefore presumes that speech about a public figure is *per se* of legitimate public interest.

[93] ECtHR, *Jerusalem* v. *Austria* [2001] App. no. 26958/95 [39].
[94] ECtHR, *Österreichischer Rundfunk* v. *Austria* [2006] App. no. 35841/02 [65].
[95] Chapter 2, Section 2.2.3.1. See, e.g., ECtHR, *News Verlags GmbH & Co. KG* v. *Austria* [2000] App. no. 31457/96 [54]; *Krone Verlag GmbH & Co. KG* v. *Austria (No. 1)* [2002] App. no. 34315/96 [37]; *Verlagsgruppe News GmbH* v. *Austria (No. 2)* [2006] App. no. 10520/02 [40].
[96] See below Section 7.3.4.1.1.3.
[97] ECtHR, *Flinkkilä and others* v. *Finland* [2010] App. no. 25576/04 [85].
[98] See Post (1987) 550. [99] 376 US 254 (1964).

However, the fact that personality rights are themselves protected as human rights contradicts approaches that focus too heavily on the status of the person concerned, such as the former German concept of the figure of contemporary society '*par excellence*'.[100] Rather, the crucial question is whether the impugned reporting is *in substance* capable of contributing to a debate of general concern.[101] It is part of the duties and responsibilities of the media that even a publication in the public interest must not overstep the boundaries set by the right to reputation and privacy of others. The reputation and privacy of a public figure, even a controversial one, must benefit from the protection afforded by international human rights guarantees.[102]

In this context, the distinction between factual statements on the one hand, and opinions, comments and value judgments on the other, gains particular significance.[103] Since statements of fact claim to accurately reflect reality, they bear stronger suggestive power than value judgments, which allow the possibility of a different opinion.[104] However, it can be difficult to establish *which* facts have actually been claimed. The Strasbourg Court's jurisprudence reveals a criticisable tendency towards interpreting statements against the media. In *Růžový panter, o.s.* v. *Czech Republic,*[105] the applicant, an NGO, used the term *spolčila* ('banded together') to describe the link between a politician and people who allegedly committed fraud and prepared a murder. The Strasbourg Court followed the domestic court's observation that the term carried a criminal connotation. Although the applicant was seeking, on behalf of the public, to expose the questionable connections of a politician, the term *spolčila* allegedly conveyed the false impression that this politician was part of a criminal association. More illustratively, in *Salumäki* v. *Finland*, the impugned article was entitled: 'The victim of the Vantaa homicide had connections with

[100] See ECtHR, *Von Hannover* v. *Germany (No. 1)* [2004] App. no. 59320/00 [75]; Dörr and Aernecke (2012) pp. 120–1.

[101] See, e.g., ECtHR, *News Verlags GmbH & Co. KG* v. *Austria* [2000] App. no. 31457/96 [54]; *Eerikäinen and others* v. *Finland* [2009] App. no. 3514/02 [66]; *Flinkkilä and others* v. *Finland* [2010] App. no. 25576/04 [76]; *Standard Verlags GmbH* v. *Austria (No. 3)* [2012] App. no. 34702/07 [39].

[102] See, among many other authorities, ECtHR, *Lindon, Otchakovsky-Laurens and July* v. *France* [2007] App. nos. 21279/02 and 36448/02 [57]; *Flux* v. *Moldova (No. 6)* [2008] App. no. 22824/04 [30]; *Kuliś* v. *Poland* [2008] App. no. 15601/02 [50]; *Standard Verlags GmbH* v. *Austria (No. 2)* [2009] App. no. 21277/05 [48]; *Tuşalp* v. *Turkey* [2012] App. nos. 32131/08 and 41617/08 [45]; IACtHR, *Herrera-Ulloa* v. *Costa Rica* [2004] Case 12.367 [128]; *Ricardo Canese* v. *Paraguay* [2004] Case 12.032 [100]; *Fontevecchia and D'Amico* v. *Argentina* [2011] Case 12.524 [53].

[103] See Chapter 4, Section 4.1.2.

[104] Grote and Wenzel (2013) para. 118.

[105] ECtHR, *Růžový panter, o.s.* v. *Czech Republic* [2012] App. no. 20240/08.

K. U. [*the name of a well-known Finnish businessman*]?'. The Court followed the domestic court's finding that this title, although formulated as a question, 'created a connection between K. U. and the homicide, implying that he was involved in it'.[106] Although the main text of the article only stated that the victim of the homicide *may* have had connections with the businessman and further clarified that the homicide suspect had no connections with K. U., the Strasbourg Court criticised that the article 'contained a false insinuation and that this false insinuation was capable of causing suffering to K. U.'[107] The Court found that the newspaper violated K. U.'s presumption of innocence, and thus decided against the newspaper.

For two reasons, this decision cannot be followed. The first reason is related to this case in particular: it appears rather contrived to deduce an insinuation of K. U.'s involvement in the crime by the mere conjecture that he may have known the *victim*. Second, and more generally, it appears rather paternalistic to allow a claim solely because of a headline, the function of which is merely to attract the reader's attention. The audience can be expected to read and understand a text as a whole, taking 'bane' and 'antidote' together.[108] The article expressly mentioned that the *suspect* had no connection with K. U. The fact that this information 'only appeared towards the end of the article'[109] is irrelevant; the readership can even be trusted to read a text to the end. The same applies to a series of articles, which must be understood in their general context and not singled out.[110]

7.3.4.1 Factual statements

The most important factor relevant to the balancing exercise between media freedom and the protection of a person's honour or privacy with regard to a factual statement is the authenticity of the information disclosed. Therefore, a distinction must be made between four categories of statements of fact:

Category I: true statements;
Category II: statements that are untrue and which the publisher knew to be untrue;

[106] ECtHR, *Salumäki* v. *Finland* [2014] App. no. 23605/09 [57].
[107] ECtHR, *Salumäki* v. *Finland* [2014] App. no. 23605/09 [58].
[108] *Chalmers* v. *Payne* [1835] 2 CM&R156, 159; *Charleston* v. *News Group Newspapers Ltd* [1995] UKHL 6; see also ECtHR, *Gutiérrez Suárez* v. *Spain* [2010] App. no. 16023/07 [36].
[109] ECtHR, *Salumäki* v. *Finland* [2014] App. no. 23605/09 [58].
[110] ECtHR, *Brunet Lecomte et Lyon Mag* v. *France* [2010] App. no. 17265/05 [44].

Category III: statements that the publisher believed to be true when issued, but which later turned out to be untrue; and

Category IV: statements that have been proven neither true nor untrue.

7.3.4.1.1 True statements of fact: the conflict between media freedom and the right to privacy

If statements of fact are found to be true (Category I), then there is usually no room left for a violation of a person's honour, since honour may only be affected by untrue statements and derogatory opinions.[111] However, the gathering and dissemination of true information may violate a person's right to privacy, because the concept of 'privacy' includes the right to control the release and circulation of information about oneself.[112]

Both the Strasbourg Court and the Parliamentary Assembly therefore recognised with disapproval that 'the private lives of those in the public eye have become a highly lucrative commodity for certain sectors of the media'.[113] In so far as media newsgathering and reporting pertains to the private life even of a public figure, it enjoys little protection. By contrast, if, and as far as, the exercise of their public functions is concerned, the public interest in publication usually supersedes any privacy interest. This approach is rooted in the functional understanding of media freedom in its significance for public discourse. Freedom of the media serves to support delivering what the public *needs* to know, and not merely what (a part of) the public *wants* to know.[114] Not everything that is in the interest of the public is necessarily of public concern.

The seminal test is, therefore, whether the victim had a 'reasonable' or 'legitimate' expectation of privacy outweighing the public interest in receiving the information. In order to establish whether there has been a reasonable expectation of privacy superseding public interest, it is suggested that five categories can be distinguished: the disclosure of private information protected by data protection provisions or received in confidence (see Section 7.3.4.4.1.1), the publication of photos (see Section

[111] This is at least the approach of English law, where the truth of a statement constitutes an absolute defence. Under German law, by contrast, Section 192 Criminal Law Code states that '[p]roof of truth of the asserted or disseminated fact shall not exclude punishment [for insult] if the insult results from the form of the assertion or dissemination or the circumstances under which it was made.' (Translation provided by M. Bohlander, juris GmbH, 2009)

[112] Compare Warren and Brandeis (1890); Prosser (1960) 392; Solove (2002) 1109; Hughes (2012) 809; Volokh (2000) 1050.

[113] ECtHR, *Mosley* v. *United Kingdom* [2011] App. no. 48009/08 [131]; Council of Europe, Parliamentary Assembly, Resolution 1165 (1998) on the Right to Privacy, para. 6.

[114] Compare Bezanson (1998) 176.

7.3.4.4.1.2), reportings on accidents, crimes and criminal proceedings (see Section 7.3.4.4.1.3), cases where children are concerned (see Section 7.3.4.4.1.4) and, finally, the dissemination of private information that does not fall under one of these categories (see Section 7.3.4.4.1.5).

7.3.4.1.1.1 Disclosure of confidential private information and personal data Information privacy is an important aspect of the right to private life. One sub-category of an interference with information privacy is the disclosure of personal information, such as private information received in confidence, and personal information that is confidential under data protection rules. Being the most recent international human rights codification, Article 8 EUChFR expressly guarantees the right to protection of personal data. Similarly, Article 16(1) TFEU states that everyone has the right to protection of personal data concerning them.

The laws protecting personal data[115] and confidentiality[116] impose limitations on others who want to publish certain information by restricting access to, or disclosure of, this information. However, data protection and confidentiality rules do not *per se* supersede freedom of expression and media freedom. Where the law grants protection of specific data, this restriction must itself be justified in light of freedom of expression and media freedom. Data protection and confidentiality rules have to allow for conflicting rights and interests to be properly balanced.[117] Legislation and case-law should therefore acknowledge the importance of media freedom by providing exemptions for journalists from data protection provisions, as is the case, for instance, with Article 9 of the EU Data Protection Directive.[118] Recital 37 to the Directive states:

[115] For example, Directive 95/46/EC of the European Parliament and of the Council of 24 October 1995 on the Protection of Individuals with regard to the Processing of Personal Data and on the Free Movement of such Data, OJ 1995, L281/31, and Directive 2002/58/EC of the European Parliament and of the Council of 12 July 2002 concerning the Processing of Personal Data and the Protection of Privacy in the Electronic Communications Sector (Directive on Privacy and Electronic Communications), OJ 2002, L201/37.

[116] Such as breach of confidence under English law; see *Prince Albert* v. *Strange* [1848] 1 Mac & G 25; *Coco* v. *A. N. Clark Ltd.* [1968] FSR 415 Ch D; *Attorney General* v. *Guardian Newspapers (No. 2)* [1990] 1 AC 109 HL; *Metall und Rohstoff AG* v. *Donaldson Lufkin & Jenrette Inc* [1990] 1 QB 391; *Kitechnology BV and others* v. *Unicor GmbH Plastmaschinen and others* [1995] FSR 765 (CA); Aplin *et al.* (2012).

[117] ECJ, *Lindqvist* [2003] ECR I-12971, Case C-101/01 [85–7]; *Rechnungshof* v. *Österreichischer Rundfunk and others* [2003] ECR I-04989, Joined Cases C-465/00, C-138/01 and C-139/01 [76]; *Tietosuojavaltuutettu* v. *Satakunnan Markkinapörssi Oy and Satamedia Oy* [2008] ECR I-09831, Case C-73/07 [53]; Barnes (2011) p. 271.

[118] Article 9 states:'Processing of personal data and freedom of expression.

Member States shall provide for exemptions or derogations from the provisions of this Chapter, Chapter IV and Chapter VI for the processing of personal data carried out

[T]he processing of personal data for purposes of journalism or for purposes of literary or artistic expression, in particular in the audiovisual field, should qualify for exemption from the requirements of certain provisions of this Directive in so far as this is necessary to reconcile the fundamental rights of individuals with freedom of information and notably the right to receive and impart information, . . .;

Member States should therefore lay down exemptions and derogations necessary for the purpose of balance between fundamental rights as regards general measures on the legitimacy of data processing, measures on the transfer of data to third countries and the power of the supervisory authority.

The right to privacy gains particular importance where confidentiality of personal information relating to medical issues is concerned.[119] The confidentiality of medical data is crucial not only for the protection of a patient's privacy, but also for the maintenance of the confidence in the medical profession and in the health services in general.[120] The ECtHR case of *Plon* v. *France* was a breach of confidentiality case involving the publication of a book containing revelations by President Mitterrand's former private doctor about the deceased President's state of health. An interim injunction prevented the publication of the book *Le Grand Secret* ten days after President Mitterrand's death. The Strasbourg Court agreed with the domestic court that the distribution of the book so soon after the President's death could only have intensified the legitimate emotions of the deceased's relatives, who 'inherited the rights vested in him'.[121] However, the Court also held in *Plon* that the continued ban on the distribution of the book no longer met a pressing social need and was therefore disproportionate to the aims pursued.[122] When the Paris Tribunal de Grande Instance decided on the continued ban, François Mitterrand had been dead for nine and a half months. The ECtHR thus found that the more time had elapsed, the more the public interest in discussion of the history of President Mitterrand's terms of office

solely for journalistic purposes or the purpose of artistic or literary expression only if they are necessary to reconcile the right to privacy with the rules governing freedom of expression.'

On the application of this provision, see ECJ, *Tietosuojavaltuutettu* v. *Satakunnan Markkinapörssi Oy and Satamedia Oy* [2008] ECR I-09831, Case C-73/07. Article 80(1) of the Commission Proposal for a Regulation on the Protection of Individuals with regard to the Processing of Personal Data and on the Free Movement of such Data (General Data Protection Regulation), COM(2012) 11 final, corresponds to this provision. Under domestic law, see, e.g. Sections 32, 3(a) UK Data Protection Act 1998.

119 See ECtHR, *Armonienė* v. *Lithuania* [2008] App. no. 36919/02 [40]; *Biriuk* v. *Lithuania* [2008] App. no. 23373/03 [39]; *Ageyevy* v. *Russia* [2013] App. no. 7075/10 [175].

120 See, e.g., ECtHR, *Biriuk* v. *Lithuania* [2008] App. no. 23373/03 [43].

121 ECtHR, *Éditions Plon* v. *France* [2004] App. no. 58148/00 [53].

122 ECtHR, *Éditions Plon* v. *France* [2004] App. no. 58148/00 [51].

prevailed over the requirements of protecting the President's rights to medical confidentiality. Furthermore, since at this stage the book had already been disseminated on the internet, some 40,000 copies had been sold and the book had been the subject of considerable media comment, the information in the book was to a large extent no longer confidential in reality.[123] As a general rule, there is usually no need for information to be kept confidential if the information is already available to the public anyway.[124]

An obligation to keep information confidential may not only arise from professional ethics, as is the case with medical information or the client–attorney relationship. There may also be implicit agreements of confidentiality in personal relations. It is therefore a breach of confidentiality and a violation of privacy if a person publishes intimate information about their sexual life with a former partner, even if the ex-partner happened to be a well-known politician.[125]

7.3.4.1.1.2 Publication of photos The question of whether the subject-matter of newsgathering and reporting contributes to a debate of general concern is particularly problematic with regard to publications of photographs or video recordings. The publication of photos is basically protected as a form of news reporting.[126] However, a person's image 'constitutes one of the chief attributes of his or her personality, as it reveals the person's unique characteristics and distinguishes the person from his or her peers'.[127] The right to privacy thus also encompasses the individual's right to control the taking and use of an image, including the right to refuse its publication.[128] In the absence of express consent, photo journalism stands in conflict with two privacy interests: the interest of being free from intrusion to privacy and the interest of information privacy. While the publication of a photo may interfere with a person's information privacy, the taking of a photo may already constitute an

[123] ECtHR, *Éditions Plon* v. *France* [2004] App. no. 58148/00 [53].

[124] See, e.g., ECtHR, *Weber* v. *Switzerland* [1990] App. no. 11034/84 [51]; *Observer and Guardian* v. *United Kingdom* [1991] App. no. 13585/88 [66]; *Vereniging Weekblad Bluf!* v. *Netherlands* [1995] App. no. 16616/90 [41]. See also ECJ, *Tietosuojavaltuutettu* v. *Satakunnan Markkinapörssi Oy and Satamedia Oy* [2008] ECR I-09831, Case C-73/07 [61]; House of Lords, *Attorney General* v. *Observer Ltd* [1990] 1 AC 109.

[125] Compare ECtHR, *Ruusunen* v. *Finland* [2014] App. no. 73579/10 [50].

[126] See, e.g, ECtHR, *Verlagsgruppe News GmbH* v. *Austria (No. 2)* [2006] App. no. 10520/02 [29]; *Von Hannover* v. *Germany (No. 2)* [2012] App. nos. 40660/08 and 60641/08 [103]; IACtHR, *Fontevecchia and D'Amico* v. *Argentina* [2011] Case 12.524 [66].

[127] See ECtHR, *Von Hannover* v. *Germany (No. 2)* [2012] App. nos. 40660/08 and 60641/08 [96]; IACtHR, *Fontevecchia and D'Amico* v. *Argentina* [2011] Case 12.524 [66].

[128] See ECtHR, *Von Hannover* v. *Germany (No. 2)* [2012] App. nos. 40660/08 and 60641/08 [96].

intrusion of a person's privacy.[129] The right to privacy therefore requires not only the examination of whether the publication of the picture itself contributes to a debate of general concern, but also the circumstances in which the picture was taken.

Consequently, a proper balancing exercise between the media's right to take and publish a photo and a person's right to privacy has to be based on a three-step test. First, one needs to examine the content of the pictures, especially whether the images contain very personal or even intimate information about an individual.[130] The non-consensual publication of pictures of nakedness, wardrobe malfunctions, sexual activity, ill or dead persons hardly ever contribute a discourse on a matter of public concern. In *Hachette Filipacchi Associés* v. *France*, the Strasbourg Court therefore rightly held that the publication of the photo of a murdered politician's body constitutes an unlawful intrusion into the privacy of his family.[131] Similarly, in *National Archives & Records Administration* v. *Favish,*[132] the US Supreme Court denied FOIA access to several photos of a high-ranking White House lawyer who had committed suicide. The Court held that the family's interest in the privacy of the deceased outweighed the public interest in seeing pictures from his death scene.

Regard must also be had to the gravity of the intrusion and the consequences of the publication of the photo for the person concerned: particularly for a private individual, unknown to the public, the publication of a photo may amount to an even more substantial interference than a written article.[133] In turn, politicians must show a broader degree of tolerance concerning the publication of their picture.[134]

Second, and related to the first step, the publication of a photo in addition to an article has to be necessary to ensure the credibility of the story.[135] The publication of the photograph of a murdered politician is

[129] See Moreham (2011) p. 431; Oster (2012b) p. 203.

[130] See, e.g., ECtHR, *Von Hannover* v. *Germany (No. 1)* [2004] App. no. 59320/00 [59]; *Mosley* v. *United Kingdom* [2011] App. no. 48009/08 [115]; see also, *mutatis mutandis*, *Krone Verlag GmbH & Co. KG* v. *Austria (No. 1)* [2002] App. no. 34315/96 [37]; *Eerikäinen and others* v. *Finland* [2009] App. no. 3514/02 [62].

[131] ECtHR, *Hachette Filipacchi Associés* v. *France* [2007] App. no. 71111/01 [46].

[132] US Supreme Court, *National Archives & Records Administration* v. *Favish*, 124 S Ct 1570 (2004).

[133] See ECtHR, *Egeland and Hanseid* v. *Norway* [2009] App. no. 34438/04 [61]; *Eerikäinen and others* v. *Finland* [2009] App. no. 3514/02 [70]; *A.* v. *Norway* [2009] App. no. 28070/06 [72]. See also *Karantsalis* v. *Department of Justice*, No. 10-10229, 11 March 2011, where the Court of Appeals in Atlanta (11th Cir.) held that the release of police mug shot photographs under a FOIA request would violate the personal privacy rights of those depicted.

[134] See ECtHR, *Schüssel* v. *Austria* [2002] App. no. 42409/98.

[135] See ECtHR, *Fressoz and Roire* v. *France* [1999] App. no. 29183/95 [54]; *MGN Ltd* v. *United Kingdom* [2011] App. no. 39401/04 [151].

usually not necessary to prove that he is in fact dead. The possibly newsworthy information that a child was born does not require visual proof that his mother was in labour. A report may also not be used as a pretext to publish photos of a person that are unrelated to the content of the text.[136]

Third, one must examine the circumstances under which the pictures have been taken. Even the fact that pictures haven been taken in a public place or in relation to an event in public does not automatically exclude a violation of a person's privacy.[137] At this point the approach taken by the Strasbourg Court differs significantly from First and Fourth Amendment jurisprudence of the US Supreme Court. In the seminal *von Hannover* v. *Germany (No. 1)* decision, the Strasbourg Court noted that the photos of the applicant in various German magazines showed her in scenes from her daily life, thus involving activities of a purely private nature: on holiday, engaging in sport or leaving a restaurant.[138] By contrast, while the US Supreme Court has acknowledged that a person may generally have a reasonable expectation of privacy,[139] the idea that a person can be private in public is alien to US law.

Yet a person may have a legitimate expectation of privacy even in public places and even if this person is known to the general public. To be sure, a person who walks down the street or sits in a restaurant is inevitably visible to any member of the public who is also present. It is another thing, however, whether this person is acting in an official function or in the exercise of their profession, or whether he is engaged in an activity that by cultural convention *is* private, such as having a conversation with a friend over dinner or taking out the trash. If the latter is the case, then there is no warrant to visually record the person's behaviour for the general public, as it is not conducive to any reasonable public discourse. The public does not have a legitimate interest in knowing where other individuals are and how they behave generally in their private life, even if they appear in places that cannot be described as secluded and despite the fact that they are well-known to the public.[140] The mere taking of such a photograph or video recording may already violate a person's privacy, that is, their 'freedom from intrusion' interest. In particular, the right to privacy requires that private information must

[136] See, *mutatis mutandis*, ECtHR, *Von Hannover* v. *Germany (No. 3)* [2013] App. no. 8772/10 [49–52].

[137] See ECtHR, *Peck* v. *United Kingdom* [2003] App. no. 44647/98 [62]; *Egeland and Hanseid* v. *Norway* [2009] App. no. 34438/04 [61]; Moreham (2006).

[138] ECtHR, *Von Hannover* v. *Germany (No. 1)* [2004] App. no. 59320/00 [61].

[139] US Supreme Court, *Katz* v. *United States*, 389 US 347 (1967).

[140] ECtHR, *Von Hannover* v. *Germany (No. 1)* [2004] App. no. 59320/00 [77].

not be obtained by subterfuge or other illicit means, or through the use of secret recording devices.[141] This applies even more where celebrities are continuously besieged and harassed. Photos 'appearing in the "sensationalist" press or in "romance" magazines, which generally aim to satisfy the public's curiosity regarding the details of a person's strictly private life are', according to the Strasbourg Court, 'often taken in a climate of continual harassment which may induce in the person concerned a very strong sense of intrusion into their private life or even of persecution'.[142]

In turn, an individual may under three exceptions have a lesser expectation of privacy even if the information concerned is private. First, because the person consented to the intrusion into his private sphere, as is the case with so-called 'homestories'. Second, there is no reasonable expectation of privacy if individuals intentionally and ostentatiously conduct private activities in public places, and do not arrange for protection of their privacy. This was the case, for example, in *Lillo-Stenberg and Sæther* v. *Norway*,[143] in which a well-known musician and an actress got married at a popular holiday location, where the bride arrived in an open boat on an islet. Third, a person does not have a legitimate expectation of privacy if the information concerned refutes prior public statements of the person, which served to build a positive reputation. If, for example, a celebrity publicly declared herself to be a vegetarian, the public has a legitimate interest to be informed that the person ate meat in a restaurant, although this would usually be a private matter. Privacy is a shield against unjustified intrusion, but not a cover for a false reputation.

7.3.4.1.1.3 Reporting on accidents, crimes and criminal proceedings Accidents, natural disasters and norm violations, especially if criminal in nature, receive particular public attention.[144] However, the media has

[141] See, e.g., ECtHR, *Hachette Filipacchi Associés ("Ici Paris")* v. *France* [2009] App. no. 12268/03 [47]; *Flinkkilä and others* v. *Finland* [2010] App. no. 25576/04 [81]; *Saaristo and others* v. *Finland* [2010] App. no. 184/06 [65]; *Von Hannover* v. *Germany (No. 1)* [2004] App. no. 59320/00 [68]; *MGN Ltd* v. *United Kingdom* [2011] App. no. 39401/04 [151]; *mutatis mutandis*, *Wizerkaniuk* v. *Poland* [2011] App. no. 18990/05 [75] and IACtHR, *Fontevecchia and D'Amico* v. *Argentina* [2011] Case 12.524 [68].

[142] ECtHR, *Von Hannover* v. *Germany (No. 2)* [2012] App. nos. 40660/08 and 60641/08 [103]. See, e.g., *Von Hannover* v. *Germany (No. 1)* [2004] App. no. 59320/00 [59]; *Hachette Filipacchi Associés ("Ici Paris")* v. *France* [2009] App. no. 12268/03 [40]; *mutatis mutandis*, IACtHR, *Fontevecchia and D'Amico* v. *Argentina* [2011] Case 12.524 [68].

[143] ECtHR, *Lillo-Stenberg and Sæther* v. *Norway* [2014] App. no. 13258/09. See also *Peck* v. *United Kingdom* [2003] App. no. 44647/98 [62]; *Shabanov and Tren* v. *Russia* [2006] App. no. 5433/02 [46].

[144] Luhmann (1996) p. 29.

to abide by certain standards of conduct when reporting on such incidents and on criminal proceedings.

When reporting tragic incidents and actual or threatened commissions of crimes, the media has to carefully balance the public's interest in information against the interests of victims, their relatives and other people involved. 'Victims of misfortune must not be made to suffer a second time by their portrayal in the media.'[145] Furthermore, the media must neither interfere with the work of the police nor allow itself to be made the tool of criminals.[146]

Reportings on criminal court proceedings are of significant public interest beyond the interest in the crime itself: the public has a right to be informed about the administration of justice. The principle of open justice, which is an essential component for any state governed by the rule of law,[147] is not only required by the public's right to receive information, but also a right of the parties involved. Trials under the watching eyes of the public are less susceptible to arbitrary judgments than secret proceedings.

However, the public's interest in being informed may be superseded by the parties' interest not to be subjected to public monitoring, or by overriding state interests.[148] Articles 14(1) ICCPR and 6(1) ECHR recognise that open justice may have to yield to privacy under certain circumstances. According to Article 14(1) ICCPR,

> [t]he press and the public may be excluded from all or part of a trial for reasons of morals, public order (*ordre public*) or national security in a democratic society, or when the interest of the private lives of the parties so requires, or to the extent strictly necessary in the opinion of the court in special circumstances where publicity would prejudice the interests of justice; but any judgment rendered in a criminal case or in a suit at law shall be made public except where the interest of juvenile persons otherwise requires or the proceedings concern matrimonial disputes or the guardianship of children.

[145] German Press Council, German Press Code, Guideline 11.3.

[146] See German Press Council, German Press Code, Guideline 11.2. As a lesson from the 1988 Gladbeck hostage crisis in Germany, where representatives of the media conducted interviews with the abductors and the hostages, the German German Press Council also prohibited any interviews with hostage-takers during a hostage situation.

[147] Compare *G and G* v. *Wikimedia Foundation Inc.* [2009] EWHC 3148 (QB) [16], providing further references; Master of the Rolls, Report of the Committee on Super-Injunctions: Super-Injunctions, Anonymised Injunctions and Open Justice, 2011. See Article 14(1) ICCPR, Article 6(1) ECHR and Article 8(5) ACHR.

[148] At common law, the requirements for an exception to public hearing were stated in *Scott* v. *Scott* by Lord Haldane LC: 'unless it is strictly necessary for the attainment of justice, there can be no power in the Court to hear in camera either a matrimonial cause or any other where there is a contest between the parties.' (*Scott* v. *Scott* [1913] AC 417, 438). See, e.g., *Ntuli* v. *Donald* [2010] EWCA Civ 1276 [47].

Similarly, under Article 6(1) ECHR,

> the press and public may be excluded from all or part of the trial in the interests of morals, public order or national security in a democratic society, where the interests of juveniles or the protection of the private life of the parties so require, or to the extent strictly necessary in the opinion of the court in special circumstances where publicity would prejudice the interests of justice.

Therefore courts have to balance the interest of the media and of the public against those of the persons involved in the court proceedings.[149] The aspects to be considered in this balancing exercise are:

- The right of the media to inform the public on ongoing criminal proceedings as matters of significant public concern;
- the right of the public to be informed on ongoing criminal proceedings;
- the state's positive obligations to protect the privacy of accused and convicted persons in criminal proceedings;
- the requirement under Article 14(1) ICCPR, Article 6(1) ECHR and Article 8(5) ACHR that hearings be public, and the fact that reporting and commenting on court proceedings may contribute to their publicity;
- the particular interests of minors;[150]
- the need to safeguard due process and to maintain the authority and impartiality of the judiciary;[151] and
- the fact that a person has a right to be presumed innocent of any criminal offence until proven guilty.[152]

One particular limitation on media freedom arises with regard to news reporting on the criminal history of a person. Several courts have prohibited publishing information about criminal convictions of people who served their sentence.[153] The rationale for those prohibitions is the fact

[149] See, e.g., ECtHR, *Eerikäinen and others* v. *Finland* [2009] App. no. 3514/02; *Egeland and Hanseid* v. *Norway* [2009] App. no. 34438/04; *News Verlags GmbH & Co. KG* v. *Austria* [2000] App. no. 31457/96; Council of Europe, Committee of Ministers, Recommendation Rec(2003)13 on the Provision of Information through the Media in relation to Criminal Proceedings.

[150] See below Section 7.3.4.1.1.4. [151] See Chapter 10.

[152] Article 14(2) ICCPR, Article 6(2) ECHR, Article 7(1)(b) AfCHPR and Article 8(2) ACHR. See, e.g., ECtHR, *Bladet Tromsø and Stensaas* v. *Norway* [1999] App. no. 21980/93 [65]; *Pedersen and Baadsgaard* v. *Denmark* [2004] App. no. 49017/99 [78]; *White* v. *Sweden* [2006] App. no. 42435/02 [21]; *Axel Springer AG* v. *Germany (No. 1)* [2012] App. no. 39954/08 [96]; Council of Europe, Committee of Ministers, Recommendation Rec(2003)13 on the Provision of Information through the Media in relation to Criminal Proceedings.

[153] See, e.g., Supreme Court of California, *Briscoe* v. *Reader's Digest Association*, 93 Cal. Rptr. 866, 873 (1971); German Federal Constitutional Court, '*Lebach*' [1973] Case 1 BvR 536/72.

that such reporting may threaten to jeopardise the released person's social rehabilitation. Having served a sentence means that the person has paid for his crime and should receive a chance to reintegrate into society. On the other hand, one should consider that the commission of crimes is *per se* a matter of public concern. Furthermore, one might also argue that members of society have a right to have such information available in order to get an undistorted picture of a person.[154]

This conflict between the freedom of the media and the public's right to be informed, on the one hand, and the former convict's right to respect for privacy, on the other hand, is not susceptible to a clear yes/no answer. Rather, the conflicting rights should be balanced in a way that each right can be realised to the optimal extent. The ECtHR decision *Österreichischer Rundfunk* v. *Austria*, which concerned a broadcaster's publication of a picture of a convicted person after his release on parole, provides commendable guidance for this balancing exercise. The Strasbourg Court considered the degree of notoriety of the person concerned, the lapse of time since the conviction and the release, the nature of the crime, the connection between the contents of the report and the picture shown and the completeness and correctness of the accompanying text.[155] The Court found in this case that the prohibition of the publication of the picture had been disproportionate, because the domestic courts had attached too great a weight to the long lapse of time since the person's conviction, but did not pay any particular attention to the fact that only a few weeks had elapsed since his release. Furthermore, they did not take into account his notoriety and the political nature of the crime of which he had been convicted.[156]

The Court also distinguished the case from the comparable 2004 admissibility decision *Österreichischer Rundfunk* v. *Austria*.[157] In that case, the Court found that the prohibition on publishing a convict's picture after his release on parole did not violate Article 10 ECHR. The Court had regard to the fact that the picture of the convicted person had been shown in a different context, namely in connection with the investigations into a series of attacks with letter bombs. However, the broadcaster neither mentioned that the person concerned had been acquitted of any involvement in these attacks, nor that he had served his sentence and had been released on parole.[158] This admissibility

[154] See Volokh (2000) 1091.
[155] ECtHR, *Österreichischer Rundfunk* v. *Austria* [2006] App. no. 35841/02 [68].
[156] ECtHR, *Österreichischer Rundfunk* v. *Austria* [2006] App. no. 35841/02 [69].
[157] ECtHR, *Österreichischer Rundfunk* v. *Austria* [2004] App. no. 57597/00 (admissibility decision).
[158] See ECtHR, *Österreichischer Rundfunk* v. *Austria* [2006] App. no. 35841/02 [70].

decision is indeed justifiable, because the omission of relevant facts may have the same impact as the statement of untrue facts.

7.3.4.1.1.4 Reportings involving children Particular vigilance is called for where privacy of minors is concerned. According to Article 16 of the UN Convention on the Rights of the Child, '[e]very child has the right to privacy. The law should protect the child's private, family and home life.' Against this background, it is not acceptable for the media to publish intimate details about children's lives or to publish a picture of a minor from which he or she could be recognised without his or her parents' consent, even if the parents are well-known.[159]

This applies even more in criminal proceedings against minors.[160] Article 40 of the UN Convention on the Rights of the Child emphasises that the privacy of a child accused or guilty of breaking the law must be respected at all times. Similarly, Principle 8 Recommendation of the Council of Europe on the provision of information through the media in relation to criminal proceedings requires that particular protection of privacy 'should be given to parties [to criminal proceedings] who are minors or other vulnerable persons'.[161]

7.3.4.1.1.5 Dissemination of private information that does not fall under one of these categories There are further cases that do not fall under one of the aforementioned categories, which may nonetheless constitute a violation of privacy. These are cases in which the publication did not significantly contribute to a matter of public concern, but had as its aim to satisfy the curiosity of a particular readership. In these cases, entertainment is presented as news rather than news being presented as entertainment. Examples are reportings of details of the private life of an individual who does not exercise public functions,[162] the love affair between a noblewoman and a banker[163] and the financial difficulties of a famous singer.[164]

[159] ECtHR, *Kurier Zeitungsverlag und Druckerei GmbH* v. *Austria (No. 2)* [2012] App. no. 1593/06 [57]; *Ageyevy* v. *Russia* [2013] App. no. 7075/10 [175].

[160] ECtHR, *S. and Marper* v. *United Kingdom* [2008] App. nos. 30562/04 and 30566/04 [124].

[161] Council of Europe, Committee of Ministers, Recommendation Rec(2003)13 on the Provision of Information through the Media in relation to Criminal Proceedings.

[162] ECtHR, *Von Hannover* v. *Germany (No. 1)* [2004] App. no. 59320/00 [63].

[163] ECtHR, *Campmany y Diez de Revenga and Lopez-Galiacho Perona* v. *Spain* [2000] App. no. 54224/00, p. 8.

[164] ECtHR, *Hachette Filipacchi Associés ("Ici Paris")* v. *France* [2009] App. no. 12268/03 [43].

Courts have to examine on a case-by-case basis whether aspects of the private life of public figures, even when they are not exercising official functions, may nonetheless give cause for legitimate public interest. In *Standard Verlags GmbH* v. *Austria*, the Strasbourg Court found that the award of damages for a publication concerning alleged marital difficulties of the then-Federal President of Austria did not violate Article 10 ECHR. However, it seems more convincing to follow the dissenting opinion by Judges Jebens and Spielmann, who argued that the state of the marriage of the Federal President is indeed a topic of public interest.[165] It may raise sincere concerns about the President's well-being and the question as to whether these difficulties hamper the prudent exercise of his functions. Furthermore, in this particular case, the President himself had kept the public informed about his first divorce and his remarriage. It was probably less the content of the publication that enticed the Court to its rather paternalistic approach, but the tongue-in-cheek way in which it was presented.

The public interest in publication outweighs any expectation of privacy where persons publicly exhibit or otherwise 'mediatise' aspects of their private life. Whoever fails to keep their private life separate from their business makes themself subject to legitimate scrutiny.[166] In the ECtHR decision *Kuliś* v. *Poland*, the fact that a politician himself publicly displayed the kidnapping of his daughter and got involved in the prosecution of this kidnapping made this affair, although in the first place a family matter, a case of public interest.[167] Another important and illustrative case in this context is the Inter-American Court's decision *Fontevecchia and D'Amico* v. *Argentina*.[168] The case involved the conviction and order to pay damages of two journalists for the disclosure of personal information about the life of the then-President of Argentina, Carlos Saúl Menem. The journalists' magazine *Noticias* published a report to the effect that President Menem had a child out of wedlock, born in 1981. The magazine also reported details about the source of the child's mother's assets and about her personal relationship with President Menem, and included allegations of money and favours being given to the child's family because of their connection to the President. President Menem successfully sued the journalists for invading his family's privacy in the Argentinian courts. Similar to the ECtHR, the Inter-American Court considered several factors for its balancing exercise between freedom of expression and the

165 ECtHR, *Standard Verlags GmbH* v. *Austria (No. 2)* [2009] App. no. 21277/05, dissenting opinion of Judge Jebens, joined by Judge Spielmann [4].
166 Walker (2012) pp. 65–6.
167 ECtHR, *Kuliś* v. *Poland* [2008] App. no. 15601/02 [48].
168 ECtHR, *Fontevecchia and D'Amico* v. *Argentina* [2011] Case 12.524; see Alvira (2013).

right to respect for private life, in particular the limited protection of public figures and the public interest in the publication.[169] As the then-President of Argentina, the highest elective public official in his country, President Menem 'was subject to greater scrutiny not only regarding his official activities or the exercise of official functions, but also regarding aspects that, in principle, could be linked to his private life but revealed matters of public interest'.[170] Concerning the public interest in the presentation, the Court held that the information concerned related to the integrity of a political leader, and thus a legitimate social interest.[171] Moreover, the Court observed that the facts giving rise to this controversy had been made widely available in print media in Argentina and abroad, and that President Menem 'adopted, prior to the publications that he later questioned, behavior patterns favourable that let out that personal relationships, sharing acts and public situations with these people ... even receiving the child and his mother in official places like the Government House and the presidential residences.'[172]

7.3.4.1.2 *Knowingly false statements of fact*

If the content provider knew that a defamatory statement was false (Category II), then there is little room for freedom of expression protection, and even less room for media freedom. As a consequence, the Strasbourg Court regularly upholds interferences with a false defamatory statement made in bad faith, which cannot be reasonably perceived as satire or parody.[173] Similarly, even under First Amendment doctrine public figures succeed in a defamation lawsuit if they can prove that the defamatory statement was made with 'actual malice' – that is, with knowledge that it was false or with reckless disregard of whether it was false or not.[174]

7.3.4.1.3 *Statements that turn out to be untrue or cannot be proven to be true*

The most difficult cases of statements of fact are those where neither the truth nor the falsity of the statement could be established (Category III), and those where the publisher believed the statement to be true when

[169] ECtHR, *Fontevecchia and D'Amico* v. *Argentina* [2011] Case 12.524 [59].
[170] ECtHR, *Fontevecchia and D'Amico* v. *Argentina* [2011] Case 12.524 [60].
[171] ECtHR, *Fontevecchia and D'Amico* v. *Argentina* [2011] Case 12.524 [62].
[172] ECtHR, *Fontevecchia and D'Amico* v. *Argentina* [2011] Case 12.524 [63] and [64].
[173] ECtHR, *Alithia Publishing Company Ltd and Constantinides* v. *Cyprus* [2008] App. No. 17550/03 [67]; see also *Pedersen and Baadsgaard* v. *Denmark* [2004] App. No. 49017/99 [78].
[174] US Supreme Court, *New York Times Co.* v. *Sullivan* 376 US 254, 279-80 (1964).

issued, but which later turned out to be untrue (Category IV). In these categories, the First Amendment jurisprudence of the US Supreme Court differs most significantly from the approaches taken by international courts and tribunals. Under First Amendment doctrine, public figures succeed in a defamation lawsuit only if they can prove that the defamatory statement was made with 'actual malice'.[175] By contrast, international adjudicators have accepted it as principally compatible with freedom of expression to place the onus of proving the truth of defamatory statements even concerning a public figure on a defendant in libel proceedings.[176]

To be sure, the mass media has the power to shape public opinion, and libellous statements disseminated by the mass media have a more devastating effect than defamation in private circles. Furthermore, under international human rights conventions, the right to respect for one's reputation is in itself protected as a human right with equal value to freedom of expression and media freedom. Imposing on a defamation claimant the burden of proving the falsity of a publication may thus be perceived as a violation of their right to respect for reputation, as it is usually more difficult to prove the falsity than the veracity of a statement of fact. In addition, the argument that the best remedy against false speech is true speech applies only to a minimum extent to the modern mass media. Even politicians do not always have the forum to counter false reporting by powerful and influential media conglomerates, which have the power to shape, but also to destroy, political careers.

However, to impose the burden of proof regarding the full veracity of a factual statement on the media defendant would not only be contrary to the general rule that the claimant in civil proceedings or the state in criminal proceedings has the burden of proving that a wrongful act has been committed.[177] In addition, such a reversal of the burden of proof would have an intolerable chilling effect on news reporting of matters of public concern, and thus on public discourse itself. The media must have 'breathing space'[178] when reporting on matters of public concern; media freedom includes the right to make mistakes. Consequently, there can be

175 US Supreme Court, *New York Times Co.* v. *Sullivan*, 376 US 254, 279–80 (1964).

176 See Human Rights Committee, *Marques de Morais* v. *Angola* [2005] Communication no. 1128/2002 [6.8]; General Comment no. 34, para. 47; ECtHR, *McVicar* v. *United Kingdom* [2002] App. no. 46311/99 [87]; *Steel and Morris* v. *United Kingdom* [2005] App. no. 68416/01 [93]; IAComHR, *Dudley Stokes* v. *Jamaica* [2008] Case 12.468 [80].

177 See Pasqualucci (2006) 406.

178 US Supreme Court, *New York Times Co.* v. *Sullivan*, 376 US 254, 272 (1964).

no absolute obligation on a defendant in libel proceedings to establish the truth of their publication.[179] In particular, domestic courts may not require a publisher to present 'compelling proof' and thus a degree of precision that comes close to the one usually required for justifying a criminal sentence.[180]

Yet, following from the argument from public discourse, the media not only has an obligation towards potential victims of its publications, but also towards its audience in general, to publish *prudently researched* information. Consequently, the media has an obligation not to absolutely verify, but to attempt to verify factual statements that are defamatory of private individuals.[181] If a publisher issues a defamatory factual statement without showing any attempt to prove the statement, for instance, because he believed that it was merely a value judgment, this may lead to a violation of the claimant's right to respect for his reputation and make the publisher subject to liability.[182] But this also means that courts must allow the defendant to establish the truth of his or her statement.[183] If this is not the case, then not only the freedom of the media but also the right to a fair trial has been violated.[184] In addition, regard must be had to the right of journalists not to disclose information identifying their sources. In defamation proceedings against a journalist, courts may not require the disclosure of information identifying a source by the journalist for the purposes of establishing the truth.[185]

[179] See, e.g., ECtHR, *Thorgeir Thorgeirson* v. *Iceland* [1992] App. no. 13778/88 [65]; *Dalban* v. *Romania* [1999] App. no. 28114/95 [49]; *Gutiérrez Suárez* v. *Spain* [2010] App. no. 16023/07 [37]; Human Rights Committee, General Comment no. 34, para. 47; IACtHR, *Herrera-Ulloa* v. *Costa Rica* [2004] Case 12.367 [132]; AfComHPR, *Scanlen & Holderness* v. *Zimbabwe* [2009] App. no. 297/05 [120].

[180] See ECtHR, *Scharsach and News Verlagsgesellschaft mbH* v. *Austria* [2003] App. no. 39394/98 [43]; *Karman* v. *Russia* [2006] App. no. 29372/02 [42]; *Brosa* v. *Germany* [2014] App. no. 5709/09 [48].

[181] See, e.g., ECtHR, *De Haes and Gijsels* v. *Belgium* [1997] App. no. 19983/92 [39]; *Pedersen and Baadsgaard* v. *Denmark* [2004] App. no. 49017/99 [78]; *Karsai* v. *Hungary* [2009] App. no. 5380/07 [32]; *Kaperzyński* v. *Poland* [2012] App. no. 43206/07 [64].

[182] See, e.g., ECtHR, *Perna* v. *Italy* [2003] App. no. 48898/99 [47]; *Pfeifer* v. *Austria* [2007] App. no. 12556/03 [47]; *Flux* v. *Moldova (No. 6)* [2008] App. no. 22824/04 [27–9]; *Růžový panter, o.s.* v. *Czech Republic* [2012] App. no. 20240/08.

[183] Human Rights Committee, *Marques de Morais* v. *Angola* [2005] Communication no. 1128/2002 [6.8]; General Comment no. 34, para. 47; ECtHR, *Castells* v. *Spain* [1992] App. no. 11798/85 [48]; *Sürek* v. *Turkey (No. 2)* [1999] App. no. 24122/94 [39]; *Dalban* v. *Romania* [1999] App. no. 28114/95 [50]; *Colombani and others* v. *France* [2002] App. no. 51279/99 [66].

[184] See ECtHR, *Folea* v. *Romania* [2008] App. no. 34434/02 [29–32] and [42].

[185] See Council of Europe, Committee of Ministers, Recommendation No. R(2000) 7 on the Right of Journalists not to Disclose their Sources of Information, Principle 4; compare ECtHR, *Kasabova* v. *Bulgaria* [2011] App. no. 22385/03 [65].

In turn, in order for liability in defamation to be proportionate to the aim of protecting the reputation of others, a person suing for defamation has to prove that it was the defendant's statement that was damaging to his or her reputation. This requires the claimant to establish a clear link between themselves and the impugned statement. Mere personal conjecture or a subjective perception of a statement as defamatory is not sufficient. Rather, from the perspective of an ordinary recipient, the statement must have referred directly to the claimant, or he or she must have been targeted by the criticism.[186]

Therefore, Categories III and IV can be treated equally with regard to civil liability, since both a publisher who cannot prove the truth of his statement and a publisher who unintentionally issued a false statement must have the opportunity to establish a defence based on the importance of the publication for public discourse. Hence, the relevant test is not whether the defendant journalist can prove the veracity of the statements. Rather, the journalist has to establish that he abided by his duties and responsibilities. The factors that have to be taken into account and properly balanced with regard to defamatory publications are:

- The degree to which the reporting is of public concern;[187]
- Whether the journalist communicated remaining doubts;[188]
- Whether the journalist has taken all reasonable steps to verify the factual basis of the allegations. The media must themselves ascertain whether allegations are true by obtaining further information.[189] This includes a reasonable amount of research before publication.[190] Whether all reasonable steps have been taken depends on several factors, such as:
  - (i) The extent to which the publisher can reasonably regard his sources as reliable:[191] this has to be determined in the light of the situation *ex ante*, rather than on the basis of the findings of fact

[186] ECtHR, *Dyuldin and Kislov* v. *Russia* [2007] App. no. 25968/02 [44]; reiterated in *Filatenko* v. *Russia* [2007] App. no. 73219/01 [45] and *OOO 'Vesti' and Ukhov* v. *Russia* [2013] App. no. 21724/03 [62].

[187] See Chapter 2, Section 2.2.3.1 and Chapter 6, Section 6.3.3.2.

[188] ECtHR, *Pedersen and Baadsgaard* v. *Denmark* [2004] App. no. 49017/99 [77 ff.]; *Wizerkaniuk* v. *Poland* [2011] App. no. 18990/05 [66].

[189] ECtHR, *Europapress Holding d.o.o.* v. *Croatia* [2010] App. no. 25333/06 [68]; IACtHR, *Kimel* v. *Argentina* [2008] Case 12.450 [79].

[190] ECtHR, *Prager and Oberschlick* v. *Austria* [1995] App. no. 15974/90 [37]; IACtHR, *Kimel* v. *Argentina* [2008] Case 12.450 [79].

[191] See, e.g., ECtHR, *Bladet Tromsø and Stensaas* v. *Norway* [1999] App. no. 21980/93 [66]; *McVicar* v. *United Kingdom* [2002] App. no. 46311/99 [84]; *Pedersen and Baadsgaard* v. *Denmark* [2004] App. no. 49017/99 [78 ff.]; *Ringier Axel Springer Slovakia, AS* v. *Slovakia* [2011] App. no. 41262/05 [97].

made thereafter.[192] However, the media is entitled to rely on the contents of official reports[193] or investigations by professionals specialised in a certain area[194] without having to undertake independent research. Particularly problematic in this context is whether internet material may constitute a 'reliable source'.[195] The ECtHR held that 'the policies governing reproduction of material from [the internet] undeniably have to be adjusted according to the technology's specific features in order to secure the protection and promotion of the rights and freedoms concerned'.[196]

(ii) The seriousness of the defamation in question: the more serious the allegation is, the more solid the factual basis has to be.[197]

(iii) Whether the media gave the defamed persons the opportunity to defend themselves prior to publication.[198]

(iv) The topicality, because news is a perishable commodity:[199] however, journalists must not focus in a sensationalist fashion on being the first paper to print the story.[200] In this context, a distinction can be made between daily news and reports that are not dependent upon daily events, such as in books.[201] The news value of reports is to a lesser degree based on its topicality than on its accuracy.

(v) Authors of historical texts are required to respect the fundamental rules of historical method.[202]

192 ECtHR, *Bladet Tromsø and Stensaas* v. *Norway* [1999] App. no. 21980/93 [66]; *Alithia Publishing Company Ltd and Constantinides* v. *Cyprus* [2008] App. no. 17550/03 [65]; *Flux* v. *Moldova (No. 6)* [2008] App. no. 22824/04 [26].

193 ECtHR, *Bladet Tromsø and Stensaas* v. *Norway* [1999] App. no. 21980/93 [68]; *Colombani and others* v. *France* [2002] App. no. 51279/99 [65]; *Selistö* v. *Finland* [2004] App. no. 56767/00 [60]; *Pipi* v. *Turkey* [2009] App. no. 4020/03, p. 7; *Tănăsoaica* v. *Romania* [2012] App. no. 3490/03 [50]; *mutatis mutandis, Rumyana Ivanova* v. *Bulgaria* [2008] App. no. 36207/03 [65].

194 ECtHR, *Ungváry and Irodalom Kft* v. *Hungary* [2013] App. no. 64520/10 [75].

195 See ECtHR, *Editorial Board of Pravoye Delo and Shtekel* v. *Ukraine* [2011] App. no. 33014/05 [63–4].

196 ECtHR, *Editorial Board of Pavoye Delo and Shtekel* v. *Ukraine* [2011] App. No. 33014/05 [63]; *Węgrzynowski and Smolczewski* v. *Poland* [2013] App. No. 33846/07 [58].

197 ECtHR, *Pedersen and Baadsgaard* v. *Denmark* [2004] App. no. 49017/99 [78]; *Dyundin* v. *Russia* [2008] App. no. 37406/03 [35]; *Rumyana Ivanova* v. *Bulgaria* [2008] App. no. 36207/03 [64]; *Kasabova* v. *Bulgaria* [2011] App. no. 22385/03 [65].

198 ECtHR, *Bergens Tidende and others* v. *Norway* [2000] App. no. 26132/95 [58]; *mutatis mutandis, Flux* v. *Moldova (No. 6)* [2008] App. no. 22824/04 [29].

199 ECtHR, *Observer and Guardian* v. *United Kingdom* [1991] App. no. 13585/88 [60].

200 ECtHR, *Novaya Gazeta and Borodyanskiy* v. *Russia* [2013] App. no. 14087/08 [37]; *Ageyevy* v. *Russia* [2013] App. no. 7075/10 [227].

201 See Luhmann (1996) p. 35.

202 ECtHR, *Chauvy and others* v. *France* [2004] App. no. 64915/01 [77].

- Where allegations of having committed a crime are at issue, the media has to respect the presumption of innocence.[203] Furthermore, media publications must not include statements which are likely to prejudice the chances of a person to be acquitted, or to undermine the confidence of the public in the role of the courts in the administration of criminal justice.[204] However, where the media publishes allegations that someone had committed a criminal offence, it can neither be expected to adduce compelling evidence like a public prosecutor, nor may it be obliged to wait for a final conviction.[205] Moreover, while a final conviction in principle amounts to incontrovertible proof that a person has committed an offence,[206] the fact that a person was neither prosecuted nor convicted does not mean that the media may not report on the issue and describe the person's role in the case.[207]
- Whether the publisher corrected false statements of fact after he learned of their falsity;[208] this is particularly relevant for articles in internet archives. A daily news report in an internet archive may, after a certain lapse of time, lose its news value. Consequently, it is reasonable to impose a higher burden on the accuracy of an article in an internet archive than on breaking news.[209] The publisher can be requested to add an appropriate qualification to an article contained in an internet archive, where he has been informed that a libel action has been initiated against the article published in the written press.[210] Such a request is a less intrusive, and therefore more proportionate, interference with media freedom than requiring the removal of potentially defamatory articles from archives altogether, as it is not for courts to rewrite history and to treat articles as if they never existed.[211]

[203] Article 14(2) ICCPR, Article 6(2) ECHR, Article 8(2) ACHR and Article 7(1)(b) AfCHPR. See ECtHR, *Flux* v. *Moldova (No. 6)* [2008] App. no. 22824/04 [31]; *Salumäki* v. *Finland* [2014] App. no. 23605/09 [58].

[204] See ECtHR, *Worm* v. *Austria* [1997] App. no. 83/1996/702/894 [50]; *Du Roy and Malaurie* v. *France* [2000] App. No. 34000/96 [43]; *News Verlags GmbH & Co. KG* v. *Austria* [2000] App. no. 31457/96 [56]; *Krylov* v. *Russia* [2013] App. no. 36697/03 [38].

[205] ECtHR, *Kasabova* v. *Bulgaria* [2011] App. no. 22385/03 [62].

[206] ECtHR, *Kasabova* v. *Bulgaria* [2011] App. no. 22385/03 [62].

[207] EComHR, *Barril* v. *France* [1997] App. no. 32218/96, p. 157.

[208] See ECtHR, *Ristamäki and Korvola* v. *Finland* [2013] App. no. 66456/09 [57].

[209] Compare ECtHR, *Times Newspapers Ltd (Nos 1 and 2)* v. *United Kingdom* [2009] App. nos. 3002/03 and 23676/03 [47].

[210] ECtHR, *Węgrzynowski and Smolczewski* v. *Poland* [2013] App. no. 33846/07 [59].

[211] ECtHR, *Times Newspapers Ltd* v. *United Kingdom (Nos. 1 and 2)* [2009] App. nos. 3002/03 and 23676/03 [47]; *Węgrzynowski and Smolczewski* v. *Poland* [2013] App. no. 33846/07 [65].

According to the CJEU's *Google Spain* decision, this is different for internet search engines.[212]

- The context of the allegations: in 'the course of a lively political debate', journalists should enjoy a wide freedom to criticise the actions of public officials, even where the statements may lack a clear factual basis.[213] This applies especially to statements that have been issued in live broadcasting, where a person has but a limited possibility of reformulating, refining or retracting any statements before they are made public.[214]
- The tone of the publication: the civility rules of public discourse require a minimum degree of moderation and propriety. Journalists should consider different points of view, in particular those of the person concerned.[215] Facts have to be presented in an objective and reasonably balanced manner and not with recourse to excessive language.[216]

7.3.4.2 Value judgments

Freedom of the media does not only include the right to offer a factual account of events. It also encompasses the right to issue value judgments and thus shape public opinion. In contrast to statements of fact, a requirement to prove the truth of a value judgment is impossible to fulfil. Such a requirement would *per se* infringe freedom of expressing one's opinion.[217]

Freedom of the media even protects defamatory statements of opinion, if they constitute fair comment and do not overstep the boundaries of acceptable criticism. The decisive factors for the establishment of a fair comment defence are:

- The degree to which the reporting is of public concern.[218]

[212] CJEU, *Google Spain SL* v. *AEPD* [2014] (not yet reported), Case C-131/12.
[213] ECtHR, *Lombardo and others* v. *Malta* [2007] App. no. 7333/06 [60].
[214] Compare ECtHR, *Fuentes Bobo* v. *Spain* [2000] App. no. 39293/98 [46]; *Gündüz* v. *Turkey* [2003] App. no. 35071/97 [49]; *Filatenko* v. *Russia* [2007] App. no. 73219/01 [41].
[215] ECtHR, *Bladet Tromsø and Stensaas* v. *Norway* [1999] App. no. 21980/93 [63]; *Bergens Tidende and others* v. *Norway* [2000] App. no. 26132/95 [58]; *Selistö* v. *Finland* [2004] App. no. 56767/00 [62] and [66].
[216] ECtHR, *Bergens Tidende and others* v. *Norway* [2000] App. no. 26132/95 [57]; *Lindon, Otchakovsky-Laurens and July* v. *France* [2007] App. nos. 21279/02 and 36448/02 [66]; *Saaristo and others* v. *Finland* [2010] App. no. 184/06 [65]; *Kaperzyński* v. *Poland* [2012] App. no. 43206/07 [64].
[217] See, e.g., ECtHR, *Lingens* v. *Austria* [1986] App. no. 9815/82 [46]; *Jerusalem* v. *Austria* [2001] App. no. 26958/95 [42]; *Ferihumer* v. *Austria* [2007] App. no. 30547/03 [24]; IACtHR, *Kimel* v. *Argentina* [2008] Case 12.450 [93]; *Usón Ramírez* v. *Venezuela* [2009] Case 12.554 [86].
[218] See Chapter 2, Section 2.2.3.1 and Chapter 6, Section 6.3.3.2.

- Whether the comment was based on a sufficiently factual basis to support it, since a value judgment without any factual basis to support it may be excessive.[219]
- The facts on which the value judgment is founded must be true, or there must have been at least sufficient efforts to establish the truth. The ability to argue in a public discourse presupposes accurate facts.[220] The test of whether there have been sufficient efforts to establish the truth is identical with the factors applicable to untrue statements of fact.[221] Consequently, courts must allow an 'effective opportunity to adduce evidence to support [the] statements and thereby show that they constituted fair comment'.[222]
- Even if the factual basis of a value judgment is correct, a true statement, coupled with additional comments or innuendo, may create a false image to the public and may thus go beyond the limits of acceptable criticism.[223]
- The tone of the publication: whether the value judgment constituted insult rather than criticism.[224] However, the use of strong polemical terms is allowed where the impugned statement constitutes a reaction to a provocative statement by the allegedly defamed person in a robust and heated public discussion.[225] The precise words used in the precise context are thus of crucial importance.[226]
- The way facts and comments are presented to the public and the impression they could produce in the reader.[227]

A singular area of value judgment is the stylistic device of satire and caricature. Media freedom covers a certain degree of exaggeration and even provocation, including vulgar phrases and a satirical style.[228] Satire

[219] See, e.g., ECtHR, *De Haes and Gijsels* v. *Belgium* [1997] App. no. 19983/92 [47]; *Unabhängige Initiative Informationsvielfalt* v. *Austria* [2002] App. no. 28525/95 [47]; *Lindon, Otchakovsky-Laurens and July* v. *France* [2007] App. nos. 21279/02 and 36448/02 [55]; IACtHR, *Kimel* v. *Argentina* [2008] Case 12.450 [79].
[220] Post (1990) 659. [221] See above Section 7.3.4.1.3.
[222] ECtHR, *Jerusalem* v. *Austria* [2001] App. no. 26958/95 [45].
[223] ECtHR, *Vides Aizsardzības Klubs* v. *Latvia* [2004] App. no. 57829/00 [45]; *Růžový panter, o.s.* v. *Czech Republic* [2012] App. no. 20240/08 [32].
[224] See ECtHR, *Mustafa Erdoğan and others* v. *Turkey* [2014] App. nos. 346/04 and 39779/04 [44].
[225] See, e.g., ECtHR, *Oberschlick* v. *Austria (No. 2)* [1997] App. no. 20834/92 [33] and [34]; *Nilsen and Johnsen* v. *Norway* [1999] App. no. 23118/93 [52]; *Unabhängige Initiative Informationsvielfalt* v. *Austria* [2002] App. no. 28525/95 [43].
[226] See, e.g., ECtHR, *Tammer* v. *Estonia* [2001] App. no. 41205/98 [68]; *Karhuvaara and Iltalehti* v. *Finland* [2004] App. no. 53678/00 [45]; *Kobenter and Standard Verlags GmbH* v. *Austria* [2006] App. no. 60899/00 [31].
[227] ECtHR, *Růžový panter, o.s.* v. *Czech Republic* [2012] App. no. 20240/08 [31].
[228] See Chapter 4, Section 4.1.3.

may contribute to debates of general interest in a particular way by using wit as a weapon, yet its capability to ridicule is often more distinct compared to an unvarnished comment. Acceptable satirical comment seeks to make a critical contribution to an issue of general concern rather than insulting the other person, and the humorous character must be cognisable for the average reader.[229]

Concerning the publication of the novel *Jean-Marie Le Pen on Trial*, the Court held in *Lindon, Otchakovsky-Laurens and July* v. *France* that referring to a politician as the 'chief of a gang of killers', to assert that a murder – even one committed by a fictional character – was 'advocated' by him, and to describe him as a 'vampire who thrives on the bitterness of his electorate, but sometimes also on their blood', oversteps limits of acceptable criticism.[230] This judgment, however, is unconvincing. First, the Court categorised these statements partly as statements of fact, thereby ignoring their fictional, satirical character. Second, the Court did not properly consider Mr Le Pen as the highly controversial politician he then was, and thereby as a particularly prominent public figure. Third, the Court disregarded the fact that Mr Le Pen could himself have answered the attacks by the characters of Mr Lindon, a solitary novelist, in political debate.[231]

7.3.4.3 No right to prior notification

The European Court of Human Rights has proven to be a bulwark in protecting media freedom against initiatives for new restrictions of that freedom to protect personality rights.[232] In *Mosley* v. *United Kingdom*, the applicant complained that the United Kingdom had violated its positive obligations under Article 8 ECHR by failing to impose a legal duty on a newspaper to notify him in advance of a publication allegedly violating his right to respect for his private life. Therefore, he saw himself deprived of the opportunity to seek an interim injunction and thus prevent publication of certain material. Yet the Court accepted that *ex post facto* damages provide an adequate remedy for violations of Article 8 rights arising from the publication of private information by a newspaper.[233] Despite the judges' obvious disapproval of the impugned publication, which included very intimate details about the applicant, the Court held that concerns regarding the effectiveness of a pre-notification duty 'are not unjustified',

229 See ECtHR, *Nikowitz and Verlagsgruppe News GmbH* v. *Austria* [2007] App. no. 5266/03 [25].
230 ECtHR, *Lindon, Otchakovsky-Laurens and July* v. *France* [2007] App. nos. 21279/02 and 36448/02 [57].
231 Millar (2009) 288. 232 See Voorhoof (2014) p. 7.
233 ECtHR, *Mosley* v. *United Kingdom* [2011] App. no. 48009/08 [129].

and indicated the chilling effect of such a duty.[234] In any case to which a pre-notification requirement applied, the newspaper in question could choose to run the risk of either notifying and getting an injunction, or declining to notify, preferring to risk an *ex post facto* fine instead.[235]

7.3.5 Summary

'Personality rights' are an aspect of 'rights of others', and thus civility rules limiting media freedom. They encompass the rights related to privacy, including the protection of private information, and honour, especially reputation. Under the ECHR, privacy and honour are sub-categories of the right to private life according to Article 8 ECHR, and as such they need to be balanced against freedom of expression rather than being mere defensive rights under Article 10(2) ECHR.

While the dissemination of defamatory false information and comments or value judgments usually affect a person's reputation and honour, the publication of true statements of fact can violate a person's privacy. An interference with the dissemination of a true statement of fact is justified where the interest in keeping certain information private outweighs the public interest in its distribution. Furthermore, the media may not maliciously disseminate false statements of fact. If the media unintentionally publishes false information, media freedom has to be balanced against the personality rights of the person affected by the publication. The same applies to derogatory comment (value judgments). However, it is not sufficient for the media to claim that certain statements have been value judgments and therefore do not need to be proven: first, a court may find that a statement which was intended to be a comment amounted to a factual allegation and therefore requires proof. Second, even a value judgment must be based on a sufficient factual basis to support it, since a value judgment without any factual basis to support it may be excessive. Third, the factual basis must be correct or at least all reasonable attempts must have been made to verify the publication.

7.4 Intellectual property and other exclusive rights

A special category of rights of others preventing the dissemination of information is the protection of intellectual property rights and other exclusive rights. Intellectual property rights, especially copyright, impose limitations on others who want to publish certain information by granting the creator of

[234] ECtHR, *Mosley* v. *United Kingdom* [2011] App. no. 48009/08 [126].
[235] ECtHR, *Mosley* v. *United Kingdom* [2011] App. no. 48009/08 [128].

an original work exclusive rights to it. Intellectual property rights thus do not fall squarely into the fact–opinion dichotomy, but pertain to creative work, which is often fictional in nature. The right to protection of intellectual property is a sub-category of the right to property.[236]

Yet, intellectual property rights are not absolute. Provisions restricting the use of copyright protected material and their enforcement may constitute an interference with the user's right of freedom of expression or media freedom and must thus be in accordance with the conditions for restrictions of these rights.[237] Restrictions based on intellectual property rights are not justified if the use of the protected information contributes to a debate of general concern.[238] Furthermore, the rights and interests of those affected by an enforcement measure to protect intellectual property rights need to be considered. An injunction to install an internet blocking system as a measure of enforcement of copyright must thus also be measured against the rights of affected internet users to receive information.[239]

As a consequence, legislation protecting intellectual property has to provide mechanisms for conflicting rights and interests to be duly balanced, especially by providing exemptions for journalists from copyright provisions. For instance, Article 5(3)(c) EU Copyright Directive[240] stipulates that Member States may provide for exceptions or limitations to the reproduction right provided for in Article 2 and the right of communication to the public provided for in Article 3 of the Directive with regard to, *inter alia*, 'reproduction by the press'. Furthermore, access to telecommunications networks and services may conflict with intellectual property rights of the network operator. The domestic regulatory authorities must therefore duly balance and reconcile conflicting interests, as is the case, for example, under Article 12(2) EU Access Directive.[241]

[236] Article 17 UDHR, Article 17(2) EUChFR, Article 1 First Protocol to the ECHR, Article 14 AfCHPR and Article 21 ACHR. Compare ECtHR, *Melnychuk* v. *Ukraine* [2005] App. no. 28743/03, p. 7; *Anheuser-Busch Inc.* v. *Portugal* [2007] App. no. 73049/01 [72]; *Ashby Donald and others* v. *France* [2013] App. no. 36769/08 [40]; ECJ, *Promusicae* v. *Telefónica de España SAU* [2008] ECR I-00271, Case C-275/06 [62].

[237] ECtHR, *Ashby Donald and others* v. *France* [2013] App. no. 36769/08 [34]; *Neij and Sunde Kolmisoppi* v. *Sweden* [2013] App. no. 40397/12; CJEU, *Scarlet Extended* v. *SABAM and others* [2011] ECR I-11959, Case C-70/10 [43]; Volokh (2003a); see also Volokh (2003b).

[238] See, *mutatis mutandis*, ECtHR, *Ashby Donald and others* v. *France* [2013] App. no. 36769/08; *Neij and Sunde Kolmisoppi* v. *Sweden* [2013] App. no. 40397/12.

[239] CJEU, *UPC Telekabel Wien GmbH* v. *Constantin Film Verleih and others* [2014] (not yet reported), Case C-314/12 [47].

[240] Directive 2001/29/EC of the European Parliament and of the Council of 22 May 2001 on the Harmonisation of Certain Aspects of Copyright and Related Rights in the Information Society, OJ 2001, L167/10.

[241] Directive 2002/19/EC of the European Parliament and of the Council of 7 March 2002 on Access to, and Interconnection of, Electronic Communications Networks and

The same considerations apply to other rights that cannot be regarded as intellectual property rights because they do not relate to creations classifiable as works, but which are nonetheless exclusive in their nature.[242] These are, in particular, rights based on exclusive licence agreements on transmission of certain events. In the 2013 case of *Sky Österreich*, the Court of Justice of the EU had to examine the validity of Article 15 AVMS Directive.[243] This provision essentially requests broadcasters holding rights on exclusive transmission of events of high interest to enable competitors to broadcast short extracts of this event (usually 90 seconds[244]). The holder of exclusive rights may not seek compensation exceeding the additional costs directly incurred in providing access to the signal.

Although rights on exclusive transmission have an asset value, the Luxembourg Court held that such contractually acquired rights cannot confer an established legal position on a broadcaster protected by Article 17(1) EUChFR (protection of property).[245] However, since Article 15 AVMS Directive prevents the holder of exclusive broadcasting rights from deciding freely with which broadcasters it may wish to enter into an agreement regarding the granting of the right to make short news reports, the Court held that this constituted an interference with Article 16 EUChFR (freedom to conduct a business).[246] Nonetheless, the CJEU held that interference to be justified. Article 15 AVMS Directive puts any broadcaster in a position to be able to make short news reports and thus to inform the general public of events of high interest, irrespective of their commercial power and financial capacity. Thus the provision promotes pluralism of the media, protected under Article 11(2) EUChFR, and safeguards the public's right to receive information according to Article 11(1) EUChFR, since 'the marketing on an exclusive basis of events of high interest to the public is increasing and liable to restrict considerably the access of the general public to information relating to those

Associated Facilities (Access Directive), OJ 2002, L108/7; see van Rooijen (2010) pp. 170–90.

242 Compare CJEU, *Football Association Premier League Ltd and others* v. *Karen Murphy and others* [2011] ECR I-09083, Joined Cases C-403/08 and C-429/08 [99] and [105–17].

243 CJEU, *Sky Österreich* v. *Österreichischer Rundfunk* [2013] (not yet reported), Case C-283/11.

244 Directive 2010/13/EU of the European Parliament and of the Council of 10 March 2010 on the Coordination of Certain Provisions laid down by Law, Regulation or Administrative Action in Member States concerning the Provision of Audiovisual Media Services (Audiovisual Media Services Directive), OJ 2010, L95/1, Recital 55.

245 CJEU, *Sky Österreich* v. *Österreichischer Rundfunk* [2013] (not yet reported), Case C-283/11 [38].

246 CJEU, *Sky Österreich* v. *Österreichischer Rundfunk* [2013] (not yet reported), Case C-283/11 [44].

events'.[247] Furthermore, since short news reports on the event being exclusively retransmitted may not be produced for any kind of television programme, but only for general news programmes, Article 15 AVMS Directive ensures 'that the extent of the interference with the freedom to conduct a business and the possible economic benefit which broadcasters might draw from making a short news report are confined within precise limits'.[248] In the light of the importance of safeguarding the fundamental freedom to receive information and the freedom and pluralism of the media guaranteed by Article 11 EUChFR, the CJEU thus held that the EU legislature was entitled to adopt Article 15 AVMS Directive. In doing so, the Luxembourg Court, without mentioning it, differed from an earlier judgment of the German Federal Constitutional Court, according to which broadcasters holding exclusive transmission rights of events of high interest are obliged to enable competitors to broadcast short extracts of this event, but have a right to seek reasonable compensation beyond the additional costs incurred in providing access to the signal.[249] In contrast to the European Court, the German Court emphasised that the right to short extract reporting did not only enure to the benefit of the general public, but also to the rights holder's competitors, who may therefore be obliged to pay reasonable compensation in addition to the costs of providing access.[250] Yet in light of the necessity to safeguard a pluralistic media,[251] the CJEU's approach is to be preferred. It also finds support in Article 9 of the European Convention on Transfrontier Television. Accordingly, the Convention States shall protect the right of the public to information from being undermined by a broadcaster having exclusive rights for the transmission or retransmission of events of high interest for the public. Competitors may not be in a financial position to pay a compensation fee for short news reporting on events of general interest. This may undermine the public's right to be properly informed. In addition, the 'damage' incurred by the exclusive rights-holder is marginal: people interested in an event are arguably more interested in watching the entire event live rather than a mere 90 second short news report on the event.

[247] CJEU, *Sky Österreich* v. *Österreichischer Rundfunk* [2013] (not yet reported), Case C-283/11 [51–3].

[248] CJEU, *Sky Österreich* v. *Österreichischer Rundfunk* [2013] (not yet reported), Case C-283/11 [61–2].

[249] German Federal Constitutional Court, '*Short extract reporting*' [1998] Case 1 BvF 1/91.

[250] German Federal Constitutional Court, '*Short extract reporting*' [1998] Case 1 BvF 1/91 [129].

[251] See Chapter 14.

8 Threats to public order interests: national security, territorial integrity, public safety and prevention of disorder and crime

Media freedom is based on the idea that a free and open discourse on matters of public concern is more conducive to a democratic society than the suppression of unpalatable speech. Freedom of expression and media freedom do not only protect information and ideas that are favourably received or regarded as inoffensive or as a matter of indifference, but also those that offend, shock or disturb the state or any sector of the population.[1] Because of its dominant position in public discourse, the government especially has to abstain from interfering with media freedom via governmental channels of communication.[2]

Nevertheless, in their capacity as guarantors of public order, state authorities must be able to adopt measures to react appropriately to remarks which themselves overstep the boundaries of civilised discourse by threatening public order.[3] Therefore, Article 19(3)(b) ICCPR and Article 13(2)(b) ACHR allow restrictions on freedom of expression for the protection of national security or public order. Similarly, Article 27(2) AfCHPR requires that the rights and freedoms of each individual shall be exercised 'with due regard to collective security . . . and common interest'. Although the notion of 'public order' is not expressly provided by Article 27(2), it is included in the term 'common interest'.[4] Finally, Article 10(2) ECHR may justify an interference in the interests of national security, territorial integrity or public safety, and for the prevention of disorder or

[1] See Chapter 4, Section 4.1.2.

[2] See ECtHR, *Sürek* v. *Turkey (No. 2)* [1999] App. no. 24122/94 [34]; *Sürek* v. *Turkey (No. 3)* [1999] App. no. 24735/94 [37].

[3] Compare ECtHR, *Incal* v. *Turkey* [1998] App. no. 41/1997/825/1031 [54]; *Sürek* v. *Turkey (No. 2)* [1999] App. no. 24122/94 [34]; *Sürek* v. *Turkey (No. 3)* [1999] App. no. 24735/94 [37].

[4] Compare AfComHPR, *Media Rights Agenda, Constitutional Rights Project, Media Rights Agenda and Constitutional Rights Project* v. *Nigeria* [1998] App. nos. 105/93, 128/94, 130/94 and 152/96 [73]; *Constitutional Rights Project, Civil Liberties Organisation and Media Rights Agenda* v. *Nigeria* [1999] App. nos. 140/94, 141/94 and 145/95 [43]; *Scanlen & Holderness* v. *Zimbabwe* [2009] App. no. 297/05 [109].

crime.[5] Further interests related to public order will be discussed in separate chapters: the protection of health and morals (Chapter 9), the authority and impartiality of the judiciary (Chapter 10), the prevention of incitement to hatred (Chapter 11) and of religiously offensive publications (Chapter 12).

8.1 The notion of 'public order'

The concept of 'public order' encompasses fundamental interests the state needs to preserve in order to guarantee public safety and to protect the interests of society as a whole.[6] The Strasbourg Court has reiterated that the press must not overstep the bounds set, *inter alia*, 'for the protection of the vital interests of the State, such as the protection of national security or territorial integrity against the threat of violence or the prevention of disorder or crime'.[7] Similarly, the Human Rights Committee and the AfComHPR have identified safeguarding and strengthening national unity under difficult political circumstances as a legitimate objective.[8]

The IACtHR has provided the most sophisticated definition of public order so far, interpreting this term as 'the conditions that assure the normal and harmonious functioning of [democratic] institutions based on a coherent system of values and principles'.[9] Thus public order is not only a legitimate aim allowing an interference with freedom of expression; rather, public order itself 'requires the broadest possible circulation of information, opinions, news and ideas – that is, the maximum degree of exercise of freedom of expression'.[10] Both public order and freedom of

[5] The French version speaks of '*à la défense de l'ordre et à la prévention du crime*' (emphasis added). However, the Court's interpretation tends towards the English version, thus seeing 'prevention of disorder' and 'prevention of crime' as two different concepts; see ECtHR, *Engel and others* v. *Netherlands* [1976] App. nos. 5100/71, 5101/71, 5102/71, 5354/72 and 5370/72 [98]. 'Prevention of disorder' and 'prevention of crime' therefore do not have to be invoked cumulatively, as suggested by the French version.

[6] Grote and Wenzel (2013) para. 85.

[7] See, e.g., ECtHR, *Sürek* v. *Turkey (No. 1)* [1999] App. no. 26682/95 [59]; *Şener* v. *Turkey* [2000] App. no. 26680/95 [41]; *Özgür Gündem* v. *Turkey* [2000] App. no. 23144/93 [58]. See also Warbrick (2002).

[8] See, *mutatis mutandis*, Human Rights Committee, *Mukong* v. *Cameroon* [1994] Communication no. 458/91 [9.7]; AfComHPR, *Article 19* v. *Eritrea* [2007] App. no. 275/03 [108]; see also UN Economic and Social Council, Siracusa Principles on the Limitation and Derogation Provisions in the International Covenant on Civil and Political Rights, UN Doc. E/CN.4/1985/4, Annex (1985), no. 29.

[9] IACtHR, Advisory Opinion OC-5/85 [64].

[10] Office of the Special Rapporteur for Freedom of Expression with the Inter-American Commission on Human Rights, Inter-American Legal Framework Regarding the Right to Freedom of Expression, 2009, CIDH/RELE/INF. 2/09 [81]; see also IACtHR,

expression, and thus also media freedom, are intrinsically connected with each other and with democracy itself.

Accordingly, where public order interests are invoked to interfere with freedom of expression and media freedom, they have to be interpreted in strict adherence to the just demands of a democratic society.[11] Public order as a justification to limit freedom of expression and media freedom must therefore 'be based on real and objectively verifiable causes that present the certain and credible threat of a potentially serious disturbance of the basic conditions for the functioning of democratic institutions'.[12] Mere conjecture regarding possible disturbances of public order or hypothetical circumstances that do not clearly present a reasonable threat of serious disturbances are therefore not sufficient to justify an interference with media freedom.[13]

The concept of 'order' encompasses order in the public sphere, such as on public streets and in public places.[14] It also includes the order that must prevail within a specific group, for instance, the armed forces,[15] the civil service[16] and prison inmates.[17] This appears at first glance inconsistent with the idea of free public discourse, because those groups are substantially subject to the state's authority and thus must be able to open public debates on their situation. However, the regulation of discourse within such groups is necessary when disorder in that group can have a negative impact on order in society as a whole. As Kant observed, 'for many affairs conducted in the interest of a commonwealth a certain mechanism is necessary, by means of which some members of the commonwealth must behave merely passively, so as to be directed by

Advisory Opinion OC-5/85 [69]; AfComHPR, *Scanlen & Holderness* v. *Zimbabwe* [2009] App. no. 297/05 [109].

11 Office of the Special Rapporteur for Freedom of Expression with the Inter-American Commission on Human Rights, Inter-American Legal Framework Regarding the Right to Freedom of Expression, 2009, CIDH/RELE/INF. 2/09, para. 80.

12 Office of the Special Rapporteur for Freedom of Expression with the Inter-American Commission on Human Rights, Inter-American Legal Framework Regarding the Right to Freedom of Expression, 2009, CIDH/RELE/INF. 2/09, para. 82.

13 Office of the Special Rapporteur for Freedom of Expression with the Inter-American Commission on Human Rights, Inter-American Legal Framework Regarding the Right to Freedom of Expression, 2009, CIDH/RELE/INF. 2/09, para. 82.

14 ECtHR, *Chorherr* v. *Austria* [1993] App. no. 13308/87 [28].

15 ECtHR, *Engel and others* v. *Netherlands* [1976] App. nos. 5100/71, 5101/71, 5102/71, 5354/72 and 5370/72 [98]; *Kazakov* v. *Russia* [2008] App. no. 1758/02 [27]; *Szima* v. *Hungary* [2012] App. no. 29723/11 [25]; IAComHR, *José Francisco Gallardo Rodríguez* v. *Mexico* [1996] Case 11.430 [85]; *Rodolfo Robles Espinoza* v. *Peru* [1999] Case 11.317 [148]; *Tomás Eduardo Cirio* v. *Uruguay* [2006] Case 11.500 [75].

16 ECtHR, *Vogt* v. *Germany* [1995] App. no. 17851/91 [51–3].

17 Compare ECtHR, *Silver and others* v. *United Kingdom* [1983] App. nos. 5947/72, 6205/73, 7052/75, 7061/75, 7107/75, 7113/75 and 7136/75 [96].

the government, through an artful unanimity, to public ends (or at least prevented from destroying such ends).'[18] However, even members of those groups must be able to communicate their experiences if this does not constitute a threat to order in that group anymore. According to Kant, 'it would be ruinous if an officer, receiving an order from his superiors, wanted while on duty to engage openly in subtle reasoning about its appropriateness or utility; he must obey. But he cannot fairly be prevented, as a scholar, from making remarks about errors in the military service and from putting these before his public for appraisal.'[19]

'Prevention of crime' is essentially a sub-category of public order. However, the term 'prevention' should not be taken too literally. The 'prevention of crime' justification encompasses the prevention of specific crimes, the deterrence and control of crime in general, and the investigation of crimes allegedly already committed.[20]

8.2 Legal framework

The qualifications of freedom of expression and media freedom based on the prevention of disorder or crime rationales have gained particular significance in restrictions of publications, as well as orders to reveal journalistic sources, for reasons of national security, the protection of state secrets and the fight against terrorism. Not just since 11 September 2001 have national security and the fight against terrorism belonged to the most controversial political issues; they are as such subject to considerable debate, and, as a consequence, have had an impact on media law as well. UN Security Council Resolution 1624 (2005), which, according to its preamble, '[condemns] in the strongest terms the incitement of terrorist acts and [repudiates] attempts at the justification or glorification (*apologie*) of terrorist acts that may incite further terrorist acts', calls in its Article 1(a) upon all States 'to adopt such measures as may be necessary and appropriate and in accordance with their obligations under international law to prohibit by law incitement to commit a terrorist act or acts'.[21] Notably, Article 1 of the Resolution does therefore not call upon the states to adopt measures to prohibit justification or glorification of terrorist acts, as can be deduced, *e contrario*, from its preamble.[22]

[18] Kant (1784). [19] Kant (1784).
[20] ECtHR, *Orban and others* v. *France* [2009] App. no. 20985/05 [42].
[21] Resolution 1624 (2005), Adopted by the Security Council at its 5261st meeting, on 14 September 2005, S/RES/1624 (2005). On this resolution, see Ronen (2010).
[22] For the distinction between incitement and glorification, see Murray (2009) 340–5.

In addition, Article 5 of the Council of Europe Convention on the Prevention of Terrorism requires the Convention States to punish as a criminal offence 'public provocation to commit a terrorist offence', that is, 'the distribution, or otherwise making available, of a message to the public, with the intent to incite the commission of a terrorist offence, where such conduct, whether or not directly advocating terrorist offences, causes a danger that one or more such offences may be committed'. Similarly, Article 4(1) EU Framework Decision on combating terrorism[23] requests Member States to take the necessary measures to ensure that inciting or aiding or abetting certain terrorist offences are made punishable.

Nevertheless, the Strasbourg Court has also emphasised that it is 'incumbent on the press to convey information and ideas on political issues, even divisive ones'.[24] In the same vein, UN Security Council Resolution 1624 recalls the right to freedom of expression reflected in Article 19 UDHR and Article 19 ICCPR, and 'that any restrictions thereon shall only be such as are provided by law and are necessary on the grounds set out in [Article 19(3) ICCPR]'. States must avoid any use of the notion of 'threat to the State security' that would repress freedom of expression.[25] Eventually, Recital 10 EU Framework Decision on Combating Terrorism highlights that nothing in the Framework Decision may be interpreted as being intended to reduce or restrict fundamental rights or freedoms, including freedom of expression. In addition, Recital 14 Framework Decision amending the Framework Decision on Combating Terrorism[26] re-emphasises that the Framework Decision may not be interpreted as being intended to reduce or restrict the dissemination of information for scientific, academic or reporting purposes. Thus, 'the expression of radical, polemic or controversial views in the public debate on sensitive political questions, including terrorism, falls outside the scope of this Framework Decision and, in particular, of the definition of public provocation to commit terrorist offences [according to Article 3(1) (a) of the amended Framework Decision]'. Moreover, the amending Framework Decision stipulates in Article 2 that it

[23] Council Framework Decision 2002/475/JHA of 13 June 2002 on Combating Terrorism, OJ 2002, L164/3, amended by Council Framework Decision 2008/919/JHA of 28 November 2008 amending Framework Decision 2002/475/JHA on Combating Terrorism, OJ 2002, L330/21.

[24] ECtHR, *Özgür Gündem* v. *Turkey* [2000] App. no. 23144/93 [58]; *Şener* v. *Turkey* [2000] App. no. 26680/95 [41]; see also Human Rights Committee, General Comment no. 34, para. 46.

[25] Concluding observations on Democratic People's Republic of Korea (CCPR/CO/72/PRK), para. 23.

[26] Council Framework Decision 2008/919/JHA of 28 November 2008 amending Framework Decision 2002/475/JHA on Combating Terrorism, OJ 2008, L330/21.

shall not have the effect of requiring Member States to take measures in contradiction of fundamental principles relating to freedom of expression, in particular freedom of the press and the freedom of expression in other media as they result from constitutional traditions or rules governing the rights and responsibilities of, and the procedural guarantees for, the press or other media where these rules relate to the determination or limitation of liability.

As a consequence, the aforementioned pieces of legislation all confirm that there is little scope for restrictions on political publications or on other debates on matters of public concern even in the interest of national security or public order.

8.3 Principles

In a democratic society, the limits of permissible criticism are wider with regard to the government and public officials than in relation to private individuals. The actions or omissions of governments and politicians must be subject to the close scrutiny of public opinion. This applies not only to the media's right and duty to *inform* the public on measures taken against disturbances of public order and crimes, including terrorism, but also to *form* public opinion on such activities.

However, due to historical experiences, international conventions are also based on the idea of democracies that must be able to defend themselves. A democratic society must be tolerant, but also vigilant and not inert. It has to be in a position to fight against abuses which are directed at democratic values themselves. As a consequence, both the Human Rights Committee and the Strasbourg Court have granted a rather broad margin of appreciation for the State authorities 'to adopt, in their capacity as guarantors of public order, measures, even of a criminal-law nature, intended to react appropriately and without excess to [remarks that] incite to violence against an individual or a public official or a sector of the population'.[27] This margin of appreciation is basically justified because of the international adjudicators' epistemic deficits regarding the suitability and effectiveness of state measures against threats to public order interests.[28] Whether certain means are suitable to protect, for instance, national security or public safety, requires a careful analysis of the situation and a prediction of further developments, and consequently a high degree of factual uncertainty. It is the responsibility of the domestic

[27] ECtHR, *Sürek* v. *Turkey (No. 1)* [1999] App. no. 26682/95 [61]; *Şener* v. *Turkey* [2000] App. no. 26680/95 [40]; *Erdoğdu* v. *Turkey* [2000] App. no. 25723/94 [62]; see also Human Rights Committee, *A.K. and A.R.* v. *Uzbekistan* [2009] Communication no. 1233/2003 [7.2].

[28] See Chapter 6, Section 6.2.

authorities to decide on the suitability of certain envisaged means. International courts must therefore grant a means-selecting margin of appreciation to states where national security or public safety interests should serve to justify an interference with media freedom. However, since the uncertainty is only factual and not normative, the margin of appreciation only applies to the suitability and necessity tests within the principle of proportionality, and not to the normative proportionality *sensu stricto* test. Whether aims pursued by the domestic authorities justify the sacrifice of civil liberties is entirely for the courts to decide. Even in the struggle against espionage and terrorism, states may not adopt whatever measures they think appropriate: states must not destroy democracy on the ground of defending it.[29]

Three categories of legally problematic media coverage can be distinguished in the field of threats to public order interests: first, reporting of allegedly threatening statements by third parties; second, alleged incitement to criminal acts by the media itself; and third, the disclosure of secret state information.

8.3.1 Publication of third-party statements

The European Commission of Human Rights allowed rather severe restrictions on the dissemination of speech by certain organisations associated with terrorism related to conflicts in Northern Ireland. In *Purcell and others* v. *Ireland*, broadcasters were directed to refrain from broadcasting any interview, or report on an interview, with spokesmen for particular organisations, including the IRA or Sinn Féin. Although the Commission recognised that these restrictions may cause the applicants 'inconvenience in the exercise of their professional duties', it did not find that these restrictions violated Article 10 ECHR.[30] Live statements could 'involve a special risk of coded messages being conveyed, a risk which even conscientious journalists cannot control within the exercise of their professional judgment'.[31]

Brind and others v. *United Kingdom* pertained to the request of the British Home Department *vis-à-vis* British broadcasters to broadcast a statement by a representative of certain terrorist organisations only with a voice-over account spoken by an actor. By doing so, the government intended to reduce the impact and influence of the advocates and supporters of terrorist acts in the United Kingdom. According to the Commission,

[29] ECtHR, *Klass and others* v. *Germany* [1978] App. no. 5029/71 [49].
[30] EComHR, *Purcell and others* v. *Ireland* [1991] App. no. 15404/89.
[31] EComHR, *Purcell and others* v. *Ireland* [1991] App. no. 15404/89, p. 17.

the interference was not disproportionate given the 'limited extent of the interference' of the applicants' rights and the importance of measures to combat terrorism.[32]

On the one hand, it is understandable that states do not want to provide a forum for terrorists to disseminate their ideology or coded messages. On the other hand, the public has a right to be informed about threats to public order in order to make informed decisions on how to react to such threats. Therefore, a sweeping concession to the Convention States as in *Brind* constitutes a severe obstacle to public discourse on a matter of paramount importance to society. Instead of such a paternalistic approach, it should be examined on a case-by-case basis whether the words used and the context in which they were published could incite criminal activity or may include coded messages.[33] If this is the case, a publisher cannot be exonerated from any liability for the content of the third-party statements. This is because a publisher is subject to the 'duties and responsibilities' of journalists in the gathering and dissemination of information to the public, which incur an even greater importance in situations of conflict and tension.[34] Thus, in *Özgür Gündem* v. *Turkey*, the Strasbourg Court has rightly held with regard to media dissemination of statements by alleged terrorists – declarations of PKK-related organisations and an interview with PKK leader Abdullah Öcalan – that 'the fact that interviews or statements were given by a member of a proscribed organisation cannot in itself justify an interference with the newspaper's freedom of expression. Nor can the fact that the interviews or statements contain views strongly disparaging of government policy'.[35]

8.3.2 *Alleged advocacy of illegal action by the media itself*

Because of its special duties and responsibilities, the media is under a general obligation not to advocate the use of violence, glorify war or intend to stigmatise one side of a conflict, for example, by the use of labels such as 'fascists' or 'murder gang'.[36] The media must also take

[32] EComHR, *Brind and others* v. *United Kingdom* [1994] App. no. 18714/91.

[33] Compare ECtHR, *Sürek and Özdemir* v. *Turkey* [1999] App. nos. 23927/94 and 24277/94 [61]; *Sürek* v. *Turkey (No. 1)* [1999] App. no. 26682/95 [62]; *Şener* v. *Turkey* [2000] App. no. 26680/95 [44 ff.]; *Özgür Gündem* v. *Turkey* [2000] App. no. 23144/93 [63] and [65].

[34] ECtHR, *Sürek* v. *Turkey (No. 1)* [1999] App. no. 26682/95 [63]; *Şener* v. *Turkey* [2000] App. no. 26680/95 [42].

[35] ECtHR, *Özgür Gündem* v. *Turkey* [2000] App. no. 23144/93 [63].

[36] Compare ECtHR, *Sürek* v. *Turkey (No. 1)* [1999] App. no. 26682/95 [62]; *Sürek* v. *Turkey (No. 3)* [1999] App. no. 24735/94 [40]; *Özgür Gündem* v. *Turkey* [2000] App. no. 23144/93 [70]; *Balsytė-Lideikienė* v. *Lithuania* [2008] App. no. 72596/01 [79].

account of the particular situation of the region a publication refers to.[37] Conversely, a use of terms that does not in itself incite unlawful action, but is merely unpalatable for the government, such as the term 'Kurdistan' for a region in south-east Turkey and the associated idea of an independent Kurdish state, may not justify an interference with media freedom.[38] The extensive ECtHR case-law on the Turkish Prevention of Terrorism Act 1991 and the conflicts in south-east Turkey may serve as exemplary precedences in this context.[39] The European Commission of Human Rights and the Court have taken a similar case-by-case approach with regard to prohibitions on criticising military service.[40]

As a general rule, speech that is likely to cause harm may be restricted. However, both the necessary degree of likeliness and the extent to which speech potentially causes harm is subject to controversy. Hence the question is: what are the allowed dangers to be accepted as the price to be paid for freedom of expression and a free media?[41] This requires a balancing exercise between suppression of speech that would, if allowed, be harmless, and speech that, having been allowed, causes unlawful action.[42] In addition to the general rules on the justification of an interference with media freedom,[43] the following factors should be considered as relevant for the balancing exercise:

- The extent to which the publication contributes to a matter of public concern.

[37] See, e.g., ECtHR, *Şener* v. *Turkey* [2000] App. no. 26680/95 [35]; *Özgür Gündem* v. *Turkey* [2000] App. no. 23144/93 [65] regarding south-east Turkey; *Balsytė-Lideikienė* v. *Lithuania* [2008] App. no. 72596/01 [78] concerning the situation after the re-establishment of the independence of the Republic of Lithuania on 11 March 1990.

[38] See, e.g., ECtHR, *Sürek* v. *Turkey (No. 3)* [1999] App. no. 24735/94 [40]; *Şener* v. *Turkey* [2000] App. no. 26680/95 [45]; *Erdoğdu* v. *Turkey* [2000] App. no. 25723/94 [64]; see also Human Rights Committee, *Kim* v. *Republic of Korea* [1999] Communication no. 574/1994 [12.4]: distribution of material which was 'seen as coinciding' with the policy statements of the DPRK (North Korea).

[39] EComHR, *Başkaya and Okçuoğlu* v. *Turkey* [1999] App. nos. 23536/94 and 24408/94; ECtHR, *Arslan* v. *Turkey* [1999] App. no. 23462/94; *Ceylan* v. *Turkey* [1999] App. no. 23556/94; *Erdoğdu and İnce* v. *Turkey* [1999] App. nos. 25067/94 and 25068/94; *Gerger* v. *Turkey* [1999] App. no. 24919/94; *Karataş* v. *Turkey* [1999] App. no. 23168/94; *Okçuoğlu* v. *Turkey* [1999] App. no. 24246/94; *Polat* v. *Turkey* [1999] App. no. 23500/94; *Sürek* v. *Turkey (No. 1)* [1999] App. no. 26682/95; *Sürek* v. *Turkey (No. 2)* [1999] App. no. 24122/94; *Sürek* v. *Turkey (No. 3)* [1999] App. no. 24735/94; *Sürek* v. *Turkey (No. 4)* [1999] App. no. 24762/94; *Sürek and Özdemir* v. *Turkey* [1999] App. nos. 23927/94 and 24277/94; *Özgür Gündem* v. *Turkey* [2000] App. no. 23144/93; *Şener* v. *Turkey* [2000] App. no. 26680/95. From academic literature, see, e.g., Davis (2005).

[40] See, among other decisions, EComHR, *Arrowsmith* v. *United Kingdom* [1977] App. no. 7050/75, p. 5; ECtHR, *Ergin* v. *Turkey (No. 6)* [2006] App. no. 47533/99 [28].

[41] Compare Schauer (1982) p. 141. [42] Schauer (1982) p. 142. [43] See Chapter 6.

- Whether the publication is directed to inciting or producing lawless action. The content of publications may vary along the following spectrum:[44]
  - (i) Non-inflammatory criticism, which is always permitted.
  - (ii) Publications that do not incite lawless action, but the tone and context of the criticism may encourage disobedience to the law. Such publications are usually permitted.
  - (iii) General criticism coupled with incitement to violate the criticised laws: the criticism should be allowed, but the exhortation may be prohibited. This corresponds to the general principle that the search for less intrusive alternative ways of publication is part of the media's duties and responsibilities.[45]
  - (iv) Publications specifically, directly and exclusively devoted to inciting disobedience: such publications are inconsistent with the principles of rational discourse, which include that the force of the better argument is the only force.[46] They might be justifiable under the individual autonomy rationale – the idea that freedom of expression includes the right to 'let off steam' – but, as has been shown, this rationale applies only marginally to the media.
- The probability of causing harm: courts should examine whether there is room for public discourse to separate truth from error, or whether lawless action is imminent. The Strasbourg Court required in a decision that the impugned expression represent a 'clear and imminent danger' in order for an interference to be justified.[47] This requirement moves the Court close to the US Supreme Court's 'imminent lawless action' test, as established in Brandenburg v. Ohio.[48]
- The degree of potential harm to be caused: the more serious the effect, the less likelihood that the harm actually occurs is required.
- Timing and place of the publication: the history, geopolitical situation or instability of a country or a region.[49]
- Whether a criminal penalty, if imposed, was proportionate.

Moreover, offences such as 'encouragement of terrorism'[50] and 'extremist activity',[51] as well as offences of 'praising', 'glorifying' or 'justifying'

[44] Schauer (1982) pp. 192–5. [45] See Chapter 6, Section 6.3.3.3.
[46] See Chapter 2, Section 2.2.1.
[47] ECtHR, *Gül and others* v. *Turkey* [2010] App. no. 4870/02 [42].
[48] US Supreme Court, *Brandenburg* v. *Ohio*, 395 US 444 (1969). Compare Murray (2009) 340.
[49] Keller and Sigron (2010) 160.
[50] Human Rights Committee, Concluding observations on the United Kingdom of Great Britain and Northern Ireland (CCPR/C/GBR/CO/6), para. 26.
[51] Human Rights Committee, Concluding observations on the Russian Federation (CCPR/CO/79/RUS), para. 20.

terrorism, should be clearly defined in order to ensure that they fulfil the requirement of being 'prescribed by law' and do not lead to an unnecessary and disproportionate interference with freedom of expression and media freedom.[52] Furthermore, states must specify the exact nature of the threat that the publisher's exercise of media freedom allegedly poses for national security.[53] In particular, it is incompatible with media freedom to convict journalists on treason charges for having disseminated information of preponderant public concern.[54] Even legitimate objectives of national security or public order may not justify attempts 'to muzzle advocacy of multi-party democracy, democratic tenets and human rights'.[55]

8.3.3 Disclosure of state secrets

The media may also come into conflict with state authorities where it reveals classified information. This has been the case, for example, with the publication of US diplomatic cables and classified files by several newspapers with support of WikiLeaks, or following Edward Snowden's leak of details regarding top-secret US and British government mass surveillance programmes to the press. Related to the right of the media to publish confidential information is the question as to whether the person who leaked confidential or secret documents, the 'whistleblower', is protected by freedom of expression.

8.3.3.1 Protection of the media

Media freedom assumes particularly great importance in circumstances in which the state avoids public scrutiny behind the veil of confidentiality or secrecy. The prevention of, or conviction for, disclosing information considered to be confidential or secret prevents investigative journalists from informing the public on matters of public security, and thus inhibits public discourse on matters of paramount public concern. As a result, the ability of the press to provide accurate and reliable information is diminished, and journalists are no longer able to play their role

[52] Human Rights Committee, General Comment no. 34, para. 46. On the principle of legality, see Chapter 6, Section 6.1.1.

[53] Human Rights Committee, *Park* v. *Republic of Korea* [1998] Communication no. 628/1995 [10.3]; *Kim* v. *Republic of Korea* [1999] Communication no. 574/1994 [12.4]; *Shin* v. *Republic of Korea* [2004] Communication no. 926/2000 [7.2].

[54] See Human Rights Committee, Concluding observations on the Russian Federation (CCPR/CO/79/RUS), para. 21.

[55] Human Rights Committee, *Mukong* v. *Cameroon* [1994] Communication no. 458/91 [9.7]; AfComHPR, *Article 19* v. *Eritrea* [2007] App. no. 275/03 [108].

as 'public watchdog'.[56] In his powerful concurring opinion to the landmark decision *New York Times Co.* v. *United States*, which confirmed the *New York Times*' and the *Washington Post*'s right to publish the then-classified leaked Pentagon Papers on US involvement in Vietnam, Justice Black wrote:

> The press was protected [in the First Amendment] so that it could bare the secrets of government and inform the people. Only a free and unrestrained press can effectively expose deception in government. And paramount among the responsibilities of a free press is the duty to prevent any part of the government from deceiving the people and sending them off to distant lands to die of foreign fevers and foreign shot and shell. In my view, far from deserving condemnation for their courageous reporting, the *New York Times*, the *Washington Post*, and other newspapers should be commended for serving the purpose that the Founding Fathers saw so clearly.[57]

However, there may also be a significant public interest in secrecy that has to be balanced against the freedom of the media to publish information and the public interest in receiving that information. Even a democratic state governed by the rule of law must be able to have recourse to confidentiality and secrecy, so that its functions are not undermined.[58] In order to be effective, certain institutions must be able to operate in secret. For instance, the provisions on the inviolability of archives and documents contained in the Vienna Convention on Diplomatic Relations (Articles 24 ff.) serve to protect the archives and documents of the accredited state against interference from the receiving state. The publication of a report written by an ambassador and classified as 'confidential' or 'secret' might not only have an adverse effect on a country's foreign policy, but might also make the official concerned *persona non grata* in the host country.[59]

Yet, a state interfering with a disclosure of information that has been officially declared as confidential or even as a state secret may not automatically rely on 'national security' or 'public safety'. This would imply too broad a margin of appreciation for the state. Rather, the state has to ensure that its powers to suppress the release of certain information are restricted to matters that have been *proven* to be necessary for the protection of national security.[60] Therefore, courts have to decide on a

[56] ECtHR, *Stoll* v. *Switzerland* [2007] App. no. 69698/01 [110]; see also *Goodwin* v. *United Kingdom* [1996] App. no. 17488/90 [39].
[57] US Supreme Court, *New York Times Co.* v. *United States*, 403 US 713, 717 (1971) (Black J, concurring).
[58] Compare ECtHR, *Vereniging Weekblad Bluf!* v. *Netherlands* [1995] App. no. 16616/90 [35].
[59] ECtHR, *Stoll* v. *Switzerland* [2007] App. no. 69698/01 [159].
[60] See Human Rights Committee, Concluding observations on the United Kingdom of Great Britain and Northern Ireland (CCPR/C/GBR/CO/6), para. 24; ECtHR, *Stoll* v. *Switzerland* [2007] App. no. 69698/01 [54].

case-by-case basis whether interferences are indeed justified by national security and public safety concerns. The burden of proof for secrecy of certain information is on the state; it is not for the media to prove that the disclosure of the information was of public concern. Transparency is the rule and secrecy the exception which has to be justified. The Tacitean and Machiavellian *arcana imperii*, serving to maintain the dominance of the ruler,[61] are diametrically opposed to the idea of democratic self-governance by the people. Informed democratic decisions, especially voting, are not possible without full information on governmental activity. Secrecy can hence only be justified in those few cases where the public interest in the non-disclosure of certain information outweighs the public interest in its publicity.

One clarification needs to be made with regard to the 'information *received* in confidence' clause in Article 10(2) ECHR. This phrasing suggests that the provision relates only to a bilateral situation with the author of a document and another person who receives this document from the author. Accordingly, the information received in confidence clause would not encompass third parties, such as journalists, who have not directly received the information in confidence. However, the French wording of Article 10(2) ECHR speaks of measures necessary '*pour empêcher la divulgation d'informations confidentielles*', thus emphasising the confidentiality of the information itself and not merely of the reception of the information. Article 33(4) Vienna Convention on the Law of Treaties provides that when a comparison of the authentic texts – in this case the French and the English text – discloses a difference of meaning, the meaning which best reconciles the texts, having regard to the object and purpose of the treaty, shall be adopted. Here the French text appears to best reconcile both versions, based on the principle that within the same category the greater includes the lesser: while information received in confidence is at the same time also confidential information (at least for the party who received the information), confidential information does not necessarily have to be received in confidence, as the example of the journalist who receives information from a person subject to a duty of confidence shows. On that account, Article 10(2) ECHR has to be interpreted as 'preventing the disclosure of confidential information'.[62]

A number of different aspects need to be considered in order to ascertain whether a state measure aiming at preventing a disclosure

[61] See Donaldson (1988) pp. 111–40.
[62] See ECtHR, *Stoll* v. *Switzerland* [2007] App. no. 69698/01 [58–60].

of, or punishing a journalist for, revealing classified information was 'necessary in a democratic society':

- The extent to which the publication contributed to a debate of general concern.
- Whether the information in question had already been known to the public. If this is the case, the information had ceased to be confidential, and it becomes unnecessary to prevent the disclosure.[63]
- The gravity of the repercussions of a publication and the degree of secrecy of an official document.[64]
- The manner in which the applicant obtained the information in question:[65] whether the journalist himself leaked the documents, whether he obtained them by illegal means, or whether he acted in good faith. A journalist cannot be punished merely because he published information which someone else had obtained illegally.[66]
- Whether a criminal penalty, if imposed, was proportionate.

The leading ECtHR cases on the conflict between freedom of the press and governmental secrecy originated in the *Spycatcher* litigation: *Observer and Guardian* v. *United Kingdom* and *Sunday Times* v. *United Kingdom (No. 2)*.[67] A former senior member of the British Security Service (MI5) wrote his memoirs, entitled *Spycatcher*, and made arrangements for their publication in Australia in 1985. The book dealt with the operational organisation, methods and personnel of MI5 and included an account of alleged illegal activities by the Security Service, such as activities calculated to undermine the 1974–9 Labour Government, 'bugging' of embassies of allied and hostile countries and an unsuccessful plot to assassinate President Nasser of Egypt. Furthermore, the book alleged that an MI5 Director General was a Soviet agent. The Attorney General of England and Wales instituted proceedings in an Australian court to restrain the publication of *Spycatcher*. Whilst the Australian proceedings were still pending, the *Observer* and the *Guardian* published short articles

[63] See, e.g., ECtHR, *Weber* v. *Switzerland* [1990] App. no. 11034/84 [51]; *Vereniging Weekblad Bluf!* v. *Netherlands* [1995] App. no. 16616/90 [45]; *Observer and Guardian* v. *United Kingdom* [1991] App. no. 13585/88 [69]; *Dammann* v. *Switzerland* [2006] App. no. 77551/01 [53]; Council of Europe, Parliamentary Assembly, Resolution 1551 (2007): Fair Trial Issues in Criminal Cases concerning Espionage or Divulging State Secrets; *mutatis mutandis*, ECtHR, *Pasko* v. *Russia* [2009] App. no. 69519/01 [85].

[64] ECtHR, *Stoll* v. *Switzerland* [2007] App. no. 69698/01 [136]; *Vereniging Weekblad Bluf!* v. *Netherlands* [1995] App. no. 16616/90 [41].

[65] ECtHR, *Stoll* v. *Switzerland* [2007] App. no. 69698/01 [140].

[66] ECtHR, *Radio Twist a.s.* v. *Slovakia* [2006] App. no. 62202/00 [62].

[67] ECtHR, *Observer and Guardian* v. *United Kingdom* [1991] App. no. 13585/88; *Sunday Times* v. *United Kingdom (No. 2)* [1991] App. no. 13166/87.

on inside pages of the reporting on the forthcoming hearing in Australia, giving details of some of the contents of the manuscript of *Spycatcher*. The Attorney General obtained an interlocutory injunction restraining any further publication of the kind in question pending the substantive trial of the actions brought to the High Court in London in July 1986.

During the trial, however, more and more information about the content of the *Spycatcher* book was published by the media, including a first instalment of extracts from *Spycatcher* by the *Sunday Times* in July 1987. The Attorney General thus successfully applied for an injunction to restrain the *Sunday Times* from publishing further extracts for contempt of court, since the publication frustrated the purpose of the injunctions against the *Observer* and the *Guardian*. Eventually, on 14 July 1987, *Spycatcher* was published in the United States of America.

Reviewing the compatibility of the High Court's injunction with Article 10 ECHR, the Strasbourg Court distinguished between the time periods July 1986 and July 1987, on the one hand, and the time period following July 1987, on the other hand. The Court found that the interests of national security and the Attorney General's right as a litigant outweighed the public interest in learning more about the content of the book in the time period between July 1986 and July 1987. However, the interest in confidentiality ceased to exist after the book was published in the United States. The Court held, in particular, that maintaining the 'efficiency and reputation of the Security Service', which may still be tarnished by a publication after July 1987, and deterring other former MI5 members who might want to follow in the author's footsteps, were not sufficient objectives to justify the interference with Article 10 ECHR.[68] In *Observer and Guardian* the Court thus held by a majority that there was no violation of Article 10 ECHR during the period from July 1986 to July 1987, and held unanimously that Article 10 ECHR was violated for the second time period after July 1987. Yet, with ten(!) judges partly dissenting with regard to the first period where there was arguably no violation of Article 10, *Observer and Guardian* v. *United Kingdom* was highly controversial. In *Sunday Times* v. *United Kingdom (No. 2)*, by contrast, the Court unanimously held that Article 10 ECHR was violated, as this decision only pertained to the second time period.

Sixteen years later, in *Stoll* v. *Switzerland*, the ECtHR missed the opportunity to clarify its approach to the disclosure of confidential

[68] ECtHR, *Observer and Guardian* v. *United Kingdom* [1991] App. no. 13585/88 [69]; *Sunday Times* v. *United Kingdom (No. 2)* [1991] App. no. 13166/87 [55].

information in the media. The applicant had published articles that included confidential ambassador correspondence on negotiations between the World Jewish Congress and Swiss banks concerning compensation for Holocaust victims for unclaimed assets deposited in Swiss bank accounts. The Court accepted at the outset that, while the confidentiality of diplomatic reports is justified in principle, it cannot be protected at any price.[69] The applicant's articles were published in the context of a public debate on a matter which had been widely reported in the Swiss media and had divided public opinion.[70] The Court was thus ready to accept that there was a significant public interest in receiving information on this matter. However, the Grand Chamber of the Court eventually found that the articles were not published in accordance with the 'ethics of journalism', as the content of the impugned articles 'was clearly reductive and truncated'. The Grand Chamber observed that 'the applicant, in capricious fashion, started a rumour which related directly to one of the very phenomena at the root of the issue of unclaimed assets, namely the atrocities committed against the Jewish community during the Second World War'. In this context the Court reiterated 'the need to deal firmly with allegations and/or insinuations of that nature'.[71] Moreover, the Court found that the headings and sub-headings were made in a 'sensationalist style'.[72] The applicant's chief intention was not to inform the public on a topic of general interest but to make the ambassador's report 'the subject of needless scandal'.[73] In lieu thereof, it would have been possible for the applicant to accompany the articles with the full text of the leaked report, and thus to allow readers to form their own opinion.[74] Therefore the Grand Chamber overruled the judgment of the Fourth Chamber that had decided in favour of the applicant.

The Grand Chamber's decision in *Stoll* v. *Switzerland* cannot be endorsed. Neither a violation of the 'ethics of journalism' nor the 'immoral' or insincere motivation of the publisher were sufficient to justify the interference with press freedom.[75] Even more worrying is the fact that, as several judges expressed in a dissenting opinion, *Stoll* v. *Switzerland* is 'a dangerous and unjustified departure from the Court's

[69] ECtHR, *Stoll* v. *Switzerland* [2007] App. no. 69698/01 [128].

[70] ECtHR, *Stoll* v. *Switzerland* [2007] App. no. 69698/01 [150].

[71] ECtHR, *Stoll* v. *Switzerland* [2007] App. no. 69698/01 [148]; see, *mutatis mutandis*, *Lehideux and Isorni* v. *France* [1998] App. no. 55/1997/839/1045 [53]; *Garaudy* v. *France* [2003] App. no. 65831/01.

[72] ECtHR, *Stoll* v. *Switzerland* [2007] App. no. 69698/01 [149].

[73] ECtHR, *Stoll* v. *Switzerland* [2007] App. no. 69698/01 [151].

[74] ECtHR, *Stoll* v. *Switzerland* [2007] App. no. 69698/01 [147].

[75] See Chapter 2, Section 2.2.3.3.

well-established case-law concerning the nature and vital importance of freedom of expression in democratic societies'.[76] It is an important tenet that journalistic freedom protects not only the substance of the ideas and information expressed, but also the form in which they are conveyed, including a certain degree of provocation and exaggeration, immoderate statements and the use of strong terms. Courts should not act in place of journalists and decide on the methods and techniques of reporting.[77] Yet this is exactly what the Grand Chamber did by reproving the applicant for the 'sensationalist style' of the headings and subheadings. What would have been necessary was a proper balancing between the interest in the confidentiality of the documents and the public interest in being informed about them. And this balance would clearly have been in favour of freedom of expression, as the dissenting opinion convincingly argued. The majority held that the breach of the confidentiality of the document was '*capable* of undermining the climate of discretion necessary to the successful conduct of diplomatic relations in general and of having negative repercussions on the negotiations being conducted by Switzerland in particular' (emphasis added).[78] Not only is a 'climate of discretion' as such a questionable concept to justify an interference with freedom of expression. In addition, the majority did not even regard it as *established* that the disclosure undermined the 'climate of discretion', but based its findings on a mere hypothesis.[79] Both aspects render the reasons adduced by the majority of the Grand Chamber to justify an interference with public discourse on a matter of significant public concern insufficient.

Similarly, the Strasbourg Court found that punishment of a member of the armed forces for the disclosure of information on an arms project classified as 'secret' did not amount to a violation of Article 10 ECHR.[80] However, the Human Rights Committee criticised that powers under the UK Official Secrets Act 1989 have been exercised to frustrate former employees of the Crown from bringing into the public domain issues of genuine public interest, and that the enforcement of the Act can prevent the media from publishing such matters. Disclosures of information could be punished even where they are not harmful to national security.[81]

[76] ECtHR, *Stoll* v. *Switzerland* [2007] App. no. 69698/01, dissenting opinion of Judge Zagrebelsky, joined by Judges Lorenzen, Fura-Sandström, Jaeger and Popović.

[77] See Chapter 4, Section 4.1.3.

[78] ECtHR, *Stoll* v. *Switzerland* [2007] App. no. 69698/01 [136].

[79] ECtHR, *Stoll* v. *Switzerland* [2007] App. no. 69698/01, dissenting opinion of Judge Zagrebelsky, joined by Judges Lorenzen, Fura-Sandström, Jaeger and Popović.

[80] ECtHR, *Hadjianastassiou* v. *Greece* [1992] App. no. 12945/87.

[81] Concluding observations on the United Kingdom of Great Britain and Northern Ireland (CCPR/C/GBR/CO/6), para. 24.

8.3.3.2 Protection of whistle-blowers

Although whistle-blowers themselves cannot directly rely on media freedom if they are not journalists, they should indirectly participate in the protection afforded to the media, because without their revelations the media would not be able to publish the information in the first place. A punishment of a civil servant or employee – in both the public and the private sector[82] – for leaking information would have a chilling effect on future information disclosures and, consequently, would affect the media's ability to gather and publish such information.

However, the protection of whistle-blowers is not absolute. Rather, the public interest in the disclosure of the confidential information has to be balanced with a civil servant's or employee's duty of loyalty and discretion as well as the public interest in keeping certain information confidential. The African Commission rightly summarised the conflicting interests the following way: 'no one shall be subject to any sanction for releasing in good faith information on wrongdoing, or that which would disclose a serious threat to health, safety or the environment save where the imposition of sanctions serves a legitimate interest and is necessary in a democratic society'.[83]

The following factors should be taken into consideration in this balancing exercise:

- The extent to which the information is of public concern,[84] especially – but not exclusively – whether the information concerns misconduct or an illegal activity of public officials[85].
- Whether the whistle-blower was the only person, or part of a small group of persons, who were aware of the occurrences at their workplace, and 'thus best placed to act in the public interest by alerting the employer or the public at large'.[86]
- Whether any other effective means to remedy the wrongdoing was available to the whistle-blower, especially whether it was practicable

[82] On the impact of freedom of expression on employment law, see Chapter 5, Section 5.2.3.

[83] AfComHPR, Declaration of Principles on Freedom of Expression in Africa, Section IV.

[84] See ECtHR, *Guja* v. *Moldova* [2008] App. no. 14277/04; *Kayasu* v. *Turkey (No. 1)* [2008] App. nos. 64119/00 and 76292/01 [93]; *Kudeshkina* v. *Russia* [2009] App. no. 29492/05 [94]; *Sosinowska* v. *Poland* [2011] App. no. 10247/09 [83]; *Bucur and Toma* v. *Romania* [2013] App. no. 40238/02 [101]; IACtHR, *Palamara-Iribarne* v. *Chile* [2005] Case 11.571 [77]; IAComHR, *Rodolfo Robles Espinoza* v. *Peru* [1999] Case 11.317 [104]; *Tomás Eduardo Cirio* v. *Uruguay* [2006] Case 11.500 [71].

[85] See, *mutatis mutandis*, ECtHR, *Tierbefreier e.V.* v. *Germany* [2014] App. no. 45192/09 [54].

[86] ECtHR, *Guja* v. *Moldova* [2008] App. no. 14277/04 [72]; *Marchenko* v. *Ukraine* [2009] App. no. 4063/04 [46].

to report to the person's superior or any other competent authority or body.[87]

- The authenticity of the information disclosed.[88] Where the information turns out to be false, it is decisive whether the whistle-blower acted in good faith and whether he attempted to verify, to the extent permitted by the circumstances, that the information is accurate and reliable.[89]
- Whether the damage inflicted upon the state's interest outweighs the interest of the public in having the information revealed.[90]
- Whether a sanction, if imposed, was proportionate.[91]

The Strasbourg Court also regards the motive behind the actions of the reporting employee or civil servant as a determinant factor in deciding whether a particular disclosure should be protected or not.[92] Accordingly, an act motivated by a personal grievance, a personal antagonism or the expectation of personal advantage should not justify a particularly strong level of protection. However, it is submitted that this factor should only be applied if the information turns out to be false. If the information was false, then the whistle-blower may nonetheless have a defence if he acted in good faith. But if the information was true and of public concern, then the motives of the employee or civil servant should be irrelevant: freedom of expression does not require an act of altruism.

[87] ECtHR, *Guja* v. *Moldova* [2008] App. no. 14277/04 [73]; *Bucur and Toma* v. *Romania* [2013] App. no. 40238/02 [97]; compare *Zakharov* v. *Russia* [2006] App. no. 14881/03 [26]; Council of Europe, Parliamentary Assembly, Resolution 1729 (2010): Protection of 'Whistle-blowers', para. 6.2.3.

[88] ECtHR, *Guja* v. *Moldova* [2008] App. no. 14277/04 [75]; *Frankovicz* v. *Poland* [2008] App. no. 53025/99 [50]; *Sosinowska* v. *Poland* [2011] App. no. 10247/09 [81]; *Bucur and Toma* v. *Romania* [2013] App. no. 40238/02 [105].

[89] ECtHR, *Guja* v. *Moldova* [2008] App. no. 14277/04 [75]; *Bucur and Toma* v. *Romania* [2013] App. no. 40238/02 [105]; Council of Europe, Parliamentary Assembly, Resolution 1729 (2010): Protection of 'Whistle-blowers', para. 6.2.4.

[90] ECtHR, *Guja* v. *Moldova* [2008] App. no. 14277/04 [76]; *Pasko* v. *Russia* [2009] App. no. 69519/01 [86]; *Bucur and Toma* v. *Romania* [2013] App. no. 40238/02 [114].

[91] ECtHR, *Guja* v. *Moldova* [2008] App. no. 14277/04 [95]; *Bucur and Toma* v. *Romania* [2013] App. no. 40238/02 [119]; *Kayasu* v. *Turkey (No. 1)* [2008] App. nos. 64119/00 and 76292/01 [106]; *Kudeshkina* v. *Russia* [2009] App. no. 29492/05 [99].

[92] ECtHR, *Guja* v. *Moldova* [2008] App. no. 14277/04 [77]; *Kudeshkina* v. *Russia* [2009] App. no. 29492/05 [95].

9 The protection of health and morals

Article 19(3)(b) ICCPR, Article 10(2) ECHR and Article 13(2)(b) ACHR all provide that the exercise of freedom of expression may be subject to restrictions for the protection of, *inter alia*, health and morals. The African Charter states in Article 27(2) that the rights and freedoms of the Charter shall be exercised with due regard to, *inter alia*, morality. However, the AfCHPR does not provide a limitation on freedom of expression based on health. Since Articles 11 and 12(2) of the Charter include such a health clause, one could argue, *argumentum e contrario*, that restrictions on freedom of expression based on the protection of health are not permissible. In practice, it is nevertheless to be expected that the African Commission would base an interference with freedom of expression and media freedom pursuing public health rationales on the 'common interest' clause in Article 27(2) AfCHPR. Yet this example reveals another conceptual deficit of the freedom of expression provision in the African Charter.

9.1 'Health'

The protection of 'health' as justification for an interference with freedom of expression and media freedom becomes relevant where a publication allegedly prompts harmful conduct. An interference to which the 'health' rationale applies is especially the regulation of advertising, for example, for harmful products, such as tobacco or alcohol,[1] and of practitioners of medical professions.[2] For example, in *Women on Waves and others*

[1] ECtHR, *Société de Conception de Presse et d'Edition et Ponson* v. *France* [2009] App. no. 26935/05 [53]; compare ECJ, *Aragonesa de Publicidad Exterior SA* v. *Departamento de Sanidad y Seguridad Social de la Generalitat de Cataluña* [1991] ECR I-04151, Joined Cases C-1/90 and C-179/90 [16]; *Germany* v. *Parliament and Council ('Tobacco Advertisng II')* [2006] ECR I-11573, Case C-380/03 [154]; *Commission* v. *France ('Loi Évin')* [2004] ECR I-06613, Case C-262/02 [24]. From academic literature, see Ferguson (2003).

[2] ECtHR, *Stambuk* v. *Germany* [2002] App. no. 37928/97 [30]; ECJ, *Deutscher Apothekerverband eV* v. *0800 DocMorris NV* [2003] ECR I-14887, Case C-322/01 [103].

v. *Portugal*, the ECtHR held that the interference by the Portuguese authorities – the banning of the applicants' ship from entering Portuguese territorial waters to prevent them from holding meetings on the prevention of sexually transmitted diseases, family planning and the decriminalisation of abortion – pursued the legitimate aim of protection of health.[3]

9.2 'Morals'

The consideration of 'morals' as civility rules limiting freedom of expression in Article 19(3) ICCPR, Article 13(2)(b) ACHR and Article 10(2) ECHR[4] is remarkable. It is the only limitation that is not based on a factual (e.g., health, security) or legal-factual (e.g., rights of others, authority and impartiality if the judiciary) phenomenon, but on a primarily *social* obligation. By incorporating the concept of morals into the positive law, these provisions translate them into the legal code.

The main problems to be associated with the protection of morals as limitations on freedom of expression and media freedom are the following. First, morality claims may include civility rules that public discourse has to observe. In addition, most speech that allegedly violates morality concerns, such as pornography and alleged obscenity,[5] is predominantly based on the argument from individual autonomy, because it usually does not make a contribution to public discourse on matters of general concern.[6] The case for media freedom where pornography and obscenity is concerned is therefore basically rather weak.

Second, however, morality claims themselves must be subject to public discourse, too. And one of the most effective ways to challenge morality claims is to violate them. The intention of a publisher to open up a debate on existing morality claims must therefore be taken into account in the balancing exercise between media freedom and the protection of morals.

Third, as an originally pre-legal concept, the standpoint for the definition of morals is difficult to find: are the relevant morality claims the norms of a dominant group (assimilationism), of one of many groups (pluralism) or even of single individuals (individualism)?[7] The risks associated with each of these perspectives are obvious: although assimilationism suggests

[3] ECtHR, *Women on Waves and others* v. *Portugal* [2009] App. no. 31276/05; however, the Court found the interference to be disproportionate to the aims pursued.
[4] See also 'the moral well being of society' in Article 29(7) AfCHPR.
[5] See ECtHR, *Handyside* v. *United Kingdom* [1976] App. no. 5493/72; *Wingrove* v. *United Kingdom* [1996] App. no. 17419/90; *Perrin* v. *United Kingdom* [2005] App. no. 5446/03. The Convention State's argument that morals were at stake was rejected in *Vereinigung Bildender Künstler* v. *Austria* [2007] App. no. 68354/01 [31].
[6] Dworkin (1996) p. 228. [7] The terminology is taken from Post (1988) 295.

itself from a democratic perspective, it would support the norms of a dominant culture, and thus suppress 'otherness'. It could eventually lead to Adams' and Mill's 'tyranny of the majority'. Pluralism and individualism would safeguard the diversity of cultures, but would in turn allow minorities to impose their values on the majority, which might eventually lead to an overstretched 'political correctness' to the detriment of public discourse on moral principles themselves.

Particularly for the third reason it not surprising that international courts and tribunals allow Member States a wide margin of discretion in the field of morals. In the same vein, EU law provides substantial public policy exceptions from Internal Market provisions where morals are concerned.[8] The Strasbourg Court explained the reason for its self-restraint in *Handyside* v. *United Kingdom*:

> [I]t is not possible to find in the domestic law of the various Contracting States a uniform European conception of morals. The view taken by their respective laws of the requirements of morals varies from time to time and from place to place, especially in our era which is characterised by a rapid and far-reaching evolution of opinions on the subject. By reason of their direct and continuous contact with the vital forces of their countries, State authorities are in principle in a better position than the international judge to give an opinion on the exact content of these requirements as well as on the 'necessity' of a 'restriction' or 'penalty' intended to meet them.[9]

Similar to the Strasbourg Court, the Human Rights Committee observed that the notion of public morals differs widely and that there is no universally applicable common standard: '[T]he concept of morals derives from many social, philosophical and religious traditions; consequently, limitations ... for the purpose of protecting morals must be based on principles not deriving exclusively from a single tradition'.[10]

The approaches by the Inter-American Court and the African Court are not clearly identifiable yet. However, it is to be expected that these courts will adopt a stance similarly deferential to that of the Human Rights Committee and the ECtHR, since the rationale underlying their jurisprudence – the difficulty to establish internationally accepted standards for morals – equally applies in the Americas and in Africa.

[8] See Articles 36 and 52 (in conjunction with Article 62) TFEU; Articles 3(4), 9, 12 and 27 AVMS Directive; Article 3(4) e-commerce Directive.

[9] ECtHR, *Handyside* v. *United Kingdom* [1976] App. no. 5493/72 [48].

[10] Human Rights Committee, General Comment no. 22; see also *Hertzberg and others* v. *Finland* [1985] Communication no. 61/1979 [10.3]; UN Economic and Social Council, Siracusa Principles on the Limitation and Derogation Provisions in the International Covenant on Civil and Political Rights, U.N. Doc. E/CN.4/1985/4, Annex (1985), no. 27.

Since states lack common standards regarding morals, the margin of appreciation is justified because of a normative epistemic deficit of international courts. As a consequence, the margin of appreciation allowed to states only applies to the relative importance attached to morals within the proportionality *sensu stricto* test, but not to the factual tests of suitability and necessity.[11] Furthermore, the margin of appreciation does not apply with a view to the estimation of the importance of the impugned publication.[12]

Against this background, the moral-related Strasbourg Court's decisions *Handyside* v. *United Kingdom* and *Müller* v. *Switzerland* have to be criticised. *Handyside* involved the prohibition of a book called *The Little Red Schoolbook*, which was intended for children and adolescents of the age of twelve and upwards. The book contained information on all matters of adolescence, such as education and learning, but in particular on sexuality, including homosexuality. The Court conceded that the book basically 'contained purely factual information that was generally correct and often useful'.[13] However, the book also included sentences that, according to the Court, 'young people at a critical stage of their development could have interpreted as an encouragement to indulge in precocious activities harmful for them or even to commit certain criminal offences'.[14] The English judges were thus 'entitled, in the exercise of their discretion, to think at the relevant time that the Schoolbook would have pernicious effects on the morals of many of the children and adolescents who would read it'.[15]

It is questionable whether *Handyside* would be decided the same way if the case occurred in the twenty-first century. This is not only due to the changed concept of 'morals'; the decision was already controversial when it was adopted. In addition, the original edition of *The Little Red Schoolbook* was not the object of any proceedings in Northern Ireland, the Isle of Man and the Channel Islands and not of any conviction in Scotland; moreover, it appeared freely in the majority of the Member States of the Council of Europe, and even in England and Wales thousands of copies circulated. The prohibition was thus hardly effective.[16] However, the fact that the rather wide circulation of the book did not deter the Court from upholding the prohibition reveals that the Court granted a margin of appreciation also with regard to the suitability and necessity of the

[11] On this distinction, see Chapter 6, Section 6.2. [12] See Chapter 6, Section 6.3.3.2.
[13] ECtHR, *Handyside* v. *United Kingdom* [1976] App. no. 5493/72 [52].
[14] ECtHR, *Handyside* v. *United Kingdom* [1976] App. no. 5493/72 [52].
[15] ECtHR, *Handyside* v. *United Kingdom* [1976] App. no. 5493/72 [52].
[16] See ECtHR, *Handyside* v. *United Kingdom* [1976] App. no. 5493/72, separate opinion of Judge Mosler [2]

measure. Therefore, it is sufficient that the Convention State comprehensibly purports that the moral standards in this particular jurisdiction justify the interference.

The ECtHR went even further in the case of *Müller* v. *Switzerland*, a case concerning the seizure of allegedly obscene paintings. The Court, 'having inspected the original paintings', did '*not find unreasonable* the view taken by the Swiss courts that those paintings, with their emphasis on sexuality in some of its crudest forms, were "liable grossly to offend the sense of sexual propriety of persons of ordinary sensitivity"' (emphasis added).[17] The Swiss courts were thus '*entitled to consider it "necessary"* for the protection of morals to impose a fine on the applicants for publishing obscene material' under their margin of appreciation (emphasis added).[18] First, *Müller* thus confirms the Court's *Handyside* approach not to second-guess the domestic decision whether the protection of morals were actually at issue. Second, the Court merely reviewed whether possible *objections* against the decisions of national authorities are justified, as opposed to those cases where the Court applies strict scrutiny, testing whether the interference itself is justified. The Court thus does not only grant a margin of appreciation with regard to the question whether morals are at issue, but also whether the interference was necessary. This lenience is to be criticised, because – unlike the concept of 'morals' – the concept of 'necessity' is a fact-related, autonomous step in the proportionality analysis.[19]

The ECtHR's approach was then different in *Open Door and Dublin Well Woman* v. *Ireland*. Here the Court found that an injunction preventing the applicants from providing information to pregnant women concerning abortion facilities outside Ireland, where abortion is constitutionally and statutorily prohibited, breached Article 10 ECHR. The Court conceded that 'the protection afforded under Irish law to the right to life of the unborn is based on profound moral values concerning the nature of life'.[20] However, three factors rendered the injunction disproportionate: first, the fact that it is not a criminal offence under Irish law for a pregnant woman to travel abroad in order to have an abortion; second, that abortion services are lawful in other Convention countries; and third, the absolute nature of the domestic court's injunction regardless of age or state of health of the woman seeking information on termination of pregnancy.[21]

[17] ECtHR, *Müller and others* v. *Switzerland* [1988] App. no. 10737/84 [36].
[18] ECtHR, *Müller and others* v. *Switzerland* [1988] App. no. 10737/84 [36].
[19] Compare Grote and Wenzel (2013) para. 101.
[20] ECtHR, *Open Door and Dublin Well Woman* v. *Ireland* [1992] App. nos. 14234/88 and 14235/88 [63].
[21] ECtHR, *Open Door and Dublin Well Woman* v. *Ireland* [1992] App. nos. 14234/88 and 14235/88 [72–4].

In contrast to *Müller*, in *Vereinigung Bildender Künstler* v. *Austria*, the Court did not refuse to grant strong Article 10 ECHR protection, although the impugned picture was allegedly obscene. The painting showed, amongst other persons, Mother Teresa, an Austrian cardinal and several politicians, in sexual positions. One politician, Mr Meischberger, was shown gripping the ejaculating penis of another politician while at the same time being touched by two other politicians and ejaculating on Mother Teresa. The naked bodies of these figures were painted, but the heads and faces were depicted using photos taken from newspapers. The eyes of some of the persons were hidden under black bars. Although the Court found that Mr Meischberger was depicted 'in a somewhat outrageous manner', the Court nonetheless emphasised that he, in his capacity as politician, had to exhibit a wider degree of tolerance against criticism.[22] Furthermore, the Court followed the view taken by the court of first instance that the scene in which Mr Meischberger was portrayed could be understood to constitute some sort of counter-attack against his political party, whose members had strongly criticised the painter's work.[23] The Court thus found that the injunction against the applicant association prohibiting it from continuing to exhibit the painting violated Article 10 ECHR. This decision reminds us of the US Supreme Court's findings in *Hustler Magazine* v. *Falwell*.[24]

In *Hertzberg and others v. Finland*, the applicants were precluded from disseminating information on homosexuality via broadcasting. The Human Rights Committee decided:

> [The Committee] cannot question the decision of the responsible organs of the Finnish Broadcasting Corporation that radio and TV are not the appropriate forums to discuss issues related to homosexuality, as far as a programme could be judged as encouraging homosexual behaviour. ... As far as radio and TV programmes are concerned, the audience cannot be controlled. In particular, harmful effects on minors cannot be excluded.[25]

Accordingly, the Human Rights Committee held that there had been no violation of Article 19(2) ICCPR. Similar to the ECtHR decision in *Handyside*, *Hertzberg* must be analysed against the background of the interpretation of 'morals' at the time the decision was made, here in 1985. It is unlikely that homosexuality could justify an interference based on 'morality' today. Furthermore, the Human Rights Committee faces

[22] ECtHR, *Vereinigung Bildender Künstler* v. *Austria* [2007] App. no. 68354/01 [34].
[23] ECtHR, *Vereinigung Bildender Künstler* v. *Austria* [2007] App. no. 68354/01 [34].
[24] US Supreme Court, *Hustler Magazine* v. *Falwell* 485 US 46 (1988).
[25] Human Rights Committee, *Hertzberg and others* v. *Finland* [1985] Communication no. 61/1979 [10.4].

even greater difficulties to find common standards for morals, as the Committee would have to establish globally accepted standards, whereas the ECtHR 'only' has to examine a common denominator for Europe. Furthermore, the *Hertzberg* case pertained to the question of access to broadcasting transmission. No human rights catalogue has established a right to express oneself through a *particular* medium owned by another person, such as a broadcasting channel.[26] It may nevertheless be assumed that the Committee would take a different decision today, taking into account the more liberal approach to homosexuality and the obligation of the State Parties to safeguard media pluralism. The Individual Opinion appended to the Committee's views at the request of Mr Opsahl, who indicated that the concept of 'public morals' should not be applied so as to perpetuate prejudice or promote intolerance, would presumably prevail today.[27]

While adult pornography can be seen as basically protected by freedom of expression and media freedom (although it may be subject to considerable state interference[28]), child pornography is prohibited in absolute terms by several international Conventions, such as Article 34(c) Convention on the Rights of the Child, the Optional Protocol to the Convention on the Rights of the Child on the Sale of Children, Child Prostitution and Child Pornography, ILO Convention No. 182 on the Worst Forms of Child Labor (Article 3-b), and, under EU Law, the Directive 2011/92/EU on combating the sexual abuse and sexual exploitation of children and child pornography.[29] Likewise, the US Supreme Court excludes child pornography from First Amendment protection.[30]

[26] Human Rights Committee, *Hertzberg and others* v. *Finland* [1985] Communication no. 61/1979 [10.2]; see also EComHR, *Tete* v. *France* [1987] App. no. 11123/84, p. 69; *Huggett* v. *United Kingdom* [1995] App. no. 24744/94; *Haider* v. *Austria* [1995] App. no. 25060/94; ECtHR, *VgT Verein gegen Tierfabriken* v. *Switzerland (No. 1)* [2001] App. no. 24699/94 [75].

[27] Human Rights Committee, *Hertzberg and others* v. *Finland* [1985] Communication no. 61/1979, individual opinion appended to the Committee's views at the request of Mr. Torkel Opsahl.

[28] Some scholars even argue for a complete exclusion of pornography from free speech; see, e.g., Maitra and McGowan (2007). On this debate, see Dworkin (1981); Sunstein (1986); Koppelman (2008); Allen (2003).

[29] Directive 2011/92/EU of the European Parliament and of the Council of 13 December 2011 on Combating the Sexual Abuse and Sexual Exploitation of Children and Child Pornography, and replacing Council Framework Decision 2004/68/JHA, OJ 2011, L335/1. From academic literature, see, e.g., Akdeniz (2008).

[30] US Supreme Court, *New York* v. *Ferber*, 458 US 747 (1982).

10 Maintaining the authority and impartiality of the judiciary

Unlike Article 10(2) ECHR, Article 19(3) ICCPR, Article 13(2) ACHR and Article 27(2) AfCHPR do not provide a qualification of 'maintaining the authority and impartiality of the judiciary'. This notwithstanding, provisions protecting order and dignity in court are encompassed by the public order or common interest grounds in these provisions.[1] The purpose of 'maintaining the authority and impartiality of the judiciary' is closely linked to the obligations under Article 14 ICCPR, Article 6 ECHR, Article 7 AfCHPR and Article 8 ACHR to ensure fair administration of justice.[2]

10.1 The concepts of 'authority' and 'impartiality' of the judiciary

The term 'judiciary' includes both the judicial branch of government as such as well as the judges in their official capacity. 'Authority' of the judiciary has an objective and a subjective dimension: objectively, it includes the notion that the courts are the proper forum for the ascertainment of rights and obligations as well as the settlement of disputes; subjectively, courts are accepted and respected by the public at large in their capacity to fulfil that function.[3] 'Impartiality' describes the lack of prejudice or bias.[4] The distinction between 'authority' and 'impartiality' is significant, as an alleged interference with a court's impartiality is even harder to justify than an interference with a court's authority. Impartiality of the judiciary serves to protect the confidence which courts must inspire

[1] Compare Human Rights Committee, *Fernando* v. *Sri Lanka* [2005] Communication no. 1189/2003 [9.2]; *Dissanayake* v. *Sri Lanka* [2005] Communication no. 1373/2005 [8.2].
[2] See, e.g., ECtHR, *Sunday Times* v. *United Kingdom (No. 1)* [1979] App. no. 6538/74 [54]; *Observer and Guardian* v. *United Kingdom* [1991] App. no. 13585/88 [56]; *Egeland and Hanseid* v. *Norway* [2009] App. no. 34438/04 [53].
[3] Compare ECtHR, *Sunday Times* v. *United Kingdom (No. 1)* [1979] App. no. 6538/74 [55].
[4] See ECtHR, *Worm* v. *Austria* [1997] App. no. 83/1996/702/894 [40].

in the litigating parties and the public at large.[5] Hence, the discourse within the courtroom must not be influenced by the media discourse outside the courtroom. During the legal proceedings, the media's obligation is merely to transport the litigation discourse to the outside world, but not to replace it there. For example, in *C. Ltd* v. *United Kingdom*, a TV company intended to broadcast news reports on a high profile criminal trial with actors playing judges, counsel and witnesses. The European Commission of Human Rights confirmed the injunction issued by the Court of Appeal against the dissemination of this report, holding 'that the dramatic and suggestive reconstruction of court proceedings on television differs significantly from reporting of those proceedings in the press'. Although the Commission noted that such a television programme would not normally affect the judgment of the Court, the appellants nonetheless 'had the right to be assured that the Court was unaffected by external matters and that they would have understandable doubts of this if the programme was in fact shown before the judgment was given'.[6]

The historical origin of the notion of 'authority and impartiality of the judiciary' lies in the institution of contempt of court peculiar to common-law countries. However, this does not make the law of contempt the standard to examine whether a measure was justified. The interpretation of international conventions follows an autonomous concept and not the domestic classifications.[7] Although closely related, authority and impartiality of the judiciary are thus not identical with the common law concept of contempt of court. 'Authority and impartiality of the judiciary' generally include the functioning of the courts and the judicial procedure,[8] the protection of the rights of the litigants,[9] the confidentiality of judicial deliberations of jurors[10] and limitations on reports critical on the judiciary itself, especially criticism of judges.[11]

10.2 In particular: restrictions on court reporting

The principles of freedom of expression and media freedom apply equally to the field of the administration of justice. Courts are entitled

[5] ECtHR, *Worm* v. *Austria* [1997] App. no. 83/1996/702/894 [40].
[6] EComHR, *C. Ltd* v. *United Kingdom* [1989] App. no. 14132/88, p. 8.
[7] See ECtHR, *Sunday Times* v. *United Kingdom (No. 1)* [1979] App. no. 6538/74 [60].
[8] ECtHR, *Sunday Times* v. *United Kingdom (No. 1)* [1979] App. no. 6538/74 [55].
[9] ECtHR, *Sunday Times* v. *United Kingdom (No. 1)* [1979] App. no. 6538/74 [56]; *Observer and Guardian* v. *United Kingdom* [1991] App. no. 13585/88 [56]; *Weber* v. *Switzerland* [1990] App. no. 11034/84 [44].
[10] ECtHR, *Seckerson* v. *United Kingdom* and *Times Newspapers Ltd* v. *United Kingdom* [2012] App. nos. 32844/10 and 33510/10 [43].
[11] See Chapter 7, Section 7.3.2.2.

to exercise power and serve the interests of the community at large; hence, they should be subject to public scrutiny. This applies even more as the judiciary is independent from interferences by the other two branches of government. As the Strasbourg Court succinctly expressed, '[t]here is general recognition of the fact that the courts cannot operate in a vacuum. Whilst they are the forum for the settlement of disputes, this does not mean that there can be no prior discussion of disputes elsewhere, be it in specialised journals, in the general press or amongst the public at large.'[12]

Thus the media has a duty to impart information and ideas on matters relating to the functioning of the judiciary, and the public has a corresponding right to be properly informed.[13] When 'authority of the judiciary' is invoked as a reason for justifying an interference with media freedom, courts have to balance the public interest in the impugned reporting with the public interest in the fair administration of justice. Moreover, it is of crucial importance how the reporting is presented: whether it was balanced or partial, in moderate terms or sensational.[14]

The public has a legitimate interest in the reception of information about criminal proceedings in order to exercise scrutiny over the functioning of the criminal justice system.[15] Consequently, the media must be able to freely report and comment on such proceedings. 'The press is one of the means by which politicians and public opinion can verify that judges are discharging their heavy responsibilities in a manner that is in conformity with the aim which is the basis of the task entrusted to them.'[16] As a consequence, even the protection of rights of others or the maintenance of the authority of the judiciary cannot justify an absolute prohibition on reporting aspects of court proceedings.[17]

[12] ECtHR, *Sunday Times* v. *United Kingdom (No. 1)* [1979] App. no. 6538/74 [65]; see also *Worm* v. *Austria* [1997] App. no. 83/1996/702/894 [50]; EComHR, *Atkinson, Crook and The Independent* v. *United Kingdom* [1990] App. no. 13366/87.

[13] ECtHR, *Sunday Times* v. *United Kingdom (No. 1)* [1979] App. no. 6538/74 [65]; *De Haes and Gijsels* v. *Belgium* [1997] App. no. 19983/92 [37]; *Mustafa Erdoğan and others* v. *Turkey* [2014] App. nos. 346/04 and 39779/04 [41].

[14] See, e.g., ECtHR, *Sunday Times* v. *United Kingdom (No. 1)* [1979] App. no. 6538/74 [63]; *Barfod* v. *Denmark* [1989] App. no. 11508/85 [33]; *Brunet Lecomte et Lyon Mag* v. *France* [2010] App. no. 17265/05 [44].

[15] ECtHR, *July and SARL Liberation* v. *France* [2008] App. no. 20893/03 [66].

[16] ECtHR, *July and SARL Liberation* v. *France* [2008] App. no. 20893/03 [66].

[17] Compare ECtHR, *Du Roy and Malaurie* v. *France* [2000] App. No. 34000/96 [36]. In this particular case the law even distinguished between criminal proceedings instituted on a complaint accompanied by a civil-party application, where a ban applies, and criminal proceedings instituted on an application by the public prosecutor's office, where the ban did not apply. The Court rightly observed that '[s]uch a difference in the treatment of the right to inform does not seem to be based on any objective grounds' (para. 35 of the judgment).

However, court proceedings, especially criminal trials, may have a damaging effect on the accused person, family members and third parties' personality rights.[18] The limits of permissible comment by journalists on pending criminal proceedings must, in particular, not extend 'to statements which are likely to prejudice, whether intentionally or not, the chances of a person receiving a fair trial or to undermine the confidence of the public in the role of the courts in the administration of criminal justice'.[19] Furthermore, the media – and the public in general – may under certain specified circumstances be excluded from court proceedings. Article 14(1) ICCPR, Article 6(1) ECHR and Article 13(5) ACHR provide such exceptions to the principle of public hearing. In addition, the Strasbourg Court upheld a general prohibition of broadcasting in court proceedings.[20]

[18] See Chapter 7, Section 7.3.4.1.1.3 and 7.3.4.1.1.4.

[19] ECtHR, *Worm* v. *Austria* [1997] App. no. 83/1996/702/894 [50]; *Ageyevy* v. *Russia* [2013] App. no. 7075/10 [225].

[20] ECtHR, *P4 Radio Hele Norge ASA* v. *Norway* [2003] App. no. 76682/01.

11 Incitement to hatred

Media freedom finds its rationale in the concept of public discourse for the general benefit of a democratic society rather than the individual autonomy of the speaker. Public discourse is based on the idea of a non-coercive debate aimed at reaching understanding, in which the authority of the better argument is the only authority. As a consequence, publications that do not aim at reaching understanding, but incite hatred, and are thus directed *against* fundamental values of a democratic society, such as human dignity, tolerance and peacefulness, enjoy very little protection under international human rights law.

Academic literature has coined the term 'hate speech' for such speech acts. However, a clear and generally accepted definition of what 'hate speech' actually is has not yet been found. The Committee of Ministers of the Council of Europe defined 'hate speech' as 'covering all forms of expression which spread, incite, promote or justify racial hatred, xenophobia, anti-Semitism or other forms of hatred based on intolerance, including: intolerance expressed by aggressive nationalism and ethnocentrism, discrimination and hostility against minorities, migrants and people of immigrant origin.'[1] Similarly, the ECtHR referred to 'all forms of expressions which spread, incite, promote or justify hatred based on intolerance (including religious intolerance)'.[2] According to Anne Weber's 'Manual on Hate Speech', the concept of 'hate speech' encompasses a multiplicity of situations:

- firstly, incitement of racial hatred or in other words, hatred directed against persons or groups of persons on the grounds of belonging to a race;
- secondly, incitement to hatred on religious grounds, to which may be equated incitement to hatred on the basis of a distinction between believers and non-believers;

[1] Council of Europe, Committee of Ministers, Recommendation No. R (97) 20 on 'Hate Speech'.

[2] ECtHR, *Gündüz* v. *Turkey* [2003] App. no. 35071/97 [40].

– and lastly, to use the wording of the Recommendation on 'hate speech' of the Committee of Ministers of the Council of Europe, incitement to other forms of hatred based on intolerance 'expressed by aggressive nationalism and ethnocentrism'.[3]

However, rather than arguing how to define 'hate speech' and whether this label can be placed on an impugned publication or not, it is more important to identify the content and context of this particular speech act and apply the underlying rationales of media freedom and its limitations. All those attempts to define 'hate speech' share one common ground, namely the idea that hate speech is a speech act which elicits hatred. Thus, 'hate speech' is, in linguistic terms, a perlocutionary speech act, that is, an act which is not aimed at reaching understanding, but a strategic action that follows another goal.[4] Therefore, hate speech does not merely incite action; hate speech *is* action. Hate speech is significant not because of what language *says*, but because of what it *does*.[5]

11.1 The legal framework

There are various international provisions and documents dealing with incitement to hatred. In November 1963, the United Nations General Assembly adopted the Declaration on the Elimination of All Forms of Racial Discrimination.[6] This declaration, which is not legally binding, served as a precursor to the International Convention on the Elimination of All Forms of Racial Discrimination (ICERD), which has a legally binding effect and which has also influenced the jurisprudence of regional human rights adjudicators.[7] According to this Convention, the States Parties shall condemn racial discrimination and undertake to pursue a policy of eliminating racial discrimination in all its forms and promoting understanding among all races and, to this end, take certain measures as provided in Article 2. The ICERD is monitored by the Committee on the Elimination of Racial Discrimination (CERD).[8] According to Article 4 ICERD, the States Parties shall 'condemn all propaganda and all organisations which are based on ideas or theories

[3] Weber (2009) p. 3.
[4] Compare Austin (1962) p. 101; Habermas (1981a) p. 292; see CJEU, *Mesopotamia Broadcast AIS and Roj TV AIS* v. *Bundesrepublik Deutschland* [2011] ECR I-08777, Joined Cases C-244/10 and C-245/10 [41].
[5] See Austin (1962).
[6] General Assembly, Resolution 1904 (XVIII): United Nations Declaration on the Elimination of All Forms of Racial Discrimination of 20 November 1963.
[7] See, e.g., ECtHR, *Jersild* v. *Denmark* [1994] App. no. 15890/89 [30].
[8] See generally Wolfrum (1999).

of superiority of one race or group of persons of one colour or ethnic origin, or which attempt to justify or promote racial hatred and discrimination in any form, and undertake to adopt immediate and positive measures designed to eradicate all incitement to, or acts of, such discrimination', and to take certain measures to combat such discrimination such as those prescribed by Article 4. However, when adopting such a measure, the State Party must have 'due regard to the principles embodied in the Universal Declaration of Human Rights' – and this includes freedom of expression according to Article 19 UDHR. The 'due regard' clause thus asks for a balancing between the rights and interests affected by hate speech and the right to freedom of expression.

According to Article 11(1) ICERD, a State Party may bring a matter to the attention of the CERD if it considers that another State Party is not giving effect to the provisions of the Convention. Furthermore, a State Party may declare that it recognises the competence of the Committee to receive and consider communications from individuals or groups of individuals within its jurisdiction claiming to be victims of a violation by that State Party of Convention right, Article 14 ICERD. The individual complaints mechanism has led to a body of jurisprudence of more than forty cases on the interpretation and implementation of the Convention.

A requirement for the admissibility of a petition under Article 14 ICERD is the characterisation of the author as a 'victim'. The Committee thereby follows a rather broad interpretation, holding it to be sufficient that the author is a member of a potential group of victims. The fact that Article 4 ICERD is couched in terms of States Parties' obligations rather than inherent rights of individuals does, according to the Committee, 'not imply that they are matters to be left to the internal jurisdiction of States parties and as such immune from review under [A]rticle 14'.[9] When considering the merits of a petition, the Committee first establishes whether the impugned statements fall within any of the categories of Article 4 ICERD. If this is the case, the Committee examines whether those statements are protected by the 'due regard' provision, as it relates to freedom of speech.[10]

In the ICCPR, Article 20 stipulates that any propaganda for war and any advocacy of national, racial or religious hatred that constitutes incitement to discrimination, hostility or violence shall be prohibited by law. Therefore, Article 20 ICCPR requires positive state action to

[9] CERD, *Jewish Community of Oslo and others* v. *Norway*, Communication no. 30/2003, 15 August 2005, para. 10.6.

[10] See, e.g., CERD, *Kamal Quereshi* v. *Denmark* [2002] CERD/C/63/D/27/2002 [9]; *Jewish Community of Oslo and others* v. *Norway* [2005] CERD/C/67/D/30/2003 [10.4].

prohibit the acts enumerated in this provision.[11] The prohibitions pursuant to Article 20 ICCPR must comply with the requirements of the other articles of the Covenant, such as Article 19(3), or the prohibition of discrimination, Article 26 ICCPR.[12] Hence it would be impermissible for any such laws to grant stronger protection in favour of one or certain religions or belief systems.[13] The United States has submitted the reservation that Article 20 ICCPR 'does not authorize or require legislation or other action by the United States that would restrict the right of free speech and association protected by the Constitution and laws of the United States'.

Documents against 'hate speech' adopted by the Council of Europe include Recommendation No. (97) 20 on 'Hate Speech' and Recommendation No. (97) 21 on the Media and the Promotion of a Culture of Tolerance. In 2002, the Council of Europe established the European Commission against Racism and Intolerance (ECRI) to combat racism and racial discrimination in Europe. The ECRI formulates general policy recommendations which provide guidelines for the Member States regarding the development of national policies and strategies in various areas, and publishes monitoring reports on domestic situations. Furthermore, Article 7(1)(b) of the Convention on Transfrontier Television stipulates that programme services shall not 'give undue prominence to violence or be likely to incite to racial hatred'.

The EU has long been committed to fighting incitement to hatred and racism, too.[14] Article 19 TFEU authorises the Council, together with the European Parliament, to take appropriate action to combat discrimination based on sex, racial or ethnic origin, religion or belief, disability, age or sexual orientation. In order to reinforce co-operation between Member States, Article 1 of the Council Framework Decision on combating racism and xenophobia[15] requires Member States to take the measures necessary to ensure that certain behaviours are punishable as criminal offences. These behaviours include public incitement to violence or hatred directed at a group of persons or a member of such a group defined by reference to race, colour, religion, descent or national

[11] On this provision, see Kearney (2005). See also Human Rights Committee, General Comment no. 11.

[12] Human Rights Committee, *Ross* v. *Canada* [2000] Communication no. 736/97 [11.1].

[13] Human Rights Committee, General Comment no. 34, para. 48.

[14] See, e.g., Joint Action 96/443/JHA of 15 July 1996 adopted by the Council on the Basis of Article K.3 of the Treaty on European Union, concerning Action to Combat Racism and Xenophobia, OJ 1996, L185/5.

[15] Council Framework Decision 2008/913/JHA of 28 November 2008 on Combating Certain Forms and Expressions of Racism and Xenophobia by means of Criminal Law, OJ 2008, L328/55.

or ethnic origin. Other EU secondary law provides public policy exceptions allowing restrictions on speech that include incitement to hatred, discrimination or violence, such as Articles 3, 6 and 9 AVMS Directive and Article 3 e-commerce Directive.

With regard to the Americas, Article 13(5) ACHR stipulates that '[a]ny propaganda for war and any advocacy of national, racial, or religious hatred that constitute incitements to lawless violence or to any other similar action against any person or group of persons on any grounds including those of race, color, religion, language, or national origin shall be considered as offenses punishable by law'. This wording has been inspired by the US Supreme Court's decision *Brandenburg* v. *Ohio*, and is narrower than Article 20 ICCPR.[16]

Finally, Article 28 AfCHPR includes the duty of each individual 'to respect and consider his fellow beings without discrimination, and to maintain relations aimed at promoting, safeguarding and reinforcing mutual respect and tolerance'. In addition, the Preamble of the African Charter emphasises that the Parties have agreed to the Convention, *inter alia*, 'undertaking to eliminate colonialism, neo-colonialism, apartheid, zionism and to dismantle aggressive foreign military bases and all forms of discrimination, particularly those based on race, ethnic group, color, sex, language, religion or political opinions'.

11.2 Rationales for suppressing 'hate speech' in the media

As has already been indicated above, the theoretical justification for protecting incitement to hatred in the media is rather weak. This is not because such speech does not contribute to matters of public concern; hateful propaganda can – and often does – pertain to matters of public concern, such as migration policy or historical debates. Rather, 'hate speech', understood as a perlocutionary speech act, does not contribute to a *free and non-coercive* and *non-excluding* argumentative public discourse.[17] Therefore, such speech acts can essentially only be based on the individual autonomy rationale: the liberty of people 'to blow off steam'. Yet, as has been analysed in Chapter 2, this rationale only marginally applies to the media.

But this in itself would not mean that hate speech is always prohibited in the media. Even if the case for media freedom is weak, interferences with this liberty still need to be justified. It would be oversimplified to argue that hate speech is elementarily wrong and thus intrinsically

[16] Pasqualucci (2006) 416. [17] Compare Post (1991) 275.

harmful.[18] Rather, the reasons for justifying interferences with media freedom in general are either actual harm done to others or those rules of civility that are necessary to safeguard public discourse as such. Against this backdrop, two reasons to justify prohibitions of hate speech in the media can be identified: first, if a member of a group suffers actual individual harm, and second, its harmful effect on social peace in general by generating or reinforcing hatred in the community, leading to hateful attitudes, discrimination, suppression and exclusion of particular groups or even physical violence.[19]

In practice, however, 'hate speech' belongs to the subjects where the differences between the US Supreme Court's jurisprudence and the approaches by international organisations and adjudicators are most obvious. The US Supreme Court permits content-based restrictions on hateful speech only under narrowly defined circumstances: advocacy intended, and likely, to incite imminent lawless action, defamation, speech integral to criminal conduct, true threats and 'fighting words'.[20] This reveals that the Supreme Court focuses exclusively on the first rationale justifying an interference with incitement to hatred: the 'harm principle'. It considers as a 'bedrock principle underlying the First Amendment' that the state may not prohibit the expression of an idea 'simply because society finds the idea itself offensive or disagreeable'.[21] The US approach is based on the confidence that the best remedy against hate speech is more speech, and that falsehoods are best encountered by true speech, which is at the heart of the 'marketplace of ideas' rationale.

By contrast, particularly because of their historical experience, European jurisdictions do not share this optimism. Attacks on the underlying values of the European Convention – equality, anti-discrimination, tolerance and democracy – are regarded as sufficient to justify an interference with freedom of expression, or even to exclude speech from the protection of Article 10 ECHR altogether. Such attacks may consist of expressions of racism, anti-Semitism, Holocaust negationism and Islamophobia.[22] In contrast to the US approach, it is not necessary that the speech incites lawless action; instead, the ECtHR also allows for the

[18] Compare Post (1991) 272 and 291–3, with further references.

[19] For a detailed analysis, see Post (1991); Samolewicz (2002); Jaoude (2003); Hare (2006); Simpson (2006); Sottiaux (2011) 47–8.

[20] See US Supreme Court, *Brandenburg* v. *Ohio*, 395 US 444 (1969) on imminent lawless action; *Giboney* v. *Empire Storage & Ice Co.*, 336 US 490 (1949) on criminal conduct; *Watts* v. *United States*, 394 US 705 (1969) on true threats; *Chaplinsky* v. *New Hampshire*, 315 US 568 (1942) on fighting words.

[21] US Supreme Court, *United States* v. *Eichman*, 110 S. Ct. 2404, 2410 (1990).

[22] ECtHR, *Leroy* v. *France* [2009] App. no. 36109/03 [27]; *Perinçek* v. *Switzerland* [2013] App. no. 27510/08 [47].

harmful effect on social peace and political stability at large to justify an interference with freedom of expression, and *a fortiori* media freedom.[23]

This jurisprudence reflects the idea that free speech should not be allowed to those who aim at eliminating freedom of speech of others. In short, intolerance should not be tolerated. Milton himself, the often-cited champion of liberty, claimed that one cannot allow freedom to a system or ideology that itself is opposed to freedom. Dr Johnson succinctly wrote that Milton 'felt not so much the love of liberty as repugnance to authority'.[24] Therefore, Milton's argument for tolerance excluded those who, in his view, suppressed liberty and tolerance: the Roman Catholic Church.[25] In the same vein, Karl Popper argued that unlimited tolerance leads to the disappearance of tolerance: 'If we extend unlimited tolerance even to those who are intolerant, if we are not prepared to defend a tolerant society against the onslaught of the intolerant, then the tolerant will be destroyed, and tolerance with them.'[26] Popper therefore argues in favour of the right to suppress intolerant philosophies, if necessary even by force: 'any movement preaching intolerance places itself outside the law, and we should consider incitement to intolerance and persecution as criminal, in the same way as we should consider incitement to murder, or to kidnapping, or to the revival of the slave trade, as criminal'.[27]

In particular, there seems to be little room for media freedom where public denials of clearly established historical facts are concerned. Apart from the argument from individual autonomy and self-fulfilment, there seems to be no warrant in free speech doctrine to protect lies: the argument from democracy contradicts a freedom of expression protection of lies, because falsehoods may mislead the public in their decision-making, and the argument from truth seemingly contradicts free speech protection of lies *eo ipso*.

However, this aspect needs a closer examination. The argument from truth only contradicts protection of lies if one conceptualises this argument from a Platonic standpoint of the possibility of an objective truth.[28] Yet if the argument from truth is regarded from the sceptical perspective that absolute certainty cannot be reached, then even apparent lies warrant free speech protection, because they may challenge common beliefs which must defend themselves in the marketplace of ideas. Milton already observed the necessity of 'the scanning of error' for the 'confirmation of

[23] ECtHR, *Perinçek* v. *Switzerland* [2013] App. no. 27510/08 [46].
[24] Johnson (1826) p. 102. [25] See Milton (1673).
[26] Popper (1945) note 4 to Chapter 7.
[27] Popper (1945) note 4 to Chapter 7. Herbert Marcuse raised similar concerns in his essay 'Repressive Tolerance', see Marcuse (1965).
[28] See Chapter 1, Section 1.2.

truth'.[29] And Mill warned that truth will turn into a 'dead dogma', lacking the power to survive attacks, if it is not continuously challenged by error.[30] In fact, in *United States* v. *Alvarez,* the US Supreme Court established a case for freedom of speech protection even for intentionally false statements of fact, in this case false statements about having received a military medal. According to the Supreme Court, freedom of expression stands against the idea of an Orwellian 'Ministry of Truth', and the best remedy against a lie is true speech, not suppression.[31] Therefore, even a false statement may contribute to public debate, *because* it provokes true counterspeech.[32]

But the sceptical perception of the argument from truth overrates the benefits of falsehoods for public debate.[33] There is no support for the empirical claim that the truth is more likely to win the argument if free discussion is allowed.[34] Moreover, by resting its argument on the importance of free speech for truth, the sceptical perception of the argument from truth provides that 'the truth' would once have to be found.[35] At least, if intentional falsehood causes legally cognisable harm, the alleged advantages of false speech for finding 'the truth' are outweighed by the disadvantages of such speech.

11.3 Doctrinal approaches to hate speech by international adjudicators

Two approaches to hate speech are discernible. One approach excludes hate speech *a priori* from the scope of freedom of expression protection (hereinafter 'exclusionary approach'). Alternatively, a second approach regards hate speech as basically protected by freedom of expression, yet an interference with hate speech may be justified on a case-by-case basis (hereinafter 'justification approach').

11.3.1 Exclusionary approach

Based on Articles 5(1) ICCPR and Article 17 ECHR, respectively, the Human Rights Committee as well as both the European Commission on

[29] Milton (1644) p. 13. [30] Mill (1869) p. 65.

[31] US Supreme Court, *United States* v. *Alvarez* 567 US (2012) 1, 11–15 (Kennedy J). See, by contrast, German Federal Constitutional Court, *'CSU = NPD of Europe'* [1982] Case 1 BvR 1376/79.

[32] See Mill (1869) p. 15; US Supreme Court, *New York Times Co.* v. *Sullivan,* 376 US 254, 304; *United States* v. *Alvarez,* 567 US (2012), 1, 4 (Breyer J, concurring).

[33] See Schauer (1982) p. 169. [34] Compare Scanlon (1972) 218-19.

[35] See US Supreme Court, *United States* v. *Alvarez,* 567 US (2012) 1, 6 (Kennedy J).

Human Rights and the Strasbourg Court refused to grant freedom of expression protection when the right to freedom of expression was invoked to deny the Holocaust, to incite hatred or racial discrimination, or to justify or glorify a pro-Nazi or fascist policy.[36] The purpose of those abuse provisions is to prevent individuals from taking advantage of the rights guaranteed in the Covenant and the Convention to perform acts aimed at destroying the rights and freedoms themselves.[37]

According to the Human Rights Committee and the Strasbourg Court, the denial of the Holocaust is not only to be considered a negation of a clearly and legally established historical fact, but also an incitement to hatred against the Jewish community.[38] As a consequence, both the Committee and the Court upheld Holocaust denial prohibitions not because the denial of the Holocaust is a lie and *as such* not protected by freedom of expression. Rather, revisionism is also perceived as causing harm to the Jewish community.

As regards racism, the Strasbourg Court observed that, 'in view of its perilous consequences', this 'particularly invidious kind of discrimination ... requires from the authorities special vigilance and a vigorous reaction'. Authorities are requested to 'use all available means to combat racism, thereby reinforcing democracy's vision of a society in which diversity is not perceived as a threat but as a source of enrichment'.[39]

In *Norwood* v. *United Kingdom*, the Court applied Article 17 ECHR to an alleged attack directed at the Muslim community. The applicant in this case, a regional organiser for the British National Party (BNP), was convicted for having displayed in the window of his first-floor flat a large poster of the BNP, showing a photograph of the Twin Towers in flames, the words 'Islam out of Britain – Protect the British People' and a symbol of a crescent and star in a prohibition sign. The ECtHR agreed with the domestic courts' assessment that the poster was a public attack on all Muslims in the United Kingdom, linking the group with an act of

[36] See Cooper and Williams (1999); Keane (2007); Keller and Sigron (2010) 159; Cannie and Voorhoof (2011).

[37] ECtHR, *Lawless* v. *Ireland (No. 3)* [1961] App. no. 332/57 [7]; reiterated in, e.g., *Garaudy* v. *France* [2003] App. no. 65831/01; *Perinçek* v. *Switzerland* [2013] App. no. 27510/08 [44]; Human Rights Committee, *M. A.* v. *Italy* [1984] Communication no. 117/1981 [13.3].

[38] Human Rights Committee, *Faurisson* v. *France* [1996] Communication no. 550/93 [9.6]; ECtHR, *Lehideux and Isorni* v. *France* [1998] App. no. 55/1997/839/1045 [47]; *Garaudy* v. *France* [2003] App. no. 65831/01. See also German Federal Constitutional Court, '*Auschwitz denial*' [1994] Case 1 BvR 23/94; Canadian Supreme Court, *R* v. *Keegstra* [1996] 3 SCR 667.

[39] ECtHR, *Nachova and others* v. *Bulgaria* [2005] App. nos. 43577/98 and 43579/98 [145]; reiterated in *Timishev* v. *Russia* [2005] App. nos. 55762/00 and 55974/00 [56] and *Aksu* v. *Turkey* [2012] App. nos. 4149/04 and 41029/04 [44].

terrorism. Such an attack, the Court held, 'is incompatible with the values proclaimed and guaranteed by the Convention, notably tolerance, social peace and non-discrimination'.[40] Similarly, in *Pavel Ivanov* v. *Russia*, the Court decided that the applicant could not invoke Article 10 ECHR because of Article 17 ECHR. The applicant called for the exclusion of Jews from social life, asserted that there is a connection between social, economic and political discomfort and the activities of Jews, and described the alleged malignancy of the Jewish ethnic group. The Court found that these publications were aimed at inciting hatred towards the Jewish people and were therefore in contradiction with the Convention's underlying values of tolerance, social peace and non-discrimination.[41]

The Human Rights Committee also applied an 'exclusionary approach' in *J. R. T. and the W. G. Party* v. *Canada,*[42] where the Committee held that advocacy of racial or religious hatred within the meaning of Article 20(2) ICCPR renders a communication inadmissible within the meaning of Article 3 of the Optional First Protocol.[43]

Finally, the European Commission on Human Rights emphasised that the totalitarian doctrine of National Socialism is 'incompatible with democracy and human rights and that its adherents undoubtedly pursue aims of the kind referred to in Article 17'.[44] Furthermore, in its decision on the inadmissibility of *Glimmerveen and Hagenbeek* v. *Netherlands,*[45] the Commission considered that the applicants, who had been convicted for possessing leaflets addressed to 'White Dutch people' intending that everyone who was not 'white' had to leave the Netherlands, could not rely on Article 10 ECHR. In the same way, the ECtHR held *obiter* in *Lehideux and Isorni* v. *France*: '[L]ike any other remark directed against the Convention's underlying values ..., the justification of a pro-Nazi policy could not be allowed to enjoy the protection afforded by Article 10'.[46]

40 ECtHR, *Norwood* v. *United Kingdom* [2004] App. no. 23131/03, p. 4.
41 ECtHR, *Pavel Ivanov* v. *Russia* [2004] App. no. 35222/04, p. 4.
42 Communication no. 104/1981.
43 Article 3 of the First Optional Protocol states: 'The Committee shall consider inadmissible any communication under the present Protocol which is anonymous, or which it considers to be an abuse of the right of submission of such communications or to be incompatible with the provisions of the Covenant.'
44 ECtHR, *Nachtmann* v. *Austria* [1998] App. no. 36773/97; see also *B.H., M.W., H.P. and G.K.* v. *Austria* [1989] App. no. 12774/87; *Kühnen* v. *Federal Republic of Germany* [1988] App. no. 12194/86; *Schimanek* v. *Austria* [2000] App. no. 32307/96.
45 ECtHR, *Glimmerveen and Hagenbeek* v. *Netherlands* [1979] App. nos. 8348/78 and 8406/78, p. 197.
46 ECtHR, *Lehideux and Isorni* v. *France* [1998] App. no. 55/1997/839/1045 [53].

11.3.2 *Justification approach*

The categorical exclusion of certain speech from human rights protection stands in contrast to the Convention's and the Covenant's liberal *leitmotif* that freedom of expression also encompasses speech that offends, shocks or disturbs the State or any sector of the population.[47] The justification test furnishes the courts with more refined instruments to deal with such speech on a case-by-case basis, and it relieves them of the burden to categorise speech *a priori*, as is necessary under the exclusionary approach. It is therefore commendable that the Strasbourg Court refined its approach to 'hate speech' in *Vejdeland and others* v. *Sweden*, where the applicants were convicted for distributing homophobic leaflets in an upper secondary school. The Court distinguished between statements that directly recommend individuals to commit hateful acts and statements that 'only' include serious and prejudicial allegations.[48] Thus the Court acknowledged that hateful speech is not *per se* excluded from the scope of Article 10(1) ECHR. Rather, the Court distingushed between incitement to hatred and calls for acts of violence or other criminal acts. Insult, ridicule or slander of specific groups can be, but are not necessarily, sufficient for the domestic authorities to favour combating racist speech over freedom of expression.[49] This is similar to the US Supreme Court's approach, where hate speech is protected until it threatens to give rise to imminent violence.[50] Similarly, the Human Rights Committee overruled its exclusionary approach from *J. R. T. and the W. G. Party* v. *Canada* in *Ross* v. *Canada*.[51]

Furthermore, in contrast to the Holocaust, the Court held that the classification of the deportations and massacres perpetrated against the Armenian population on the territory of the former Ottoman Empire in 1915 and the following years as 'genocide' cannot be perceived as a legally established historical fact.[52] Therefore, the Court concluded in *Perinçek* v. *Switzerland* that there was no 'pressing social need' for the criminal conviction of the applicant for his denial of the qualification of the perpetrations as 'genocide', as he did not deny the commission of

47 Keane (2007) 661; Cannie and Voorhoof (2011) 68–72; Grabenwarter and Pabel (2012) § 23 para. 5.

48 ECtHR, *Vejdeland and others* v. *Sweden* [2012] App. no. 1813/07 [54]; see also *Féret* v. *Belgium* [2009] App. no. 15615/07 [73].

49 ECtHR, *Vejdeland and others* v. *Sweden* [2012] App. no. 1813/07 [55].

50 US Supreme Court, *Brandenburg* v. *Ohio*, 395 US 444 (1969); see the critical concurring opinion to ECtHR, *Vejdeland and others* v. *Sweden* by Judge Yudkivska joined by Judge Villiger [6].

51 Human Rights Committee, *Ross* v. *Canada* [2000] Communication no. 736/97 [10.6].

52 ECtHR, *Perinçek* v. *Switzerland* [2013] App. no. 27510/08 [119].

perpetrations as such.[53] Yet the Court also conceded, and this is to be appreciated, that it is not for the Court to decide on controversial historical debates in the absence of clearly established historical facts.[54] Rather, the Strasbourg Court has regularly granted Article 10(1) ECHR protection to contributions that are part of an ongoing debate among historians, such as the policy of the head of the Vichy government, Maréchal Philippe Pétain, as having collaborated with the Nazi regime[55], or the Khojaly massacre of 26 February 1992 during the Nagorno-Karabakh War[56].

Yet the question remains what the factors for adjudicators' balancing exercise with regard to hateful speech are. In the light of media freedom's rationale from public discourse, the relevant factors for this balancing exercise, in addition to the general rules on the justification of an interference with media freedom,[57] should be the following:

- the extent to which the publication contributes to a matter of public concern;
- whether the publication reflects the media's own opinion, or whether it is a third-party statement;[58]
- the tone of the publication: whether it is composed in a balanced manner, merely 'shocking' or 'disturbing', or gratuitously offensive;[59]
- the victims of the publication;
- whether less offensive means would have been available to get the message across;
- timing and place;
- whether the media ensured, to the broadest extent possible, the veracity of the underlying facts of its story;[60] and
- the social and historical context of the publication concerned.

The motivation of the publisher, that is, whether the statement was *intended* to incite antagonism, hatred or violence, is irrelevant if it is a factual statement and pertains to a matter of public concern.[61]

Media freedom is based on the notion of a free argumentative discourse rather than suppression of certain expressions. Publications that are merely disrespectful or create uneasiness must not be subjected

[53] ECtHR, *Perinçek* v. *Switzerland* [2013] App. no. 27510/08 [51] and [126].
[54] ECtHR, *Perinçek* v. *Switzerland* [2013] App. no. 27510/08 [99].
[55] ECtHR, *Lehideux and Isorni* v. *France* [1998] App. no. 55/1997/839/1045 [47].
[56] ECtHR, *Fatullayev* v. *Azerbaijan* [2010] App. no. 40984/07 [81].
[57] See Chapter 6.
[58] See ECtHR, *Jersild* v. *Denmark* [1994] App. no. 15890/89.
[59] ECtHR, *Soulas and others* v. *France* [2008] App. no. 15948/03 [43].
[60] Compare ECtHR, *Aksu* v. *Turkey* [2012] App. nos. 4149/04 and 41029/04 [72].
[61] See Chapter 2, Section 2.2.3.3.

to the heckler's veto.[62] The state is even under an obligation to enable publication of such speech. This applies to a greater extent the more a publication contributes to a matter of public concern. However, there is no warrant under media freedom theory to protect speech that aims at violence or hatred instead of verbal exchange of ideas: the force of the better argument shall be the only force in public discourse.[63] Furthermore, media freedom finds its limits in those rules of civility that serve to protect the rights of others or that public discourse itself presupposes. This is reflected in the notion of 'duties and responsibilities' that go hand in hand with the media's privileges.

In the seminal ECtHR decision *Jersild* v. *Denmark*, the applicant did not make the objectionable statements himself but assisted in their dissemination as a television journalist. The ECtHR drew a distinction between the statements of the interviewees – a group of young people calling themselves 'the Greenjackets' – and the alleged violation of the law by the journalist. The Court found that 'the remarks of the "Greenjackets" were more than insulting to members of the targeted groups and did not enjoy the protection of Article 10'.[64] Regarding the journalist, the Strasbourg Court noted that he knew that racist statements were likely to be made during the interview and even encouraged such statements. However, the Court did not agree with the national courts that the racist speech was presented without any attempt to counterbalance the extremist views expressed, but was broadcast as part of a serious Danish news programme and was intended for a well-informed audience. An important factor in the Court's evaluation was whether the interview appeared to have had as its purpose the propagation of racist views and ideas.[65] The TV presenter introduced the programme by referring to a recent public debate and press comments on racism in Denmark, thus inviting the audience to see the interview in that context. Taken as a whole, the feature sought to expose, analyse and explain this particular group of youths with criminal

[62] ECtHR, *Vajnai* v. *Hungary* [2008] App. no. 33629/06 [57]; *Fáber* v. *Hungary* [2012] App. no. 40721/08 [57].

[63] Compare ECtHR, *Gündüz* v. *Turkey* [2003] App. no. 35071/97 [37]; *Balsytė-Lideikienė* v. *Lithuania* [2008] App. no. 72596/01 [78]; *Soulas and others* v. *France* [2008] App. no. 15948/03 [43]; *Le Pen* v. *France* [2010] App. no. 18788/09, p. 7; *mutatis mutandis*, *Falakaoğlu* v. *Turkey* [2005] App. no. 77365/01 [35]; *Aksu* v. *Turkey* [2012] App. nos. 4149/04 and 41029/04 [70]; AfComHPR, *Malawi Africa Association, Amnesty International, Ms Sarr Diop, Union interafricaine des droits de l'Homme and RADDHO, Collectif des veuves et ayants-Droit, Association mauritanienne des droits de l'Homme* v. *Mauritania* [2000] App. nos. 54/91, 61/91, 96/93, 98/93, 164/97, 196/97 and 210/98 [102].

[64] ECtHR, *Jersild* v. *Denmark* [1994] App. no. 15890/89 [35].

[65] ECtHR, *Jersild* v. *Denmark* [1994] App. no. 15890/89 [31].

records, violent attitudes and frustration with their social situation, thus dealing with a matter that was of great public concern.[66] Although the item 'did not explicitly recall the immorality, dangers and unlawfulness of the promotion of racial hatred and of ideas of superiority of one race', in view of the above-mentioned counterbalancing elements and the natural limitations on spelling out such elements in a short item within a longer programme, as well as the journalist's discretion as to the form of expression used, the Court did not consider the absence of such precautionary reminders to be relevant.[67] Probably the most important aspect in the *Jersild* case was the Court's observation that news reporting based on interviews constitutes one of the most important means whereby the media is able to play its vital role of 'public watchdog'. Therefore, 'the punishment of a journalist for assisting in the dissemination of statements made by another person in an interview would seriously hamper the contribution of the press to discussion of matters of public interest and should not be envisaged unless there are particularly strong reasons for doing so'.[68]

Another factor in the balancing exercise is the victim the statement is targeted at. If hate speech violates the right of an individual or a particular group, such as anti-Semitic and racist statements, states are under a positive obligation to protect the rights of others and to enjoin and prosecute the speech. Specific types of disadvantaged and vulnerable minorities, such as Sinti and Roma, require special protection.[69] For example, in the Human Rights Committee case *Faurisson* v. *France*, the author of the communication was convicted under the French Gayssot Act for revisionist statements, because he doubted the existence of gas chambers for extermination purposes in Nazi concentration camps in an interview. The Committee concluded that the restriction of the author's freedom of expression was justified under Article 19(3)(a) of the Covenant, holding that '[s]ince the statements made by the author, read in their full context, were of a nature as to raise or strengthen anti-Semitic feelings, the restriction served the respect of the Jewish community to live free from fear of an atmosphere of anti-Semitism'.[70] Furthermore, the Committee acknowledged that the introduction of the Gayssot Act

66 ECtHR, *Jersild* v. *Denmark* [1994] App. no. 15890/89 [33].
67 ECtHR, *Jersild* v. *Denmark* [1994] App. no. 15890/89 [34].
68 ECtHR, *Jersild* v. *Denmark* [1994] App. no. 15890/89 [35]; see also ECtHR, *July and SARL Liberation* v. *France* [2008] App. no. 20893/03 [69]; IACtHR, *Herrera-Ulloa* v. *Costa Rica* [2004] Case 12.367 [134].
69 ECtHR, *Aksu* v. *Turkey* [2012] App. nos. 4149/04 and 41029/04 [44].
70 Human Rights Commission, *Faurisson* v. *France* [1996] Communication no. 550/93 [9.6].

was intended to serve in the struggle against racism and anti-Semitism, and that the denial of the existence of the Holocaust is the principal vehicle for anti-Semitism.[71] Yet the Committee also noted *obiter* that 'the application of the terms of the Gayssot Act, which, in their effect, make it a criminal offence to challenge the conclusions and the verdict of the International Military Tribunal at Nuremberg, may lead, under different conditions than the facts of the instant case, to decisions or measures incompatible with the Covenant.'[72]

Citing *Faurisson* v. *France*, the Committee held in *Ross* v. *Canada* that restrictions on statements which raise or strengthen anti-Semitic feeling may be justified in order to protect Jewish communities from religious hatred. Such restrictions were supported by the principles codified in Article 20(2) ICCPR.[73] The Committee noted that 'the author's statements were discriminatory against persons of the Jewish faith and ancestry and that they denigrated the faith and beliefs of Jews and called upon true Christians to not merely question the validity of Jewish beliefs and teachings but to hold those of the Jewish faith and ancestry in contempt as undermining freedom, democracy and Christian beliefs and values'.[74] The Committee therefore concluded that the restrictions imposed on the author were for the purpose of protecting the 'rights or reputations' of persons of Jewish faith. This includes the right to have an education in the public school system free from bias, prejudice and intolerance as the author worked as a modified resource teacher.

In its decision on *J. R. T. and W. G. Party* v. *Canada*, the Human Rights Committee held that the authors' application against a prohibition to communicate anti-Semitic opinions by telephone is inadmissible, since the opinions which the author sought to disseminate through the telephone system 'clearly constitute the advocacy of racial or religious hatred which Canada has an obligation to prohibit under article 20(2) of the Covenant'.[75]

In the case of *Jewish Community of Oslo and others* v. *Norway*, the Committee on the Elimination of Racial Discrimination found that 'the principle of freedom of speech has been afforded a lower level of protection in cases of racist and hate speech dealt with by other international

[71] Human Rights Commission, *Faurisson* v. *France* [1996] Communication no. 550/93 [9.7]. But see also Weaver, Delpierre and Boissier (2009).

[72] Human Rights Commission, *Faurisson* v. *France* [1996] Communication no. 550/93 [9.3].

[73] Human Rights Commision, *Ross* v. *Canada* [2000] Communication no. 736/97 [11.5].

[74] Human Rights Commission, *Ross* v. *Canada* [2000] Communication no. 736/97 [11.5].

[75] Human Rights Commission, *J. R. T. and W. G. Party* v. *Canada* [1984] Communication no. 104/1981 [8].

bodies, and that the Committee's own General recommendation No. 15 clearly states that the prohibition of all ideas based upon racial superiority or hatred is compatible with the right to freedom of opinion and expression'.[76] The acquittal of a neo-Nazi leader by a Norwegian Court on freedom of speech grounds was thus found to be a violation of the ICERD. In the course of a speech, the neo-Nazi leader stated that his 'people and country are being plundered and destroyed by Jews, who suck our country empty of wealth and replace it with immoral and un-Norwegian thoughts'. He then referred to Rudolf Hess, in whose commemoration the speech was made, and to Adolf Hitler, stating that his group will 'follow in their footsteps and fight for what (we) believe in'. The Committee considered these statements to 'contain ideas based on racial superiority or hatred; the deference to Hitler and his principles and "footsteps" must, in the Committee's view, be taken as incitement at least to racial discrimination, if not to violence'.[77]

On a sidenote, a procedural problem connected to hate speech targeted at particular groups is the question whether individual members of that group have victim status and thus fulfil the requirement of standing (see Article 2 First Optional Protocol to the ICCPR, Article 34 ECHR, Article 14 ICERD) in order to bring a complaint to an international court or tribunal against a media publication – or more precisely, against the state failing to protect their rights against a media publication. To claim to be a victim of such a violation, a person must be directly affected by the impugned measure, as opposed to bringing an *actio popularis* for the interpretation of the rights set out in a particular Convention or Covenant.[78] As stated above, the Committee on the Elimination of Racial Discrimination applies a rather generous interpretation, letting it suffice that the author is a member of a potential group of victims. Similarly, the Strasbourg Court held in *Aksu* v. *Turkey* that although the applicant, a member of the Roma community, had not been directly targeted in person in two governmentally funded publications allegedly reflecting anti-Roma sentiments, 'he could, however, have felt offended by the remarks concerning the ethnic group to which he belonged'.[79] The Court's additional argument, namely the fact that the applicant's standing before the domestic court was undisputed, is

[76] CERD, *Jewish Community of Oslo and others* v. *Norway* [2005] CERD/C/67/D/30/2003 [10.5].

[77] CERD, *Jewish Community of Oslo and others* v. *Norway* [2005] CERD/C/67/D/30/2003 [10.4].

[78] See, e.g., ECtHR, *Burden* v. *United Kingdom* [2008] App. no. 13378/05 [33]; *Aksu* v. *Turkey* [2012] App. nos. 4149/04 and 41029/04 [50].

[79] ECtHR, *Aksu* v. *Turkey* [2012] App. nos. 4149/04 and 41029/04 [53].

certainly more convincing to accept standing rather than the mere feeling of having been offended.

The proximity in time between expression and opportunity to act, and the circumstances of the speech, is another factor a court has to take into consideration. In *Leroy* v. *France*, the applicant had published a cartoon in a Basque weekly newspaper depicting the attacks on the World Trade Centre, accompanied by a parody on an advertising slogan of Sony: 'We have all dreamt of it ... Hamas did it.'[80] The cartoon was published two days after the attacks. After the newspaper received enraged letters and e-mails reacting to the cartoon, it published a reaction of the applicant, in which he explained that he did not take into account the suffering caused by the attacks. He also remarked that his intention was to convey his anti-Americanism through a satirical image. The ECtHR nonetheless upheld the ensuing conviction of the applicant for complicity in the glorification of terrorism. It refused to apply Article 17 ECHR, as the cartoon did not attack the fundamental values underlying the Convention.[81] However, the Court held that the applicant had expressed his moral support for who he thought were the perpetrators of the attacks. He thus glorified destruction and violence perpetrated against thousands of civilians and violated their dignity.[82] The Court also held the timing of the publication two days after the attack and the place of the publication – the politically sensitive Basque region – against the applicant.[83]

In *Gündüz* v. *Turkey*, the applicant uttered offensive statements on secularism in Turkey using pejorative terms in a live broadcasting debate. The Court recognised that the applicant was taking an active part in a 'lively public discussion', his statements were counterbalanced by other participants in the discussion, and his views were expressed as part of a pluralist debate.[84] The Court observed that 'the applicant's statements were made orally during a live television broadcast, so that he had no possibility of reformulating, refining or retracting them before they were made public'.[85] Therefore a number of remarks made by the applicant that could be regarded as insulting were held by the Court to be justified.

Lastly, a court has to consider the social and historical context of the publication concerned. Where historical debates are concerned, the lapse of time between the historical event and the publication plays a

[80] The original slogan said 'Sony did it'.
[81] ECtHR, *Leroy* v. *France* [2009] App. no. 36109/03 [27].
[82] ECtHR, *Leroy* v. *France* [2009] App. no. 36109/03 [43].
[83] ECtHR, *Leroy* v. *France* [2009] App. no. 36109/03 [45].
[84] ECtHR, *Gündüz* v. *Turkey* [2003] App. no. 35071/97 [51].
[85] ECtHR, *Gündüz* v. *Turkey* [2003] App. no. 35071/97 [49].

significant role.[86] Even if impugned remarks may reopen a controversy among the public, the passage of time must be taken into account in assessing whether a measure is compatible with freedom of expression: 'That forms part of the efforts that every country must make to debate its own history openly and dispassionately.'[87]

Topical issues which may stir emotions, such as the question how countries cope with migration and the integration of immigrants, should be treated with care and moderation.[88] At the same time, courts have to consider that publications on topical political issues are at the core of a democratic society; therefore, restrictions should be applied only with the utmost reservation.

To conclude, it is recommendable that courts distinguish carefully on a case-by-case basis between shocking and offensive language which is protected by freedom of expression and media freedom, on the one hand, and that which forfeits its right to participate in the public discourse, on the other hand. Such an approach should be preferred to an exclusion of certain forms of speech *a priori* from the protection of freedom of expression and media freedom.[89]

86 Compare ECtHR, *Vajnai* v. *Hungary* [2008] App. no. 33629/06 [49]; *Orban and others* v. *France* [2009] App. no. 20985/05 [49].

87 ECtHR, *Monnat* v. *Switzerland* [2006] App. no. 73604/01 [64]; *Vajnai* v. *Hungary* [2008] App. no. 33629/06 [49]; see also *Orban and others* v. *France* [2009] App. no. 20985/05 [49].

88 Compare ECtHR, *Soulas and others* v. *France* [2008] App. no. 15948/03 [43]; *Le Pen* v. *France* [2010] App. no. 18788/09, p. 7.

89 Cannie and Voorhoof (2011) 83.

12 Religiously offensive publications

For a long time, many sociologists believed that the 'disenchantment'[1] of the (Western) world through enlightenment and rationalisation led to a privatisation of religious faith.[2] The 'authority of the holy' had been replaced by the authority of consensus.[3] However, the debates following the murder of Theo van Gogh in 2004, the Muhammad cartoon controversy in 2005 and the outrage caused by the 'Innocence of Muslims' video in 2012 are just a few well-known examples of fierce conflicts between freedom of expression and religious feelings. The law of freedom of expression and media freedom has the important task of keeping public discourse on religious matters civil, despite the long underestimated significance and plurality of religious denominations in 'post-secular societies'.[4]

Countries' attitudes towards the conflict between freedom of speech and religious freedom oscillate between 'religious traditionalism' and 'secularist fundamentalism'.[5] Religious traditionalism would suppress any speech that affects religious feelings. In April 1999, the UN Human Rights Commission approved a resolution entitled 'Defamation of Religions', which had originally been brought before the Commission by Pakistan under the draft title 'Defamation of Islam'.[6] On the initiative particularly of countries with a predominantly Muslim population, the Human Rights Commission and subsequently the UN Human Rights Council adopted several resolutions in opposition to 'defamation of religion'.[7]

1 Weber (1922) p. 536. 2 See Habermas (1981a) p. 341; Habermas (2008) 17.
3 Habermas (1981b) p. 77. 4 Habermas (2008) 17. 5 See Habermas (2008) 24.
6 UN Commission on Human Rights, Resolution 1999/82: Defamation of Religions of 30 April 1999.
7 UN Commission on Human Rights, Resolution 2000/84: Defamation of Religions of 26 April 2000; Resolution 2001/4: Combating Defamation of Religions as a Means to Promote Human Rights, Social Harmony and Religious and Cultural Diversity of 18 April 2001; Resolution 2002/9: Combating Defamation of Religions of 15 April 2002; Resolution 2003/4: Combating Defamation of Religions of 14 April 2003; Resolution 2004/6: Combating Defamation of Religions of 13 April 2004; Resolution

Similar resolutions were adopted between 2005 and 2010 by the UN General Assembly.[8]

However, the concept of 'defamation of religions' is problematic. It is at odds with human rights doctrine, because human rights serve to protect individuals, not institutions or religions. Freedom of religion protects believers, not beliefs. Furthermore, it seems unjustifiable to distinguish 'religion' as particularly worthy of protection, as opposed to, say, ethnic origins. The concept of 'defamation of religions' should thus be rejected in favour of prohibition of incitement to hatred in general, including religious hatred, as developed in Chapter 11.

By contrast, secularist fundamentalism defends the right to say everything, even if it intentionally hurts religious feelings. Especially in 'Western' countries, where religion is still perceived as an essentially private matter, people often misjudge the importance religion has in other countries on the globe. The 2012 'Innocence of Muslims' video and the reactions it caused are proof of that.[9]

Media freedom, if properly conceptualised not as an absolute right to print everything, but as a means to foster public discourse in a pluralistic and tolerant democratic society, has to find a third way between these extremes.

12.1 Limitations to religiously offensive publications

Religious faith carries elements of a person's identity, which other individuals have to respect. Hence, similar to the 'legitimate expectation of privacy',[10] freedom of the media has to be weighed against a 'legitimate expectation of respect for one's religious feelings' on a case-by-case basis. This right derives from freedom of religion as a right not to be offended in one's religious beliefs as an aspect of 'rights of others'. Furthermore, interferences with religiously offensive speech may, under certain circumstances, also be justified based on public order interests.

The first approach, however, is controversial. It is contested whether freedom of religion, as protected by Article 18 ICCPR, Article 9 ECHR,

2005/3: Combating Defamation of Religions of 12 April 2005; UN Human Rights Council, Decision 1/107: Incitement to Racial and Religious Hatred and the Promotion of Tolerance of 30 June 2006; Resolution 4/9: Combating Defamation of Religions of 30 March 2007; Resolution 7/19: Combating Defamation of Religions of 27 March 2008; Resolution 10/22: Combating Defamation of Religions of 26 March 2009.

[8] UN General Assembly, Resolution 60/150 of 16 December 2005, Resolution 61/164 of 19 December 2006, Resolution 62/154 of 18 December 2007, Resolution 63/171 of 18 December 2008, Resolution 64/156 of 18 December 2009 and Resolution 65/224 of 21 December 2010, all entitled 'Combating Defamation of Religions'.

[9] Garcia (2012). [10] See Chapter 7, Section 7.3.4.1.

Article 10 EUChFR, Article 8 AfCHPR and Article 12 ACHR does indeed include a right not to be offended in one's religious beliefs. This question is not of mere academic interest, but of significant practical importance. If interferences with religiously offensive speech may only be based on public order concerns, then there is a presumption that freedom of expression and media freedom prevail, since public interest exceptions to these rights must be construed narrowly.[11] However, if one accepts a right not to be offended in one's religious beliefs as an aspect of freedom of religion, then this requires a fair balancing of conflicting equal rights. In addition, states may then even be under a positive obligation to prohibit speech that violates the religious feelings of others. In their joint dissenting opinion to *Otto-Preminger-Institut* v. *Austria*, Judges Palm, Pekkanen and Makarczyk thus wrote: 'The Convention does not, in terms, guarantee a right to protection of religious feelings. More particularly, such a right cannot be derived from the right to freedom of religion, which in effect includes a right to express views critical of the religious opinions of others.'[12]

However, it is submitted that freedom of religion, like honour and privacy, is one aspect of a person's personality rights. As a consequence, freedom of religion should be conceptualised as a right not to be offended in one's religious feelings.[13] Freedom of thought, conscience and religion is 'in its religious dimension, one of the most vital elements that go to make up the identity of believers and their conception of life'.[14] Yet, freedom of religion is not absolute in nature. As the ECtHR stated: 'Those who choose to exercise the freedom to manifest their religion, irrespective of whether they do so as members of a religious majority or a minority, cannot reasonably expect to be exempt from all criticism. They must tolerate and accept the denial by others of their religious beliefs and even the propagation by others of doctrines hostile to their faith.'[15] Similarly, the Human Rights Committee explained that prohibitions of displays of lack of respect for a religion or other belief system, including blasphemy laws, are incompatible with Article 19(2) ICCPR.[16]

[11] See Chapter 6, Section 6.3.3.2.

[12] ECtHR, *Otto-Preminger-Institut* v. *Austria* [1994] App. no. 13470/87, joint dissenting opinion of Judges Palm, Pekkanen and Makarczyk [6]. From legal scholarship, see, e.g., Ahdar and Leigh (2005) pp 395–396; Temperman (2008); Khan (2012).

[13] Compare ECtHR, *Otto-Preminger-Institut* v. *Austria* [1994] App. no. 13470/87 [48]; Keller (2011) p. 204; Oliva (2007) 85.

[14] ECtHR, *Kokkinakis* v. *Greece* [1993] App. no. 14307/88 [31]; *Otto-Preminger-Institut* v. *Austria* [1994] App. no. 13470/87 [47].

[15] ECtHR, *Otto-Preminger-Institut* v. *Austria* [1994] App. no. 13470/87 [47]; *İ.A.* v. *Turkey* [2005] App. no. 42571/98 [28].

[16] Human Rights Committee, General Comment no. 34, para. 48.

The particular methods of opposing or denying religious beliefs may require states to balance the right to peaceful enjoyment of one's faith with freedom of expression. Although media freedom is also applicable to information or ideas that shock, offend or disturb, the 'duties and responsibilities' of the media include a duty to avoid, as far as possible, an expression that is gratuitously offensive to others or profanatory.[17] Especially if speech is targeted at insulting other people's religious beliefs rather than contributing to a debate of general interest, then there is no reason to grant more protection to such speech than to the interest in not being offended in one's faith. This does not presuppose that freedom of religion necessarily prevails over freedom of expression and media freedom; rather, this question is for the justification level to decide. Although freedom of religion, like media freedom, has no direct horizontal effect, religious freedom has to be taken into account by domestic courts when applying the law.[18]

Second, publications that are offensive against religious feelings may violate the interests of society as a whole, and not only of individual persons.[19] Article 20(2) ICCPR therefore expressly states that freedom of expression must not be used to advocate religious hatred that constitutes incitement to discrimination, hostility or violence. Furthermore, the Strasbourg Court refers to the legitimate aims of public morals and public order in addition to the 'rights of others' when dealing with the protection of religious beliefs against interferences by third persons.[20]

12.2 Margin of appreciation

Interferences with freedom of speech aiming at protecting religious beliefs allow for a rather wide margin of appreciation. Similar to the notion of 'morals', a uniform global or even regional conception of the significance of religion in society does not exist. Hence, it is not possible to define in abstract terms what constitutes a permissible interference with media freedom where a publication hurts the religious feelings of others.[21]

[17] Compare ECtHR, *Otto-Preminger-Institut* v. *Austria* [1994] App. no. 13470/87 [49]; *Wingrove* v. *United Kingdom* [1996] App. no. 17419/90 [52].

[18] See Chapter 5, Section 5.2.3.

[19] ECtHR, *Otto-Preminger-Institut* v. *Austria* [1994] App. no. 13470/87 [55].

[20] ECtHR, *Murphy* v. *Ireland* [2003] App. no. 44179/98 [63]; *İ. A.* v. *Turkey* [2005] App. no. 42571/98 [22]. See also Sandberg and Doe (2008).

[21] See EComHR, *X. Ltd. and Y.* v. *United Kingdom* [1982] App. no. 8710/79 [12]; ECtHR, *Otto-Preminger-Institut* v. *Austria* [1994] App. no. 13470/87 [50]; *Wingrove* v. *United Kingdom* [1996] App. no. 17419/90 [58]; *Murphy* v. *Ireland* [2003] App. no. 44179/98 [81]; *İ. A.* v. *Turkey* [2005] App. no. 42571/98 [25].

What is likely to offend persons of a particular religious conviction varies significantly from time to time and from place to place.[22]

In *Otto-Preminger-Institut* v. *Austria*, the Strasbourg Court thus held that the Austrian courts did not overstep their margin of appreciation when they ordered the seizure and subsequently the forfeiture of the 1982 film 'Das Liebeskonzil' (officially translated as 'Council in Heaven'), which portrayed 'God as old, infirm and ineffective, Jesus Christ as a "mummy's boy" of low intelligence and the Virgin Mary, who is obviously in charge, as an unprincipled wanton'. The domestic courts acted to ensure religious peace in a particular Austrian region (Tyrol) and preventing people from feeling that they are the object of attacks on their religious beliefs in an unwarranted and offensive manner. 'It is', the Strasbourg Court stated, 'in the first place for the national authorities, who are better placed than the international judge, to assess the need for such a measure in the light of the situation obtaining locally at a given time'.[23]

Due to the lack of a uniform conception of the significance of religion in society, which is even greater on the global than on the European level, domestic authorities are in a better position to estimate the relative importance attached to religious feelings. This part of the Court's judgment can be agreed with. Yet the knowledge-based deficit which allows granting a margin of appreciation to the Member States is only normative, not factual. States are in a better position to estimate the importance of religious feelings in their society. However, they are not in a better position to decide on the 'necessity' of an interference with freedom of expression and media freedom. As a consequence, the margin of appreciation only applies to the relative weight attached to religious feelings in the proportionality *sensu stricto* analysis, but not to the factual suitability and necessity test, and especially not to the evaluation of the relative importance of the exercise of media freedom. Therefore, the Court's reasoning in *Otto-Preminger-Institut* is not commendable. Granting a margin of appreciation for the entire assessment of 'the need for such a measure' goes too far. The Austrian authorities had a margin of appreciation concerning the importance attached to religious feelings of people in the Austrian region of Tyrol. However, the estimation of the 'necessity' of the interference within the meaning of the proportionality test and of the relative importance of freedom of expression in this case was for the Court, not for the Austrian authorities. Such supervision is all the more necessary with a view to the breadth of the notion of 'blasphemy' in

[22] See ECtHR, *Wingrove* v. *United Kingdom* [1996] App. no. 17419/90 [58]; *Murphy* v. *Ireland* [2003] App. no. 44179/98 [67].

[23] ECtHR, *Otto-Preminger-Institut* v. *Austria* [1994] App. no. 13470/87 [56].

several jurisdictions and the ensuing risks of arbitrary or excessive interferences with freedom of expression and media freedom.[24]

12.3 Balancing freedom of the media and religious interests

Similar to the notion of 'hate speech', which has already been subject to criticism, 'religious speech' as a label to categorise a certain content of expression should be applied with the utmost reservation. To be sure, religiously motivated expression is often more of individual than of public concern, and thus not political in nature.[25] However, particularly religiously *offensive* speech can at the same time touch on a matter of public and even political concern, such as the Muhammad cartoons published by the Danish newspaper *Jyllands-Posten* in 2005.[26] A distinction between 'religious speech' and 'political speech' is thus not sustainable. Instead, courts should balance on a case-by-case basis whether the offence cause by a publication outweighs the importance to protect media freedom. Akin to the balancing exercise regarding 'incitement to hatred', media freedom and religious interests have to be balanced according to the following factors:

- the extent to which the publication contributes to a matter of public concern;
- whether the publication reflects the media's own opinion, or whether it is a third-party statement;
- the tone of the publication: whether it is composed in a balanced manner, merely 'shocking' or 'disturbing', or gratuitously offensive;
- the victims of the publication, especially whether the publication insults specific believers or sacred symbols;
- whether less offensive means would have been available to get the message across;
- timing and place;[27]
- whether the media ensured, to the broadest extent possible, the veracity of the underlying facts; and
- the social and historical context of the publication concerned.

For example, in *Giniewski* v. *France*, the impugned article challenged a number of principles of the Catholic faith. The Strasbourg Court acknowledged that the article was part of a view which the applicant wished to

[24] See ECtHR, *Wingrove* v. *United Kingdom* [1996] App. no. 17419/90 [58].
[25] Lewis (2007) 398–9; see also Geddis (2004).
[26] See Rösler (2008); Nathwani (2008); Keane (2008); Parmar (2009).
[27] See Chapter 11, Section 11.3.2.

express as a journalist and historian on the possible reasons behind the extermination of the Jews in Europe, and thus on a matter of great public interest in a democratic society.[28] Furthermore, the Court emphasised that the applicant's article was not gratuitously offensive or insulting, and did not incite disrespect or hatred.[29] The Court thus held that an order to pay damages to the complainant association – the General Alliance against Racism and for Respect for the French and Christian Identity (*Alliance générale contre le racisme et pour le respect de l'identité française et chrétienne* (AGRIF)) – and, in particular, to publish a notice of the ruling in a national newspaper at his own expense, violated Article 10 ECHR.

By contrast, in *İ.A.* v. *Turkey*, the Court held that Muslim believers legitimately felt to be the object of offensive attacks through the following passages of the applicant's novel: 'Some of these words were, moreover, inspired in a surge of exultation, in Aisha's arms. … God's messenger broke his fast through sexual intercourse, after dinner and before prayer. Muhammad did not forbid sexual intercourse with a dead person or a live animal.'[30]

In the case *Aydın Tatlav* v. *Turkey*, however, the impugned book that included comments critical of the Qur'an was reprinted for the fifth time after the Turkish authorities had authorised the first four editions. The Court decided that the decision to prosecute the fifth edition of the book lacked consistency in the attitude of the Turkish authorities. Moreover, the Court neither observed an insulting tone aimed directly at believers, nor an injurious attack against sacred symbols, especially concerning Muslims, who on reading the book could nonetheless feel offended by the 'somewhat caustic commentary on their religion'.[31]

In *Murphy* v. *Ireland*, a bible based Christian ministry submitted an advertisement for a video 'on the evidence of the resurrection' to a radio station for transmission. Having particular regard to 'the country-specific religious sensitivities' in Ireland and the margin of appreciation accorded to the state in religious matters, the Court found that the prohibition on disseminating this broadcast by the Independent Radio and Television Commission – the ruling did not affect the later transmission of the video by satellite – did not violate the applicant's right to freedom of expression.[32]

[28] ECtHR, *Giniewski* v. *France* [2006] App. no. 64016/00 [51].
[29] ECtHR, *Giniewski* v. *France* [2006] App. no. 64016/00 [52].
[30] ECtHR, *İ. A.* v. *Turkey* [2005] App. no. 42571/98 [29].
[31] ECtHR, *Aydın Tatlav* v. *Turkey* [2006] App. no. 50692/99 [28] (original in French).
[32] ECtHR, *Murphy* v. *Ireland* [2003] App. no. 44179/98 [73] and [82]; see also *United Christian Broadcasters Ltd* v. *United Kingdom* [2000] App. no. 44802/98.

In *Klein* v. *Slovakia*, the applicant journalist had been convicted for publishing an article criticising an archbishop for his call in a TV broadcast for the withdrawal of both the film '*The People* vs. *Larry Flint*' and the poster accompanying that film. The ECtHR found that the conviction violated Article 10 ECHR, because the article 'neither unduly interfered with the right of believers to express and exercise their religion, nor did it denigrate the content of their religious faith'. The Strasbourg Court held that the strongly worded opinion only concerned the archbishop, but did not denigrate the content of the Catholic faith as such, although some members of the Catholic Church could have been offended by the applicant's criticism.[33]

Finally, the right not to be offended in one's religious beliefs should not serve to stifle criticism of church dignitaries or religious debates which are of considerable interest to the religious community concerned.[34] High-ranking church officials are in their influence and public perception – at least in religious communities – comparable to politicians in general. Therefore, similar freedom of expression standards should apply to religious figures.

[33] ECtHR, *Klein* v. *Slovakia* [2006] App. no. 72208/01 [52].
[34] Compare ECtHR, *Albert-Engelmann-Gesellschaft mbH* v. *Austria* [2006] App. no. 46389/99 [30]; US Supereme Court, *Hustler Magazine* v. *Falwell*, 485 US 46, 50 (1988).

13 Restrictions on commercial publications

The media is protected in a particularly strong way if it contributes to the public discourse on matters of general concern. Consequently, speech that is primarily disseminated for commercial or financial interests rather than with the aim of contributing to a debate of general concern, often named 'commercial speech', enjoys less protection.[1] Remarkably, Article 7(4) Dutch Constitution even excludes commercial advertising entirely from the protection of the freedom of expression provision.

However, a distinction between 'commercial speech' and 'publications on matters of public concern' is not as clear-cut as it seems at first glance. Neither the public interest nor the publisher's intentions to achieve commercial success are *as such* suitable criteria to distinguish between, say, investigative news reporting and advertising. That is because, on the one hand, even advertising may relate to matters of public concern, because the public needs to be informed about the availability and characteristics of products and services on the market. Thus, commercial speech merits protection because it serves to inform consumers to enable intelligent opinions, and thus affects their economic well-being.[2] On the other hand, even core investigative journalism is not altruistic. Newspaper companies print articles on matters of public interest because they want people to buy their newspapers. As the then-ECJ rightly observed in

[1] See ECtHR, *Markt intern Verlag GmbH and Klaus Beermann* v. *Germany* [1989] App. no. 10572/83; *Jacubowski* v. *Germany* [1994] App. no. 15088/89 [26]; *Hertel* v. *Switzerland* [1998] App. no. 59/1997/843/1049 [47]; but see also, *mutatis mutandis*, *VgT Verein gegen Tierfabriken* v. *Switzerland (No. 1)* [2001] App. no. 24699/94 [66]; ECJ, *RTL* v. *Niedersächsische Landesmedienanstalt für privaten Rundfunk* [2003] ECR I-12489, Case C-245/01 [73]; *Herbert Karner Industrie-Auktionen GmbH* v. *Troostwijk GmbH* [2004] ECR I-03025, Case C-71/02 [51]. For analyses of commercial speech in academic scholarship, see Ferguson (2003); Munro (2003); Barendt (2005) pp. 392–416; Randall (2006); Johnson and Youm (2009).

[2] Volokh (2000) 1082.

Satakunnan Markkinapörssi Oy and Satamedia Oy, a 'degree of commercial success may even be essential to professional journalistic activity'.[3]

Consequently, rather than categorising certain forms of speech under labels, in this case as 'commercial speech', one should apply a contextual approach, scrutinising the particular impugned statement.

13.1 When are publications 'commercial'?

'Commercial speech' and 'speech on matters of public concern' are usually distinguished based on the motivation of the publisher. A producer of, for example, cosmetics publishes an advertisement because he intends to achieve commercial success by selling his products. Advertising rarely ever aims at inspiring criticism or a public debate; rather, advertising usually seeks to manipulate the viewer's opinion in favour of a certain product.[4] In these cases, the human rights-related centre of gravity is the producer's freedom to conduct a business, as protected by Article 16 EUChFR and by equivalent domestic provisions, such as Article 12 German Basic Law, but not freedom of expression. By contrast, an investigative journalist researches and publishes an article because he wants to achieve commercial success by selling the article. In this case, the article *is* the product.

However, the motivation of the publisher is as such not a permissible criterion to justify interferences with media freedom.[5] Even if the publisher intends to promote the supply of a product, the publication nonetheless deserves strong protection, if it is based on true facts and contributes to a discourse on matters of public concern. Against this backdrop, the Human Rights Committee in *Ballantyne and others* v. *Canada* rightly interpreted Article 19 ICCPR as encompassing 'every form of subjective ideas and opinions capable of transmission to others … of news and information, of commercial expression and advertising, of works of art, etc.' Furthermore, the Committee disagrees with the perception 'that any of the above forms of expression can be subjected to varying degrees of limitation, with the result that some forms of expression may suffer broader restrictions than others'.[6]

The Human Rights Committee raised a valid point. The category of 'commercial speech' should indeed not be taken too dogmatically. Commercial speech may relate not only to a company's interest in informing customers of their products and services, but also to consumers' interest

[3] ECJ, *Tietosuojavaltuutettu* v. *Satakunnan Markkinapörssi Oy and Satamedia Oy* [2008] ECR I-09831, Case C-73/07 [59].

[4] Compare Luhmann (1996) p. 44. [5] See Chapter 2, Section 2.2.3.3.

[6] ECtHR, *Ballantyne and others* v. *Canada* [1993] Communication no. 359, 385/89 [11.3].

in being accurately informed about these commodities. In addition, even commercial speech may raise matters of general importance. Credit ratings issued by credit rating agencies, for instance, are, in the first place, disseminated for commercial purposes. However, such credit ratings may nonetheless affect debates of public interest, especially where credit ratings of states – so-called sovereign ratings – are concerned. Sovereign ratings pertain to an important political issue of outstanding public interest, affecting both today's, and following, generations: the ability of states to repay their loans or bonds.[7] Furthermore, the distinction between 'selling a product' and 'selling a publication' may be blurred where the intention of the publisher is to contribute to a debate of public interest *in addition* to selling a product. This is the case where the contribution to a matter of public interest other than the information about the product itself should help selling the product. An example is so-called shock advertising, which attracts attention to products by bringing awareness to a certain public issue through startling or provoking imagery or slogans.[8] Eventually, one should also consider that restrictions on 'commercial speech' in the form of advertising constitute an interference with media freedom, because advertising is one of the main sources of income for the media.

The label 'commercial speech', which allegedly deserves less protection than speech on matters of public concern, should thus be applied with reservation. Instead, the general principles of media speech – accuracy, good faith, journalistic independence, etc. – should apply. Accordingly, consumers and competitors must be protected from false or misleading information. Examples for regulation of advertising are the EU law rules on 'audiovisual commercial communications' in the AVMS Directive,[9] Directive 2006/114/EC concerning misleading and comparative advertising[10] and Directive 2003/33/EC relating to the advertising and sponsorship of tobacco products.[11]

[7] See Oster (2012a) 212.

[8] See, for instance, the *United Colours of Benetton* decisions of the German Federal Constitutional Court, '*Benetton I*' [2000] Cases no. 1 BvR 1762/95 and 1 BvR 1787/95 and '*Benetton II*' [2003] Case 1 BvR 426/02.

[9] See Articles 1(1)(h), (i) and (j), 9, 19 to 26 AVMS Directive; with regard to the frequency of advertising breaks, see ECJ, *RTL* v. *Niedersächsische Landesmedienanstalt für privaten Rundfunk* [2003] ECR I-12489, Case C-245/01.

[10] Directive 2006/114/EC of the European Parliament and of the Council of 12 December 2006 concerning Misleading and Comparative Advertising (codified version), OJ 2006, L376/21. On the preceding Directive, see ECJ, *Herbert Karner Industrie-Auktionen GmbH* v. *Troostwijk GmbH* [2004] ECR I-03025, Case C-71/02.

[11] Directive 2003/33/EC of the European Parliament and of the Council of 26 May 2003 on the Approximation of the Laws, Regulations and Administrative Provisions of the Member States relating to the Advertising and Sponsorship of Tobacco Products, OJ

Furthermore, where commercial broadcasting is at issue, the powerful impact of the audiovisual media and the necessity to safeguard pluralism in broadcasting has to be considered.[12] The commercial character of certain publications also justifies rules requiring separation between advertising and editorial content, for example, Article 19 AVMS Directive. As the ECJ decided in *Stichting Collectieve Antennevoorziening Gouda*, a limitation on the duration or frequency of advertisements, and restrictions designed to enable listeners or viewers not to confuse advertising with other parts of the programme, may be justified by overriding reasons relating to the general interest. Such reasons may be, for instance, consumer protection or the maintenance of a certain level of programme quality.[13]

13.2 Restrictions on advertisements

International adjudicators are rather deferential where states impose restrictions on advertising. And also the US Supreme Court decided that false statements in commercial advertising are more susceptible to regulation than other false statements. The 'truth of commercial speech' is, according to the Court, more easily verifiable by its disseminator compared to news reporting or political commentary, because the advertiser knows more about the product or service he provides than anyone else.[14] Consequently, even the Supreme Court allows the suppression of misleading advertising.[15]

In Europe, the Strasbourg Court held in the seminal case of *Casado Coca* v. *Spain* that the near absolute ban on advertising by lawyers based on unfair competition rules did not amount to a violation of Article 10

2003, L152/16. The ECJ in *Germany* v. *Parliament and Council ('Tobacco Advertising II')* [2006] ECR I-11573, Case C-380/03 dismissed an action for annulment of this Directive. See also *Commission* v. *France ('Loi Évin')* [2004] ECR I-06613, Case C-262/02 [24]: French law prohibiting TV advertising for alcoholic beverages justified by the aim of protecting public health.

12 ECtHR, *Demuth* v. *Switzerland* [2002] App. no. 38743/97 [43] and [44].

13 *Stichting Collectieve Antennevoorziening Gouda and others* v. *Commissariaat voor de Media* [1991] ECR I-04007, Case C-288/89 [27]. However, since the provisions of the Dutch Media Act at issue restricted the competition to which the Dutch broadcasting advertising foundation STER was exposed, the Court held that the restriction was not justified by overriding requirements relating to the general interest: *Stichting Collectieve Antennevoorziening Gouda and others* v. *Commissariaat voor de Media* [1991] ECR I-04007, Case C-288/89 [29–30].

14 US Supreme Court, *Virginia State Bd. of Pharmacy* v. *Virginia Citizens Consumer Council, Inc.*, 425 US 748, 771 n. 25 (1976).

15 US Supreme Court, *Central Hudson Gas & Elec.* v. *Public Serv. Comm'n*, 447 US 557, 566 (1980).

ECHR. Indicating that the rules governing the profession, particularly in the sphere of advertising, vary from one country to another according to cultural tradition, and with a view to lawyers' central position in the administration of justice as intermediaries between the public and the courts, the Court granted a rather broad margin of appreciation to the Spanish authorities.[16] However, the Court made an exception to this principle in *Stambuk* v. *Germany*.[17] There the Court decided in favour of an ophthalmologist who had been fined for disregarding a ban on advertising under the provisions of rules of professional conduct for medical practitioners. The applicant in this case made the alleged advertising in a newspaper interview on a new laser operation technique, which had taken place on the initiative of the journalist. Consequently, the 'advertising' did not only contain information of the public on a matter of general medical interest, but also participated in the protection of the press. Yet such a distinction according to the form of publication – placing an advertisement versus conducting an interview – cannot convince. Rather, it should be the content of the publication, its accuracy and the extent to which it is a matter of public concern that should be decisive.

This approach was more closely followed in *Demuth* v. *Switzerland*. In this case, the applicant intended to broadcast 'Car TV AG', a television programme on automobiles, in particular news on cars, car accessories and private-vehicle transport. The Court rightly observed 'that such aspects would have contributed to the ongoing, general debate on the various aspects of a motorised society'. However, the Court then recurred to an analysis of the motivation of the publisher, finding that 'the purpose of Car TV AG was primarily commercial in that it intended to promote cars and, hence, further car sales'.[18] The Court then re-emphasised the Contracting State's broad margin of appreciation in the area of regulation of commercial speech and eventually found that refusal to grant the required broadcasting licence did not breach Article 10 ECHR. Yet, as has been indicated before, the motivation of the publisher alone hardly serves as a permissible criterion to justify interferences with media freedom.

In *Murphy* v. *Ireland*, the applicant was prevented from transmitting an advertisement for a video with religious content. There were thus three reasons for the ECtHR to grant a rather broad margin of appreciation: first, the applicant's contribution was 'commercial speech'; second, it

[16] ECtHR, *Casado Coca* v. *Spain* [1994] App. no. 15450/89 [50] and [54].
[17] ECtHR, *Stambuk* v. *Germany* [2002] App. no. 37928/97.
[18] ECtHR, *Demuth* v. *Switzerland* [2002] App. no. 38743/97 [41].

referred to 'religious speech'; and third, the applicant sought access to broadcasting as a means of dissemination.[19] Consequently, the Court found that Article 10 ECHR was not violated.

By contrast, the Court held that the domestic courts overstepped their margin of appreciation in *Krone Verlag GmbH* v. *Austria (No. 3)*. In an advertisement, the applicant's newspaper *Neue Kronenzeitung* claimed to be 'the best' local newspaper. Based on the Austrian Unfair Competition Act, a competitor newspaper successfully applied for a court order to prevent publication of the advertisement. The Strasbourg Court observed that the national courts based their decision 'on the assumption that the two newspapers were not of comparable quality and that a comparison of their prices would therefore be misleading'. However, the domestic courts also held that 'the two newspapers were competitors in the same market and for the same circle of readers'. The Strasbourg Court rightly found these two statements inconsistent.[20] Accordingly, the Court decided that in this case the restriction on comparative advertising breached Article 10 ECHR. In addition, it would have been welcomed if the Court had also emphasised that the quality of local newspapers is an important matter of public concern, and that the applicant newspaper, with its advertising, might have caused or contributed to a public debate on this issue.

With regard to the assessment of commercial speech under the ICCPR, the Human Rights Committee had to decide in the above-mentioned application *Ballantyne and others* v. *Canada*, whether the prohibition of public advertising in any language other than French in the province of Quebec violated Article 19 ICCPR. In contrast to the Government of Quebec, the Committee held that commercial activity falls within the ambit of Article 19 ICCPR.[21] Furthermore, the Committee emphasised that it does not distinguish between commercial speech and other forms of speech. The Committee then decided that the rights of the francophone minority within Canada under Article 27 ICCPR as 'rights of others' are not jeopardised by the freedom of others to advertise in a language other than French. Moreover, the Committee did not follow the argument that public order would be jeopardised by commercial advertising outdoors in a language other than French: 'A State may choose one or more official languages, but it may not exclude, outside

[19] See Chapter 4, Section 4.1.4.2.

[20] ECtHR, *Krone Verlag GmbH & Co. KG* v. *Austria (No. 3)* [2003] App. no. 39069/97 [32].

[21] Human Rights Committee, *Ballantyne and others* v. *Canada* [1993] Communication no. 359, 385/89 [11.3].

the spheres of public life, the freedom to express oneself in a language of one's choice'.[22] Accordingly, the Committee concluded that Article 19 (2) ICCPR had been violated.

13.3 Restrictions of publications critical of products and competitors

Although undertakings inevitably expose themselves to close scrutiny of their practices by their competitors and may give rise to criticism by consumers and the specialised press[23], the right to criticise products or competitors – or both – may be lawfully limited by rules on unfair competition. The ECtHR emphasised that 'there is a competing interest in protecting the commercial success and viability of companies, for the benefit of shareholders and employees, but also for the wider economic good'.[24]

If, however, the given statement is not 'purely commercial' but pertains to a debate affecting the general interest, the extent of the margin of appreciation afforded to the domestic authorities is reduced. In *Hertel* v. *Switzerland*, the Court found that a publication critical of the effects of microwaves on human health contributed to such a debate.[25] Furthermore, if the criticised company is a state-owned company providing vital public services such as institutional care for the elderly, the public interest in having information about shortcomings is so important in a democratic society that it outweighs the interest in protecting the company's business reputation and interests.[26]

[22] Human Rights Committee, *Ballantyne and others* v. *Canada* [1993] Communication no. 359, 385/89 [11.4]; see also De Varennes (1993) 176–7.
[23] See Oster (2011).
[24] ECtHR, *Steel and Morris* v. *United Kingdom* [2005] App. no. 68416/01 [94]; *Heinisch* v. *Germany* [2011] App. no. 28274/08 [89].
[25] ECtHR, *Hertel* v. *Switzerland* [1998] App. no. 59/1997/843/1049 [47].
[26] ECtHR, *Heinisch* v. *Germany* [2011] App. no. 28274/08 [89]. The case was not related to a media report, but to a 'whistle-blower'. However, the Court's reasoning may be transferred to media publications as well.

14 Media pluralism

Pluralism, or plurality, is a wide and ambiguous concept. Its content varies depending on the analytical framework. The notion of pluralism includes, for example, value or moral pluralism in philosophical ethics, social, linguistic, religious and political pluralism. The concept of *media* pluralism absorbs these different notions of pluralism by requiring that as many voices as possible should be heard in the public discourse: different moral and political viewpoints as well as voices from different social and cultural backgrounds. It thus requires both the widest possible circulation of news and opinions and the widest access to information by the public at large.[1] Democracy itself is inconceivable without such pluralism.

The importance of media pluralism has also been recognised in human rights texts and jurisprudence. Article 11(2) EUChFR now expressly codifies that the freedom and pluralism of the media 'shall be respected'. Furthermore, Article 13(3) ACHR states that freedom of expression may not be restricted, *inter alia*, by private controls over newsprint, radio broadcasting frequencies or equipment used in the dissemination of information. Under the ICCPR, the obligation to secure media pluralism is closely connected to Article 27 ICCPR, which provides: 'In those States in which ethnic, religious or linguistic minorities exist, persons belonging to such minorities shall not be denied the right, in community with the other members of their group, to enjoy their own culture, to profess and practice their own religion, or to use their own language'. Finally, the Strasbourg Court expressed that '[i]t is of the essence of democracy to allow diverse political programmes to be proposed and debated, even those that call into question the way a State is currently organised, provided that they do not harm democracy itself.'[2]

[1] Compare IACtHR, Advisory Opinion OC-5/85 [69]; reaffirmed in *Ivcher-Bronstein* v. *Peru* [2001] Case 11.762 [151]; Human Rights Committee, General Comment no. 34, para. 14; Craufurd Smith (2004) 653; Westphal (2002) 467 ff.

[2] ECtHR, *Manole and others* v. *Moldova* [2009] App. no. 13936/02 [95]; reiterated in *Centro Europa 7 Srl and Di Stefano* v. *Italy* [2012] App. no. 38433/09 [129]; see also ECtHR, *United Communist Party of Turkey and others* v. *Turkey* [1998] App. no. 133/1996/752/951 [57].

As a consequence, states are not just compelled not to harm existing media pluralism. Rather, they are under a positive obligation to safeguard media pluralism.[3] In *Fontevecchia and D'Amico* v. *Argentina*, the Inter-American Court recognised that 'the State must not only minimize restrictions on the dissemination of information, but also extend equilibrium, to the greatest possible extent, to the participation in the public debate of different types of information, fostering informative pluralism. Consequently, equity must regulate the flow of information.'[4] The policy of media pluralism may thus not only support media freedom; it may, on the contrary, also justify an interference with the freedom of too powerful media conglomerates.

14.1 The relationship between media freedom and media pluralism

Unlike media freedom, media pluralism is not a right, but a mere policy – a 'principle' within the meaning of the EUChFR. As the ECJ observed, media pluralism is a 'cultural policy' aiming at safeguarding 'the freedom of expression of the various – in particular social, cultural, religious and philosophical – components of a Member State in order that that freedom may be capable of being exercised in the press, on the radio or on television'.[5] In turn, media pluralism is too broad a concept to be interpreted as a subjective, individual right. It includes different aspects, such as diversity of ownership, variety in the sources of information as

[3] See, e.g., Human Rights Committee, Concluding observations on Lebanon (CCPR/CO/79/Add.78), para. 24; Concluding observations on Sri Lanka (CCPR/CO/79/LKA), para. 17; Concluding observations on the Russian Federation (CCPR/CO/79/RUS), para. 18; *Mavlonov et al.* v. *Uzbekistan* [2009] Communication no. 1334/2004 [8.6]; ECtHR, *Informationsverein Lentia and others* v. *Austria* [1993] App. nos. 13914/88; 15041/89; 15717/89; 15779/89; 17207/90 [32–34]; *VgT Verein gegen Tierfabriken* v. *Switzerland (No. 1)* [2001] App. no. 24699/94 [77]; *TV Vest AS & Rogaland Pensjonistparti* v. *Norway* [2008] App. no. 21132/05 [78]; *Manole and others* v. *Moldova* [2009] App. no. 13936/02 [99]; Article 10*bis* of the European Convention on Transfrontier Television (1989); IACtHR, Advisory Opinion OC-5/85 [34]; Office of the Special Rapporteur for Freedom of Expression with the Inter-American Commission on Human Rights, Inter-American Legal Framework Regarding the Right to Freedom of Expression, 2009, CIDH/RELE/INF. 2/09, para. 160; AfComHPR, Declaration of Principles on Freedom of Expression in Africa, Section III. See also Garry (1989); Komorek (2009).

[4] IACtHR, *Fontevecchia and D'Amico* v. *Argentina* [2011] Case 12.524 [45].

[5] ECJ, *Stichting Collectieve Antennevoorziening Gouda and others* v. *Commissariaat voor de Media* [1991] ECR I-04007, Case C-288/89 [22–3]; *Commission* v. *Netherlands* [1991] ECR I-04069, Case C-353/89 [29–30]; *Veronica Omroep* v. *Commissariaat voor de Media* [1993] ECR I-00487, Case C-148/91 [9]; *TV 10 SA* v. *Commissariaat voor de Media* [1994] ECR I-04795, Case C-23/93 [18].

well as in the range of contents available, and so-called 'internal pluralism', providing diversity of output or content.

The relationship between the right to media freedom and media pluralism as a policy is twofold. On the one hand, media pluralism may serve as a value *supporting* media freedom. This is especially the case where media companies seek access to a particular market. Consequently, the aim of achieving a high level of media pluralism may require states to take measures breaking up existing media monopolies or oligopolies.[6] Furthermore, 'internal pluralism' may gain significance as a value bolstering freedom of expression and media freedom.[7] Eventually, the state has to protect an independent media in order to guarantee media pluralism.[8]

On the other hand, although it is not explicitly mentioned as one of the aims set out in Article 19(3) ICCPR, Article 9(2) AfCHPR and Article 10 (2) ECHR, a high level of media pluralism may constitute an unwritten legitimate aim *justifying an interference* with media freedom. This observation finds support in the case-law of both the ECJ and the ECtHR. With regard to the freedom to provide services under EC/EU law, the Luxembourg Court has recognised media pluralism as an overriding requirement relating to the general interest, capable of justifying a restriction on the freedom to provide media services.[9] The Court thus principally allowed a receiving Member State to take measures preventing a provider of services established in another Member State from avoiding obligations under national law designed to ensure the pluralist and non-commercial content of programmes. For example, the ECJ decision *Stichting Collectieve Antennevoorziening Gouda* concerned the new Dutch Media Act (Mediawet), which restricted cable network operators from transmitting radio or television programmes containing advertisements that were supplied by broadcasters established in other Member States.

6 Compare ECJ, *ERT* v. *DEP and others* [1991] ECR I-02925, Case C-260/89 [20].

7 See below Section 14.2.3.

8 See Garry (1989); Komorek (2009). See also ECtHR, *Informationsverein Lentia and others* v. *Austria* [1993] App. nos. 13914/88; 15041/89; 15717/89; 15779/89; 17207/90 [32–4]; *TV Vest & Rogaland Pensjonistparti* v. *Norway* [2008] App. no. 21132/05 [78].

9 ECJ, *Stichting Collectieve Antennevoorziening Gouda and others* v. *Commissariaat voor de Media* [1991] ECR I-04007, Case C-288/89 [23]; *Commission* v. *Netherlands* [1991] ECR I-04069, Case C-353/89 [30]; *Veronica Omroep* v. *Commissariaat voor de Media* [1993] ECR I-00487, Case C-148/91 [10]; *TV 10 SA* v. *Commissariaat voor de Media* [1994] ECR I-04795, Case C-23/93 [19]; *Familiapress* v. *Heinrich Bauer Verlag* [1997] ECR I-03689, Case C-368/95 [26]; *United Pan-Europe Communications Belgium SA and others* v. *Belgium and others* [2007] ECR I-11135, Case C-250/06 [41]. See also *Bond van Adverteerders* v. *Netherlands* [1988] ECR 02085, Case 352/85 [38]: The maintenance of a pluralistic broadcasting system may constitute a justification for an indistinctly applicable measure, but not for discrimination. On EU media pluralism policy, see Valcke *et al.* (2010).

Furthermore, the Mediawet restricted the opportunities afforded to those broadcasters to include in their programmes advertising intended specifically for the public in the Netherlands. The Court found that the maintenance of media pluralism which the Mediawet seeks to safeguard may constitute an overriding requirement relating to the general interest which justifies a restriction on the freedom to provide services.[10] And almost simultaneously to the preliminary ruling in *Stichting Collectieve Antennevoorziening Gouda*, the ECJ decided on the Treaty infringement procedure case *Commission* v. *Netherlands*.[11] The Court found that the Mediawet's obligation to use the technical resources (recording studios, set workshops, technicians, etc.), provided by a public limited company incorporated under Dutch law, prevented broadcasters from using the services of providers established in other Member States.[12] The Court acknowledged again that cultural policy may constitute an overriding requirement relating to the general interest which is capable of justifying a restriction on the freedom to provide services, and reiterated that the maintenance of media pluralism which this Dutch policy seeks to safeguard is connected to freedom of expression, as protected by Article 10 ECHR.[13] However, the Court eventually decided in both cases that the restrictions imposed by the Mediawet were disproportionate.[14]

But also the ECtHR has confirmed that the maintenance of media pluralism may justify an interference with Article 10(1) ECHR. In the 1993 decision *Informationsverein Lentia and others* v. *Austria*, the Court had to decide whether the Austrian public broadcasting monopoly was in accordance with Article 10(2) ECHR. The Court thereby underlined that the state is the ultimate guarantor for media pluralism.[15] A public broadcasting monopoly may constitute a justified measure to guarantee media pluralism; however, it also imposes restrictions on the freedom of expression of other potential broadcasters. The Court found that there is no longer a 'pressing social need' to maintain a public broadcasting monopoly, in particular because technological progress made available

[10] ECJ, *Stichting Collectieve Antennevoorziening Gouda and others* v. *Commissariaat voor de Media* [1991] ECR I-04007, Case C-288/89 [23].

[11] ECJ, *Commission* v. *Netherlands* [1991] ECR I-04069, Case C-353/89.

[12] ECJ, *Commission* v. *Netherlands* [1991] ECR I-04069, Case C-353/89 [23].

[13] ECJ, *Commission* v. *Netherlands* [1991] ECR I-04069, Case C-353/89 [30].

[14] ECJ, *Stichting Collectieve Antennevoorziening Gouda and others* v. *Commissariaat voor de Media* [1991] ECR I-04007, Case C-288/89 [25] and *Commission* v. *Netherlands* [1991] ECR I-04069, Case C-353/89 [31].

[15] ECtHR, *Informationsverein Lentia and others* v. *Austria* [1993] App. nos. 13914/88, 15041/89, 15717/89, 15779/89 and 17207/90 [38]; see also *VgT Verein gegen Tierfabriken* v. *Switzerland (No. 1)* [2001] App. no. 24699/94 [73]; *Manole and others* v. *Moldova* [2009] App. no. 13936/02 [99].

a number of frequencies and channels.[16] The Court also rejected the Government's argument that the Austrian market was too small to sustain a sufficient number of stations to avoid the constitution of 'private monopolies': private and public stations coexist in several European states of a comparable size to Austria, but the development of private monopolies could nonetheless be prevented there.[17]

14.2 Policy areas of media pluralism

Media pluralism includes many policy areas, a detailed analysis of which would be worth a study in its own right. Three policy areas, which rank among the most important ones, should briefly be sketched: first, media competition policy; second, the active support of pluralism by either providing public broadcasting or by subsidising private companies; and third, internal media pluralism. These policy areas require legislation to adequately respond to threats to media pluralism, especially in the areas of competition law, state aid law and employment law.

14.2.1 Competition policy

Press and broadcasting companies are usually commercial institutions, and as such subject to competition rules. However, competition policy is also an important instrument for safeguarding media pluralism. The demands of a democratic society may justify *additional* competition rules and policies specifically tailored to the media. This implies media control concentration and restrictions on multilateral agreements in the media sector and abuses of a dominant position in the media market. At the same time, it has to be taken into account that media competition policy may interfere with the owners' rights to conduct a business and especially *their* media freedom. However, limits on media ownership and anti-pluralistic behaviour in addition to general competition rules are based on superseding democratic and social concerns: the media has a higher social responsibility compared to other commercial activities, because journalism is not just another 'consumer item'.[18]

First, one threat to media freedom and thus to democracy in general is the concentration of media control, especially of media ownership.

[16] ECtHR, *Informationsverein Lentia and others* v. *Austria* [1993] App. nos. 13914/88, 15041/89, 15717/89, 15779/89 and 17207/90 [39].

[17] ECtHR, *Informationsverein Lentia and others* v. *Austria* [1993] App. nos. 13914/88, 15041/89, 15717/89, 15779/89 and 17207/90 [42].

[18] Habermas (1962) p. 164. See also Sunstein (2000) 506 and 518; Thorgeirsdóttir (2004).

Concentration of media control needs to be considered with respect to both specific media segments, such as the press or broadcasting, and across different media sectors. Therefore, states have to prevent influential economic or political groups from obtaining a dominant position over the media and interfering with editorial freedom.[19] The mass media has to be saved from the pressure of economically powerful institutions and must remain capable of maintaining public discourse without external or internal constraints. Situations such as in Italy under the former Prime Minister Silvio Berlusconi, who not only owned several private television channels but also exercised political influence on the board of the public broadcaster RAI, are therefore an alarming threat to media pluralism.

Against this backdrop, it would be insufficient to approach media competition policy only with purely market-based considerations. Rather, media pluralism may require media-specific restrictions on media cartels and on mergers in order to avoid media ownership or control concentration, such as stipulated in Article 21(4) Merger Regulation.[20] This may require public authorities, for example, to apply the competition rules on significant market power considering the dominance of a cartel or a company with regard to the influence on public opinion. This can be estimated based on the average audience or reader share, thereby considering broadcasting time allocated to independent third parties.[21] Moreover, media ownership has to be transparent to ensure that the regulatory authorities and the public can take informed decisions.[22]

Second, media pluralism has to be promoted by media-specific interpretation of provisions on anti-competitive unilateral behaviour. Therefore, media pluralism may, under certain circumstances, ask for a positive obligation to enact appropriate domestic legislation to enable certain groups to disseminate their information and ideas via

[19] Human Rights Committee, Concluding observations on the Russian Federation (CCPR/CO/79/RUS), para. 18; Concluding observations on Guyana (CCPR/CO/79/Add.121), para. 19; Concluding observations on Italy (CCPR/C/79/Add. 37); General Comment no. 34, para. 40; ECtHR, *VgT Verein gegen Tierfabriken* v. *Switzerland (No. 1)* [2001] App. no. 24699/94 [73] and [75]; *Manole and others* v. *Moldova* [2009] App. no. 13936/02 [98]; *Centro Europa 7 Srl and Di Stefano* v. *Italy* [2012] App. no. 38433/09 [133]. On the European Commission's policy on media concentration, see Westphal (2002) 464–5; Bania (2013).

[20] Council Regulation (EC) No. 139/2004 of 20 January 2004 on the Control of Concentrations between Undertakings, OJ 2004, L24/1. See Part 5 Chapter 2 UK Communications Act 2003.

[21] Compare, for example, Section 26 German Interstate Treaty on Broadcasting and Telemedia (Rundfunkstaatsvertrag); Section 375 UK Communications Act 2003.

[22] Council of Europe, Committee of Ministers, Recommendation CM/Rec(2007)2 on Media Pluralism and Diversity of Media Content, para. III; compare Sunstein (2000) 506, 531–8.

broadcasting. This includes, for example, obligations of broadcasters to grant transmission time to third parties, in order to reflect a variety of opinions in their channels. This idea is based on the rationales of the 'essential facility doctrine' in competition law. This doctrine describes a type of behaviour in which a firm with market power uses a 'bottleneck resource' in a market to deny competitors entry into that market.[23] Broadcasting channels represent such 'essential facilities' on the market of mass communication. Therefore, they may be obliged to award access to their transmission facilities under 'must carry obligations' or in order to enable third parties to contribute to matters of general interest, for example, for candidates running for political office prior to elections.[24]

Two objections may be raised against an obligation to provide access to broadcasting facilities. First, one could argue that everyone could use the internet to disseminate his content. Therefore, access to broadcasting channels and networks is not necessary anymore to reach a mass audience. However, even the opportunity to reach a mass audience via the internet does not replace the powerful effect of broadcasting. The internet does not have the same impact as broadcasted information. In light of Marshall McLuhan's observation 'The medium is the message', the Strasbourg Court has rightly perceived that 'there is no evidence of a sufficiently serious shift in the respective influences of the new and of the broadcast media'.[25] The second objection, namely that an obligation for broadcasters to award transmission time to third parties stands in conflict

[23] The essential facility doctrine originates from Section 2 US Sherman Act (see *United States* v. *Terminal Railroad Association*, 224 US 383 (1912); *Associated Press* v. *United States*, 326 US 1 (1945); *Lorain Journal Co.* v. *United States*, 342 US 143, 146–9 (1951); *Otter Tail Power Co.* v. *United States*, 410 US 366, 377–9 (1973); *Verizon* v. *Trinko*, 540 U.S. 398 (2004); *MCI Communications Corp.* v. *AT&T*, 708 F2d 1081, 1132–3 (7th Cir. 1982)), and has been implemented into EU law by Commission decisions and ECJ case-law based on Article 102 TFEU (ex Article 82 EC); see ECJ, *RTE and ITP* v. *Commission* [1995] ECR I-00743, Joined Cases C-241/91 P and C-242/91 P; *Bronner* v. *Mediaprint Zeitungs-und Zeitschriftenverlag* [1998] ECR I-07791, Case C-7/97; *IMS Health GmbH & Co. OHG* v. *NDC Health GmbH & Co. KG* [2004] ECR I-05039, Case C-418/01; Commission Decision 94/19/EC of 21 December 1993 relating to a Proceeding pursuant to Article 86 of the EC Treaty (IV/34.689 – Sea Containers v. Stena Sealink), OJ 1994, L15/8; Commission Decision 94/119/EC of 21 December 1993 concerning a Refusal to Grant Access to the Facilities of the port of Rødby (Denmark), OJ 1993, L55/52. See generally van Rooijen (2008) p. 64.

[24] See, e.g., Section 312(a)(7) US Communications Act 1934: 'The [FCC] may revoke any station license or construction permit ... for willful or repeated failure to allow reasonable access to or to permit purchase of reasonable amounts of time for the use of a broadcasting station, other than a non-commercial educational broadcast station, by a legally qualified candidate for Federal elective office on behalf of his candidacy.' On the enforcement of this provision, see *CBS, Inc.* v. *FCC*, 453 US 367 (1981).

[25] ECtHR, *Animal Defenders International* v. *United Kingdom* [2013] App. no. 48876/08 [119].

with broadcasters' editorial independence, cannot convince either: it is left to the broadcaster to simply distance himself from the content that he 'must carry'.

The implementation of media pluralism has played an important role in adjudicators' practice. In *Hertzberg and others* v. *Finland*, the Human Rights Committee indicated *obiter* that a right of access to broadcasting may be established if a programme has been produced for transmission within the framework of a broadcasting organisation with the general approval of the responsible authorities.[26] A more refined, but unfortunately rather inconsistent, body of case-law on this subject is provided by the ECtHR. In the seminal case *VgT Verein gegen Tierfabriken* v. *Switzerland (No. 1)*, the applicant NGO sought to broadcast a nationwide TV commercial for the protection of animals on Swiss Radio and Television Company (Schweizerische Radio-und Fernsehgesellschaft) programmes. The Commercial Television Company (AG für das Werbefernsehen, now called Publisuisse), a company established under Swiss private law and responsible for television advertising, refused to broadcast the commercial because of its 'clear political character'. The Court observed that the applicant association had no other means available for its purpose than the national television programmes.[27] The Court thus applied the 'bottleneck' rationale, and held that the prohibition preventing the applicant from broadcasting the advertisement violated Article 10 ECHR.

In contrast to *VgT Verein gegen Tierfabriken (No. 1)*, the Court then refused the right of access to broadcasting in *Murphy* v. *Ireland*, where the applicants asked for the transmission of a religious advertisement.[28] This decision, however, could be regarded as an exception to the rule because of the margin of appreciation granted to the Convention States when religious concerns are at issue. To be specific, in *TV Vest* v. *Norway*, the Strasbourg Court confirmed the *VgT (No. 1)* ruling when reviewing the application of a Norwegian blanket-ban on political advertising. The First Section held that the blanket-ban, as applied to the advertisement of a pensioners' political party, and the fine imposed on a broadcaster for broadcasting the advertisement, violated Article 10 ECHR. Following *VgT (No. 1)*, the Court applied a 'strict scrutiny' standard of review. The Court unanimously held that the applicant party did not belong

[26] Human Rights Commission, *Hertzberg and others* v. *Finland* [1985] Communication no. 61/1979 [10.2].

[27] ECtHR, *VgT Verein gegen Tierfabriken* v. *Switzerland (No. 1)* [2001] App. no. 24699/94 [77].

[28] ECtHR, *Murphy* v. *Ireland* [2003] App. no. 44179/98. See Chapter 12.

to the 'primary targets' of the disputed prohibition, namely those which, because of their financial strength, might have obtained an unfair advantage over those with fewer resources by being able to spend more on television advertising.[29]

However, the Strasbourg Court then changed its standard of scrutiny in the case *Animal Defenders International* v. *United Kingdom*, decided in 2013. In this case, the applicant NGO submitted an advertisement for a TV broadcast describing ill-treatment of primates.[30] The Broadcast Advertising Clearance Centre concluded that the advertisement breached the Communications Act 2003, which prohibits advertisements 'directed towards a political end'. Although *TV Vest* and especially the nearly identical case *VgT* v. *Switzerland (No. 1)* would have been expected to be the guiding authorities, the majority opinion departed from the Court's previous case-law on political advertising and presented a new standard for reviewing the proportionality of such blanket-bans: a distinction between 'general measures' and prior restraints. This approach, which brings with it a too deferential standard of judicial review, has already been subject to criticism.[31] The Court eventually concluded that the reasons brought forward by the domestic authorities justified the prohibition of the applicant's advertisement.

While the application of the Court's 'general measure' doctrine on freedom of expression and media freedom is to be rejected at the outset, the reasoning on upholding blanket-bans on political advertising warrants attention. The maintenance of a free and pluralist debate on matters of public interest may require granting access to broadcasting in order to enable certain groups to disseminate their ideas. At the same time, as has been stated above, the public discourse has to be protected from distortion by financially powerful groups with privileged access to influential mass media. In a democratic society, states are under an obligation to protect the media, and thus public opinion, from undue partial influence by particular interests. Limitations on political advertising may thus impede, but also preserve, pluralism in broadcasting, a particularly powerful medium in the formation of public opinion. Therefore, it needs to be carefully scrutinised on a case-by-case basis whether the democratic order does indeed justify a prohibition on political advertising – or whether such bans are misused to suppress

[29] ECtHR, *TV Vest AS & Rogaland Pensjonistparti* v. *Norway* [2008] App. no. 21132/05 [72].
[30] ECtHR, *Animal Defenders International* v. *United Kingdom* [2013] App. no. 48876/08.
[31] See Chapter 6, Section 6.2.

political opposition. A court also needs to examine whether the advertiser qualifies as a financially powerful group, which might obtain an unfair advantage over those with fewer resources, or whether, on the contrary, the applicant belongs to a category for whose protection the ban is actually in force, such as cultural, linguistic, ethnic, religious and other minorities.[32] In contrast to *TV Vest*, the Court did not even mention this aspect in *Animal Defenders International*, where it was questionable whether the applicant NGO did pose such a threat. Furthermore, it should be considered whether time limitations on political advertising are to be preferred as the less intrusive measure to an outright ban.

14.2.2 Public broadcasting and media subsidies

Broadcasting dualism, that is, the co-existence of public and private broadcasting, may contribute to the quality and balance of programmes.[33] However, there is no obligation to install a public broadcasting service if other means can be used to the same end. *If* a state decides to create a public broadcasting system, the domestic law and practice has to safeguard that the public broadcaster provides a pluralistic line-up of programming.[34]

In addition to providing public broadcasting, states may also support media pluralism via state subsidies for suffering media companies or journalists. Yet the risks involved in media subsidy policy are obvious: first, state subsidies may distort competition, a risk that is inherent in any state subsidy, as is apparent from Article 107(1) TFEU. Second, state aid for the media sector in particular jeopardises the independence of the media, which might be more inclined towards

[32] See ECtHR, *TV Vest AS & Rogaland Pensjonistparti* v. *Norway* [2008] App. no. 21132/05 [72]; Council of Europe, Committee of Ministers, Recommendation CM/Rec(2007)2 on Media Pluralism and Diversity of Media Content.

[33] See Protocol (No. 29) to the TEU and the TFEU on the System of Public Broadcasting in the Member States; Council of Europe, Committee of Ministers, Recommendation CM/Rec(2007)2 on Media Pluralism and Diversity of Media Content: 'Recalling the importance of transparency of media ownership so as to ensure that the authorities in charge of the implementation of regulations concerning media pluralism can take informed decisions, and that the public can make its own analysis of the information, ideas and opinions expressed by the media'.

[34] ECtHR, *Manole and others* v. *Moldova* [2009] App. no. 13936/02 [101]. See also Council of Europe, Committee of Ministers, Recommendation No. R (96) 10 on the Guarantee of the Independence of Public Service Broadcasting; Recommendation No. R (94) 13 on Measures to Promote Media Transparency; Katsirea (2012) 420.

government-friendly reporting, according to the motto 'He who pays the piper calls the tune'. Therefore, state subsidies for the media, which are particularly often called for to save the declining newspaper industry, are a double-edged sword. Media pluralism requires that governmental benefits of any kind granted to media undertakings, such as state subsidies, placing of government advertisements and allocation of broadcasting frequencies, must not be used to stifle criticism of the government and media pluralism in general.[35] Financing of public broadcasting and subsidies for private media companies have to be in accordance with the rules on state aid, such as Article 107–9 TFEU. Furthermore, they must not discriminate between media companies.[36]

14.2.3 Internal pluralism

In contrast to external media pluralism, which describes the media landscape as a whole, internal pluralism refers to pluralism within a particular media organisation. Journalists must not be obliged to self-censorship when approaching delicate subjects – in particular when issues are delicate for the owners of the media company that employs them or when they work for state broadcasters. Media freedom applies to every journalist, both self-employed and employed. Although human rights do not have direct effect between private individuals, employment law has to be legislated and interpreted in a media freedom and pluralism-friendly way. Media freedom does not only foster discourse *between* media undertakings, but also *within* them.

Internal media pluralism oscillates between two conflicting principles: on the one hand, employed journalists should not be prevented from imparting a plurality of news and opinions.[37] This requires the enforcement of domestic provisions guaranteeing internal diversity and editorial independence. The concept of internal media pluralism therefore applies particularly to public broadcasters, which are required to neutrally reflect a wide range of political views and interests of minorities or other parts of the population.

On the other hand, it has to be acknowledged that, given the pressure of a free market economy, owners of media organisations should have

[35] Human Rights Committee, Concluding observations on Ukraine (CCPR/CO/73/UKR), para. 22; Concluding observations on Lesotho (CCPR/CO/79/Add. 106), para. 22.
[36] See Chapter 4, Section 4.2.4.
[37] ECtHR, *Manole and others* v. *Moldova* [2009] App. no. 13936/02 [100].

the ability to determine the strategy of their companies, including an editorial line and a certain political slant. Therefore, employment law has to ensure that the standards for diversity and neutrality of private media companies are not set too high.[38]

[38] See, for instance, Section 118 German Works Constitution Act (Betriebsverfassungsgesetz), translation provided by the Language Service of the Federal Ministry of Labour and Social Affairs:

(1) The provisions of this Act shall not apply to companies and establishments that directly and predominantly

1. pursue political, coalition, religious, charitable, educational, scientific or artistic objectives; or
2. serve purposes of publishing or expressing opinions covered by the second sentence of section 5 (1) of the Basic Law in so far as their application would not be in keeping with the specific nature of the company or establishment.

Conclusion: tenets of a Media Freedom Principle

A Media Freedom Principle has to be conceptualised according to the following tenets:

1. Media freedom has to be recognised as a distinct fundamental right.
2. The rationale for media freedom is the significance of the media for rational public discourse.
3. 'Public discourse' is to be understood in a normative sense. It shall be defined as an open, free and argumentative communicative process aimed at reaching understanding and forming public opinion on matters of public concern. Public discourse shall be 'open' in the sense that it is non-exclusive. It shall be 'free' in that it is non-coercive. It shall be 'argumentative' in that the only authority is the authority of the better argument. It shall aim at reaching understanding, which is not the case if communication is based on intentional deception and insincerity. Finally, public discourse shall aim at the formation of public opinion on matters of public concern.
4. As a consequence, media freedom is, in the first place, an instrumental and functional right, rather than an inherent one. The media is protected for fulfilling a beneficial function for society in general.
5. 'The media' should be defined in functional terms. 'The media' is any person or institution generating information and ideas on a journalistic basis and disseminating them via facilities of mass communication to an undefined number of recipients. Consequently, 'the media' as a legal concept:
   (a) is a content provider rather than a mere speech intermediary;
   (b) provides mass communication rather than individual communication; and
   (c) is based on journalistic work, that is, the adherence of certain standards of conduct. However, 'journalism' should in this context not be confused with a requirement of 'professionalism', but should be open to encompass non-professional writers, such as bloggers, who regularly contribute to the public discourse.

6. In order to fulfil its function, the media enjoys considerable liberties, but is subject to enhanced duties and responsibilities. These duties and responsibilities relate to those content and conduct-related norms that public discourse itself presupposes. These 'norms of civility' can be furcated into two categories: individual rights of others and indispensable social norms necessary for the public discourse.
7. Freedom of expression and media freedom are overlapping concepts, but they are not identical. Media freedom is partly a derivative right from freedom of expression, and partly a self-standing right. Thus, media freedom is more than merely freedom of expression for journalists.
   (a) As a derivative right, media freedom is *lex specialis* to freedom of expression. Freedom of the media is special in the sense that a person or institution, by virtue of being media and acting as media, is governed by a different set of factors concerning the intensity of protection when issuing a publication, compared to freedom of expression afforded to private individuals or non-media entities. The fact that an impugned statement is 'media speech', rather than speech by any other individual or institution, adds to the burden of justifying its restrictions.
   (b) In addition, media freedom encompasses certain rights that are not available under freedom of expression at all. Here, media freedom differs from freedom of expression not only concerning the *intensity* of protection, as is the case with media speech, but also regarding the *scope* of protected action. This institutional protection of the media guarantees rights that are not directly related to the content of a publication or the way in which it is presented, but are related to the media in its newsgathering, editorial or distribution process, or even to the mere existence of an independent media. The best-known example is a journalist's protection from being compelled to give testimony of confidential information or sources.
8. Interferences with media freedom are allowed if such limitations are prescribed by law (principle of legality), pursue a legitimate aim (principle of legitimacy) and are necessary in pursuit of this aim (principle of proportionality). The proportionality test requires balancing media freedom with conflicting rights or interests according to the principle of practical concordance. In this balancing exercise, the 'weight' attached to media freedom depends on whether the media fulfils its function as a contributor to public discourse: the extent to which the media reports on matters of public concern, the media's conduct prior to publication and whether the media acted in good faith.

(a) 'Public concern' is not susceptible to an exhaustive definition. Instead, courts should be allowed to develop the notion of public concern on a case-by-case basis. International adjudicators have delivered many precedents in their case-law. However, the question should not be whether a matter *is* of public concern, but rather to which *extent* it is of public concern.
(b) The media's privileged protection is subject to the proviso that it is acting on an accurate factual basis. However, to require a journalist to ensure that each factual statement he publishes is correct would have an intolerable chilling effect on the media to the detriment of public discourse itself. Consequently, the media may deviate from the obligation to verify factual information it discloses if it has taken all reasonable steps to verify the accuracy of its statements prior to publication. If the media adheres to its duties and responsibilities, then media freedom also includes the right to make mistakes.
(c) In addition, journalists must always act in good faith. Liability for a false, harmful statement made in bad faith is justified. However, the requirement of good faith relates only to the veracity of the statement, and not to the integrity of the motivation of the publisher.
(d) The consideration of 'ethics of journalism' or 'responsible journalism' as a factor in the balancing exercise should be rejected. The law determines what the media may *legally* do and what it is *legally* prohibited from doing, but not what the media should or should not do in journalistic-ethical terms. Media law and 'responsible journalism' or 'ethical journalism' are overlapping, but not identical, concepts: a violation of media ethics can only be vindicated in a court if the ethical command has been absorbed into a *legal* obligation. In turn, a merely ethical obligation without legal underpinning can only be vindicated under media self-regulation or in the court of public opinion, but not in a court of law.

9. The Media Freedom Principle should overcome the hitherto accepted categories of speech, such as 'hate speech' and 'commercial speech'. Instead, the protection of the media should be established by balancing the relevant factors that have been developed throughout this book.

Bibliography

Abramowicz, D., (2009) 'Calculating the Public Interest in Protecting Journalists' Confidential Sources' 108 *Columbia Law Review* 101

Adams, J., (1856), 'A Defence of the Constitutions of the Government of the United States of America', in C. F. Adams (ed.), *The Works of John Adams, Second President of the United States: with a Life of the Author, Notes and Illustrations, by his Grandson Charles Francis Adams, vol.* 6 (Boston, MA: Little, Brown and Co.), p. 3

Addo, M. K., (1998) 'Are Judges beyond Criticism under Article 10 or the European Convention of Human Rights?' 47 *International & Comparative Law Quarterly* 425

(ed.), (2000) *Freedom of Expression and the Criticism of Judges: A Comparative Study of European Legal Standards* (Dartmouth: Aldershot)

Ahdar, R. and Leigh, I., (2005) *Religious Freedom in the Liberal State* (Oxford University Press)

Akdeniz, Y., (2008) *Internet Child Pornography and the Law: National and International Responses* (Aldershot: Ashgate)

Alder, J., (2006) 'The Sublime and the Beautiful: Incommensurability of Human Rights' *Public Law* 697

Alexy, R., (2002) *A Theory of Constitutional Rights* (Oxford University Press)

(2005) 'Balancing Constitutional Review and Representation' 3 *International Journal of Constitutional Law* 572

Alkema, E. A., (1988) 'The Third-Party Applicability or "*Drittwirkung*" in the European Convention on Human Rights', in F. Matscher, H. Petzold and G. J. Wiarda (eds.), *Protecting Human Rights: The European Dimension. Studies in Honour of G.J. Wiarda* (Cologne: Carl Heymanns), p. 33

Allen, B., (2003) 'Freedom of Expression and the Protection of Public Morals in the United Kingdom and the United States' 8 *Coventry Law Journal* 16

Alonzo, J. S., (2006) 'Restoring the Ideal Marketplace: How Recognizing Bloggers as Journalists Can Save the Press' 9 *Legislation and Public Policy* 751

Alvira, G., (2013) '*Fontevecchia v Argentina:* The "Ink Assassins," Self-Censorship, and Self-Preservation' 21 *Tulane Journal of International & Comparative Law* 545

Amar, V. D., (1999) 'From Watergate to Kenn Starr: Potter Stewart's "Or of the Press" A Quarter Century Later' 50 *Hastings Law Journal* 711

Anderson, D. A., (1983) 'The Origins of the Press Clause' 30 *UCLA Law Review* 455

(2002) 'Freedom of the Press' 80 *Texas Law Review* 429

Anonymous author, (2007) 'Developments in the Law—The Law of the Media' 120 *Harvard Law Review* 990

Anonymous author, (2011) 'The News Industry: Bulletins from the Future', *The Economist*, 9 July 2011, Special Report, p. 4

Aplin, T., Bently, L., Johnson, P. and Malynicz, S., (2012) *Gurry on Breach of Confidence* (Oxford University Press, 2nd edn)

Arendt, H., (1958) *The Human Condition* (2nd edn) (republished The University of Chicago Press, 1998)

Austin, J. L., (1962) *How to Do Things with Words* (Oxford University Press)

Baker, C. E., (1978) 'Scope of the First Amendment Freedom of Speech' 25 *UCLA Law Review* 964

(1989) *Human Liberty and Freedom of Speech* (Oxford University Press)

(2007) 'The Independent Significance of the Press Clause under Existing Law' 35 *Hofstra Law Review* 955

(2011) 'Press Performance, Human Rights, and Private Power as a Threat' 5 *Law & Ethics of Human Rights* 219

Bania, K., (2013) 'European Merger Control in the Broadcasting Sector: Does Media Pluralism Fit?' *Competition Law Review* 49

Barak, A., (2001) 'Constitutional Human Rights and Private Law', in D. Friedmann and D. Barak-Erez (eds.), *Human Rights in Private Law* (Oxford: Hart Publishing), p. 13

(2012) *Proportionality – Constitutional Rights and their Limitations* (Cambridge University Press)

Barendt, E., (2005) *Freedom of Speech* (Oxford University Press, 2nd edn)

(2009) 'Bad News for Bloggers' 2 *Journal of Media Law* 141

Barnes, J., (2011) 'Data Protection and the Media', in M. Warby, N. A. Moreham and I. Christie (eds.), *Tugendhat and Christie The Law of Privacy and the Media* (Oxford University Press, 2nd edn)

Bassani, L. M., (2002) 'The Bankruptcy of the Republican School' 124 *Telos* 131

Beck, G., (2008) 'Human Rights Adjudication under the ECHR Between Value Pluralism and Essential Contestability' *European Human Rights Law Review* 214

Berger, L. L., (2003) 'Shielding the Unmedia: Using the Process of Journalism to Protect the Journalist's Privilege in an Infinite Universe of Publication' 39 *Houston Law Review* 1371

Berlin, I., (1969) 'Two Concepts of Liberty', in I. Berlin (ed.), *Four Essays on Liberty* (Oxford University Press), p. 118

Bernstein, M., (1955) *Regulating Business by Independent Agencies* (Princeton University Press)

Bertoni, E. A., (2009) 'The Inter-American Court of Human Rights and the European Court of Human Rights: A Dialogue on Freedom of Expression Standards' *European Human Rights Law Review* 332

Bezanson, R. P., (1977) 'The New Free Press Guarantee' 63 *Virginia Law Review* 731

(1998) 'The Atomization of the Newspaper: Technology, Economics and the Coming Transformation of Editorial Judgments about News' 3 *Communication Law and Policy* 175

(2012) 'Whither Freedom of the Press?' 97 *Iowa Law Review* 1259
Black, H. L., (1960) 'The Bill of Rights' 35 *New York University Law Review* 882
Blasi, V., (1977) 'The Checking Value in First Amendment Theory' *American Bar Foundation Research Journal* 521
Blocher, J., (2012) 'Public Discourse, Expert Knowledge, and the Press' 87 *Washington Law Review* 409
Bork, R. H., (1971) 'Neutral Principles and some First Amendment Problems' 47 *Indiana Law Journal* 1
Bossuyt, M. J., (1987) *Guide to the "Travaux Préparatoires" of the International Covenant on Civil and Political Rights* (Dordrecht: Martinus Nijhoff Publishers)
Bradley, A. and Ewing, K., (2011) *Constitutional & Administrative Law* (Harlow: Pearson Education, 15th edn)
Calvert, C. and Torres, M., (2011) 'Putting the Shock Value in First Amendment Jurisprudence: When Freedom for the Citizen-Journalist Watchdog Trumps the Right of Informational Privacy on the Internet' 23 *Vanderbilt Journal of Entertainment and Technology Law* 323
Cannie, H. and Voorhoof, D., (2011) 'The Abuse Clause and Freedom of Expression in the European Human Rights Convention: An Added Value for Democracy and Human Rights Protection?' 29 *Netherlands Quarterly of Human Rights* 54
Carney, D., (2009) 'Theoretical Underpinnings of the Protection of Journalists' Confidential Sources: Why an Absolute Privilege Cannot be Justified' 1 *Journal of Media Law* 97
Carter, S. L., (1984) 'Technology, Democracy, and the Manipulation of Consent' 93 *Yale Law Journal* 581
(1992) 'Does the First Amendment Protect More than Free Speech?' 33 *William and Mary Law Review* 871
Chang, R. (ed.), (1997) *Incommensurability, Incomparability and Practical Reason* (Harvard University Press)
Chemerinsky, E., (2000) 'Protect the Press: A First Amendment Standard for Safeguarding Aggressive Newsgathering' 33 *University of Richmond Law Review* 1143
Chesterman, M., (2000) *Freedom of Speech in Australian Law: A Delicate Plant* (Dartmouth: Ashgate)
Clapham, A., (1993) *Human Rights in the Private Sphere* (Oxford University Press)
Collins, M., (2010) *The Law of Defamation and the Internet* (Oxford University Press, 3rd edn)
Cooper, J. and Williams, A. M., (1999) 'Hate Speech, Holocaust Denial and International Human Rights Law' *European Human Rights Law Review* 593
Craig, P. and de Búrca, G., (2011) *EU Law, Text, Cases, and Materials*, (Oxford University Press, 5th edn)
Craufurd Smith, R., (2004) 'Rethinking European Union Competence in the Field of Media Ownership: The Internal Market, Fundamental Rights and European Citizenship' *European Law Review* 652
Curran, J. and Seaton, J., (2010) *Power Without Responsibility—Press, Broadcasting and the Internet in Britain* (London: Routledge, 7th edn)

Davis, H. (2005) 'Lessons from Turkey: Anti-Terrorism Legislation and the Protection of Free Speech' *European Human Rights Law Review* 75
De la Rasilla del Moral, I., (2006) 'The Increasingly Marginal Appreciation of the Margin-of-Appreciation Doctrine' 7 *German Law Journal* 611
De Schutter, O., (2010) *International Human Rights Law* (Cambridge University Press)
De Varennes, F., (1993) 'Language and Freedom of Expression in International Law' 15 *Human Rights Quarterly* 163
Dicey, A. V., (1889) *An Introduction to the Study of Law of the Constitution* (London: Macmillan, 3rd edn)
Dillon, J. and Gergel, T., (2003) *The Greek Sophists* (London: Penguin Classics)
Diogenes Laërtius, (2003) 'The Life of Protagoras' (*c. 200 AD*) (republished in J. Dillon and T. Gergel, *The Greek Sophists*; London: Penguin Classics)
Donaldson, P. S., (1988) *Machiavelli and Mystery of State* (Cambridge University Press)
Dörr, D. and Aernecke, E., (2012) 'A Never Ending Story: Caroline v. Germany', in D. Dörr and R. Weaver (eds.), *The Right to Privacy in the Light of Media Convergence – Perspectives from Three Continents* (Berlin/Boston, MA: De Gruyter), p. 114
Drzemczewski, A. Z., (1979) 'The European Human Rights Convention and Relations between Private Parties' 2 *Netherlands International Law Review* 168
Durity, L., (2006) 'Shielding Journalist-"Bloggers": The Need to Protect Newsgathering Despite the Distribution Medium' 11 *Duke Law & Technology Review*, iBrief
Dworkin, R., (1977) *Taking Rights Seriously* (republished London: Duckworth, 1996)
(1981) 'Is there a Right to Pornography?' 1 *Oxford Journal of Legal Studies* 177
(1996) *Freedom's Law: The Moral Reading of the American Constitution* (Harvard University Press)
Emerson, T. I., (1963) 'Toward a General Theory of the First Amendment' 72 *Yale Law Journal* 877
Fargo, A. L. and Alexander, L. B., (2009) 'Testing the Boundaries of the First Amendment Press Clause: A Proposal for Protecting the Media From Newsgathering Torts' 32 *Harvard Journal of Law & Public Policy* 1094
Fenwick, H. and Phillipson, G., (2006) *Media Freedom under the Human Rights Act* (Oxford University Press)
Ferguson, P., (2003) 'Tobacco Advertising and Freedom of Speech – Why the Greater does not Include the Lesser' 10 *UCL Jurisprudence Review* 315
Flanagan, A., (2005) 'Blogging: A Journal Need Not a Journalist Make' 16 *Fordham Intellectual Property, Media and Entertainment Law Journal* 395
Fraser, N., (1992) 'Rethinking the Public Sphere: A Contribution to the Critique of Actually Existing Democracy', in C. Calhoun (ed.), *Habermas and the Public Sphere* (Cambridge, MA: MIT Press), p. 109
Frey, D., Rudolph, M. and Oster, J., (2012) 'Internetsperren und der Schutz der Kommunikation im Internet' *Multimedia und Recht* (Beilage 3) 1
Fried, C., (1968) 'Privacy' 77 *Yale Law Journal* 475

Friedman, I., (2006) 'Where Public and Private Spaces Converge: Discriminatory Media Access to Government Information' 75 *Fordham Law Review* 253

Garcia, F. J., (2012) 'Yelling "Fire" in a Crowded Planet' available at www.huffingtonpost.com/frank-j-garcia/innocence-of-muslims-protests_b_1912834.html (last accessed 30 August 2014)

Garry, P., (1989) 'The First Amendment and Freedom of the Press: A Revised Approach to the Marketplace of Ideas Concept' 72 *Marquette Law Review* 187

Gavison, R., (1980) 'Privacy and the Limits of Law' *Yale Law Journal* 421

Geddis, A., (2004) 'You Can't Say "God" on the Radio: Freedom of Expression, Religious Advertising and the Broadcast Media after Murphy v Ireland' *European Human Rights Law Review* 181

Gittleman, R., (1982) 'The African Charter on Human and Peoples' Rights: A Legal Analysis' 22 *Virginia Journal of International Law* 667

Goldberg, D., (2009) 'Freedom of Information in the 21st Century: Bringing Clarity to Transparency' 14 *Communications Law* 50

Grabenwarter, C. and Pabel, K., (2012) *Europäische Menschenrechtskonvention* (Munich: C.H. Beck Verlag, 5th edn)

Greer, S., (2004) '"Balancing" and the European Court of Human Rights: A Contribution to the Habermas-Alexy Debate' 63 *Cambridge Law Journal* 412

Grossman, C., (2001) 'Freedom of Expression in the Inter-American System for the Protection of Human Rights' 7 *ILSA Journal of International and Comparative Law* 619

Grote, R. and Wenzel, N., (2013) 'Meinungsfreiheit', in T. Marauhn and R. Grote (eds.), *EMRK/GG Konkordanzkommentar zum europäischen und deutschen Grundrechtsschutz* (Tübingen: Mohr Siebeck, 2nd edn), Chapter 18

Habermas, J., (1981a) *The Theory of Communicative Action, vol. 1: Reason and the Rationalization of Society* (translation by McCarthy, T.; Boston, MA: Beacon Press, 1984)

(1981b) *The Theory of Communicative Action, vol. 2: Lifeworld and System: A Critique of Functionalist Reason* (translation by McCarthy, T.; Boston: Beacon Press, 1987)

(1962) *The Structural Transformation of the Public Sphere* (translation by Burger, T.; Cambridge: Polity Press, 1992)

(1992) *Between Facts and Norms* (translation by Rehg, W.; Cambridge, MA: MIT Press, 1996)

(2008) 'Notes on Post-Secular Society' *Fall New Perspectives Quarterly* 17

Hare, I., (2006) 'Crosses, Crescents and Sacred Cows: Criminalising Incitement to Religious Hatred' *Public Law* 521

Helle, S., (1982) 'The News-Gathering/Publication Dichotomy and Government Expression' *Duke Law Journal* 1

Hesse, K., (1999) *Grundzüge des Verfassungsrechts der Bundesrepublik Deutschland* (Heidelberg: C.F. Müller, 20th edn)

Lord Hoffmann, L., (2009) 'The Universality of Human Rights' 125 *Law Quarterly Review* 416

Hughes, K., (2012) 'A Behavioural Understanding of Privacy and its Implications for Privacy Law' 75 *Modern Law Review* 806

Ingber, S., (1984) 'The Marketplace of Ideas: A Legitimizing Myth' *Duke Law Journal* 1

Jackson, D. M., (2001) 'The Corporate Defamation Plaintiff in the Era of SLAPPs: Revisiting New York Times v Sullivan' 9 *William and Mary Bill of Rights Journal* 491

Janis, M. W., Kay, R. S. and Bradley, A. W., (2008) *European Human Rights Law* (Oxford University Press, 3rd edn)

Jaoude, P. A., (2003) 'Racist Speech – the Ultimate Challenge for Toleration? A Philosophical Exploration of Justifications for Hate Speech Protection' *UCL Jurisprudence Review* 340

Jeffery, A. J., (1986) 'Free Speech and Press: An Absolute Right?' 8 *Human Rights Quarterly* 197

Jellinek, G., (1892) *System der Subjektiven Öffentlichen Rechte* (Freiburg i. Br.: J. C. B. Mohr)

Johnson, S., (1826) *The Lives of the English Poets*, vol. 1 (London: J. F. Dove)

Johnson, B. E. H. and Youm, K. H., (2009) 'Commercial Speech and Free Expression: The United States and Europe Compared' 2 *Journal of International Media and Entertainment Law* 159

Kant, I., (1784) 'An Answer to the Question: What is Enlightenment?', in *Immanuel Kant. Practical Philosophy* (translation by Gregor, M. J., Cambridge University Press, 1996)

(1785) *Groundwork for the Metaphysics of Morals* (translation by Wood, A. W., New Haven and London: Yale University Press, 2002)

(1793) 'Principles of Political Right', in *Kant's Principle of Politics including his Essay on Perpetual Peace* (translation by Hastie, W.; Edinburgh: T. & T. Clark, 1891)

(1797) *The Metaphysics of Morals* (translation by Gregor, M. J., Cambridge University Press, 1996)

Katsirea, I., (2012) 'Who is Afraid of Public Service Broadcasting? The Digital Future of an Age-Old Institution Under Threat' 31 *Yearbook of European Law* 416

Kay, R. S., (2005) 'The European Convention on Human Rights and the Control of Private Law' *European Human Rights Law Review* 466

Keane, D., (2007) 'Attacking Hate Speech under Article 17 of the European Convention on Human Rights' 25 *Netherlands Quarterly of Human Rights* 641

(2008) 'Cartoon Violence and Freedom of Expression' 30 *Human Rights Quarterly* 84

Kearney, M., (2005) 'The Prohibition of Propaganda for War in the International Covenant on Civil and Political Rights' 23 *Netherlands Quarterly of Human Rights* 551

Keller, P., (2011) *European and International Media Law* (Oxford University Press)

Keller, H. and Sigron, M., (2010) 'State Security v Freedom of Expression: Legitimate Fight against Terrorism or Suppression of Political Opposition?' 10 *Human Rights Law Review* 151

Kelsen, H., (1928) *General Theory of Law and State* (translation by Wedberg, A.; New York: Russell & Russell, 1961)

Khan, A., (2012) 'A "Right not to be Offended" under Article 10(2) ECHR? Concerns in the Construction of the "Rights of Others"' *European Human Rights Law Review* 191

Knight, C. J. S., (2013) 'Article 10 and a Right of Access to Information' *Public Law* 468

Komorek, E., (2009) 'Is Media Pluralism a Human Right? The European Court of Human Rights, the Council of Europe and the Issue of Media Pluralism' *European Human Rights Law Review* 395

Koppelman, A., (2008) 'Is Pornography "Speech"?' 14 *Legal Theory* 71

Lange, D., (1975) 'The Speech and Press Clauses' 23 *UCLA Law Review* 77

Lazarsfeld, P. F. and Merton, R. K., (1948) 'Mass Communication, Popular Taste, and Organized Social Action', in *The Communication of Ideas* (republished in P. Marris and S. Thornham (eds.), *Media Studies*, (New York University Press, 2002)), p. 18

Lee, D. E., (1987) 'Public Interest, Public Figures, and the Corporate Defamation Plaintiff: Jadwin v Minneapolis Star & Tribune' 81 *Northwestern University Law Review* 318

Lewis, A., (1979) 'A Preferred Position for Journalism?' 7 *Hofstra Law Review* 595

Lewis, T., (2007) 'What not to Wear: Religious Rights, the European Court, and the Margin of Appreciation' *International and Comparative Law Quarterly* 395

Locke, J., (1689) *Two Treatises of Government, Second Treatise* (London: A. Millar *et al.*)

Luhmann, N., (1996) *The Reality of the Mass Media* (translation by Cross, K.; Cambridge: Polity Press, 2000)

Lusky, L., (1972) 'Invasion Of Privacy: A Clarification Of Concepts' 72 *Columbia Law Review* 693

Maitra, I. and McGowan, M. K., (2007) 'The Limits of Free Speech: Pornography and the Question of Coverage' 13 *Legal Theory* 41

Marcuse, H., (1965) 'Repressive Tolerance', in R. P. Wolff, B. Moore, Jr., and H. Marcuse, *A Critique of Pure Tolerance* (Boston, MA: Beacon Press), p. 95

Marshall, G., (1992) 'Press Freedom and Free Speech Theory' *Public Law* 40

Marauhn, T., (2009) 'Kommunikationsgrundrechte', in D. Ehlers (ed.), *Europäische Grundrechte und Grundfreiheiten* (Berlin/Boston: De Gruyter, 3rd edn), § 4

McCrudden, C., (2008) 'Human Dignity and Judicial Interpretation of Human Rights' *European Journal of International Law* 655

McDonald, B. P., (2004) 'The First Amendment and the Free Flow of Information: Towards A Realistic Right to Gather Information in the Information Age' 65 *Ohio State Law Journal* 249

McLuhan, M., (1964) *Understanding Media* (republished London and New York: Routledge, 2001)

Meiklejohn, A., (1948) *Free Speech and its Relation to Self-Government* (New York: Harper Brother Publishers)

(1961) 'The First Amendment is an Absolute' *Supreme Court Review* 245

Mill, J. S., (1869) *On Liberty* (republished London and Felling-on-Tyne: The Walter Scott Publishing Co., 1989)
Millar, G., (2009) 'Whither the Spirit of Lingens?' *European Human Rights Law Review* 277
Mills, J. L, (2008) *Privacy – The Lost Right* (Oxford University Press)
Milo, D., (2008) *Defamation and Freedom of Speech* (Oxford University Press)
Milton, J., (1644) *Areopagitica; A Speech of Mr. John Milton For the Liberty of Unlicenc'd Printing, To the Parliament of England* (London: unknown publisher)
(1673) *Of True Religion, Hæresie, Schism, Toleration, and what best Means may be us'd against the Growth of Popery* (London: unknown publisher)
Mitchell, P., (2011) 'The Nature of Responsible Journalism' 3 *Journal of Media Law* 19
Monk, C. C., (1986) 'Evidentiary Privilege for Journalists' Sources: Theory and Statutory Protection' 51 *Missouri Law Review* 1
Moore, V., (2005) 'Free Speech and the Right to Self-Realisation' 12 *UCL Jurisprudence Review* 95
Moreham, N. A., (2006) 'Privacy in Public Places' *Cambridge Law Journal* 606
(2011) 'Intrusion', in M. Warby, N. A. Moreham and I. Christie (eds.), *Tugendhat and Christie – The Law of Privacy and the Media* (Oxford University Press, 2nd edn)
Munro, C. R., (2003) 'The Value of Commercial Speech' 62 *Cambridge Law Journal* 134
Murray, D., (2009) 'Freedom of Expression, Counter-Terrorism and the Internet in Light of the UK Terrorist Act 2006 and the Jurisprudence of the European Court of Human Rights' 27 *Netherlands Quarterly of Human Rights* 331
Nathwani, N., (2008) 'Religious Cartoons and Human Rights – a Critical Legal Analysis of the Case Law of the European Court of Human Rights on the Protection of Religious Feelings and its Implications in the Danish Affair concerning Cartoons of the Prophet Muhammad' *European Human Rights Law Review* 488
Nestler, J. S., (2005) 'The Underprivileged Profession: The Case for Supreme Court Recognition of the Journalist's Privilege' 154 *University of Pennsylvania Law Review* 201
Nicol, A., Millar, G. and Sharland, A., (2009) *Media Law & Human Rights* (Oxford University Press, 2nd edn)
Nimmer, M. B., (1968) 'The Right to Speak from *Times* to *Time*: First Amendment Theory Applied to Libel and Misapplied to Privacy' 56 *California Law Review* 935
(1975) 'Introduction—Is Freedom of the Press a Redundancy: What Does it Add to Freedom of Speech?' 26 *Hastings Law Journal* 639
Nowak, M., (2005) *UN Covenant on Civil and Political Rights Commentary* (Kehl am Rhein: Engel, 2nd edn)
O'Fathaigh, R., (2013) 'Article 10 and the Chilling Effect Principle' *European Human Rights Law Review* 3
Oliva, J. G., (2007) 'The Legal Protection of Believers and Beliefs in the United Kingdom' 9 *Ecclesiastical Law Journal* 66

Oster, J., (2011) 'The Criticism of Trading Corporations and their Right to Sue for Defamation' 2 *Journal of European Tort Law* 255

(2012a) 'The Commission Proposal to Amend the Regulation on Credit Rating Agencies' 19 *Maastricht Journal of European and Comparative Law* 206

(2012b) 'Breach of Confidence Claims under English and European Private International Law', in D. Dörr and R. Weaver (eds.), *The Right to Privacy in the Light of Media Convergence – Perspectives from Three Continents* (Berlin/Boston, MA: De Gruyter), p. 194

(2013) 'Theory and Doctrine of "Media Freedom" as a Legal Concept' 5 *Journal of Media Law* 57

(2015) 'Communication, Defamation, and Liability of Intermediaries' *Legal Studies* (forthcoming)

Oswald, M., (2012) 'Freedom of Information in Cyberspace: What now for Copyright?' 26 *International Review of Law, Computers & Technology* 245

Parmar, S., (2009) 'The Challenge of "Defamation of Religions" to Freedom of Expression and the International Human Rights' *European Human Rights Law Review* 353

Pasich, K. A., (1978) 'The Right to the Press to Gather Information under the First Amendment' 12 *Loyola of Los Angeles Law Review* 357

Pasqualucci, J. M., (2006) 'Criminal Defamation and the Evolution of the Doctrine of Freedom of Expression in International Law: Comparative Jurisprudence of the Inter-American Court of Human Rights' 39 *Vanderbilt Journal of Transnational Law* 379

Plato, (c. 369 BC) *Theaetetus* (translation by Waterfield, R. A. H., London: Penguin Classics, 2004)

Popper, K., (1945) *The Open Society and Its Enemies* (republished London and New York: Routledge, 2002)

Post, R. C., (1987) 'Defaming Public Officials: On Doctrine and Legal History' *American Bar Foundation Research Journal* 539

(1988) 'Blasphemy, The First Amendment and the Concept of Intrinsic Harm' 8 *Tel Aviv University Studies in Law* 293

(1990) 'The Constitutional Concept of Public Discourse: Outrageous Opinion, Democratic Deliberation, and *Hustler Magazine v Falwell*' 103 *Harvard Law Review* 601

(1991) 'Racist Speech, Democracy, and the First Amendment' 32 *William and Mary Law Review* 267

(1993) 'Meiklejohn's Mistake: Individual Autonomy and the Reform of Public Discourse' 64 *University of Colorado Law Review* 1109

(1995) 'Recuperating First Amendment Doctrine' 47 *Stanford Law Review* 1249

(2000) 'Reconciling Theory and Doctrine in First Amendment Jurisprudence' 88 *California Law Review* 2353

(2011) 'Participatory Democracy and Free Speech' 97 *Virginia Law Review* 477

(2012) *Democracy, Expertise, and Academic Freedom, A First Amendment Jurisprudence for the Modern State* (New Haven, CT and London: Yale University Press)

Prosser, W. L., (1960) 'Privacy' 48 *California Law Review* 383
Pugh, S. C., (1995) 'Checkbook Journalism, Free Speech, and Fair Trials' 143 *University of Pennsylvania Law Review* 1739
Ramsay, M., (2012) 'The Status of Hearers' Rights in Freedom of Expression' 18 *Legal Theory* 31
Randall, M. H., (2006) 'Commercial Speech under the European Convention on Human Rights: Subordinate or Equal?' 6 *Human Rights Law Review* 53
Rawls, J., (1971) *A Theory of Justice* (Cambridge, MA: Harvard University Press)
Raz, J., (1984) 'Legal Rights' 4 *Oxford Journal of Legal Studies* 1
Redish, M. H., (1982) 'The Value of Free Speech' 130 *University of Pennsylvania Law Review* 591
Richards, D. A. J., (1986) *Toleration and the Constitution* (Oxford University Press)
(1999) *Free Speech and the Politics of Identity* (Oxford University Press)
Richardson, M., (2002) 'Whither Breach of Confidence: A Right of Privacy For Australia?' 26 *Melbourne University Law Review* 381
(2013) 'Reforming Privacy Law – Again' 5 *Journal of Media Law* 345
Rogers, E. M., (1994) *A History of Communication Study* (New York: The Free Press)
Ronen, Y., (2010) 'Incitement to Terrorist Acts and International Law' 23 *Leiden Journal of International Law* 645
Rooney, M. J., (1983) 'Freedom of the Press: An Emerging Privilege' 67 *Marquette Law Review* 34
Rösler, H., (2008) 'Caricatures and Satires in Art Law: the German Approach in Comparison with the United States, England and the Human Convention on Human Rights' *European Human Rights Law Review* 463
Rousseau, J.-J., (1762) *The Social Contract* (translation by Tozer, H. J., Ware: Wordsworth Editions, 1998)
Rubenfeld, J., (2001) 'The First Amendment's Purpose' 53 *Stanford Law Review* 767
Russell, B., (1946) *History of Western Philosophy* (republished London and New York: Routledge, 2004)
Samolewicz, P., (2002) 'Limiting Freedom to Hate: the Case for Banning Racist Speech' *UCL Jurisprudence Review* 188
Sandberg, R. and Doe, N., (2008) 'The Strange Death of Blasphemy' 71 *Modern Law Review* 971
Sanderson, M. A., (2004) 'Is Von Hannover v Germany a Step Backward for the Substantive Analysis of Speech and Privacy Interests?' *European Human Rights Law Review* 631
Scanlon, T. M., (1972) 'A Theory of Freedom of Expression' 1 *Philosophy & Public Affairs* 204
(1979) 'Freedom of Expression and Categories of Expression' 40 *University of Pittsburgh Law Review* 519b
Schauer, F., (1982) *Free Speech: A Philosophical Enquiry* (Cambridge University Press)
(1983) 'Must Speech Be Special?' 78 *Northwestern University Law Review* 1284

(2005a) 'Towards an Institutional First Amendment' 89 *Minnesota Law Review* 1256

(2005b) 'Freedom of Expression Adjudication in Europe and the United States: A Case Study in Comparative Constitutional Architecture', in G. Nolte (ed.), *European and US Constitutionalism* (Cambridge University Press)

Schonsteiner, J., Beltran y Puga, A. and Lovera, D. A., (2011) 'Reflections on the Human Rights Challenges of Consolidating Democracies: Recent Developments in the Inter-American System on Human Rights' 11 *Human Rights Law Review* 362

Seelye, K. Q., 7 March 2005, 'White House Approves Press Pass for Blogger', *NY Times*

Shannon, C. E., (1948) 'A Mathematical Theory of Communication' 27 *The Bell System Technical Journal* 379

Shannon, C. E. and Weaver, W., (1949) *The Mathematical Theory of Communication* (Champaign, IL: University of Illinois Press)

Simpson, E., (2006) 'Responsibilities for Hateful Speech' 12 *Legal Theory* 157

Solove, D. J., (2002) 'Conceptualizing Privacy' 90 *California Law Review* 1087

Sottiaux, S., (2011) '"Bad Tendencies" in the ECtHR's "Hate Speech" Jurisprudence' 7 *European Constitutional Law Review* 40

Stewart, P., (1975) 'Or of the Press' 26 *Hastings Law Journal* 631

Sunstein, C. R., (1986) 'Pornography and the First Amendment' 35 *Duke Law Journal* 589

(1992) 'Free Speech Now' 59 *University of Chicago Law Review* 255

(2000) 'Television and the Public Interest' 88 *California Law Review* 499

Temperman, J., (2008) 'Blasphemy, Defamation of Religions and Human Rights Law' 26 *Netherlands Quarterly of Human Rights* 517

Thorgeirsdóttir, H., (2004) 'Journalism Worthy of the Name: Affirmative Reading of Article 10 of the ECHR' 22 *Netherlands Quarterly of Human Rights* 601

Ugland, E., (2008) 'Demarcating the Right to Gather News: A Sequential Interpretation of the First Amendment' 3 *Duke Journal of Constitutional Law and Public Policy* 118

Valcke, P., Picard, R., Sükösd, M., Klimkiewicz, B., Petkovic, B., dal Zotto, C. and Kerremans, R., (2010) 'The European Media Pluralism Monitor: Bridging Law, Economics and Media Studies as a First Step towards Risk-Based Regulation in Media Markets' 2 *Journal of Media Law* 85

Van Alstyne, W. W., (1977) 'The Hazards to the Press of Claiming a "Preferred Position"' 28 *Hastings Law Journal* 761

van Rooijen, A., (2008) 'The Role of Investments in Refusals to Deal' 31 *World Competition* 63

(2010) *The Software Interface between Copyright and Competition Law: A Legal Analysis of Interoperability in Computer Programs* (Alphen an den Rijn: Wolters Kluwer)

Volokh, E., (2000) 'Freedom of Speech and Information Privacy: The Troubling Implications of a Right to Stop People From Speaking About You' 52 *Stanford Law Review* 1049

(2003a) 'Freedom of Speech and Intellectual Property: Some Thoughts after *Eldred, 44 Liquormart*, and *Bartnicki*' 40 *Houston Law Review* 697
(2003b) 'Freedom of Speech and the Right of Publicity' 40 *Houston Law Review* 903
(2010) 'Tort Liability and the Original Meaning of the Freedom of Speech, Press, and Petition' 96 *Iowa Law Review* 249
(2011a) 'In Defense of the Marketplace of Ideas/Search for Truth as a Theory of Free Speech Protection' 97 *Virginia Law Review* 595
(2011b) 'The Trouble with "Public Discourse" as a Limitation on Free Speech Rights' 97 *Virginia Law Review* 567
(2012) 'Freedom for the Press as an Industry, or For the Press as a Technology? From the Framing to Today' 160 *University of Pennsylvania Law Review* 459
Voorhoof, D., (2014) 'The Right to Freedom of Expression and Information under the European Human Rights System: Towards a more Transparent Democratic Society' *EUI Working Paper RSCAS 2014/12*
Voorhoof, D. and Humblet, P., (2014) 'Human Rights and the Employment Relation – The Right to Freedom of Expression at Work' *Les e-publi de l'Europe en mutation – La CEDH et la relation auf travail*
Wacks, R., (2013) *Privacy and Media Freedom* (Oxford University Press)
Walker, R., (2012) 'When is There a Public Interest in Private Life?' in J. Casadevall, E. Myjer, M. O'Boyle and A. Austin (eds.), *Freedom of Expression – Essays in Honour of Nicolas Bratza, President of the European Court of Human Rights* (Nijmegen: Wolf Legal Publishers), p. 61
Warbrick. C., (2002) 'The Principles of the European Convention on Human Rights and the Response of States to Terrorism' *European Human Rights Law Review* 287
Warren, S. and Brandeis, L., (1890) 'The Right to Privacy' 4 *Harvard Law Review* 193
Weaver, R. L., (2006) 'Speech and Technology' 110 *Penn State Law Review* 703
Weaver, R. L. and Partlett, D. F., (2005–2006) 'Defamation, Free Speech, and Democratic Governance' 50 *New York Law School Law Review* 57
Weaver, R. L., Delpierre, N. and Boissier, L., (2009) 'Governmentally Imposed Truth: An Examination of France's Holocaust Denial Law' 41 *Texas Tech University Law Review* 495
Webber, G., (2013) 'Rights and the Rule of Law in the Balance' 129 *Law Quarterly Review* 399
Weber, A., (2009) *Manual on Hate Speech* (Strasbourg: Council of Europe Publishing)
Weber, M., (1922) 'Wissenschaft als Beruf', in M. Weber (ed.) *Gesammelte Aufsätze zur Wissenschaftslehre* (Tübingen: J.C.B. Mohr) p. 524
Weinstein, J., (2011a) 'Participatory Democracy as the Central Value of American Free Speech Doctrine' 97 *Virginia Law Review* 491
(2011b) 'Participatory Democracy as the Basis of American Free Speech Doctrine: A Reply' 97 *Virginia Law Review* 633

Wells, C. E., (1997) 'Reinvigorating Autonomy: Freedom and Responsibility in the Supreme Court's First Amendment Jurisprudence' 32 *Harvard Civil Rights – Civil Liberties Law Journal* 159
West, S. R., (2011) 'Awakening the Press Clause' 58 *UCLA Law Review* 1025
Westin, A. F., (1967) *Privacy and Freedom* (New York: Atheneum)
Westphal, D., (2002) 'Media Pluralism and European Regulation' 13 *European Business Law Review* 459
Whitman, J. Q., (2004) 'The Two Western Cultures of Privacy: Dignity Versus Liberty' 113 *Yale Law Journal* 1151
Wolfrum, R., (1999) 'The Committee in the Elimination of Racial Discrimination' 3 *Max Planck Yearbook of United Nations Law* 489
Wragg, P., (2013) 'Mill's Dead Dogma: The Value of Truth to Free Speech Jurisprudence' *Public Law* 363
Zucca, L., (2007) *Constitutional Dilemmas: Conflicts of Fundamental Legal Rights in Europe and the USA* (Oxford University Press)

Index

Cambridge Intellectual Property and Information Law

Titles in the series (formerly known as *Cambridge Studies in Intellectual Property Rights*)

Brad Sherman and Lionel Bently
The Making of Modern Intellectual Property Law

Irini A. Stamatoudi
Copyright and Multimedia Products: A Comparative Analysis

Pascal Kamina
Film Copyright in the European Union

Huw Beverly-Smith
The Commercial Appropriation of Personality

Mark J. Davison
The Legal Protection of Databases

Robert Burrell and Allison Coleman
Copyright Exceptions: The Digital Impact

Huw Beverly-Smith, Ansgar Ohly and Agnès Lucas-Schloetter
Privacy, Property and Personality: Civil Law Perspectives on Commercial Appropriation

Catherine Seville
The Internationalisation of Copyright Law: Books, Buccaneers and the Black Flag in the Nineteenth Century

Philip Leith
Software and Patents in Europe

Geertrui Van Overwalle
Gene Patents and Clearing Models

Lionel Bently, Jennifer Davis and Jane C. Ginsburg
Trade Marks and Brands: An Interdisciplinary Critique

Jonathan Curci
The Protection of Biodiversity and Traditional Knowledge in International Law of Intellectual Property

Lionel Bently, Jennifer Davis and Jane C. Ginsburg
Copyright and Piracy: An Interdisciplinary Critique

Megan Richardson and Julian Thomas
Framing Intellectual Property: Legal Constructions of Creativity and Appropriation 1840–1940

Dev Gangjee
Relocating the Law of Geographical Indications

Andrew Kenyon, Megan Richardson and Ng-Loy Wee-Loon
The Law of Reputation and Brands in the Asia Pacific Region

Annabelle Lever
New Frontiers in the Philosophy of Intellectual Property

Sigrid Sterckx and Julian Cockbain
Exclusions from Patentability: How the European Patent Office is Eroding Boundaries

Sebastian Haunss
Conflicts in the Knowledge Society: The Contentious Politics of Intellectual Property

Helena R. Howe and Jonathan Griffiths
Concepts of Property in Intellectual Property Law

Rochelle Cooper Dreyfuss and Jane C. Ginsburg
Intellectual Property at the Edge: The Contested Contours of IP

Normann Witzleb, David Lindsay, Moira Paterson and Sharon Rodrick
Emerging Challenges in Privacy Law: Comparative Perspectives

Paul Bernal
Internet Privacy Rights: Rights to Protect Autonomy

Peter Drahos
Intellectual Property, Indigenous People and their Knowledge

Susy Frankel and Daniel Gervais
The Evolution and Equilibrium of Copyright in the Digital Age

Edited by Kathy Bowrey and Michael Handler
Law and Creativity in the Age of the Entertainment Franchise

Sean Bottomley
The British Patent System and the Industrial Revolution 1700–1852: From Privileges to Property

Susy Frankel
Test Tubes for Global Intellectual Property Issues: Small Market Economies

Jan Oster
Media Freedom as a Fundamental Right